HOLY FATHERS, SECULAR SONS

HOLY FATHERS,

SECULAR SONS

CLERGY, INTELLIGENTSIA, AND THE MODERN SELF IN REVOLUTIONARY RUSSIA

Laurie Manchester

Northern
Illinois
University
Press

DeKalb

Studies of the Harriman Institute, Columbia University

The W. Averell Harriman Institute for Advanced Study of the Soviet Union, Columbia University, sponsors the Studies in the Harriman Institute in the belief that their publication contributes to scholarly research and public understanding. In this way the Institute, while not necessarily endorsing their conclusions, is pleased to make available the results of some of the research conducted under its auspices.

Library of Congress Cataloging-in-Publication Data

Manchester, Laurie.

Holy fathers, secular sons : clergy, intelligentsia, and the modern self in revolutionary Russia / Laurie Manchester.

   p.   cm.

Includes bibliographical references (p.   ) and index.

ISBN 978-0-87580-380-7 (clothbound : alk. paper)

1. Russkaia pravoslavnaia tserkov'—Clergy—Political activity. 2. Russia—Church history—1801–1917. 3. Russia—Church history —20th century. 4. Church and state—Russia. 5. Intellectuals—Russia—History—19th century. I. Title.

BX540.M36 2008

305.6'81947—dc22

2007034863

To the Memory of My Parents

Julia Marshall Manchester (1922–1998)

and William Manchester (1922–2004)

Contents

Illustrations and Tables

Preface

This book is about a cultural revolution that was fueled by traditions. In nineteenth-century Russia, sons of Orthodox parish clergymen, or *popovichi,* departed from the castelike clerical estate and entered into virtually every Russian profession and political movement. Popovichi introduced into secular society a new ethos and a new way of looking at oneself and one's role in the world. They were modern selves, self-reliant agents distinguished by both introspection and the belief that they could and should change their world—themselves included. Yet these modern men also collectively fashioned themselves according to traditional clerical estate models and religious values, including adhering to respect for family and nation. The seeming contradiction that characterized the self-understanding of this sectarian and specifically Russian group forces us to rethink many commonly accepted dichotomies at the heart of the discourse of modernity.

This project originated at Columbia University, where I was fortunate to study with a remarkable group of graduate students and professors. I came to Russian history via my passion for Russian literature, and from the start I knew I wanted to study the Russian intelligentsia. It was in my first semester of graduate school, in the last colloquium Marc Raeff taught on Imperial Russia, that I was introduced to educated Russians I had never considered: Orthodox parish clergymen and their sons. At the time, before the collapse of Communism sparked an interest in religion amongst Russianists, Raeff was one of the few professors whose courses included an examination of the clergy (and of nationalities, for that matter). Having just returned from studying in Moscow, where I couldn't help but see that Orthodox churches were one of the most prominent symbols of pre-revolutionary Russia, and curious to learn something about a subject I knew nothing about, I chose to present on the clergy. Reading the two memoirs Raeff assigned on clerical life, I was struck that they were written not by priests but by priests' sons employed in secular professions who, despite their differences, shared a remarkably similar attitude toward their clerical pasts and other social estate groups. Around this same time, as I became more familiar with the historiography on the Russian intelligentsia, I realized that although many historians made passing references to popovichi as a ubiquitous group—given the prominence of individual popovichi among Russian revolutionaries and academics they could not be ignored, and biographies had been written about the most renowned popovichi—no one had studied their collective ethos. In part this was because of the widespread acceptance of theories of social mobility that dictated that lowly popovichi would have assimilated (or at least tried their best to fit) into the noble dominated society they entered. They were also neglected because most historians assumed that their juridical status—they were officially grouped under the catch-all term *"raznochintsy,"* defined as "persons of various rank"—denoted a particular set of "commoner" values that they shared with other non-nobles. These assumptions led historians to overlook the connection between popovichi and their clerical heritage, an error that was also fueled by widespread negative stereotypes about the clergy that made it hard for many to believe they had borne an educated culture worth passing on. Once I began researching this topic, Evgenii Beshenkovskii, the Slavic librarian at Columbia, provided me with the bibliographical tools essential to trace my popovichi (it was he who informed me about the uniformity of clerical last names) and I began to understand yet another reason why no one had studied them—studying such a diverse, self-constructed group presented many challenges, including how to find them.

Like many recent scholarly books on Russian history, this book benefited from the opening of archives following the collapse of the Soviet Union. When I embarked on my research in post-Soviet Russian archives, I was allowed unfettered access to all archives, including those in the provinces. Most importantly, I was not dependent on archivists to interpret my topic and bring me files; I was given access to all archival inventories. Yet because I was studying an aspect of Russian history that had been denied to its citizens, no matter how odd some archivists found my approach (my periodization of the *longue durée,* for example) most were fascinated with my research. Unlike Western historians of Russia, some of whom still have a hard time accepting that educated Russians (besides the Slavophiles), as opposed to "premodern" peasants, were religious, Russians rediscovering their religious heritage were keen to see popovichi as pious sons of Russia; however, they were much less interested in my popovichi—revolutionaries who, I argue, were also drawing on their clerical past. In most of the archives I worked in, archivists hunted down popovichi and helped me decipher handwriting. But the warmest welcome I received was in the archive of Vladimir province, where the archivists literally adopted me into their work collective. Nina Ivanovna Diatlova was generous with her time, and Natalia Maksimova, Georgii Ovchinnikov, and Tatiana Pugina have assisted this project in countless ways, including taking me deep into the countryside to see where some of my popovichi grew up. In Petersburg, Raphael Shalomovich Ganelin has been a selfless proponent of this project from the start. I also thank Aleksandr Belousov, Alexei Maksimov, Michael Thuman, Leonid Ovanesbekov, Aleksandr Polunov, Olga Rodionova, Jennifer Spock, and Kirill Tarasov, who all assisted my research in Russia.

Almost halfway through this project I realized that the origins of popovichi's values lay not so much in their particular social milieu, as I had been taught by the Annales school, but in the cultural system that Orthodox theology provided. The time I spent at Harvard as a postdoctoral fellow was crucial in allowing me to teach myself this theology, in lieu of adequate secondary sources on the subject. I spent several years in Widener reading the same theology textbooks, pastoral theology manuals, and collections of model sermons that my seminarians had read. In Cambridge, Virigine Coulloudon and Steve Coe provided welcome companionship. I also was able to reconnect with my childhood friend Eric Greimann, and he has since made two spur-of-the-moment trips out to Arizona to assist us with child care, which will never be forgotten. Before, during, and after the move to Cambridge, Alice Yurke and Daniel Kahn, who has been the similar-age sibling I never had since the moment we first met boarding a train for Moscow in Helsinki in May 1985, provided much-needed friendship and support in New York.

Three close friends in the field deserve a special mention for having nurtured this book (and its author): Robert Geraci, Igal Halfin, and Vera Shevzov. All three have shared my professional and personal ups and downs over many years and have always been unselfish about sharing their time with me; I also owe an intellectual debt to them. Vera has shared her immense knowledge of Russian Orthodoxy with me. Bob has taught me a great deal about evolving conceptions of Russian national identity and ethnicity. Igal mentored me—to the extent I can be mentored—in philosophy and literary theory.

For their valuable comments on the first draft of the text, I thank Gregory Freeze, Boris Gasparov, Robert Geraci, Leopold Haimson, Igal Halfin, Marc Raeff, Mark von Hagen, Elise Wirtschafter, and Richard Wortman. For their insightful suggestions on subsequent drafts of specific chapters, I thank Jochen Hellbeck, Nadia Kizenko, Nathaniel Knight, Alexander Martin, Ronald Meyer, Irina Paperno, Randall Poole, Vera Shevzov, and Elena Vishlenkova. Robert Geraci, Igal Halfin, and Elise Wirtschafter were more than gracious in agreeing to read select draft chapters after commenting on the entire first draft. For reading the entire book manuscript in its closer-to-publication form, I thank Mary Bellino, Marc Raeff, Yuri Slezkine, and Richard Wortman. I also thank my editor, Mary Lincoln.

Moving across the country to Arizona has been made much easier by the warm welcome I have received from my colleagues in the history department at Arizona State University. In particular, I am thankful to those fellow Europeanists who have mentored me since my arrival: Stephen Batalden, Rachel Fuchs, Hava Samuelson, and Victoria Thompson. Rodney Ito and Hans Peter L'Orange offered invaluable computer technical assistance at Arizona State. I am grateful to fate for having Eugene Clay and Agnes Kefeli-Clay, who were my neighbors twice in Petersburg, as neighbors in Tempe.

Numerous institutions provided funding for the research and writing of this book. I am most grateful for grants from the International Research and Exchanges Board (IREX), the U.S. Department of Education Fulbright-Hays, the Social Science Research Council, the Kennan Institute for Advanced Russian Studies of the Woodrow Wilson Center, the Davis Center for Russian Studies at Harvard University, the Harriman Institute of Columbia University, and a faculty-grant-in-aid from Arizona State University.

Portions of chapters 4 and 6 were previously published as "The Secularization of the Search for Salvation: The Self-Fashioning of Orthodox Clergymen's Sons in Late Imperial Russia" in *Slavic Review* 57 (Spring 1998): 50–76. Portions of chapters 4 and 7 were published as "Harbingers of Modernity, Bearers of Tradition: *Popovichi* as a Model Intelligentsia Self in Revolutionary Russia" in *Jahrbücher für Geschichte Osteuropas* 50 (Fall 2002): 321–44. I thank both journals for allowing me to republish portions of these articles.

I regret that my parents did not live to see this book published. My father's unique pronunciation of "popovich" was charming. Though I have lost them, I now have my own family, and I am grateful to the patience of my loving husband, Brian, and our children, Eli and Julia, who entered my life (or in the case of Brian, reentered) in the midst of the drafting stage of this project. This book is about, in part, the stories people tell about their families and childhoods. Though my mother did not live to meet my children, and my father met only my son, through my stories about them, my children are getting to know their maternal grandparents. Just as popovichi, long gone, and their collective story will now live on through this book, my parents will live on through my children.

HOLY FATHERS, SECULAR SONS

Introduction

In the mid-nineteenth century a horde of "new men" entered virtually all the professions in Russia. These "new men" didn't look like other educated Russians: they didn't speak Western languages, had been educated separately in special schools, and were unfashionably dressed. These "new men," despite their distinctiveness, didn't come from another country or ethnic group: they were Orthodox clergymen's sons (*popovichi*), most of whom were raised in poverty-stricken villages throughout the Russian empire. Just as these popovichi were foreign to Russian secular society, they loathed the "foreignness" of the nobles who dominated it. Eulogizing his friend and fellow popovich Irinarkh Vvedenskii in 1857, the publicist Grigorii Blagosvetlov (1824–1880) contrasted their upbringing to that of Russian nobles: "it had its good and moral side, compared with the upbringing of other children, thrown straight out of the cradle into the arms of foreigners, who had been cast upon the Russian land from God knows where. Let us assume that the young popovich did not learn how to babble in French from his earliest years, that he could not master tens of thousands of Chinese ceremonies, but that is not yet a great loss." Popovichi considered nobles corrupted by the influence of foreign cultures. By contrast, they were proud bearers of a "native" culture inculcated in them directly by their beloved parents, as Blagosvetlov's description of clerical upbringing further illustrates: "there were many other advantages to Vvedenskii's upbringing. He was nursed at the breast of his own mother; he was lulled to sleep in his cradle by the sounds of his native language; his first teacher was his father, 'who dearly loved his son,' and there, where there wasn't sufficient skill, nature completed the task."[1] Popovichi considered themselves more Russian than Russia's nobility. They were Russia's alternative intelligentsia, ordained to be Russia's rightful moral leaders. Yet the only feature shared by these diverse individuals—including Bolshevik revolutionaries as well as monarchist professors of theology—was their clerical origins, upon which they not insignificantly fashioned themselves as a group.

The mass exodus of popovichi from the castelike clerical estate was possible because of attempts by the Russian state to dismantle its estate-based social structure during the modernizing Great Reforms of the 1860s. Many Russian statesmen, however, were ambivalent and divided about creating a class-based society, and subsequent counter-reforms, added to the incompleteness of the initial reforms, essentially preserved key aspects of an old regime European social estate system until 1917. Despite these hurdles, the trickle of popovichi who managed to leave the clerical estate before the 1860s grew to a flood during and after the period of the Great Reforms. Once popovichi entered secular society they acted as agents of change, just as educated, professional "sons of commoners" and marginalized groups who reach the center have done throughout the modern world. Faced with adversity from both noble-dominated society and an often hostile state, popovichi affiliated themselves with clerical traditions. They did not become citizens who subscribed to universalism, and as such, they can be seen as another example of the Russian state's incomplete modernization, a source of the social instability that weakened the country on the eve of 1917. Yet popovichi were not simply unfinished products of a modernization orchestrated by Russia's seemingly omnipotent state. Most of them chose voluntarily to leave their native estate, and they failed to assimilate into the majority culture because they chose not to. They helped shape the new practices and ways of thinking in Russia associated with the era of modernity as they shaped themselves into dissenters.[2]

The secular milieu popovichi entered was the intelligentsia, a term Russian *intelligenty* (self-professed members of the intelligentsia) coined as they created the concept in the mid-nineteenth century. It described a small but significant group of Russians who, faced with an authoritarian government, began to see themselves as belonging to a society independent from the state, a society representing public opinion and the broader nation. In part, stalled (or non-existent) political reforms gave rise to the intelligentsia, but so did the dramatic changes that accompanied modernization: urban growth, the rise of the free professions, the rapid spread of print culture, greater exposure to Western ideas, and increases in educational opportunities. Deprived of unions and aided by few official independent professional organizations, the nineteenth-century intelligentsia formed, in the words of one scholar, a "nascent civil society." Membership in the pre-revolutionary Russian intelligentsia was always subjective: individuals from a variety of social backgrounds, political affiliations, professions, and educational levels might consider themselves members of the intelligentsia. Thus, although it is often defined in the historiography as either an ideological or a sociological group, the intelligentsia was not a social group, nor did it ever espouse a specific political agenda or religious (or atheistic) orientation.[3] Self-styled intelligenty created a wide variety of vibrant cultural, scholarly, theological, and political movements.

This book offers a new definition of the intelligentsia that is closer to that which the intelligenty used to define themselves. The intelligentsia— particularly in the postreform period—can best be understood as critical- thinking individuals who believed they could shape themselves and control their universe. They were modern selves, and their sense of self was multi-dimensional, encompassing material, relational, and reflexive components.[4] Intelligenty expressed their ethos of modern selfhood in a particular prism of values through which they perceived themselves and the world around them, and this ethos affected their attitudes toward the major issues they grappled with: national identity, civic equality, justice, social responsibility, the integration of the largely illiterate peasant masses into society, and the inroads of the capitalist marketplace. This ethos was characterized by unconditional dedication to social activism and by service to the collective good. Although self-sacrifice lay at the core of the intelligentsia ethos, care of the self was never far from its agenda. Rejecting the Western liberal ethos whereby individuals set themselves against society, intelligenty derived their identity from their role in society. Dedication to society did not mean self-renunciation, although it might seem so, since some intelligenty were willing to die for the greater good. Rather, the betterment of society and self-improvement were parts of the same project. The intelligentsia's relentless pursuit of scholarship accomplished both. To perform their universalistic mission, members of the intelligentsia endeavored to follow ethical codes in both their professional and personal lives. Although intelligenty always thought of themselves in moral terms, self-judgment became less central as a shift in the intelligentsia ethos, from a state of consciousness to a mode of action, took place in the postreform period just as popovichi were inundating secular professions and educational institutions.

Because the traditions popovichi brought with them were new to Russian secular society, they were revolutionary and could contribute to this shift. Their traditions were so novel because in no other European country was there such a strict differentiation of the priesthood, extending from birth to marriage, education, laws, and bureaucracy. Imperial Russia's clerical estate was the most castelike of its estates, similar to the religiously sanctioned caste system of India and to the biblical Levites, to whom the clergy was not infrequently compared in the nineteenth century. Even after clergymen's sons were granted secular legal status in the 1860s, the clerical profession still remained virtually closed to persons from other estates. Clergymen's sons thus consistently inherited the birthright of moral leadership, and Russia's only two educated estates, the clergy and the nobility, developed distinct traditions.[5] Noble anti-clericalism, clerical poverty, the interest of some nobles in Western Christianity, and the multi-national composition of the nobility also explained the divergence between noble and clerical culture. Lastly, their attitudes toward Western Europe differed: the nobility defined itself according to formalized behavior largely imported from Western Europe; the clergy, because of the schism between Western and Eastern Christianity and the structure of national churches in Orthodox Christianity, defined itself in opposition to Western Europe. Clerical culture was not only distinct from noble culture; it also provided an alternative pool of identities and precepts to the culture of the nobility, Russia's ruling class, that encouraged guilt-ridden postreform "repentant" nobles to emulate popovichi, the "uncouth" sons of commoners. For although the Russian Orthodox Church was less independent than the majority of churches to its west, institutionally it was less dependent on the state than the Russian nobility was. It was the only institution that possessed independent institutional structures paralleling those of the imperial government: educational institutions and clerical courts.[6] Because of the particular circumstances that resulted from having an exodus from a castelike clerical estate, minor particularities specific to Eastern Orthodox theology, and the rise of a reformation-like pastoral care movement in the mid-nineteenth century, popovichi embodied a concept of modern selfhood, despite the fact that Russia did not experience the Renaissance and never enjoyed the protection of the inviolability of the individual codified in Western law, traditionally regarded as prerequisites for the emergence of the modern self.

In the immediate wake of the unsuccessful 1905 revolution, a number of prominent intelligenty lambasted the shift toward activism in intelligentsia ethos, arguing that the postreform intelligentsia's utopianism was hindering Russia's ability to move forward from oppression to political liberty and personal autonomy. Among them was Semen Frank, a former Marxist. Frank lamented the demise of prereform intelligenty, the vast majority of whom were nobles, and expressed hope that a new intelligentsia was coming of age that would return to the values of intelligenty of the 1830s and '40s. Although Frank did not directly name popovichi as the conduits of the postreform intelligentsia ethos he rejected, he linked this ethos to Bazarov, the infamous protagonist of Ivan Turgenev's masterpiece *Fathers and Sons*—a man of clerical descent. According to Frank, the quintessential postreform intelligent was, regardless of his political affiliation, "a stubborn, inveterate populist," whose single-minded goal was the happiness of the masses, and whose self-proclaimed moral superiority ensured that he and his fellow intelligenty alone knew what the masses needed. His moralism was characterized by "ascetic self-restraint," utilitarianism, hatred of high culture and wealth, an anti-aristocratic fervor, and a binary morality that informed his judgment of people, actions, and circumstances. Frank compared this intelligentsia to monks who employed "religion"—meaning a secularized religious sensibility—to declare war on a world they wanted to radically change.[7]

Popovichi were grounded in the religious, albeit often secularized, sensibility Semen Frank described, and they brought it with them to the intelligentsia, helping forge the emergence of modern selfhood amongst the postreform intelligentsia ethos. The clash between prereform and postreform intelligenty, depicted by Turgenev as the "sons" against the "fathers," was actually less generational than it was social. Popovichi conceived of themselves as "worldly ascetics," embarking on a mission to recast the secular world based on their clerical past, and it was this mission that energized them. Their professional and political endeavors often derived from Western and secular ideas, but their primary sense of identity was rooted in Russian clerical traditions. By secularizing clerical models, and therefore retaining aspects of their heritage, those who drew on Western or secular ideas were able to reconcile this seeming contradiction. Given the extensive professional and political diversity among popovichi, not all of them agreed on how to define their heritage; as modern men they defined it individually. Some saw clerical values as tradition; others as modernity.[8] Popovichi's diversity on the one hand—which made them ubiquitous in Russian culture, movements, and professions—and their common identity on the other help explain the scope and nature of their impact on the intelligentsia.

The existence of a clerical estate culture permitted popovichi to perceive the existence of a dual set of Orthodox values: religious values, espoused by popovichi who were believers, and clerical estate values, which permeated the heritage of all popovichi, regardless of whether they remained religious. Religious and clerical values were not necessarily mutually exclusive and, for the majority of popovichi who remained believers, often overlapped. But because these clerical values could be distinguished from religious values, they could be consciously espoused by a non-believer, and irreligious popovichi could retain spiritual values in the guise of social estate values, while discarding religious dogma. Importantly, for all popovichi clerical culture was never simply synonymous with Orthodox culture, to which any believer, regardless of their origins, belonged. On the other hand, all popovichi, even believers, were bearers of the clerical culture they shared with atheist popovichi. In this sense popovichi's identity was similar to contemporary American Jews: all may identify themselves and each other as Jewish, but many qualify their Jewish identity with the diverse labels "cultural," "secular," "religious," or "ethnic" Jew, while still preserving key characteristics of their background. In either case, whether a popovich believed his values were social values derived from the clerical estate or spiritual values rooted in his clerical heritage, these values were frequently secularized when applied to secular realms. Yet the actual values of religious and irreligious popovichi remained remarkably similar as modernization blurred the boundary between secular and religious spheres, and the irreligious continued to exhibit what Eliade called "degenerated religious behavior," unconsciously espousing vestiges of an exemplary religious upbringing that began with their births.[9]

Conventional sociologists define secularization as the process of religion becoming "privatized" during modernization, but, in contrast, the understanding of secularization employed in this book allows for a diffusion of religion—whether it is defined functionally in the Durkheimian sense as beliefs that fulfill certain social functions, or substantively as beliefs pertaining to the supernatural—into newly emergent modern public spheres such as political movements and professions. Secularization, in an inversion of its conventional sense, can therefore heighten, rather than diminish, a religion's influence. On the other hand, once religious principles are applied to secular matters, they are inevitably generalized, or "reorientated," to use Hans Blumenberg's term.[10] Rather than being restricted to the realm of personal piety in the modern world, religion—or secularized religious beliefs—is fundamentally incorporated into the professional, political, and personal lives of educated individuals.

This secularization, as well as the interplay between, rather than the juxtaposition of, religion and modernity, applies not only to "backward" Russia, where retention of religion in the early twentieth century might be seen as the result of uneven modernization, but also to the "progressive" West. Because the binary opposition of the concepts of religious and secular is usually understood as an integral part of the divide between modern and traditional, one of the most fruitful avenues for challenging these dichotomies has been recent research on religion in modern Western Europe, which undermines the false assumption that rationalism obliterated religious belief once modernity arrived.[11] Many scholars exploring the roots of the modern Western European self have argued that this selfhood was also rooted in secularized Christianity.[12] Rather than serving as a source of Russia's alleged distinctiveness, popovichi's secularization of clerical traditions can thus paradoxically be seen as rendering them *both* mediators between ancient Orthodox traditions and modernity *and* arbitrators between Russia and Western Europe.

The prejudice all popovichi faced from nobles as clerical offspring, coupled with the cultural chasm between the world they entered and the world they left, collectively inspired them to model themselves according to the anti-aristocratic, anti-Western alternative: the clerical culture in which they were raised. Religion served, as it often does in the modern world, as their "cultural defense" against the majority culture, in this case the nobility, as they followed the cardinal tenet of self-fashioning, fashioning themselves, in the words of Stephen Greenblatt, "in relation to something perceived as alien, strange or hostile."[13]

The context in which this battle was fought was textual; whereas popovichi and noble intelligenty often worked side by side in their professions and political organizations, in their personal texts and in the press they affiliated themselves with different cultural traditions. The polemics between popovichi and noble intelligenty were bitter and prolonged precisely because they both agreed on many fundamentals but disagreed, especially in the case of most non-radical nobles (including Slavophiles, who, unlike popovichi, did not accept a differentiation between Orthodox and clerical culture), as to their origins. In the case of radical nobles, they differed from popovichi because of their different attitudes toward their pasts. While noble radicals fit the widespread assumption that "all revolutionaries are patricides" and self-hating, popovichi did not complain of alienation, whether from their families, the masses, or themselves.[14] This lack of identity crisis explains a conundrum that has faced scholars who have studied the intelligentsia: if intelligenty were so alienated, why did they appoint themselves leaders of the nation? Because popovichi believed their clerical origins christened them the chosen people, they were more than willing to become the nation's self-professed leaders. The preconceived notions popovichi and their would-be noble followers had of each other, and the different values they associated with their pasts, led to overt and subtle divergences between the two groups.

The particular ethos and character of the intelligentsia was shaped by both nobles and popovichi, but it was also shaped by the conflict and interaction between the two groups, producing a single fragmented intelligentsia while retaining two separate intelligentsia lineages. Thus despite claims by leading members of the intelligentsia that it was the most universalistic of groups because of its "all-class" or "above-estate" consciousness, on the eve of the fateful events of 1917 the intelligentsia was riddled with the same complexities and divisions that plagued the rest of Russia.[15] The emergence of a civil society and a middle class was thwarted not only by conflicts between ethnic groups or between the have-nots and the haves; it was also impeded by a struggle between educated Russians over who would lead the nation based on political differences as well as an immutable feature some of them clung to: social origin. The retention by popovichi of their native estate culture raises the broader question of how historians define national cultures. Usually this query has been answered by citing binary models of "high" or educated culture, and popular or mass culture. But can a nation have more than one educated cultural tradition based on the same ethnicity?

The new selfhood popovichi helped bring to the intelligentsia is vividly illustrated by the sharp increase in the production of personal texts, including diaries, autobiographies, and letters, in the late imperial period.[16] The reasons behind this explosion of ego-documents parallels the by-products of the tangible economic and technological process of modernization that assisted the creation of the intelligentsia. These changes encouraged the sense of individual choice and heightened awareness of the self associated with the era of modernity; consequently they have also been linked to the rise of the "autobiographical habit" in Renaissance Europe. The first autobiography by a popovich appears to have been written in 1802 (it was not published until 1899); the first one published appears to have been in 1832. By the postreform period, when the majority of the texts used for this study were written, the culture of autobiography was so pervasive that autobiographies were sometimes written—and frequently collectively published—as a professional courtesy or as participation in alumni organizations. Writing in 1879, one popovich described this phenomenon: "In Russia we have four historical journals and several historical collections being published, and autobiographies or memoirs constantly appear in them. Each and every person who can hold a pen in his hand and put it to paper without fail wants to leave his descendants his past and his name."[17] The process of writing an autobiography also further promulgated the modern self that had initially spawned the genre: writing autobiographies developed educated Russians' sense of self by making them define who they were, what they had done, and where they had come from. Regardless of why they wrote autobiographical statements, popovichi employed this genre to publicly profess their clerical origins as the repository of their collective memory, a memory they sought to impose on the emerging genealogy of the intelligentsia, which they linked to the creation of a Russian national identity.

The preoccupation of educated Russians with themselves as subjects can also be found in autobiographical statements preserved in a wide variety of archival materials that usually elude studies of the self: personal texts such as suicide notes, petitions, trial testimonies, and correspondence confiscated by the authorities.[18] The relative uniformity of popovichi's self-construction in all of these various texts—published and unpublished, and designed for disparate audiences if any audience at all—is a testament to their collective cohesiveness. Because the voices of popovichi are the only source for understanding their sense of self, this book is based in large part on all types of personal texts.

Popovichi's personal texts are valuable not because they narrate what actually happened in the past (they sometimes don't), but because they reveal to us what was meaningful to their authors: how they viewed the world, themselves, the past and the present; how they wished to present themselves to different audiences; and how the recurrent narrative patterns that are particular to popovichi's personal writings link them as a group. In terms of their autobiographies, popovichi's memory, like all collective memory, was selective. As individuals choose what is important to remember and how to present it, they draw on a specific group context to recreate the past.[19] And, as will be seen, popovichi often exaggerated or omitted aspects of their pasts to fit the genre that linked them.

In assembling their group context, popovichi were aided by a common set of prescriptive norms that members of the clergy alone drew upon as "master narratives." Not coincidentally, the mass exodus of popovichi was preceded by the most significant reform movement that the Russian Orthodox Church had ever experienced. In part, these internal reforms were the defensive response of a church that felt itself under attack from a hostile secular society and was battling that society to become Russia's primary "national" educated culture and deliver Russia from the crisis she faced in the late imperial period. It was also part of the Orthodox Church's response to modernity. A by-product of this movement was the proliferation of prescriptive clerical texts written for clergymen and their family members. These ranged from clerical etiquette and child-rearing manuals to collections of model sermons and clergymen's obituaries. The Church publicists —priests, popovichi employed as theological academy professors or seminary teachers, and to a lesser extent, learned bishops—who wrote them strove to establish a more direct connection between religious precepts and personal behavior by instructing clerical estate members on how to conduct every aspect of their lives, from their intimate relations with their spouses to how they should regard foreign lands. But first and foremost, they explained how clerical estate members should perfect themselves. These texts were widely available to seminarians and their families. It was these texts that popovichi used to articulate their alternative to noble culture.

The remarkable similarity we will see between clerical prescriptive texts and popovichi's *and* clergymen's autobiographical narratives further confirms popovichi's own statements about the source of their identity. I employ theological typologies as literary scholars have used literature to elucidate the paradigms individuals utilized to fashion themselves, and as a cultural or ideological system that individuals use to structure their lives. To establish the degree to which popovichi secularized these models, this book also is based on the voices of their fathers.

Popovichi were linked, not only despite professional and political affiliations, but also despite generational differences, even in the dynamic late imperial period. Unlike noble intelligenty, whose values are divided by generation and by political differences, popovichi's collective identity was a constant, regardless of time or place. What is particularly striking is that it even bridged the cataclysmic events of 1917, as evidenced in some of the published and unpublished autobiographies written by elderly popovichi in the Soviet period. Because popovichi were defining themselves according to a tradition—albeit one that was partially invented and provided them with multiple models of interpretation—popovichi's ethos remained relatively static and homogeneous. With a few exceptions, the popovichi included in this study were born between the 1820s and the 1870s and wrote their personal texts in the period following both the import of romanticism and the Great Reforms. These were the generations that left behind the majority of written sources and had the most impact on secular society. The only popovichi not included in this study were those who came of age after the cataclysmic events that began in 1917; that is another topic in and of itself. The continuity of popovichi's ethos over a broad chronological scope substantiates that popovichi drew on clerical estate models rather than adopting the ethos of other intelligenty. To emphasize this remarkable continuity, this study makes use of quotes and examples that are ahistorical and aspatial. To further demonstrate that popovichi did not assimilate into intelligentsia circles they entered, this study employs personal texts that individual popovichi wrote at different times of their lives, specifically both before and after they left the clerical estate, as well as autobiographical narratives by intelligenty from other social estates.

Popovichi made up approximately one percent of the population of postreform European Russia.[20] The personal sources of 207 identifiable popovichi, along with hundreds of other popovichi whose biographical information eluded me, were employed. These 207 identifiable popovichi came from 39 of Russia's 50 European provinces (plus 5 of her non-European provinces), and span all secular professions, including professors at theological academies and seminaries. Even though the latter fell under the legal jurisdiction of the clerical domain (vedomstvo), they were, nevertheless, no longer members of the clerical estate, a status reserved for ordained clergymen, sacristans, and monks. Because national identity played an important role in popovichi's self-understanding and their secularized mission, this study limits the subjects to popovichi who considered themselves ethnically Russian. To assist the reader in navigating and assessing the representativeness of these hundreds of popovichi and their texts, an appendix lists these 207 identifiable popovichi, their birthdates, professions, birthplaces, political orientation, the genre(s) of their personal texts employed, the dates such texts were either written or published, whether these texts were published, and if they were commissioned.

Finding these 207 men was not an easy task: popovichi were not ascribed a single legal entity, nor did they share membership in institutionalized organizations after they left the clergy. In the case of their many published autobiographies, I was aided by bibliographical indexes and multi-volume autobiographical collections. In the case of the unpublished papers of individual popovichi, the distinctiveness of clerical family names—a symbol of the historical castelike nature of the Russian parish clergy that continues to mark descendants of the clergy in Russia today—was particularly helpful. Clerical last names were usually acquired in the late eighteenth century, when they were assigned by church school administrators to individual seminarians. The names dispensed belonged to four categories reflecting the estate's sacred mission: church holidays; virtues (including their Latin translation); fruits and products of the earth; and reference to God. On the basis of common clerical family names, along with a few published archival guides to memoirs that included social origin, I was able to trace 74 archival personal collections of popovichi.[21] This led me to 11 different archives located in three cities, including the province of Vladimir, which, given its central Russian location, provided a representative sample of rank-and-file popovichi, clerical schools, and rural clerical life.

In light of the fact that this book is ultimately about individuals—who happened to define themselves collectively—its structure roughly follows the life course of its subjects, after providing the reader with background information in chapter 1 about the "lived" experiences of the nineteenth-century parish clergy and the perceptions of popovichi by nobles. Chapter 2 discusses how popovichi—and their fathers—responded to the social prejudice described in chapter 1 by judging social estates according to prescriptive clerical norms. Chapter 3 examines the church publicists' and clergymen's views of the parish clergy as superior to monks and laity. Chapter 4 turns to popovichi's and clergymen's portrayals of their childhoods and family life as exemplifying the paradigms of virtue described in chapter 3. Chapter 5 discusses how popovichi employed their education in clerical boarding schools to cement their alternative intelligentsia lineage, despite the fact that they depicted the school universe as the polar opposite of their heavenly childhoods. Chapter 6 explores the central paradox of how popovichi justified why they left the estate they subsequently drew upon in order to fashion themselves. In the final chapter I focus on how popovichi secularized their fathers' goal of leading others to salvation in order to structure their adult lives. I also present a concluding examination of how a popovich accomplished this through his professional writings during a career that extended through the Stalinist period.

Russia—like other countries to her east—has traditionally been depicted largely as a receptacle of Western ideas. Even adherents of the idea that Russia has its own sonderweg have argued that Russian intellectuals misunderstood Western ideas, that they were compelled to adapt them, or that the importation of Western ideas forced Russia to deviate from her normative course of development. Westerners have been fascinated for centuries by "backward" Russia, but they have also been intrigued by the Russian intelligentsia, exemplified by the lofty status of Russian nineteenth-century fiction and plays in Western literary canons. This raises the question of how much influence Imperial Russia, historically an integral part of Europe, has had on countries to her west. One of the key concepts the rest of the world has imported from Russia is that of an intelligentsia. This book unveils a Russian intelligentsia that was rooted more in Russian culture than in Western European culture. The Western world has been profoundly affected by the Russian intelligentsia examined in this book but has not been formally introduced to it.

The Backdrop

Origins and Caricatures

In one of the most widely circulated Russian letters, the critic Vissarion Belinskii asked the writer Nikolai Gogol in 1847: "Whom do the Russian people call 'the idiot breed,' 'cheats,' 'stud horses'? Their priests. Is not the Russian priest regarded by everyone as a symbol of gluttony, avarice, sycophancy, bawdiness?" This negative image of the Russian Orthodox parish clergy was reiterated throughout the pre-revolutionary period by intellectuals of non-clerical origin and was later reinforced by anti-religious campaigns in Communist Russia. It was present in all forms of pre-revolutionary Russian "high" culture: poetry, plays, fiction, and pictorial art. Russian writers and artists from different schools and generations—including the father of Russian literature, Aleksandr Pushkin, the playwright Aleksandr Griboedev, the novelist Ivan Turgenev, the artist Ilya Repin, and the symbolist poet Zinaidia Gippius—derided clergymen according to the formulae Belinskii employed.[1] Anti-clerical stereotypes are also found in the memoir literature written by nobles, workers, and persons of non-clerical birth who were classified along with popovichi as *raznochintsy* (persons of various ranks). These memoirists recalled priests as detested figures who bored them to tears, were ignorant and ill-read, or were of questionable moral character. The radical Alexander Herzen depicted his childhood parish priest both as a scandalous drunk who harassed him for vodka to the point at which Herzen's only recourse was to escape by hiding in the woods and as a rabid thief who not only extorted money from peasants for the performance of religious rites but literally stole from the sacristan who served alongside him. Disdain for the clergy is also present in memoirs written by conservative nobles and was also part of the discourse of prominent Russian liberals, even in the post-1917 emigration. Lastly, this stereotype can be found in Russian popular culture, such as peasant proverbs and folklore.[2]

Yet, paradoxically, nineteenth-century Russia had the highest level of religious observance in all of Europe; anti-clericalism and atheism were not necessarily synonymous. In modern Western Europe widespread anti-clericalism was directed at denominations that were wealthy and powerful, but the abolishment of the patriarchate and the secularization of Church lands in the eighteenth century had robbed the Russian Orthodox Church of both. Anti-clerical sentiment in early modern Europe has been linked to the extent to which the clergyman is viewed as an outsider. In Russia, the clergy's sacramental role and castelike nature encouraged myths about them to proliferate among all estates. Orthodox custom also encouraged parishioners to perceive the parish community as divided not into the traditional estates but into two separate groups, lay and clerical. Ordained clergymen, required to wear their hair long and dress in their cassocks at all times in the presence of parishioners, were immediately physically discernible from the laity. The clergy's lack of kinship ties to other estates and their segregated education in the *bursa* (the general term for either primary theological education in the church school, secondary education in the seminary, or both), where they learned a dialect-like form of Russian laden with Church Slavonic and Latin words, only added to this sense of otherness. Legal restrictions further set them apart; for example, the clerical profession was almost impossible to relinquish. Widowed clergy were forbidden to remarry, yet an ordained clergyman who left the clergy was legally prohibited from joining a secular profession for five years, after which he could enter only a few low-level positions. These stipulations were enacted by the Church hierarchy to ensure that few clergymen ever renounced their vows, thus retaining the mystique of the order as eternally distinct from the laity. According to one peasant proverb, "one would know a priest even dressed in a rug woven with bast. Priests have their own distinctive manner."[3]

Conversely, clergymen's religious and social distinctiveness could also contribute to lay reverence that further isolated them. Peasant parishioners interviewed in the late nineteenth century stated that they did not want their confessor to judge them when they gathered for leisure. While declaring that they respected their priests, some were superstitiously afraid when encountering clergy on the street. In the few positive literary and memoir portraits of parish clergymen written by nobles, the priest is portrayed exclusively as a representative of the Church whose only concerns are religious and whom nobles regard purely as a spiritual father.[4]

Awe for the parish clergy created a double standard that explains the paradoxical coexistence of popular anti-clerical stereotypes amidst a largely pious population. Parishioners expected clergymen to prove their holiness by constantly meeting a higher moral and spiritual standard. To enforce this standard, their behavior was more closely monitored than that of any other group in Imperial Russia. In addition to a hierarchy of ecclesiastical authorities who recorded every indiscretion, clergymen were watched vigilantly by their parishioners, who complained to the authorities whenever their clergy did not act according to their lofty standards—for example, when they were intoxicated. The juxtaposition of the prevalent image of the pious monk or elder in nineteenth-century secular literature with the unflattering portraits of the parish clergyman is indicative of the greater respect laypersons had for those members of the clergy furthest removed from the trappings of the temporal world. Even the Slavophiles, who at least as adults could hardly be accused of anti-clericalism, demonstrated a preference for the monastic clergy.[5]

Nineteenth-century European discourse on the concept of "the other," buoyed by imperialist conquests, focused mainly on race. In Russia, the protracted enserfment of the majority of the dominant ethnicity led to a racialization of peasant serfs by Russian nobles.[6] To a lesser extent the caste-like Russian clergy was also an "other" to the laity. This racialization of social estate groups helps explain why ethnic Russians belonging to estate groups could produce the types of alternative cultures associated with national, regional, or religious minorities, despite the predominance of Orthodoxy as their faith.

At the turn of the twentieth century several members of the elite of St. Petersburg's avant-garde intelligentsia, intrigued by mysticism and apocalypticism, arranged to meet with members of the local Orthodox clergy. A leading member of this group, who was of noble origin, recalled that "the world of the clergy was new to us, an unknown world." This ignorance, along with anti-clerical stereotypes, is largely responsible for the historiographical misconception that the Russian Orthodox clergy was incapable of producing an educated culture because it was largely illiterate and completely dependent on the state.[7]

Because many aspects of clerical life still remain shrouded behind these stereotypes, this chapter begins by deconstructing these images. This is especially important because, as subsequent chapters will reveal, popovichi politicized every seemingly mundane feature of their clerical pasts to construct their alternative intelligentsia lineage. To personalize this past, this chapter draws in part on examples from the biographies of the families of three divergent popovichi who will reappear in subsequent chapters: the radical publicist Nikolai Dobroliubov, the conservative stockbroker turned art collector Ivan Tsvetkov, and the liberal doctor and ethnographer Aleksandr Smirnov. Because how popovichi and the clergy were perceived by others affected both how popovichi fashioned themselves and how historians have misconstrued the lived experience of the clerical estate, this chapter will then focus on how the otherness of the clergy tainted popovichi even after they left the clerical estate. For as Pierre Bourdieu has observed, "A class is defined as much by its *being-perceived* as by its *being*."[8] And as is the case regarding a genuine "other," the dominant culture vacillated between viewing popovichi as fiends or as saviors. What remained constant was the perception by other Russians that popovichi were their opposite, that they were representatives of the alternative culture popovichi themselves espoused.

Forefathers

The father of Nikolai Dobroliubov, Aleksandr (1812–1854), an urban archpriest, was the son of a rural deacon and the grandson of a rural priest. Nikolai's paternal great-grandfather began life as a peasant. Although many clergymen could trace their clerical roots back to an ancestor who had served as a pastor in medieval Russia, it was not until reforms enacted during the eighteenth century that entrance into the parish clergy became closed to individuals from other estate groups. Prior to the Petrine era the majority of clergymen descended from clerical families as a result of a custom born mainly from practicality: in the absence of schools, clergymen were encouraged to homeschool their sons and train them at the altar. Formal theological schools were established by Petrine legislation, but clerical positions remained largely hereditary, since to ensure an adequate number of educated clergymen, enrollment in these schools was ruled mandatory for clergymen's sons. Because the peasantry had traditionally provided the largest number of outside recruits, their complete enserfment under Peter the Great contributed to the reserving of ecclesiastical education for clergymen's sons. The state also sought to prevent individuals from the poll-tax population—drawn from both the townspeople and the peasantry—as well as merchants, who paid a special tax, from joining the clergy and gaining the tax exemption status that only the clergy shared with the nobility. Russian nobles, unlike some of their Western European counterparts, showed little interest in joining the parish clergy. By the mid-eighteenth century it was unusual for someone other than a clergyman's son to study in a seminary; by the end of the eighteenth century, when the number of seminaries had rapidly increased, it was rare.[9]

The clergy also had its own reasons for closing the estate to outsiders: hereditary claims to clerical positions helped provide for clerical children. Either a son would inherit his father's parish seat, or, more often, he would receive his father-in-law's seat as part of his bride's dowry. Because of this custom of family claims, some villages were served by the same clerical family for several generations.

Marriage to a fellow member of the clerical estate was not only the means of obtaining a parish seat, it was also in keeping with clerical tradition. Even after the theoretical abolishment of hereditary claims in 1867, endogamy among the clergy remained the norm, despite the fact that marriage to the laity was never outlawed. Clergymen were, however, legally prohibited from marrying brides who were not ethnically Russian or were non-Orthodox. By contrast, as a consequence of the Russian empire's multi-ethnicity, Russian nobles frequently married persons of other faiths, and in the mid-nineteenth century roughly half of the noble social estate did not speak Russian as their native tongue. The clergy was also the only Russian social estate group whose members tended to live in a nuclear family structure.[10]

Marriage played another key role in obtaining a clerical position: unmarried candidates were not ordained. Although Orthodox canon law merely stipulated that an ordained clergyman could not marry *after* ordination, Slavic and Greek Orthodox churches had enacted ecclesiastical legislation over the centuries prohibiting unmarried candidates from the priesthood. Despite the overturning in 1667 of Russian council rulings on this question, and the reiteration of the 1667 ruling in 1869, the custom of obligatory marriage prior to ordination prevailed throughout the imperial period. Because of this custom, the practice of hereditary family claims and the ordination of candidates for the priesthood immediately following the completion of their education in the all-male bursa, many clerical marriages were arranged, even after love marriages became standard among Russian nobles in the mid-nineteenth century.

Besides marriage, education increasingly became a requirement for ordination as the nineteenth century progressed. One of Nikolai Dobroliubov's great-grandfathers, for example, born in 1764, was ordained a priest without receiving any formal education. He was, however, literate enough to teach a small group of sacristans to read. His son attended a seminary and attained the rank of deacon. Subsequently, his son, Nikolai's father, graduated from the seminary in 1832, during a time when the expansion of clerical education ensured that almost half the priests in Russia had completed a seminary education. Although the general educational levels of the parish clergy continued to improve throughout the nineteenth century, the disparity between the education of priests and the lower clerical ranks of deacons and unordained sacristans remained. In 1860, for example, 82.6 percent of priests were seminary graduates, compared to 0.4 percent of sacristans and 15.6 percent of deacons.[11] Because of the increased importance of education for obtaining placement, this disparity sharply hampered upward mobility through the clerical ranks.

Despite these advances in clerical education, Russian priests consistently remained less educated than Protestant ministers in Western European countries, who customarily received advanced university degrees. In contrast to Western Europe, secular and clerical education was always bifurcated in Imperial Russia, and clergymen could receive a higher theological education only at one of the three theological academies (a fourth was opened in 1842). These small academies trained a fraction of the number of students Russian universities educated. The primary purpose of these academies was not to educate priests, but to produce church hierarchs and perpetuate the clerical education system by training subsequent generations of academy and seminary professors. A minority of priests attended them.[12] Nevertheless, despite the stereotype of the barely literate priest, Russian priests were much more educated than clergymen in any other Orthodox country and were far more educated than any other Russian social estate apart from the nobility.

What did the ecclesiastical duties of a priest consist of? They included officiating for all the sacraments of the church with the exception of ordination. Priests were also responsible for listening to confessions, delivering sermons, and performing religious rites and conferring blessings outside of the church, such as in parishioners' homes. In the mid-nineteenth century the average parish consisted of 1,300 parishioners.[13] Although some parishes were served by more than one priest, the demanding liturgical calendar of the Orthodox Church, which includes numerous additional services during holidays entailing all-night vigils, dictated a strenuous schedule with little respite.

Priests were assisted by ordained deacons and unordained sacristans. The responsibilities of a deacon included assisting the priest during divine services in the officiating of sacraments, reciting the common prayers, and supervising worshippers' demeanor in church. The specific responsibilities of sacristans consisted of ringing church bells and supervising the physical welfare and upkeep of the church building. They also served as clerks, maintaining parish registers. In 1855, there were 62,603 sacristans in Russia, compared to 12,570 deacons and 35,406 priests, making the lowest clerical rank by far the most numerous.[14] Unordained clergymen were legislatively less privileged. For example, sacristans were not freed from corporal punishment until 1862, a right which was accorded ordained clergymen in 1801, years after it had been granted to nobles and the first two guilds of merchants.

The vast majority of clergymen served in rural parishes where they ministered almost exclusively to peasant parishioners. Until the Great Reforms, rural clerical families were usually the only nonpeasants who resided within village borders; clerical homes were normally situated next to the church on the village outskirts. Once *zemstvo* (postreform local self-government) schools began to spread throughout rural Russia, schoolteachers joined clerical families as educated village residents. As will be seen in Chapter 6, however, many of these schoolteachers were either popovichi or their sisters (*popov'ny*).[15]

Because their flock was largely illiterate and impoverished, rural clergymen had to attend to many of their parishioners' basic needs. The supplementary functions of rural clergymen increased substantially in the 1860s when the pastoral care movement, begun in the 1840s, gained momentum. This movement was engendered by four phenomena: a newfound emphasis

Ivan Tsvetkov, seated with his mother and sister Liubov' (his wife is standing), 1892. (Courtesy of Russian State Archive of Literature and Art, Moscow, f.904, op.1, d.352, l.1)

on moralism spawned by romanticism, German Pietist texts, and translations of the Early Eastern Church Fathers; church school reforms that expanded the teaching of theology in 1840; the dramatic increase of clerical print culture in the 1860s; and a clergy emboldened by the end of serfdom, a relaxation of censorship following Nicholas I's death in 1855, and the state's invitation to society to involve itself in the Great Reform process.[16] As will be discussed, the pastoral care movement generated many of the prescriptive clerical texts that popovichi used to fashion themselves.

The primary goal of the pastoral care movement was to instill informed piety into parishioners through edification. This internal mission led to the translation of the Bible from Slavonic into the vernacular and its publication in the mid-nineteenth century. But in rural Russia, clergymen first had to render their parishioners literate. Because of the dearth of village schools in prereform Russia, rural clergymen, usually the only educated individuals in their villages, had in a number of cases taught parishioners informally, and free of charge, in their own homes. In the postreform period, the majority of ordained clergymen taught in schools, institutionalizing and expanding their role as teachers.[17]

Rural clergymen also enlightened their parishioners through paraliturgical discussions, during which they instructed and advised parishioners about living their lives according to the tenets of the Orthodox faith. The themes of the paraliturgical discussions conducted by Father Emelian Tsvetkov (1822–1888), Ivan Tsvetkov's father, included explaining how to pray and the nature of God. The number of priests engaging in these discussions increased dramatically over the course of the century, as did the number of sermons priests composed and delivered. During his career Father Emelian wrote sermons on topics such as the Mother of God, the prodigal son, and the fourteenth-century Saint Prince Aleksandr Nevskii.[18]

As a consequence of the late development of free professions and the dearth of educated citizens in Russia, clergymen performed a wide variety of the new secular civic functions created by the modernizing state. In urban areas some clergy served as members of city councils, deputies of the city police, notary publics, and after 1906, the Duma; they also sat on public library, agricultural, and charity committees. In rural villages priests served as medics, vaccinators, and scribes. Because of their intimate familiarity with their peasant parishioners, as well as the traditional role they played as repositories of local archives, rural clergymen, particularly retired priests, also collected ethnographic and statistical data for scholarly organizations such as the Imperial Geographic Society. Their performance of secular roles runs counter to standard secularization theory, which equates modernization with the clergy's ceasing to perform secular duties.[19]

But priests were forbidden to perform some secular political functions. These included giving legal advice, serving on a jury or draft board, or being an arbitrator of peace.[20] Unlike the separation of church and state in many Western countries following the French Revolution, under the doctrine of "symphony" that the Russian Orthodox Church inherited from Byzantium, the tsar remained obligated to protect the Church from internal and external enemies, and, in exchange, the Church refrained from independent political activism. Like Lutheran clergymen in Denmark-Norway, Russian priests were required by state and church law to swear an oath of loyalty to the tsar and to the welfare of the fatherland. Priests were legally required to hand over to the police parishioners who divulged political crimes during confession. No evidence exists, however, to confirm that any priest ever violated the confidentiality of the rite of confession.

Parish clergymen customarily expressed pro-monarchist sentiments in their sermons, and they could be denounced and penalized for any anti-monarchist statements they uttered. Father Emelian Tsvetkov glorified members of the royal family in commemorations marking their birthdays. Yet Father Emelian qualified his support for the monarchy. In a sermon consecrating the ascension to the throne of Alexander II, he referred to the social contract between tsar and people, outlining the responsibilities of the tsar to be the single soul of the millions of diverse people living in

Orthodox Russia and to serve the general will.[21] The increasing sense among some clergymen that the tsar had broken this social contract was one of the reasons a few young priests entered into conflict with the state by engaging in illegal political protests and conspiring with radical parties. Those clergymen who did take political action on the eve of the revolution, however, were loath to admit that their actions were political. They tended to disavow specific parties, claiming allegiance only to their nation, their church, and their estate. The clergy's hesitance to become involved in partisan politics explains why, despite the nationalistic monarchism of most clergymen, they remained absent from the leadership of ultra-nationalist parties.[22]

Rural priests were frequently assisted in pastoral care by their wives. Canon law dictated that women could fulfill only certain limited liturgical duties, such as baking communion bread, singing in the choir in religious services, and reading prayers and didactic texts. But priests' wives (*matushki*) were allowed to—and increasingly did—counsel female parishioners on marital problems and hygiene, engage in charity work, administer first aid, and teach in parish schools. In contrast to their husbands' contact with parishioners, which usually took place within the framework of Orthodox rites, the interaction of matushki with parishioners was more informal. The majority of matushki's time, however, was spent performing household chores and attending to their many children. Ivan Tsvetkov's mother, for example, gave birth to nine children; Dobroliubov's to eight. The household duties of matushki included spinning yarn, flaxing linen, and sewing clothes, even though most priests' families employed a servant. Since their husbands were struggling to meet their multitude of official duties, matushki were also usually in charge of all budgetary matters. In the prereform period the education of clerical women was restricted with few exceptions to a rudimentary domestic education, which was not universal. By the late nineteenth century, the majority of clerical daughters received some degree of formal education, and many priests' daughters attended the rapidly expanding number of women's diocesan secondary schools designed specifically for them. Yet despite these advancements over the course of the century, literacy among clerical women lagged behind that of noblewomen.[23]

The parish clergy drew their main financial support directly from parishioners in the form of voluntary contributions (*treby*) for ceremonies performed, such as weddings, funerals, baptisms, and paraliturgical blessings. Income from treby was determined by the prosperity and generosity of parishioners. Because of the greater concentration of wealth in urban areas, urban clerics tended to be more well-off than their rural counterparts, particularly if they lived in capital cities. Dobroliubov's father, for example, who lived in the capital of Nizhnii-Novgorod province, represented the high end of clerical prosperity. He was able to purchase a three-story stone house and hire a cook as well as a nanny, all of which were exceptional feats for a priest. He was also able to acquire a substantial personal library of over 650 volumes. Yet in comparison to landowning Russian nobles and wealthy merchants, the Dobroliubovs' standard of living was modest. Besides wages from teaching and the nominal dowry of money and/or goods that a wife brought to their marriage, a Russian priest's income was his family's sole subsistence. Clergymen were not allowed to own serfs or loan money, nor were they permitted to engage in trade. Dobroliubov's mother worked alongside her servant; the sole cow they owned was invaluable to their household. It took years for the Dobroliubovs to buy the land and build their stone house, and they were only able to do this after receiving a 10,000-ruble mortgage. Their house was not merely a dwelling; it generated income from the numerous tenants whom they housed.[24]

Whereas Dobroliubov's father earned 800 rubles in 1854 from treby, in 1850 the entire rural parish—consisting of a priest, deacon, and sacristan—served by the sacristan father of Aleksandr Smirnov, Vasilii (1822–1899), earned 479 rubles. In addition to this disparity between rural and urban clerical income, all earnings, whether from treby or from the meager government salaries instituted in a few regions in the postreform period, were divided hierarchically among the three clerical ranks. Priests were paid twice as much as deacons and two-thirds more than sacristans. The amount of earnings the clergy divided among themselves also fluctuated considerably from parish to parish, from year to year, and from region to region. For example, in 1870 the three clergymen in the new town parish to which the Smirnovs had relocated earned 646 rubles; by 1876 the income for this same parish had fallen to 477 rubles. By comparison, in 1884 a clerk in the Ministry of Internal Affairs earned between 1,180 to 1,500 rubles a year, and a teacher in a provincial gymnasium earned 800 rubles in 1866. To address the national dilemma of clerical poverty, the Holy Synod attempted repeatedly to regulate treby through contractual agreements with parishioners, but Russian parishioners did not accept that it was their responsibility to support the clergy. Disputes over payment for treby were a common source of anti-clericalism and spawned the stereotype of the greedy priest. In the first parish where Smirnov's father served, the priest was sworn at and beaten by peasants during such an altercation in 1842. If parishioners had to pay, they preferred to set prices on a day-to-day basis as they saw fit, reserving the right to control local parish life by rewarding and penalizing individual priests.[25]

To supplement their meager earnings some sacristans earned extra money by resorting to manual labor, such as carpentry and shoemaking. Their ability to subsist, however, was primarily the result of their agricultural labor. The clergy of each parish were collectively allotted varying amounts of land by parishioners, and this land, like their income, was divided hierarchically among clerical ranks. Smirnov's father was given six *desiatins* (just over sixteen acres) to farm in his new parish and was able to grow enough food in 1870 to earn twenty-two rubles by selling excess

grain. In the village where he had previously served, however, he was allotted less than the three-to-five desiatins that Lenin would later use to define
the land holdings of a typical *bedniak* (poor peasant) family. Not surprisingly, sacristans' families' clothing and lifestyles sometimes led them to be
mistaken for peasants, particularly in the prereform period. In the village
where Smirnov's father first served, all of the clergy worked their land allot-
ments themselves. By contrast, in 1876 Smirnov was the only member of
the clergy in his urban parish who farmed his land. The young priest and
deacon, along with an increasing number of other ordained clergymen,
rented out their land. Many ordained clergymen in rural areas, however,
continued to farm most of their land throughout the nineteenth century.
They were assisted in plowing and harrowing the fields by their adolescent
sons during school vacations and by their wives and daughters, who attended to the farm animals and helped reap the harvest and plant rye.[26]

In contrast, the celibate monastic clergy, who did not have families to
support, were financially secure. Because of the requirement of monasticism to qualify for the office of bishop, they also wielded absolute power
within the Church hierarchy. Each of the sixty-one dioceses had its own
bishop. Although they were permitted to perform sacraments, bishops
spent the bulk of their time tending to administrative functions, including
the administration of ecclesiastical schools. In addition, bishops governed
all the parish clergymen in their diocese, including appointing, transferring, ordaining, supervising, promoting, and disciplining. As monastics,
bishops were not allowed to hold any secular offices and they were frequently relocated to different dioceses, hampering their familiarity with
and loyalty to local parish clergy. With the exception of bishops, who were
required to be graduates of the theological academies, admission to which
was largely reserved for seminary graduates and therefore clergymen's sons,
monks were drawn from all estate groups, and education was not a requirement for tonsuring. In the mid-nineteenth century only half of all male
monastics were of clerical origin and many were uneducated. Compared to
the parish clergy, monks were also few in number and were almost completely isolated from the laity.[27] Subsequent chapters will discuss how
popovichi and their fathers sometimes used the monastic clergy as another
foil—in addition to the nobility—against which to define themselves.

Despite living among the laity, however, the parish clergy was relatively
socially isolated from other social estate groups. The major recreational
events in the clerical family revolved around parish holidays and religious
rites such as weddings and anniversaries of the local priest's years in service.
These activities conveyed a sense of professional identity among the clergy
and further accentuated their distinctiveness from the laity, especially since
the clergy officiated at these ceremonies. A study of the records of clergymen's sons' godparents, who were chosen from among trusted family
friends, indicates that clerical families socialized informally mainly with
other clerical families as late as the 1890s. And both of the godparents

of the radical publicist Nikolai Chernyshevskii (1828–1889), Dobroliubov's closest friend and author of *What Is to Be Done?*—the highly influential novel that served as an etiquette manual for generations of Russian radicals—were members of the clerical estate, despite the fact that his father was an urban archpriest and his mother was the rare matushka born into the nobility.[28] Because of this clerical social isolation as well as the rural origins of the vast majority of popovichi, they had little actual prior comprehension of the urban milieu, which most of them entered by virtue of their higher secular education and professions.

Early Images—

Popovichi as Bearers of a Distinct Culture

Once they entered that world, popovichi remained marked, for better or worse, by their clerical heritage. The otherness that enshrouded Orthodox clergymen was inherited by their families. According to Orthodox tradition, for example, parishioners were supposed to bow to members of a clergyman's family. In general, despite the socio-economic differences between clerical ranks, in the eyes of outsiders all members of the clergy were the same. Writing in 1872, the populist thinker Aleksandr Engel'gardt, a nobleman, noted: "By the word 'priests' the peasants mean everyone belonging to the clergy, everyone who wears long hair, and a special priest's frock; this means the priest, the deacon, the sexton, the sacristan. . . ." Engel'gardt's comment is as indicative of his own views as it is of those of the peasants he observed. Even the tsarist police shared this popular conception, often referring in official documents, such as arrest records, to sacristans' and deacons' sons as sons of priests.[29] Clerical last names, which did not differ according to clerical rank, contributed to this misconception, identifying popovichi of all ranks to the outside world as generic clergymen's sons.

But because popovichi were not legally members of the clerical estate and were enrolled in the same higher educational institutions, employed in the same professions, and active in the same movements as intelligenty from other estates, their "otherness," though grounded in anti-clericalism, was distinct from that of their clerical families. Competing on a daily basis as they did with educated nobles over membership—and leadership—of the intelligentsia, they were a threat to the noble intelligent's very sense of self. Popovichi forced the nobility to defend their right to be part of the intelligentsia, and as is always the case with a "proximate other" their battle was fiercer and more imperative than the tension between the anti-clerical nobility and clergy had ever been.[30]

Anti-clericalism colored perceptions of popovichi as a group in the prereform period. Pushkin not only slandered clergymen, he also referred to their secular sons as vulgar and degenerate. When he wanted to attack the renowned ethnographer/publicist Nikolai Nadezhdin (1804–1856) he reminded his readers of Nadezhdin's clerical parentage and seminary education. Invoking clerical stereotypes, he called him, among other things, a "drunken seminarian" from an "estate of servants." In her memoirs about her father, the daughter of the popovich publicist Maksim Antonovich (1835–1918) described the reaction of her maternal grandfather, a nobleman, to her parents' marriage. Antonovich met his noble bride when he served as her family's tutor, a customary way for seminarians to earn money. Antonovich's father-in-law never reconciled himself to the marriage. By marrying a popovich, his wife severed virtually all of her ties to her relatives and her former social circle. Antonovich's father-in-law referred to him as a *kuteinik,* a slang term derived from the word for a grain used to prepare a food eaten primarily after funerals (*kut'ia*).[31] Because secular society viewed popovichi as forever branded by their clerical origins, it was only fitting that this slang term, originally coined to insult members of the clergy, was used to ridicule popovichi.

Nobles of all political orientations in the preform period perceived popovichi as the scourge of society. Writing in 1862, the conservative literary critic Mikhail Katkov predicted that nihilism would flourish among clerical offspring due to their fathers' lack of spirituality and ignorance. The liberal bureaucrat Boris Chicherin, a nobleman who helped engineer the Great Reforms, recalled that he met Chernyshevskii only once and never imagined that a "meager seminarian" could have turned the heads of so many young people.[32]

These noble intelligenty felt threatened by popovichi, whom they believed to be the antithesis of noble identity. By the mid-nineteenth century the Russian nobility was a cohesive estate. Yet because individuals from other estates could be ennobled, as Dobroliubov's younger brother Vladimir was, the nobility's self-definition had less to do with legal status than with culture. This culture was defined by the nobility as entailing a "proper" Western-oriented education, "correct" breeding, and a "civilized" lifestyle, and it was defined in opposition to traits nobles associated with other Russian estate groups. Noble intelligenty expected individuals from other estates to be subordinate to them, and popovichi were not. Turgenev privately attacked popovichi publicists, the most visible upstarts in the preform period, for not acknowledging the superiority of noble culture. He complained to a fellow noble: "They are envious, because they grew up on Lenten oil, and therefore they insolently want to wipe from the face of the earth poetry, fine arts, all aesthetic enjoyments and establish in their place coarse seminarian principles. These are, gentlemen, literary Robespierres. . . ."[33] If popovichi had accepted their lower social standing and humbly attempted to assimilate noble intelligentsia culture, they might have been tolerated. Instead, they were the nobility's chief competitors.

As a true "other," popovichi were perceived as endowed with distinct essentialist physical features. In her description of a popovich who converted her older sister to nihilism, the noble-born mathematician Sof'ia Kovalevskaia captures this otherness:

His ungainly, lanky body, long veiny neck and pale face fringed with thin rusty-blond hair, his big red hands with their flat and not always irreproach-ably clean fingernails; and worst of all, his unpleasant, vulgar accent overem-phasizing the "o's" and bearing unmistakable witness to his clerical origins and seminary education—none of this made him a very attractive hero in the eyes of a young girl of aristocratic tastes and habits.

This conception of popovichi's deformities as physiological was not limited to noblewomen. One noble claimed that *all* popovichi were immediately recognizable due to their distinct smell.[34] The conception of culture that was so intrinsic to noble self-definition consisted of an amalgamation of an "acceptable" physical appearance—expressed simultaneously in dress, hy-giene, and bone structure—with social grace and manners. In short, popovichi were seen by noble intellectuals as a subspecies.

Even in the few positive portrayals by prereform nobles, popovichi were depicted as a group characterized by distinct traits. The neo-Slavophile Apollon Grigorev, writing in 1862, described a seminarian type that tran-scended generation, profession, and political affiliation. Highly erudite and imbued with a sense of superiority, single-mindedness, and self-centered-ness, this type was fearless, having survived great hardships in the poverty-stricken bursa.[35] While Grigorev evaluated these characteristics as benefi-cial, his portrait bears striking resemblance to the caricature of the intelligentsia lambasted by Semen Frank in 1909. Other intelligenty would castigate popovichi for these very same traits.

The literary critic Aleksandr Miliukov, the son of a townsman, was one such intelligent. Describing popovichi publicists, he wrote in the 1860s: "They brought with them hatred of all existing customs, and they revenge themselves for their past with realism and nihilism. Having engaged in lit-erary endeavors, they brought with them their bursa manners." Miliukov warned that a "continent" of seminarians was overwhelming Russian cul-ture with their particular style. He argued that this style—which he, along with others, defined as "coarse," narrow-minded, utilitarian, anti-aesthetic, devoid of feeling, critical thinking and elegance, dogmatic, and a slavish imitation of Western ideas—stemmed directly from their "medieval" scholastic seminary education. These "modern scholastics" who saw them-selves as the "literature of the future" were instead living representatives of the pseudo-poets educated in the seventeenth-century Moscow Slavonic-Latin Theological Academy, and like them, they would soon be forgotten. He implored his audience to name one writer or poet with "aesthetically developed taste" who had emerged from the seminary. He argued that no matter how talented, industrious, and dedicated these men were, because of their training they could not contribute beneficially to society.[36] Preju-dice and hostility toward popovichi was clearly not limited to the nobility.

This widespread conception of popovichi as a distinct, menacing group was even shared by foreigners. In his famous account of his trip to Russia in

1839, Marquis de Custine wrote that the sons of priests constituted "a special kind of men who should not be included among the elite, nor among the ordinary people." These men, anti-aristocratic to the core, were "Russia's plague" and "a nuisance to the state." He warned that it would be these men "who will start Russia's next revolution."[37]

Popovichi also surfaced as villains in mid-nineteenth-century Russian fiction and art. Fedor Dostoevskii, the son of a recently ennobled medic, cast his anti-hero Rakitin, in *The Brothers Karamazov,* as a popovich. Because of his clerical origins, Rakitin hates nobles; he is an atheist who believes men are capable of creating paradise. His dream is to marry a wealthy woman for her money so that he can move to the capital. Dostoevskii, despite his Orthodox nationalism, despised popovichi as a group, and in the mid-1870s noted in his diary, "I have found the enemy of Russia—seminarians." The plot of an 1863 play by a merchant playwright also plays on noble fears that popovichi intended to seduce their women to further their illicit challenge to noble power: a seminarian attempts to have an affair with a married noblewoman, whom he hopes can assist him in securing a lofty position in the bureaucracy. The noblewoman is both horrified and amused by the seminarian's proposition. After she informs her husband of the seminarian's plans, husband and wife decide to play a joke on the preposterous would-be suitor. The noblewoman cons the seminarian into pretending that he is a dispossessed nobleman. The seminarian is, of course, utterly unfit to play his role successfully, as is revealed not only by his ignorance of basic etiquette but also his unfamiliarity with Moscow, Petersburg, and the location of Western European capitals. This caricature of the greedy, immoral, uncouth popovich also appeared in the mid-nineteenth century in the classic plays of the merchant writer Aleksandr Ostrovskii, the vignettes of the noble satirist Mikhail Saltykov-Shchedrin, and the paintings of the raznochinets artist Vasilii Perov.[38]

Populist Emulation of the Popovich as "Proximate Other"

Representations of popovichi did not remain static. In the wake of the Great Reforms, attitudes toward popovichi within some intelligentsia circles changed with the advent of populism and generational strife between noble fathers and sons. By embracing uncouth popovichi, young nobles had found an appropriate means to express their rebellion against their parents. In the age of populism, popovichi were attractive to noble radicals because they were both bearers of an alternative to noble serf-owning culture and because their clerical origins were perceived as wedding them to the peasantry.

Russian populism, a widespread radical movement that emerged in the 1850s, had its heyday in the 1860s and '70s and waned in the 1890s before dying out in the 1920s. It was neither a coherent body of doctrine nor a political party. The beliefs that populists held in common included the romantic notions that the folk were the nation, that the Russian peasant was Russia's savior, that capitalism and industrialization were not progressive since they did not promote social justice and social equality, and that it was necessary to crush the autocracy and the old social structure in order to attend first and foremost to the peasantry's material needs. Although political radicalism is part of the classic definition of Russian populism, some scholars have identified a broader form of populism, which was centered around the belief that the peasantry was the repository of Russian national identity. It had a revolutionary as well as a conservative element. Conservative populism praised the peasantry as a conservative force imbued with monarchism and piety; it was widespread in the bureaucracy, as bureaucrats competed with various intelligentsia groups over who would represent the peasantry, who comprised up to 90 percent of Russia's population. It extended to reactionary parties such as the Union of Russian People, and even inspired the last two tsars, who modeled their worship, appearance, and hobbies after the peasantry.[39]

The clergy and their secular sons were widely considered to be part of the *narod*, the nebulous term denoting the "folk," masses, or common people, which was most often synonymous with the peasantry. In 1877, when the noble-born composer Alexander Borodin decided to write his opera *Prince Igor* in an average peasant dwelling, he chose the home of the father of one of his co-workers from the Military-Medical Academy, the popovich Professor Alexander Dianin (1851–1919). In a letter to Dianin, Borodin equated Dianin's priest father with the kinder, gentler world of the non-Westernized peasantry, a world which was the antithesis of his own Western-oriented, urban milieu:

> What a pity it was to have to leave Davydovo. I felt sorry for your sweet father. He personifies simplicity, kindness, and warmth, which I can only imagine in a person who has come from the narod but has never left the narod. How much there is in him that is innate, subtle, true—not bourgeois European—a delicateness, courtesy of simplicity without any kind of disparaging, helpfulness without servility. We lived with him in harmony, although we did not see each other that often or that much. He was too busy, either with his church or household affairs. And finally, his style of life was so different from ours that it was quite clear—we were like the sun and moon.

That same year the noble writer Pavel Zasodimskii described the popovich writer Aleksandr Levitov (1835–1877) as a full-fledged member of the narod: "he came from the country, from the narod . . . inside of him all of his life there existed a simple and agreeable Russian man." Zasodimskii emphasized that when you listened to Levitov, you would forget you were listening to a writer and would think you had a dressed-up *muzhik* (peasant man) in front of you, "to the extent there was preserved in him the characteristic ways of thinking and speech of the people."[40]

As individual living representatives of the faceless peasantry in the discernable guise of educated professionals, popovichi were even sometimes deemed superior to peasants. In the 1870s the poet Nikolai Nekrasov chose a deacon's son, rather than a peasant, to serve as Russia's savior in his famous poem *"Komu na Rusi zhit' khorosho."* Because he was raised among the peasants in poverty but is also educated, the deacon's son Grisha can serve *his* people and therefore bring happiness to Russia: he is simultaneously the people's past, present, and future.

This identification of popovichi as the crème de la crème of the narod lingered well into the twentieth century. In his biography of the popovich ethnographer Ivan Orlovskii (1869–1909), the conservative military judge Aleksandr Zhirkevich, son of a prominent noble family, described Orlovskii as having spent his childhood among "the simple, dark, humble narod, with the rural clergy, which had not long ago come from that narod." Consequently, according to Zhirkevich, Orlovskii personified in an exaggerated form many characteristics of the common people, suggesting that Orlovskii was more of a peasant than the peasants themselves.[41]

Because of their alleged peasant roots, the populism of popovichi was perceived by their contemporaries as fundamentally different from that of noble populists. According to the pre-revolutionary critic Dmitrii Ovsianiko-Kulikovskii, the "new men" of the 1860s, most of whom were popovichi, had every right to say "I am the narod." Since popovichi had never been alienated from the peasantry, they did not need to go and learn from the peasants as noble populists did. But their "native" knowledge of the peasantry gave them more than a head start; it was perceived at times as fostering a more genuine populism. As insiders, they suffered none of the repentance or trepidations of their noble peers. Unalienated from the peasantry, they tended not to idealize the peasants, as noble populists like Mikhail Bakunin did. This allowed them, Ovsianiko-Kulikovskii concluded, to realistically and critically discern the indignities and hardships of peasants' daily lives so they could work to alleviate peasant suffering. In 1892 a colleague born into a secular estate described the particular populism of the popovich writer Karonin (N.E. Petropavlosvkii [1853–1892]):

> . . . he was from a clerical family from Saratov province. . . . His conscious childhood years were spent in the countryside, among the already liberated peasantry, with whom his entire family came into direct and close day-to-day contact. Here his deep attachment to the countryside and the peasantry was begotten, which later developed into a sincere and highly conscious love, comprising the defining characteristic of both his personality and his talent. He lived the countryside, breathed it, ached for it and based on it all his faith in life and the future. But this does not mean that N.E. closed his eyes to the poverty and evil raining down on the village structure, that he did not see or ignored these features. However, he was able to understand them, to explain their causes.

Because noble populists preferred at times to idealize the peasantry, popovichi writers' allegedly realistic portrayal of village life was not always heralded; their populism was, however, always perceived as distinct.[42]

Peasant narratives that mention popovichi do indicate that some peasants believed that popovichi, particularly those whom they had known since childhood, had a distinctive insight into peasant life. These peasant authors, however, clearly do not regard popovichi as peasants. One peasant *starosta* (elected elder), for example, writing in 1911, recalled a popovich who had been his friend since childhood: "From his childhood years S.S. also learned how to suffer. He lived among us, carried on a friendship with us, came to visit us in our dirty little huts, witnessed the sorrow and suffering of the peasant family. One could say that all that influenced greatly his young soul, developed it, made it mild and responsive to all surrounding it."[43]

In an era in which virtually everyone claimed to be the legitimate voice of the peasantry, popovichi were the only group whom the majority of society—even rivals, and even some of the peasants themselves—accepted as authentic. They were the self-appointed vanguard of the masses, the central trait that Frank criticized as endemic to the postreform intelligentsia.

Another positive populist-related feature widely associated with popovichi beginning in the late imperial period was their "Russianness." The historian Mikhail Bogoslovskii, a bureaucrat's son, described this link between popovichi and Russian "national" tradition in his 1912 description of the popovich historian Vasilii Kliuchevskii (1841–1911):

> Kliuchevskii originated from that societal milieu in which more than in any other there remains a sense of attachment and love of the past. It is from this milieu that S.M. Solov'ev originated, and from this milieu in antiquity that our chronicles were born. . . . The stamp of that milieu lay on all of the external conditions of his domestic structure. In the rooms of his apartment . . . there was something extremely reminiscent of the home of a rural priest. Even in his own physical appearance, in his attractive head, framed by fairly long hair, in that wedge-shaped thin chin, in the sharp look of his eyes through his glasses there was something, which, despite the complete originality of his appearance, associated him with types which are found among our clergy.[44]

For Bogoslovskii, the fact that so many of Russia's prominent historians were popovichi was not a coincidence. The Russian "national" tradition he alluded to, originating in the pre-Petrine medieval chronicles, was stripped of the Western influences that permeated Russian noble culture. It was in the clergy, the only other educated Russian estate, that the "true" Russian culture had been preserved.

Vasilii Kliuchevskii in 1893.

The Enemy Reemerges—

Turn-of-the-Century Representations

Bogoslovskii's description of Kliuchevskii is reverential, yet like the gentry intelligenty who branded popovichi in the mid-nineteenth century, he still conceived of popovichi as a socially distinct group with essentialist features. Veneration of popovichi—like that of the peasantry with whom they were associated—contributed to the perpetuation of popovichi's image as an "other." And since popovichi were a true "other," conceptions of them vacillated between castigation and idealization.[45] Even after social stigma toward other estates began to dissipate in the increasingly fluid early twentieth century, the association of popovichi with the clerical "other" continued to stigmatize them.

Even members of other social estate groups who studied in the bursa and radical populists who embraced popovichi were capable of expressing this anti-clerical prejudice toward popovichi at the turn of the century. In their memoirs, seminarians who were born into secular estates, a tiny but growing minority, referred to clergymen's sons using the slur *kuteiniki* and portrayed them as drunken, exploitative, greedy, and spoiled. Because the clergy was perceived as an estate with essentialist features, even a rare non-clergyman's son who was ordained a priest vented his bias against members of the clerical estate in 1903.[46] He was now a clergyman, but because he was not born into the clerical estate, he did not consider himself tainted by the features commonly associated with the clergy. The populist writer Vladimir Korolenko, on the other hand, who was himself married to the daughter of a priest and had described the clergy sympathetically in his fiction, referred in his diary in 1894 to Kliuchevskii as a kuteinik.[47]

Popovichi also faced new opposition from radical circles following the decline of populism in the late nineteenth century. With the proliferation of Marxism in the 1890s, anti-clerical sentiment reemerged with a new, sharpened focus. The Orthodox Church was a state church, and as more and more people turned violently against the state, the church and its clergy became targets. During the 1905 revolution, when seminaries rose up in opposition to autocracy alongside the rest of society, one revolutionary exchanged correspondence with rebel seminarians. In his letters, in which he proposed organizational advice, he told his potential comrades that he doubted they would be able to contribute anything to the revolution. He had asked his comrades, he said, and they had all agreed that there wasn't much point in associating with seminarians because of their stunted mental development.[48]

Like Russian Marxists, most non-radical members of the landed nobility also heaped scorn on popovichi, even at the height of populism. In the decades following the Great Reforms, many members of the landed nobility, convinced that the dismantling of the feudal estate system was an assault on them, began to try to reassert themselves as Russia's ruling class. They lashed out at the newly mobile popovichi, their main competitors in the workplace and the cultural arena. In 1889 the nobleman Nikolai Vagner, a professor of zoology, remarked about a colleague from the clergy: "he was a person from the clerical rank knowing little, but with glib seminarian's speech." Theories of popovichi's genetic inferiority were extended to a new, albeit logical, conclusion: even the sons of popovichi were tainted. Regarding Konstantin Pobedonostsev, the ober-procurator of the Holy Synod and the grandson of a priest, the noble-born wife of a general wrote in her diary in 1881: "He has a petty soul, he is envious, in his veins runs the blood of pastors." Even pious Slavophiles were capable of hostility toward popovichi. In the 1870s the noble-born Konstantin Leontev ended an argument with his friend and fellow neo-Slavophile, the popovich Nikolai Strakhov (1828–1896), by telling him: "you are still just a seminarian!"[49]

Noble-born state officials, the bulwark of the autocracy, also worried about popovichi's pernicious influence on society. Many of these officials were behind Alexander III's counter-reforms, which aimed to restore the estate-based social order of the pre-emancipation era that prevented popovichi from exercising power. In a diary entry from 1892, Aleksandr Polovtsov, the state secretary to Alexander III, attacked popovichi:

> a denser and denser cluster emerges of popovichi, seminarians, barge haulers, greedy rascals. They fool their poor sovereign and achieve the destruction of everything which is superior to them, securing the inviability of wild, gregarious forms of survival of the gray crowd, not wishing to know the history, political economy, or any other scholarship devoted to the development and perfection of the human spirit. They establish so-called distinctiveness as the ideal of Russian political life, which amounts to the worship of the samovar, kvas, bast sandals, and a contempt toward everything that other nations have produced.[50]

Polovtsov directly contested the populist-oriented intelligentsia's assertion that popovichi deserved authority because of their affiliation with the peasantry. Nobles were superior to popovichi precisely because they represented the progressive West, the opposite of "backward" rural Russia.

Postreform government officials such as Polovtsov took steps beyond disparaging popovichi in private; they enacted legislation to protect society from them. After popovichi received secular legal status at birth in 1869, officials still continued to classify them by their social origin, ensuring that they did not assimilate into the population. Up until 1917 popovichi's clerical origins were included on military conscription lists, university diplomas, and arrest sheets. A regulation was imposed in 1889 requiring the offspring of clergymen to register their marriages and residency according to a different procedure than that followed by others who shared their legal status as hereditary and personal honorable citizens.[51] Legislation was issued periodically in the second half of the nineteenth century limiting clergymen's sons access to positions in the military and bureaucracy. As early as

1869 the secret police condemned seminarians studying in universities as particularly prone to radicalism and as corrupters of students from secular estates. Subsequent legislation sought to limit the number of seminarians in the universities. At first only a few individual seminaries were branded as hotbeds of radicalism and their students banned from entering universities. But by 1879 drastic measures were taken (see chapter 6).[52]

By the turn of the century, some noble intellectuals challenged the assertion that popovichi were representatives of Russian "national" culture. In 1901 one noble-born literary critic wrote a vicious attack on popovichi writers eerily reminiscent of Aleksandr Miliukov's charge decades earlier. To disassociate popovichi from any advantages they reaped from their widespread association with the peasantry, he focused his assault on the sons of priests, rather than the sons of deacons and sacristans, whose literary style he praised as folkish. Sons of priests, on the other hand, were the bearers of a clerical literary tradition that he claimed was at war with an older literary tradition borne by the sons of nobles. He dismissed those who mistook this "seminarian's school" for a raznochintsy literary tradition by claiming that despite the affiliation of a few non-clerical writers with this non-noble tradition, "in its entirety the school bore the mark of one estate, of one upbringing." This clerical tradition was characterized by its "rejection of Pushkin," its aesthetics, and the spirit "of everything which represents the fruits of the historical life of the narod." It represented fanaticism, "a naked, ascetic, severe realism and utilitarianism," scholasticism, and a descriptive literal-mindedness that did not even provide a correct depiction of reality. He directly connected this school to clerical culture by comparing the writings of a wide variety of popovichi to those of a priest. He portrayed noble intellectuals as anti-materialists, who had rejected their wealth and class privileges, while he claimed that popovichi were careerists who had left behind "poverty, the horrors of the bursa, beatings, cold, and hunger" to enrich themselves. In his analysis he grouped together popovichi from different generations such as the ethnographer and statesman Nikolai Nadezhdin, the radical publicist Grigorii Blagosvetlov, and the writer Fedor Reshetnikov (1841–1871)—popovichi whose only common trait was their clerical heritage.[53]

From the mid-nineteenth century on, popovichi were consistently deemed by defenders of noble culture as the enemy, as bearers of an alternative Russian culture that threatened to destroy its opponent. In early twentieth-century obituaries of noble professionals written by noble peers with a variety of political affiliations, the deceased are often praised for their European manners, orientation, and tact, which are contrasted to Russian customs, as well as for their social grace, physical attractiveness, recreational activities, and wide range of cultural interests. Despite the dramatic changes that Russian society experienced during the postreform period, these traits, virtually identical to those for which nobles were praised in the prereform period, continued to form the basis of Russian noble culture.[54]

At the turn of the century, however, yet another cultural shift occurred when a segment of Russian educated society began to reject noble culture in favor of the alternative culture that popovichi represented. In 1904, the literary critic Semen Vengerov, the son of a bank director, praised Grigorii Blagosvetlov as embodying the quintessential character of the "new man" of the 1860s. He defined this "new man" as possessing precisely the traits that defenders of noble hegemony castigated popovichi for: clerical origins, a seminary education, an inability to compromise or socialize, a need to lecture others on how to live, an intemperate industriousness, vulgarity, boundless energy, and "pureness of direction."[55] In obituaries and reminiscences written by colleagues from secular estates in the early twentieth century, individual popovichi were exalted for this heightened sense of moral conviction, self-destructive industriousness, and a seriousness that, in the words of one colleague, affected "attitude toward all questions of life, be they scholarly, political, social or even personal."[56] Because many educated Russians—including some nobles—embraced popovichi's alternative culture, it is not surprising that the obituaries of a wide range of professionals of non-clerical origins written by their peers in the late imperial period often praised the deceased for these same.[57] Noble and popovichi culture continued to co-exist, but the latter was gaining converts even among the former's brethren.

Defenders and foes of popovichi disagreed on whether their contribution to Russian society was positive or negative, but they agreed on what this culture represented. Vengerov's portrait—along with virtually every representation of popovichi we have examined—conforms to Semen Frank's definition of the postreform intelligentsia.

In his analysis of Blagosvetlov, Vengerov employed a sociological paradigm of two co-existing universalistic strains in any movement: that of a crowd and that of an elite. In this paradigm, the crowd always unseats the aristocracy, and by the early twentieth century popovichi and their alternative culture epitomized the ethos of the intelligentsia. Popovichi appeared as characters in the plays and short stories of Anton Chekhov, such as "Gusev" (1890), in which the strange-looking solider Ivanych is so confident of his moral superiority that not even the Spanish Inquisition can silence him. Popovichi became so closely associated with the image of the intelligentsia that when Mikhail Bulgakov wrote his satirical classic Heart of a Dog in 1925, he cast both the mad scientist and his assistant, who transform a street dog into a proletariat through a Frankenstein-like operation, as popovichi.

Representations of popovichi vacillated in the nineteenth and early twentieth centuries, but popovichi consistently remained an "other." The "lived" experiences of clerical families, despite some regional, hierarchical, and generational differences, also did not drastically change during the dynamic nineteenth century. Clerical daily life was characterized by social isolation, liturgical duties, segregated theological education, dependence on parishioners, lack of accumulated wealth, and powerlessness before monastic and secular authorities. Paradoxically, many of the particularities of the clerical estate allowed the clerical "other" to serve as a unique "cultural intermediary," in the words of Michel Vovelle, *between* estates, to bridge the perceived impenetrable gulf between the Russian elite and the masses and forge an alternative culture that would attract members of other estates. Certain aspects of their experience were shared by the "elite" noble ruling class, while other facets were similar to the way of life of the masses. Patriarchy, attachment to one locality, the labor of children and wives, and agricultural work—all were typical of the lifestyle of Russian peasants. Another characteristic of clerical life, learnedness, was associated only with the noble elite. The parish clergy—subservient to the State, the monastic clergy, and parishioners—was not a traditional elite, unless elites are defined by literacy alone. The clergy defies the two-tiered categorization of "elite" versus "masses" because it was exclusively an elite within the parish, the only arena that united Russians as equals regardless of estate distinctions.[58] The problem for the Russian nobility and the state was that the clergy—and even more its secular sons—perceived itself as not only an elite, but as the only legitimate elite qualified to lead Russia. As the narratives of popovichi and their fathers in upcoming chapters demonstrate, they countered their noble foes by turning the distinctiveness of the clerical milieu from a detriment in the eyes of their enemies to a prerequisite for intelligentsia leadership.

Popovichi and Their Fathers Judge Other Social Estates

In 1864 Aleksandr Tsvetkov, a student, wrote a letter to his brother Ivan about a last-minute social invitation from the noble family whose children he tutored. He recounted how horrified he was to learn, after he had already accepted, that two foreigners were to be present at the gathering. For Aleksandr, unlike his noble hosts, had never met a foreigner and could not converse in any modern language except Russian. At the party he tried unsuccessfully to avoid meeting these guests:

> Finally they flew up to me in the corner, shuffling their feet and bowing about in front of me, and they began to chatter away in the most elegant French dialect. I was completely dumbfounded, and, like a mad man, I cast my eyes upon them, opened my mouth and spread my arms. Not receiving any kind of answer from me, they again repeated their question. I panicked completely and couldn't put together even one muddled phrase.

After unsuccessfully trying to elicit assistance from his students, who were too busy to notice his desperate glances, Aleksandr attempted to utilize his bursa Latin: "I began to put together some sort of ridiculous Russian phrases together with a large smattering of Latin words and even entire phrases, such as 'aqua nitrosa utilis bibendo; o socii o *passi graviora!'* They did not understand what I said. Neither did I." Someone then came to Aleksandr's rescue and dragged him away, much to the bewilderment of the foreign guests, who asked their host what was wrong with him. This unpleasant exchange was followed by another catastrophe. Having never been at a social function, Aleksandr did not realize that he was expected to go to the ballroom. Once he realized his error and made his way there:

> I saw a glittering, huge room, filled with the most fantastic, capricious aristocrats. They were playing various types of games which I had never seen, heard, or sniffed of before; dances were beginning. . . . In a word, there was such a perturbation occurring there, that I was overcome with fever by the thought of being there. No matter what the consequences, I decided to escape.

Aleksandr hastily announced to his hosts that he had matters to attend to and bolted for the door, which he had difficulty opening. While he was struggling, he heard the other guests asking why he was leaving, speaking in blaring, agitated voices in a multitude of languages—English, German, French, and Russian. During the carriage ride home, he sighed, wrung his hands, and broke out in a sweat. The driver assumed he had lost his mind. But Aleksandr concludes by telling his brother that he is glad he left; he is sure he would have made even more of a fool of himself if he had stayed, since "I don't know any aristocratic gestures."

In subsequent letters, Aleksandr told his brother excitedly that he had conquered his shyness: "I am dealing with *boyars and the children of boyars* and I am not in the least embarrassed to socialize with them!" Yet Aleksandr continued to be amazed by the differences between the nobility's lifestyle and the one he was familiar with. He approached his employers as an ethnographer, not as a novice: "Our way of life is patriarchal, which I haven't at all noticed among the aristocracy."[1]

Even after they left the clergy, popovichi belonging to various generations continued to associate "our way of life" with the life of the parish clergy. Rather than identifying themselves primarily according to their legal classification as raznochintsy, they preferred the term "popovich."[2] Like secular observers and administrators, they rarely differentiated between the various ranks of the parish clergy when referring to themselves. They shared the widespread belief of pre-revolutionary secular society that they were a group distinguished by immutable features. In petitions written at the turn of the century, several argued that membership in the clerical estate was irrevocable and inherited through consanguineous ties, rendering them—and their offspring—members. Others claimed that they could recognize fellow popovichi from a mile away.[3] They agreed with their foes that they were a different type, but disagreed over both how to define this type and whether it was pejorative or affirmative. In turn, their definition of themselves as a collective remained consistent over a century, immune to the vacillations of others' representations of them.

The typology popovichi attributed to themselves consisted of a combination of physical, intellectual, and moral traits. In his unfinished history of his fellow popovichi written at the end of his life, the ethnographer and former gulag prisoner Aleksei Zolotarev (1879–1950) included grandsons of clergymen. He believed that the clergy was not only a socio-historical group with a shared consciousness, but a class status imbued with hereditary characteristics. Zolotarev described one clerical grandson, the scientist Vernadskii: "I personally took Vladimir Ivanovich as a typical popovich, beginning with his external features, his manner of speaking and working, and ending with his synthetic and audacious mind and thinking." Zolotarev portrayed popovichi as the embodiment of Russia's spiritual worth, talent, industriousness, and self-consciousness, as a group dedicated single-mindedly to serving her people. Despite his repudiation of the radicalism of his youth, Zolotarev insisted that radical popovichi were also products of the clergy, quoting Chernyshevskii's 1848 diary entry in which the publicist stated that he saw himself, more and more, resembling his father. To emphasize how integral and deeply rooted the image of the popovich was in Russian culture, Zolotarev reminded his potential audience of the character of "Alyosha popovich" in the classic medieval Russian folktale *Tri bogatyria*. More than the other two heroes of that tale, Alyosha was "representative of the intellectual and spiritual powers of the narod."[4]

Scores of other popovichi in the imperial period, regardless of their political affiliations, shared Zolotarev's assessment. They readily affiliated themselves and their kind with the traits Zolotarev later identified, traits that closely resemble the stereotype of the postreform intelligent coined by Semen Frank. They identified themselves proudly as "new men" ready to lead Russia and entitled to do so because they were superior to Russia's only other educated group, the nobility, who so viciously attacked them. One popovich, for example, claimed in 1906 that nobles coveted popovichi's intellectual superiority. Another argued in 1884 that he had surveyed eighteenth-century writers, and the works of popovichi stood head and shoulders above the writings of any noble writer.[5]

Popovichi readily self-professed themselves as members of a subgroup, transforming themselves into a familial community. Many referred to popovichi they befriended as their "native brothers," and in their autobiographies they mentioned renowned popovichi relatives, no matter how distant the connection.[6] In an autobiography he published in 1912, one popovich, born in 1847, recalled that when he enrolled in the Forestry Academy, he immediately addressed students who had also attended the bursa with the informal "thou" (*ty*). Many others—including radicals—demonstrated both their sense of collective identity and how highly they valued this identity by engaging, like Zolotarev, in scholarly studies on the phenomenon of popovichi.[7]

Moreover, many popovichi chose to socialize with and even marry individuals who shared their clerical background. While social prejudice may have played a role in this phenomenon in the prereform period, it was not uncommon for popovichi to continue to choose friends and brides from the clerical estate during the late nineteenth century, when they were considered fashionable in certain societal circles. Popovichi as diverse as Doctor Aleksandr Smirnov (1854–1918), the teacher Fedor Tsvetaev (1849–1902), uncle of the poet Marina Tsvetaeva, and the revolutionary Dmitrii Parlinov (b. 1875) all married clergymen's daughters.[8]

Popovichi shared a mutual and collective responsibility for each other. They assisted, encouraged, and lobbied for members of their familial community whom they did not know. Several recalled how fellow popovichi who were strangers went out of their way to assist them and other popovichi in enrolling in educational institutions and finding employment.[9] Many popovichi also established or contributed to scholarships for impoverished seminarians.[10] In a letter he wrote to a newspaper as an institute student, Nikolai Dobroliubov (1835–1861) cited Nicholas I's ban against the children of sacristans entering the civil service as one of the grave injustices committed during his reign. This sense of responsibility for each other continued after 1917. Ivan Pavlov (1849–1936) resigned his chair of physiology at the Military Medical Academy in Leningrad in 1924 after popovichi studying at the Academy were expelled. He told Soviet authorities that they could consider him "expelled" along with the other sons of clergymen. Until his death in 1936, Pavlov used his unique immunity as a Nobel Prize winner and valued Soviet asset to lobby the Soviet government on behalf of individual disenfranchised popovichi. A few months before his death in 1936, Pavlov wrote to Viacheslav Molotov demanding that any laws disenfranchising popovichi be abolished; as evidence he expressed the view, consistently shared by other popovichi regardless of era, that they were superior to other Russians:

> The former clerical estate was the strongest and healthiest Russian social estate. Really did it do so little for the general culture of our motherland? Really were the first of our teachers of literary truth and progress not from the clerical estate: Belinskii, Dobroliubov and others? Really almost 50 percent of our medical estate before the revolution did not consist of persons from the clerical estate? And really are there so few of them in the field of pure science, etc., etc. . . . ?[11]

In the imperial period, fellow popovichi felt the need to protect each other because they were acutely aware of the prejudice—on the part of society and the state—that existed against them. In his 1866 diary Ivan Tsvetkov (1845–1917) vented his rage against such prejudice:

> Society regards a tailor, a shoe-maker, and a seminarian identically. As opposed to a gentleman, a seminarian is inexperienced, timid. When I have happened to witness lofty, idiotic aristocratic bias, I, like Satan, have become inflamed with bile against them. Once on the street I stopped and interrupted one gentleman

because he spoke about my friends, who were walking ahead of me, with contempt. I almost hit him.

Other incidents that inflamed their anger included being refused admittance to universities because of their origins, being addressed by noble strangers with the informal "thou," being seated in a third-class train compartment when they were in possession of a first-class ticket, and being forced to watch their fellow popovichi be passed over for promotions in favor of unqualified nobles. Popovichi also portrayed themselves as vulnerable because they were detached from existing secular power structures. The confession of a radical popovich to the police in 1870 adduced his clerical origins as the reason for his disenfranchisement: "I studied fifteen years. I had to work to achieve each step. It was so difficult for me to survive my first year in the university—me, a seminarian, without money and without acquaintances."[12]

Popovichi generally expressed disillusionment and dissatisfaction with the "foreign" secular society they had entered. On the eve of his return from abroad to Russia in 1861, Dobroliubov, for example, wrote his friends that he knew that when he returned to Petersburg he would order clothes that would look strange on him, would go to Italian operas that he would not understand, and would spend evenings as the guest of people who bored him to pieces: "if I had the slightest chance I would leave Petersburg and all of its muck." In his official testimony following a denunciation by a noble pupil in 1856, another popovich, the publicist Blagosvetlov, then thirty-two, described his almost immediate disillusionment with the new society he had entered: "Two weeks after my arrival in Petersburg, I was left without a half-kopeck piece. I had no acquaintances. As an inexperienced boy from the provinces, I imagined the capital to be heaven on earth, and that the people there were angels. But the cold egoism soon disillusioned my naive dreams." Another popovich recounted in his 1832 autobiography the alienation he experienced when he left the clerical estate, a sentiment many other popovichi also voiced: "I felt as if I was thrown to the winds into the world. It seemed to me, that I was placed before the world to be made fun of by any old person, I saw that I was alien to everyone. I thought of myself as the prodigal son, estranged in a country far off." In his 1884 memoir of his childhood and schooling, still another popovich lamented at the age of forty-one: "Since then a great deal of time has passed. Year after year came and went, bringing and taking away joy and (especially) misfortune. My family and professional relations changed, a completely new life emerged, not the one about which I had dreamed in my youth." In a few cases, popovichi responded to their disillusionment by returning to the fold to become ordained.[13]

To feel excluded from a society, one has to desire to be a part of it. Yet rather than seek to assimilate into noble society, popovichi were angry that their "way of life" rendered them outsiders within their own country. They did not hold the clergy responsible for its poverty and powerlessness, which they had inherited; they blamed the powers that be: the nobility, and, in the case of radical popovichi, the state. Instead of joining secular society, they sought to rid it of such injustices. Few chose violence; rather, it was memory that became the weapon popovichi wielded against their foes. Deprived of a common legal status, and of professional, political, or institutional affiliation, their common culture was based exclusively on memory.

They enshrined their memories of their common heritage in their autobiographies. In the process, they cemented their community and created a second "alternative" intelligentsia lineage. Just as noble intelligenty used autobiography as a "living narrative" that provided access to intelligentsia alliances over generations, popovichi employed their personal narratives to create a Russian "national" intelligentsia tradition. But whereas noble intelligenty established this alliance by writing extensively about other intelligenty, popovichi focused in their autobiographies primarily on themselves.[14] Writing their autobiographies was a means of reestablishing links, not creating entirely new affiliations. Popovichi's intense interest in themselves as subjects stemmed from their belief that they were prototypes for the "new man" who would recast society. In defining themselves, they were also defining "Russianness," since the clergy—in contrast to the Westernized nobility—symbolized the intellectual promise of Russian nationality. Their belief in the essence of their "Russianness" was another source of their unequivocal confidence in the legitimacy of their moral leadership of Russia.

To write a story is to create a community formed by its intended audience. Unlike Russian merchants, who largely wrote their autobiographies exclusively for the private audience of their families, popovichi, like their noble counterparts, usually chose to make their private memories public. Few popovichi chose to address the question of why they decided to write an autobiography, yet most began with "I was born the son of a priest in . . ." This convention, which was also generally followed by nobles, underscores the importance that social origin continued to play in Russians' lives in the late imperial period. A few popovichi did include a statement of intent in the preface. For some the main purpose of their autobiography was to offer exemplars to readers, since they believed that their "way of life" was the prototype of the future. A popovich teacher explained in the preface to his 1904 autobiography that his life could serve, in the tradition of Christian autobiography, as a redemption plan:

> In our declining years each one of us, not awaiting anything joyful ahead, turns his ordinary mental glance to past life, recalling during a conversation with those close to him this or that event in order to make a point, drawn from life's experience. Keeping in mind that the life of a person . . . may serve as an example at least for those close to him, I decided to work on composing my autobiography, assuming that something in it will be of interest also to readers I do not know.[15]

For others, writing their autobiographies was primarily a way to rejoin their fellow popovichi, and, not less importantly, the clergy they had left behind. One popovich posited himself as representative of his community in his autobiography's 1913 preface: "Life in this village and, in part, the life of a clerical family in it . . . appears rather typical and in several ways characteristic. . . . After all, everything or almost everything that the author of these lines experienced, with only several differences in details, was endured by his peers."[16] To this end, some popovichi interspersed "we" and "I" in their autobiographical recollections, with "we" referring to clerical children in general. This notion that their story was shared by each and every one of their fellow popovichi was even present in the autobiography of the Bolshevik Panteleimon Lepeshinskii (1864–1944), a close friend of Lenin's and the official historian of the Communist Party after 1917. In a 1921 edition republished numerous times in the Soviet Union, Lepeshinskii referred to the "humble origins" of "every rural popovich," himself included.[17] Popovichi simultaneously enlightened others about the superiority of their "way of life" while reuniting with their own kind by collectively constructing their self-narratives according to clerical cultural paradigms.

Although some of these clerical paradigms overlap with ethics long associated with the Russian intelligentsia, they differ and often conflict with the values of noble culture (see chapter 4). Popovichi saw members of the society they entered as just as foreign and loathsome as they themselves often appeared to individuals from other estate groups. As national cultures define themselves through exposure to—and often condemnation of—other national cultures, the Russian clergy and nobility defined each other by finding each other alien. Popovichi's self-conception was grounded in a discourse of class. They adhered to a dichotomous view of Russian society, and in their reconstruction of society they reserved the right to decide who was to be included and excluded. They saw not only themselves, but other Russians, primarily as social elements with common characteristics, rather than as individuals. Because the sources of their moral superiority lay in their clerical past, their depictions of other social estate groups usually focused on their childhood memories of these groups. In their judgment of these groups popovichi elucidated their notions of sin and virtue, values they brought to the intelligentsia at large.

Sin and Virtue

The cultural paradigm popovichi and their clerical fathers used to judge others was based on the criteria nineteenth-century Russian Orthodox Church thinkers outlined as necessary to attain salvation. As the pastoral movement spread in the 1860s these criteria were transmitted in a proliferation of texts, such as theological journals, moral theology seminary textbooks, new translations of early church fathers, diocesan gazettes, and collections of model sermons. Their intended audience was primarily the parish clergy and seminarians. Clerical families widely subscribed to diocesan gazettes. The other texts were also available in parish and bursa libraries. It was only at the turn of the twentieth century, when literacy levels for peasant parishioners rose and mass printing began, that the Church began to publish theological literature directed at the laity in earnest.

Salvation, defined by these texts as moral and spiritual perfection, included two mandatory prerequisites: a gift from the divine and the active participation of the individual concerned. Although Russian Orthodox seminaries borrowed heavily from both Catholic and Protestant literature, Church publicists emphasized that in contrast to Western Christianity, Orthodoxy teaches that an individual, utilizing free will, plays a fundamental role in bringing about his own salvation. The metaphor of climbing a ladder was employed by one Church publicist, who preached that the higher one climbed on this ladder of self-perfection, the greater one's chances of being admitted to heaven after death. Because of one's own evil desires and the corrupting influence of the temporal world, seeking salvation was a formative task. It had to be the all-encompassing purpose of a believer's life, imbuing all of his actions, no matter how mundane, with a utilitarian purpose. Father Ioann Khalkolivanov (1814–1882), the author of one widely used postreform moral theology seminary textbook first published in 1872, wrote: "in everything one does: in work, during travel, rest, when one eats and drinks, at home when there is joy and at home when there is sorrow, there is only one goal during all of these activities . . . the salvation of one's soul."[18]

Orthodox theologians have traditionally agreed on the doctrinal level of salvation theology, but have found room for interpretation concerning the personal conduct necessary to attain salvation. This was especially the case in postreform Russia, when lively and original theological debates rocked the Church during the renaissance of Russian theology. Following the advent of the pastoral care movement, some nineteenth-century Russian Orthodox theologians drew upon a more optimistic view of man and of the temporal world in determining moral conduct, and by the turn of the century a group of priests in Petersburg even claimed that it was possible to build heaven on earth. Rather than arguing that salvation was achieved primarily through sacraments, pastoral care-oriented theologians emphasized one's contribution to improving welfare in the temporal world as a means to salvation. The form and content of nineteenth-century moral theology textbooks—the texts popovichi learned theology from—emphasized the moral nature of man and his role in the temporal world: they were structured around discussions of the obligations of a Christian to himself, God, family, society, state, and the church.[19]

Participating in one's salvation entailed a process of rational or "worldly asceticism." Few Church publicists employed the traditional definition of asceticism as withdrawal from the world.[20] Instead, ordinary believers were supposed to accompany faith with the consistent performance of good deeds. Good deeds—so reminiscent of the Pietest "good works"—were defined by a wide spectrum of values, including charity, obedience, industriousness, meekness, patience, zeal, justice, honesty, modesty, frugality, wisdom, brotherly love, and courage. One's beliefs and one's actions were seen as inseparable, and believers were expected to rationally apply moral principles to daily life. This new emphasis on reason required emotions to be subordinated to the mind. As Khalkolivanov explained, "all vices, which have covered and cover the earth, originate in the human heart."[21] Good deeds hastened salvation through an interrelated dual process of unification: of body and soul, and of oneself with one's community. Believers were supposed to take as models the good deeds performed by the exemplary figures of Christ and the saints.

One of the good deeds most frequently mentioned is work. Orthodox publicists argued that work provided the means to distract believers from sin by subjugating their passions. They explained that manual labor, a common topos in the lives of saints and in Christ's biography, was particularly effective in maintaining physical temperance. But rather than conceiving of work primarily as a punishment, Orthodox publicists argued that it provided the keys to whatever happiness was possible on earth. One Church publicist, writing in 1904, disagreed with the conservative writer Gogol's conception of temporal life as employment followed by celebration in heaven: "I think that work itself contains the means here for a holiday."[22]

Work hastened one's salvation; leisure hindered it. "Idleness is the mother of all vices," one Church publicist warned in 1841. Work was a moral imperative, not merely a material necessity. Therefore, the rich were required to work, even if they were independently wealthy. Except for church holidays, the only rest believers were allowed to take was rest required by nature to rebuild one's strength for future endeavors.[23]

Avoiding becoming imprisoned by material concerns was another good deed, one that quelled physical passions. In part, believers achieved this as they always had in the Orthodox tradition, by observing the many fast days in the Orthodox calendar. Fasting was necessary to awaken humility, to destroy pride, and to battle the devil through the subjugation of flesh (rather than the body, which was sacred) to the soul. Church publicists warned, however, that ordinary believers were not to engage in heroic feats of painful ascetic deprivation. These were reserved for saints, who, in the words of Khalkolivanov, were closer to God than ordinary believers.[24]

Living an industrious life devoid of material attachments was not adequate if one failed to regularly practice charity. Through almsgiving believers imitated the social activism that Christ practiced and preached. In sermons on charity, numerous Church publicists blatantly drew on the anti-capitalist rhetoric present in the Gospels. They argued that wealth had to be distributed and not accumulated. Everyone has a right to own property, one theologian wrote in 1886, but you are obligated to share that property with others. Even a sermon directed at peasants, written in 1884, chastened them to work only to feed their families. While they should save money, they should not be "dirty misers" who give nothing to others, strangle those who are in debt, and live off another's misery. Writing in 1872, however, Khalkolivanov felt the need to distance Orthodox teachings on social service from Communism. Communism, he stated, was when the poor and lazy would live off the rich and hard-working.[25]

Engaging in frequent acts of charity was especially essential for wealthy believers. Church publicists repeatedly stated that it was difficult for the rich to gain admittance to heaven. Wealthy people were liable to misuse their money by flaunting it and becoming addicted to it, rendering them susceptible to the cardinal sins of greed or miserliness. Wealth always had to be considered a gift from God, and the rich were reminded that this gift could be rescinded at a moment's notice. And since Church publicists depicted wealth as a state fraught with spiritual danger, the wealthy could hardly be seen as chosen, even if their material lives were trouble-free. Those who suffered from poverty, on the other hand, were almost assured entrance into heaven. Pastoral theology manuals instructed priests to soothe poor parishioners by citing the traditional Christian justification for poverty, which so inflamed modern revolutionaries: it freed the soul from the distractions of earthly attachments, providing more time for prayer and the pursuit of salvation. Church publicists praised poverty for compelling those whom it affected to work and therefore contribute to society. The poor had attained a higher moral state and thus had no reason to envy the rich. Their lives were imbued with the values of industriousness, humility, patience, and modesty, enabling them to avoid many fatal sins.[26]

This "worldly asceticism" believers were supposed to engage in entailed a simultaneous pursuit of external good deeds and inner work. Inner work was a key to moral perfection, which, Khalkolivanov explained, was intrinsically connected to self-knowledge: "To know oneself, means to know, firstly, your spiritual nature, that is, what forces and perfections exist in our soul, what kind of deficiencies and infirmities, in addition, what kind of effective means exist which can assist in the perfecting of our nature, and what means exist for the eradication of our imperfections and deficiencies." Nineteenth-century Russian Orthodox attitudes toward the self did not include the pre-Renaissance Christian pessimism about man's power to shape his identity. This Western Christian dissuasion of self-fashioning was engendered by Augustine's denial that human works could contribute to salvation, which played a lesser role in Eastern Christianity.[27]

As the century progressed, knowledge and scholarly learning were identified by Church publicists as a qualified means toward moral self-perfection. A popular Orthodox religious etiquette manual published at the turn of the century stated: "those who wish to be saved need to occupy themselves with the reading of sacred books. . . . The Holy Fathers called the reading of books and listening to the words of God the King of all good deeds." Many saints whose lives were widely published in the nineteenth century were celebrated for being well read.[28] In the postreform period, literacy was increasingly associated with morality. Religious texts were not the only means to edification, although the laity was warned to be careful in choosing which secular books to read. Historical novels and romantic poetry were preferable to works of pure fiction. Excessive reading also posed dangers, such as a compulsion to avoid reality. Once educated, believers were obligated to assist others rather than using their diplomas to enrich themselves. As one priest told a graduating class of engineers in 1904: "After all, even animals serve a purpose for mankind!"[29]

Church publicists responded to the challenges that one form of knowledge, science, could pose to their faith by dissociating it entirely from Christianity. In a treatise published at the turn of the century an anonymous priest explained that just as distinct heavenly and earthly realms exist, religion and scholarship peacefully co-exist separately. Unlike Western Christians, he continued, Eastern Christians' faith is not threatened by science. Reason rules the temporal world, while faith rules the heavenly world. Believers strive toward salvation so that they might live well beyond the grave; they engage in scholarship so that they might have a good life on earth. Because Eastern Christians understood faith and reason as entirely separate they could fearlessly pursue scholarship without threatening their faith.[30]

Education, like income, was one of many factors that differentiated believers in the temporal world. Inherent in Orthodox Christianity and Roman Catholicism is a tension between egalitarianism, epitomized by all believers being brothers in Christ, and hierarchy, implicit within the institutional structure of the church. Nineteenth-century Orthodox Church publicists resolved this tension by explaining that hierarchies were only allowed in the temporal world. The heavenly was devoid of inegalitarianism.[31] All believers were created equal, and each was assured of the chance to attain salvation, but on earth they were not all identical. The disparity between members of society resulted from inherent differences in human nature, the conditions of temporal life, and God's having created individuals with different talents.

Rather than generating unique individuals, however, these processes produced several disparate groups. To describe the asymmetrical relations between these groups, Khalkolivanov invoked two metaphors, the first incorporating age. Every civil society contains groups of individuals who are stronger spiritually or physically than others, just as age renders adults more experienced and capable than children. These groups tend to paternalistically rule other groups, as parents govern their children. Just as parents and children belong to a single unit, that of the family, all of the members of society are interconnected. Each member is subservient to another, and each contributes to the happiness of the whole while enjoying the privileges of his particular station.

Khalkolivanov's second metaphor for civil society was that of the body. He drew upon the New Testament's conception of the church as a body, headed by Christ, and also employed the medieval view of monarchy as a divinely ordained body politic, with the king as the head, the councils and courts as the organs, and limbs representing the intendants, armed forces and clergy. Like nineteenth-century conservative thinkers, who had revived this metaphor following the French Revolution, Khalkolivanov saw society as an organism that was greater than the sum total of its members. Khalkolivanov argued that both the body and society are divided into numerous parts and that each has its own specific function. Societal subgroups are comprised of either professions or social estate groups that reflect the different needs, traits, and talents of members. Just as the different parts of a body cannot perform the other parts' functions, the members of a society must each play their appointed role, otherwise society would collapse. Although Khalkolivanov argued that all parts of both society and the body are necessary for either organism to function, some parts, like the head and heart, are more vital than others. After all, a body can continue to function if a limb is amputated, but not without the head or heart.[32]

For society to function properly, its members had to obey the laws of both the church and the government. As heaven on earth, the church ruled the spiritual realm, and believers had to obey its clergy to attain salvation. Conversely, the tsar was appointed by God to rule the temporal world, and only God could judge him; however, as Father Emelian Tsvetkov's sermons demonstrate, the nineteenth-century Russian Orthodox Church also subscribed to the Enlightenment idea that rulers had a responsibility to take care of their subjects. As God's representative on earth, the tsar had responsibilities to all his people, just as each estate had responsibilities to society. The same anonymous priest who argued that faith and scholarship were independent applied this same dualism to faith and politics. Orthodox people, he explains, unlike Western Christians who place politics above faith, understand that politics is corrupt because of its association with the temporal world. Therefore Orthodox believers should never become involved with politics, even if their abstinence means having to live obediently under a foreign-faith government.[33] This disdain toward politics explains in part the peculiar nature of clerical politics (or the lack thereof).

Such peculiarities also stemmed from concurrent declarations by Church publicists that believers were supposed to stand up for what they believed in and attend to the welfare of others. A model sermon published in 1896 stated that "a Christian must speak the truth (*pravda*) without fear and without any hypocrisy." Khalkolivanov, among others, glorified both Russian Orthodox conceptions of truth: pravda, meaning moral truth and justice, and *istina,* meaning sacred truth. It was sinful for believers to violate either notion of truth.[34]

Even if they were forced to passively live under a foreign government, believers were told to always remain patriotic to their nation. Patriotism, Khalkolivanov explained, was the most natural of feelings, an extension of one's love for one's family. Church publicists warned believers never to leave their homeland to seek pleasure or happiness. The only acceptable reasons to travel abroad were illness or work. Above all, Church publicists associated patriotism with individual activism and self-sacrifice. An 1871 article in the clerical press explained that the best way to instill patriotism in children was not to teach about the great personages in history, but to instruct that each and every person "in the sphere of the activity assigned to him" should work for the good of the government. Conversely, cosmopolitanism, whereby individuals who had no tie to a single country proclaimed that the whole world was their homeland and all people were their brothers, was condemned by Church publicists as a sin. Unlike Catholicism, a universalistic church united under the international leadership of the Pope and traditionally linked by the Latin mass, Eastern Orthodoxy is divided into independent national churches, and the liturgy is conducted in a language very close to the vernacular of particular Orthodox countries. In the eyes of nineteenth-century Church publicists, therefore, "brothers" referred not to humanity, but to fellow Russian Orthodox believers. One even portrayed Christ as a nationalist who loved his homeland. Russia's status as a multi-ethnic empire was only relevant in terms of missionary work; members of national minority groups could become Russian as long as they converted to Orthodoxy. Church publicists considered Russian national identity and Russian Orthodoxy synonymous and equivalent to citizenship in the Russian empire.[35]

Because members of their homeland were united in spiritual brotherhood, regardless of implicit temporal hierarchies, the spirit of social egalitarianism was supposed to prevail. Just as a real Christian loves his enemies, Khalkolivanov explained, he also should love his brothers without differentiating on the basis of age, sex, or rank. To achieve this feat, believers had to exhibit deference to their subordinates and patiently agree with their superiors, even if they knew they were wrong. The antithesis of acting humbly was to condescend to others and to take pride in one's superiority over subordinates. Pride was depicted by Khalkolivanov as a mortal sin, comparable to the other deadly sins, which included envy, hatred of one's kin, taking advantage of the poor, acting against the Church, disobeying parental authority, and murder. Honor was considered a sin synonymous with pride. Esteeming oneself highly was sinful, as was judging others, since only God had the right to judge.[36]

The belief that all individuals are potentially redeemable lies at the heart of Christianity. Nineteenth-century Russian Orthodox Church publicists argued that salvation was possible for all believers, provided they performed good deeds and avoided mortal sins. Yet these same Church publicists also conceived of society as composed of a rigid hierarchy of social estates. The influence of one's native social estate in shaping a person was considered so formative that one Church publicist wrote in 1874 concerning social estate:

From the day of birth it already marks the spiritual physiognomy of a person and, constantly holding him under its strong influence, more and more outlines it, leaving on a person a more or less noticeable stamp. This stamp is not only external, but under the influence of estate particularities manifests itself not only in the differentiation of people according to external traits, such as manners, language, habits, inclinations, the level of education, types of ideas, but also estate differences leave a mark on the inner, so to speak, common to all mankind, side of the spirit, such that it influences the constitution of the entire spiritual nature of a person.[37]

As inherent members of these estates, the proximity of individual believers to specific sins or virtues thus differed, depending on the social estate group to which they belonged. For the parish clergy, who saw these groups through the lens of their own social prejudices, and for their popovich sons, who secularized their fathers' social bias, some Russian social estate groups were considered more sinful than others.

Noble Aliens

In addition to the general blueprint for attaining salvation discussed above, theology textbooks and religious etiquette manuals included supplementary guidelines for each social estate group. These guidelines required the noble ruling class to exercise paternalism in their leadership roles as bureaucrats, officers, landowners, and employers of servants. Such paternalism included treating their subordinates with kindness, using strictness only when it was completely necessary, and never expecting servants to do something that might harm them. They were obligated to take care of their subordinates when they were ill, were deemed responsible for their moral welfare, and were expected to pay them decently. Nobles were warned to always be honest, to be fearful of God, to love humanity, to follow the letter of the law, to be enlightened and sensible, and to fearlessly love the tsar, fatherland, church, and each and every rank. Because they occupied a lofty position, nobles were expected to display a greater degree of humility before God and were warned not to be prideful, severe, or haughty. They were required to ask God for the wisdom they needed to rule, although they were reminded that they still had to fear God and follow his commands.[38]

Popovichi, clergymen, and Church publicists argued that the nobility as an estate and most individual nobles did not live up to these expectations. Many clergymen and virtually all of their secular sons claimed that the nobility was riddled with sin and had few—if any—redeeming qualities. They employed a divisive social language to explain indirectly how nobles disqualified themselves from attaining salvation. Popovichi perceived nobles as the "proximate other," just as the reverse was true. Because nobles were their cultural rivals, popovichi and their fathers devoted more attention to noble conduct than to the demeanor of any other social estate in their personal narratives, their fiction, and their publicistic works.

Despite the disparity of wealth among members of the noble estate, popovichi and clergymen alike tended to depict the nobility as uniformly rich. Popovichi recalled being struck by awe when, as young men, they glimpsed the clothing and cuisine of noble assemblies and societies.[39] The nobility inhabited an alien world, segregated from the clergy who frequently juxtaposed noble wealth against their own standard of living. One priest recalled in 1907 a scene from his childhood during his family's return one summer night from working the fields: "An original group of travelers: one with rakes, the other with vessels, another with a barrel, that one with a bundle of hay—but everyone is tired, hungry, dressed in work-clothes . . . on the way our workers meet the children of the local landowner with their governess, they are all nicely dressed, playful, cheerful."[40]

Rather than envying the wealth and gaiety of the nobility, popovichi and their fathers depicted prosperity as drowning nobles in sin. Church publicists associated nobles with all the various sins to which the wealthy were susceptible. One wrote in 1871 that nobles exhibit "a tendency toward luxury, toward comfort and the comforts of life, which distract them from feats of selflessness and Christian good deeds . . . a passion for extravagance." This passion, he went on, led them to be too sentimental. In his 1882 autobiography one priest told a parable about a noble acquaintance to illustrate the nobility's conspicuous consumption. This nobleman defined a "respectable person" as someone who had splendid furniture and an attractive housekeeper. The priest concluded, "and that was said by a marshall of the nobility—the guardian of the people's morality!"[41]

Nobles not only indulged themselves frivolously in an immodest lifestyle, they were also too slothful and pleasure-oriented to engage in productive work. In 1866 Aleksandr Tsvetkov described the nobleman whose son he was tutoring: "Dmitrii Ivanovich is in the true sense of the word a pampered aristocrat. He is unable to do anything for more than half an hour without resting." In his famous essay on Ivan Goncharov's 1859 novel *Oblomov*, Dobroliubov coined the term "Oblomovism" ("*Oblomovshchina*"), which has been used ever since to describe the so-called Russian national disease. Dobroliubov, however, understood Oblomovism as a disease specific to the nobility, and he castigated nobles for replacing their souls with an endless cycle of oversleeping and useless lavish rituals, such as dining, hunting, and attending the theater and balls. He even went so far as to criticize Pushkin, the father of Russian literature, as a frivolous aristocrat incapable of active thought because of his noble origins. One priest in 1859 linked nobles' engaging in mindless diversions to instances of nobles' breaking Lent, skipping church services, and engaging in sexual promiscuity precisely because he believed such diversions bred gluttony and selfishness.[42]

Nobles misused their temporal authority as Russia's ruling class just as they squandered their wealth. Popovichi and their fathers portrayed the nobility as intoxicated by power over others. As one Church publicist wrote in 1871, "in the higher estate there is a noticeably exaggerated understanding of one's honor, of pride, rivalry, litigiousness." Nobles' abuse of power was nowhere more evident than in their treatment of their peasant serfs. Although the state itself is largely absent from clerical memoirs and the memoirs of childhood by popovichi, the state is indirectly present through the actions of its primary servitors, the nobility. In the eyes of anti-autocratic memoirists, the nobility was conflated with the state; in the eyes of monarchist memoirists, the nobility had hijacked the state. In turn, condemnation of the nobility's treatment of peasants was a veiled attack on the inhumane institution of serfdom, whose legacy remained long after emancipation. Popovichi who were not aligned with the radical movement were just as likely to condemn the nobility for exploiting the peasantry. In his posthumously published autobiography, the historian Sergei Solov'ev (1820–1879) recounted his revulsion when he was approached by a peasant on the estate where he was employed as a tutor. The peasant inquired whether Solov'ev would like to sleep with his fifteen-year-old daughter, who had been raped by the noble landowner and hence was ineligible for marriage. Serfdom had transformed nobles into violent tyrants. Dobroliubov reminded his readers that even Oblomov, whom educated society had embraced as a gentle buffoon, kicked his servant.[43]

Misuse of power so infected nobles that they even tried to rule their spiritual fathers. Priests deplored that nobles had the gall to tell them what sermons to deliver. In the 1860s, Church publicists were appalled when the secular press asserted that educated society should participate in clerical reforms.[44] In their autobiographies many clergymen and popovichi went further, bitterly complaining about nobles who were uncharitable or insulting toward, or even directly abused, clergymen. For example, one priest, writing in 1900, recalled an incident from the prereform period in which his father was beaten with a whip by an unknown noble company commander riding by, apparently for the sole reason that he was a clergyman. His father fought back and, as a result, was demoted from priest to sacristan and reassigned to a poorer parish. Dobroliubov, clearly affiliating himself with his native estate, summed up how the clergy was treated by nobles under serfdom: "[they] played with us as if we were checkers." Clergymen saw themselves as enserfed by the nobility, leading one Church publicist writing at the end of the nineteenth century to go so far as to argue that the clergy had suffered more under serfdom than the serfs: "and if the narod languished then under the yoke of serf slavery, then the clergy suffered doubly—for the narod, and for itself. Its slavery was more painful to bear, since juridically [by law] it was completely free, but in fact it was completely enserfed. . . ."[45]

Persecuting Russian peasants and the Orthodox clergy was not only unpatriotic, it also led the clergy and their secular sons to question whether nobles were truly Russian. Just as the Abbott Sieyès had done during the French Revolution, they accused the nobility of being foreign. Church publicists explained that Russian nobles lost their national identity following the Petrine reforms. The favorite pastime of the "despicable" foreign tutors who were subsequently imported into noble homes, one publicist wrote in 1871, "was to laugh not only at all Russians, but at all saints." One bishop, writing at the turn of the century, distinguished between pious Europe and the "pagan Europeanization" nobles had selectively imported, arguing that Europe itself was not the problem, rather, the material comforts and recreational activities nobles had chosen to import from Europe were. This Europeanization had rendered nobles strangers in their native land as they gallivanted aimlessly about the world, in clear violation of the Church's teachings on foreign travel. One priest claimed in 1882 that "many of the so-called upper strata of society are much more acquainted with some kind of Zulus than they are with their own Russian peasant, and they are better acquainted with Paris, Naples, and Nice than they are with Moscow, Novgorod, and Kazan. . . ." Dobroliubov took this notion of a cultural gulf a step further, arguing in his essay "When Will the Real Day Come?" that Russian nobles played the same role in Russia as Turks, foreign occupiers, played in Bulgaria. A half-century later, at the height of anti-semitism in Russia, one of Nikolai Dobroliubov's younger brothers, a wealthy entrepreneur, equated noble intelligenty who criticized popovichi with Jews who "slandered" the Russian people. Ironically, not all Russian noble intelligenty disagreed with popovichi's and their fathers' assessment of their foreignness; Herzen, after all, had referred to the Russian intelligentsia as "foreigners at home," a characterization popovichi intelligenty clearly did not share regarding themselves.[46]

The nobility's preference for Western languages was further evidence of their foreignness. One Church publicist lamented in 1871 that noble girls had forgotten their native tongue. He could not understand why the nobility relished speaking foreign languages, for "each nationality should speak its own language." Sergei Solov'ev recalled that during his service as a tutor to a prince's family he was teased for speaking Russian and labeled "Mr. Russian," a title he felt he alone entirely deserved: "The princes senselessly laughed at this, but I, with the pride of an eighteen-year-old boy, proclaimed that I was completely satisfied with this nickname, that it was precious to me, that I was entirely flattered that I was the only Russian in the house, or, at least, the only one who was primarily Russian."[47]

Many parish clergymen were ironically willing to confer one admirable trait to the noble estate, or at least to its educated members. They associated educated nobles with a high degree of intelligence and cultivation and believed these individuals could have a beneficial influence on anyone lucky enough to gain acceptance into their rarefied social circles. One priest's obituary, written by a fellow clergyman in 1906, described what he had gained from his noble acquaintances: "In the circle of educated society young Father Fedor acquired, along with the ability to conduct himself, knowledge of people and life, a passion for reading and skill in literary conversational speech."[48] Given the clergy's increasing association of morality and education, some degree of respect for Russia's most educated estate was only natural.

Yet as time progressed, some clergymen were less and less willing to concede greater refinement and erudition to the nobility. In 1859 a priest straightforwardly questioned how cultured nobles could be when they mistreated clergymen: "If you are a nobleman and a distinguished nobleman at that, then why do you force us to wait at the thresholds of your homes for hours before you grant us a meeting with you?" Writing in 1873, a Church publicist responded to the reverence with which some priests held enlightened nobles by warning that secular society would never accept this type of "secular" priest whom it encouraged. Instead of trying to emulate secular tastes, priests should endeavor to be better than this world and should expect secular society to kneel to them, not the other way around. A priest went a step further in his 1882 autobiography, questioning whether nobles really represented educated society, which, he argued, was much larger and more diverse than the nobility. Alluding to the meager education of some poor nobles, he questioned the image of the nobility as the "educated class." Of all the estates, he contended, the clergy was actually the best educated. By 1909 an article in a leading clerical journal referred to the conflict between clerical culture and educated society as a "fratricidal war," and ended by stating that the clergy were ready to fight and were arming themselves for this war. By the time of this 1909 attack, this ambivalence toward educated high society (*obshchestvo*) was shared by Russian workers, but in the nineteenth century, when workers were far fewer in number and the higher echelons of the merchantry aspired to adopt the trappings and refinements of the nobility, the clergy alone voiced dissent in print regarding noble cultural hegemony.[49]

Popovichi's dissent far exceeded their fathers'; they were unwilling to concede the nobility even erudition. In their autobiographies they gleefully described unintelligent and uncultured nobles they had encountered over the course of their lives.[50] Popovichi considered noble cultivation little more than an obsession with immaterial external taste and manners, and they resented that they were expected to parrot this so-called culture. One popovich, born in 1834, was employed, as many young popovichi were, as a tutor to a noble family. In his 1910 autobiography he recalled that since he did not understand which utensil to use, he continually left his employer's table hungry. At one point, the father of his pupil reprimanded him for using the wrong utensil, which embarrassed him greatly. He also resented the obligation to wear his only good suit every day, regarding this custom as pretentious. Deeply homesick, he soon returned to his native village, to wait for a teacher's position in his father's parish. In his 1832 autobiography, the bureaucrat Aleksandr Orlov (1791–1840), recalling the time he spent working as a tutor to a noble family, wrote: "I must confess, not living in a manor house, I did not like the etiquette. I taught not according to the French system, but according to the seminarian's . . . just as I did not agree with their method of teaching, I was not agreeable to these foreigners."[51] Unlike their fathers, whose cultural choice was predetermined at birth, popovichi were compelled to choose unequivocally between two cultural traditions. Any ambivalence would lessen their chances of imposing clerical culture on the secular world. Second, having obtained a secular education and first-hand knowledge of the subtleties of secular society, popovichi did not share the awed illusions of the noble "enlightenment" that some of their fathers had felt from afar. Lastly, it was easier for popovichi professionally removed from their native estate to idealize the clerical world as itself embodying the only proper enlightenment.

Popovichi did not want to be accepted by noble society, so they voiced no anger over being rebuffed by their rivals. On the contrary, it was popovichi who did the rebuffing. A conscious choice was made, as in the case of the writer Serafim Shashkov (1841–1882): at the end of his life he claimed that although as a child he was not shy in front of noble children and was in fact courted by them, he preferred instead the company of street kids. Nobles were so loathsome to popovichi that the statistician Konstantin Lavrskii, born in 1844, described in his 1905 unpublished autobiography his service as tutor to a wealthy noble family as worse than imprisonment: "I suffered terribly, seeing myself in surroundings, which were not only foreign to me, but also extremely adverse. It seems to me that when I was imprisoned I never languished from the type of loneliness that I experienced in this aristocratic house." His hatred of the nobility was so intense that later on in life he was unable to support the Kadet party, despite his affinity to parts of its platform, because of the noble origins of most of its members: "all the time I was negatively disposed toward the Kadets. For my democratic nature was able to detect gentry lordliness (*barstvo*), a smell which for me was unbearable."[52]

Popovichi's hatred of the nobility and their depiction of the estate as riddled by sin even affected their conceptions of fellow intelligenty from the nobility. The populist writer Nikolai Uspenskii (1837–1889) claimed that the gentry-born populist poet Nekrasov exploited the peasants after he purchased a large estate and installed a factory on it. Alluding to the gentry's laziness, he complained that he once visited Nekrasov at eleven in the morning only to find him still asleep. And how did Nekrasov spend his waking hours? Counting his money, Uspenskii asserted. Nekrasov's disgruntled servant readily confided in Uspenskii, whom he recognized as a fellow man of the people. It was indeed shocking that a poet would stoop to such levels, Uspenskii conceded, but given his noble origins, could one expect anything more? Nekrasov was not Uspenskii's only noble target; he also claimed that Count Lev Tolstoi, the benefactor of the peasantry, beat peasant children for not doing their arithmetic correctly. The Bolshevik popovich Lepeshinskii complained in 1921 that noble lineage even tainted Georgii Plekhanov, the founder of Russian Marxism. He recalled that

Plekhanov continued to refer to himself as a "Tambov noble" and that Plekhanov's wife told him that "if insulted [Plekhanov] will answer like a nobleman . . . he will challenge you lampoonists to a duel. . . ." Lepeshinskii lamented that Plekhanov all his life "never got rid of that side of himself which was a Tambov noble."[53]

Popovichi were not ambivalent about their rejection of noble culture, but they were ambivalent about their intelligentsia identity. Like some of their more estate-minded noble counterparts, they often vacillated between referring to themselves as members of the intelligentsia and dissociating themselves from the intelligentsia.[54] They resolved this ambivalence by dividing the intelligentsia into two: one aristocratic and the other Russian "national." By virtue of their "foreignness," the Russian noble estate was excluded from this new national intelligentsia led by popovichi. In his confession to the police in 1899, the popovich Sergei Lebedev (b. 1875) spoke of a "true" (*istinnaia*) and false intelligentsia. Christ was the father of the true intelligentsia, while the false intelligentsia luxuriated in their "easy life." Lebedev clearly branded noble intelligenty as the false intelligentsia. Although many clergymen tended to view the nobility and the intelligentsia as intertwined, the existence of popovichi and their defense of the clergy as just as—if not more—educated than the nobility led some Church publicists to conceive of dual opposing intelligentsias. One publicist in 1888 divided the intelligentsia into an "upper" intelligentsia consisting of hereditary nobles, and a "lower" intelligentsia, including, among other groups, the clergy: "the upper intelligentsia and pastors—these are two opposed poles."[55]

Popovichi writers also differentiated between two types of intelligenty, those from the clergy and those from the nobility. They contrasted their fellow popovichi, whom they portrayed as selfless, industrious intelligenty who ceaselessly served the Russian people, to noble intelligenty, who only spoke of serving the people but were too lazy, unfocused, and self-interested to follow through. A popovich writer mischievously chastised a representative of the former type of intelligent in an 1892 short story: "Petr Emel'ianov had a dignified appearance: well-groomed cheeks, a carefully shaved double chin and an esteemed stomach. In the full sense of the word this was a cultured person, whose appearance had been attended to by several generations of servants and who did not know how to do anything with his own hands."[56]

Popovichi's "national" intelligentsia included their native estate. Many popovich-writers portrayed enlightened priests as intelligenty in their fiction. Doctor Aleksandr Smirnov described society in the village where he worked as consisting of "the expected personages: the rural priest, the teacher, the medical attendant, forest ranger—here we have all of the various intelligenty." In turn, the author Dmitrii Mamin-Sibiriak (1852–1912) referred to his clerical parents as "the intelligentsia family, into which I was born. . . ." Intelligentsia members were any professionals who served the people. Popovichi's lifelong subjective affiliation with the clergy thus did not preclude their new association with the intelligentsia because unlike many noble intelligenty, popovichi did not consider the clergy and intelligentsia as mutually exclusive groups.[57]

Despite popovichi's malice toward the nobility and its culture, individual nobles could join their "national" intelligentsia. Popovichi did not demonize the nobility; they did not portray nobles in zoological terms. Nobles were sinners, but they were still human beings, and like all human beings, they were capable of attaining individual redemption. The key to redemption for nobles was rejecting noble culture and adopting the cultural norms set by popovichi. In their personal texts popovichi often described a few individual "good" nobles. In his autobiography published in 1929, Sergei Elpat'evskii (1854–1933), who complained that most landed nobles did not participate in the zemstvo because of their indifference toward peasant distress, described such a "good" noble as one who was active in the zemstvo, who read and wrote all the time. The key to his salvation was that "his noble origins somehow were removed from him." Noble Slavophiles, given their Orthodox piety and Russian nationalism, were likewise "good" nobles in the eyes of many of those popovichi who remained religious. Yet the historian Sergei Solov'ev, who considered himself a Slavophile in his youth after spending what he described as excruciating time abroad, described all of the leading Slavophiles—a few of whom he shared membership with in the Society for Lovers of Spiritual Enlightenment—as characterized by many of the same traits for which other popovichi lambasted "bad" nobles. In Solov'ev's views, some of them were really "ultra-Westernizers." Others were dilettantes, self-centered, or morally weak buffoons. Having parted with the Slavophiles, Solov'ev did not consider himself a Westernizer either, which is not surprising since both movements were noble-dominated.[58] As Solov'ev's portrayals of Slavophiles demonstrates, "good" nobles were, however, few and far between. So it was to Russia's largest, least wealthy, and least Westernized social estate group—which was, not coincidentally, the foremost victim of noble oppression—that popovichi turned to find the constituency for their alternative "national" intelligentsia.

Peasant Brothers

In his textbook, Khalkolivanov argued that the vast and diverse peasant estate was united by having been assigned by God to perform manual labor. Peasants' other obligations included obeying the tsar and their pastors, not complaining, drinking, or lying, and not engaging in theft, deceit, or perjury. Not only did the sins peasants were deemed susceptible to committing differ from those associated with the nobility, but Khalkolivanov concluded his description of peasants' obligations with a note conspicuously absent from his section on the nobility: he warned that peasants who led a dishonest life of sin and crime would be punished by unhappiness and sorrow.[59] In part, the warning to the peasantry reflects the increasing link in the minds of the clergy between morality and learnedness. Peasants lacked erudition; consequently, their morality was surely in greater danger than that of enlightened nobles. On the other hand, because priests had greater authority over their peasant parishioners, they paid more attention to improving their morality. Khalkolivanov's threat did not, therefore, necessarily imply a greater sinfulness on the part of the peasantry. Indeed, the peasantry embodied many of the general virtues required for salvation and were thus a group considered potentially redeemable. The noble estate, on the other hand, was so rife with sin that no warning could save it. And of course, because clergymen regarded the temporal world as inferior to the heavenly realm, all believers had an uphill battle to fight.

Popovichi's partial secularization of religious dualism allowed them to be more optimistic about the temporal world. Not that popovichi's conception of the temporal world was uniform. Secularization, in this case, entailed a bifurcation of the temporal world into two spheres: one the kingdom of God on earth, the other the unrighteous. Unlike noble aliens, firmly entrenched in sinful secular society, peasants belonged to the enchanted realm of popovichi's childhood villages. Thus while popovichi and their fathers largely concurred in their assessment of secular society, their fathers' lack of secularization and lesser idealization of village life—which they, unlike their sons, still inhabited, and inhabited fully aware of the peasants' sins since they heard the peasants' confessions—led to a greater discrepancy between their assessments of the peasantry. At the same time, the similarity between the traits for which popovichi and their fathers praised the peasantry indicate that popovichi still judged peasants according to clerical paradigms.

This is particularly striking when one compares the differences between the criteria popovichi and intelligenty from the nobility employed to judge the peasantry's moral superiority. The traits that everyone, including clergymen, agreed that peasants embodied included simplicity, justice, and "Russianness." Like most educated Russians, clergymen were also increasingly swept up by the spirit of populism. In his pastoral theology textbook, for example, Father Evgenii Popov stated in 1873 that by studying the narod priests would gain new spiritual and life powers. Yet the other features for which popovichi praised the peasants—honesty, industriousness, their performance of manual labor, humility, modesty, poverty, and intelligence—included almost every good deed required to attain salvation and were largely absent from the images dominant among noble populist intelligenty. Whereas the Slavophiles had depicted the peasantry as inherently anti-intellectual, even a liberal popovich such as Vasilii Kliuchevskii argued that peasants were able to understand a great deal more than educated Russians. Nor were patience and passivity, which Slavophiles and moralists alike cited as beneficial aspects of the peasant character, singled out by popovichi or clergymen to praise peasants. The dynamic peasant, an image so attractive to socialists and revolutionary populists, was required by the pastoral care movement to successfully enlighten peasants. As Father Evgenii also wrote: "our simple narod is good, down-to-earth, receptive, useful; it only needs to be more active."[60]

The most striking difference is that whereas all other intelligenty conceived of the peasantry as their cultural polar opposite and defined the term "intelligentsia" in juxtaposition to the narod, popovichi claimed that they were both intelligentsia *and* the narod. They thus accepted—and fed—this perception about themselves by others. Tracing their family back to the peasantry was a standard topos in popovichi's personal narratives, regardless of adult political affiliation. Popovichi as seemingly divergent as the populist revolutionary Mikhail Popov (1851–1909) and the conservative bureaucrat V.A. Tikhonov (1847–1912) began their autobiographies by stating that they were the grandsons or great-grandsons of serfs on both their mother's and father's side. Another popovich, a theological academy professor born in 1862, cited his distant peasant lineage on his curriculum vitae. Sergei Bulgakov (1871–1944), a professor briefly affiliated with the revolutionary movement who was later ordained a priest, described in emigration this sense of belonging: "Together with the church, I received into my soul the Russian folk, not externally, like some kind of object to respect or to bring to its senses, but from the inside, like one's own internal being . . . I was always a populist because I was one of the people from birth."[61]

To underscore their kinship with the narod, popovichi, regardless of their generation, also emphasized the similarities between the culture and household subsistence agricultural economies of the clergy and peasantry. Elpat'evskii summed up this likeness in his unpublished autobiography written in the 1920s: "In essence the entire structure of our life was like the peasants." The parallels they drew between the daily life of the two estates are so comparable that unlike noble autobiographers, who tended to write about the peasantry in great ethnographic detail, popovichi focused almost exclusively in their memoirs of childhood on describing themselves and their families. Because they saw themselves as part of the narod, writing about themselves entailed depicting the peasantry as well. The peasantry was not an enigma they needed to study to understand.[62] They were their brothers.

Instead of juxtaposing intelligentsia to narod, many late imperial popovichi juxtaposed obshchestvo, meaning high society or noble society, to narod, and their definition of narod consisted of themselves and the peasantry. To emphasize this they contrasted the similarity of clerical and peasant daily life to the gulf that separated the nobility from the narod. Sergei Solov'ev emphasized that while the gentry conversed in foreign languages and professed non-Orthodox faiths, clerical families spoke the language and practiced the religion of the narod. The conservative Tikhonov emphasized in his autobiography, published in 1913, his kinship to the peasants while ridiculing a local populist nobleman who treated the peasantry as if they were his pets:

> It is necessary to love the peasant (*muzhik*) with your head, not your heart. To love a peasant that way, is like lords loving dogs and cats, feeding them to the point of revulsion and delighting in the superiority of their own (frequently sorrowful) mind over the mind of the animals. Let me emphasize, one can not love the peasant that way. And it seems to me, that he will not permit himself to be treated like that. . . . They [the peasants] related to me as they related to one another.

Elpat'evskii explained in the 1920s how he had differed from his "repentant noble" populist peers: "I did not feel that I owed anything or that I should repent anything. I felt myself to be on the same level with the peasantry. . . ."[63] Popovichi—even radical popovichi—did not share the self-hatred that consumed other populist intelligenty because they did not consider themselves antithetical to their ideal. In an age of populism their perceived kinship to the peasantry empowered them.

Whereas any similarity between clerical and peasant daily life was a source of pride to popovichi, it was the basis of resentment for most clergymen. In part, clergymen were indignant that their agricultural chores left them too little time to devote to their pastoral duties.[64] But many clergymen also regarded the peasant way of life as beneath them. In his autobiography, one priest wrote in 1882 that it was a tragedy when priests ended up living in peasant huts. He described the village he was initially assigned to serve in ethnographic detail, explaining how awful the peasants' diet was.[65]

The different lens with which popovichi and clergymen perceived the peasantry is particularly apparent in their descriptions of their social interactions with peasants. The phrase "my childhood, spent among the peasants" in the 1929 autobiography of Apollinarii Vasnetsov (1850–1933), is commonplace in popovichi's autobiographies. Social bonding with peasant children was yet another source of superiority over their noble peers. For although noble intelligenty also claimed that they romped in the fields with peasant children, their childhood memories revolved mainly around peasant servants, and occasionally included fear of peasant uprisings and robbers. Popovichi, in contrast, recalled a mutual bond so close that many popovichi asserted that peasant boys were their best friends in childhood.[66] In his autobiography published in 1886, one conservative popovich described the roots of these childhood unions as virtually supernatural: "there was a weight on all of us which involuntarily drew us toward the lower classes (*nizy*), toward the peasantry—a faith in its customs." Regardless of their political orientation, popovichi claimed that these mutually affectionate relations with peasants followed them into adulthood.[67]

While clergymen occasionally mentioned in their autobiographies adult friendships they had with "good" noble parishioners, such relationships between adult clergymen and peasants are conspicuously absent. Clergymen did recall socializing with peasant children, but less frequently, and in most cases their closest boyhood friend was not a peasant child. They were also liable to criticize certain aspects of such friendships, which were regarded as morally harmful by Synodal reform committees and Church publicists alike. In his autobiography published in 1903, the priest Smiriagin, for example, praised his "ragged, dirty" childhood peasant friends for instilling in him love of nature, the peasantry, and good health. But he lamented that his peasant friends also taught him to swear and steal, and that they filled his head with impure images and thoughts. Smiriagin's portrait of "uncultured" peasant children was echoed by virtually every clergyman who described his adult relations with peasant parishioners. In addition to complaining about peasants' ignorance and coarseness, clergymen in the postreform era bemoaned the abuse they received from some peasants when they refused to drink vodka with them on holidays. Clergymen also lamented the peasants' lack of comprehension of clerical financial difficulties, and the unrealistic moral ideal by which peasants judged them.[68] Such sins are attributed to the peasantry in the fiction of popovichi writers such as Nikolai Uspenskii but are, significantly, largely absent from their autobiographies. Because of the close alliance of the peasantry and the clergy in their self-narratives, any censure of the peasantry would pass judgment on the clerical world as well.

There was, however, a fundamental difference between clerical accusations of peasant unculturedness and of noble sins. Individual nobles were either good or evil, and if they were evil, they had only themselves to blame, but clergymen always blamed peasants' unculturedness on their ignorance.[69] Subscribing to the liberal enlightenment ideal of shaping the population through education, Church publicists argued that peasants simply did not know right from wrong because they were uneducated. And ignorance, unlike the deadly sins of evil nobles, could easily be corrected. Civilization, in this case, provided peasants with the means to salvation, while it damned the noble estate, which had adopted it in an erroneous form. Because the clergy and their secular sons did not divide the peasants into "good" and "bad" typologies but conceived of the peasantry as a homogeneous mass, salvation for the entire estate through rational enlightenment was possible. Thus, clergymen's criticism of peasant morals did not lessen their love for them. As one priest wrote in 1901, no one loves the narod more than seminarians "who were raised amongst the narod."[70]

Peasants would, of course, be enlightened by the estate that had served them for centuries, the parish clergy. Now that noble exploitation had been curbed by emancipation, the true leaders of the people could save them. Writing in 1880, one Church publicist stated: "The clergy is not better than the other estates, but it works for the good of the narod a great deal more than the other noncaste estates."[71]

Despite the attempts to present peasants as their peers, popovichi also shared their fathers' conception of themselves as the natural leaders of the masses. Popovichi recalled both leading *and* serving the peasantry in their childhood, the two simultaneous, and yet contradictory, functions that typified the intelligentsia. In his 1913 autobiography, one popovich de-

scribed the multiple roles he had played as peasant peer, observer, attendant, and leader: "I remember how I spent all day in the summers and almost all day in the winter with my peers from among the peasant children
. . . how we, not without envy, observed peasant kids . . . how we, clerical
youngsters, accompanied the clergy on their procession to peasant homes. . . ."
Popovichi remembered other instances when they watched over peasants
of all ages, even as preschool boys: assisting their fathers in teaching peasants in the home, serving as go-betweens for nobles and peasants, and es-
corting peasants visiting their homes for advice.[72]

Because of popovichi's greater idealization of the peasantry, and their
conception of the peasants as their brothers (albeit perhaps stepbrothers),
popovichi were more likely than their fathers to portray peasants as eager
for their leadership. Two petitions, one from a popovich and one from a
priest, illustrate this point. In their replies to inquiries made in 1865 as to
whether they would like to initiate home schools for peasants in their home
province of Vladimir, a popovich replied that local peasants liked him and
thus would welcome him as their teacher. A priest answered that peasants
would prefer to study under other peasants.[73] Because they were members of
both the intelligentsia and the narod, popovichi saw themselves, and not the
peasants, as the new men required for leadership of Russia, and they were confident that the peasants would be their willing followers.

Philistines and Anti-Philistinism

From the mid-century on, as modern capitalism spread in Russia, Church
publicists assigned the merchantry and townspeople, Russia's two urban estate groups, the longest inventory of potential sins to guard against. Both
merchants and their poorer counterparts, townsmen, engaged in commerce
and trade. Although Khalkolivanov acknowledged that trade, like scholarship, art, and shipping, was one of the useful affairs of humanity, he and
other Church publicists warned that it was the most dangerous of professions. The obligations of merchants included first and foremost "honesty
and a good conscience in all activities." The second obligation, "not any
less important," was "the correct and legitimate use of wealth, for the glory
of God and for aiding one's neighbor." Because self-interest lies at the heart
of capitalist business practice, merchants had to counter the selfishness inherent in their profession by vowing that any profit they reaped would be
used to benefit the welfare of the community. Merchants were reminded
not to lie or cheat by such means as hiding the defectiveness of their goods,
fixing the scales, or misusing people's trust in them.[74] Although these publicists associated many of the trappings of wealth, such as immodesty and
slothfulness, with the nobility, the source of most noble wealth—capital
garnered passively from renting out land on inherited estates or from lucrative state salaries—appears to have troubled them less than that of merchant wealth, which was accumulated directly through the sale of goods at

inflated prices. Nobles served the state and protected the nation in their bureaucratic and military careers. Merchants, however, only made money off
others, even if they were necessary for the economy to function.

In their self-narratives popovichi wrote less about the merchantry and
the townspeople than about any other estate. This is not surprising, since
they belonged to the world of urban capitalist Russia, which was largely removed from the villages where most clerical families lived. Despite the fact
that the majority of popovichi lived in urban areas during their adult years,
when they wrote most of their personal texts, what was of primary importance to them was the clerical world they had left. Those popovichi and
clergymen who did write about the merchantry often portrayed them as
embodying the sins of gluttony, greed, inhumanity, tyranny, injustice, and
ignorance. In his famous essay "Kingdom of Darkness," Nikolai Dobroliubov described merchants as mechanical dolls who did not think twice
about selling their daughters into marriage or cheating their friends and
even family members. They loathed education, for "nothing is sacred,
nothing is pure" to them. In his autobiography published in 1882, the
popovich writer Shashkov, whose mother was the rare matushka from the
merchantry, described even his maternal relatives in such pejorative terms.
He portrayed his two maternal aunts as misers who attached such significance to their money that they wouldn't tell their own sisters where it was
hidden. He recalled them "greedily stuffing every bit that fell into their
hands into their pockets." The fact that merchants were generally more pious than other secular estate groups did not deter the clergy from judging
merchant faith as well. Writing in 1882, one priest attacked merchant piety
by concluding that "their religiosity is completely fused with speculation."
For example, they expected their parish priest to provide them with stock-
market tips gleaned from proximity to divinity. Merchants tended to follow
only the external forms of religion, he explained, fasting strictly on the one
hand, but on the other hand cheating others to obtain money that they
then donated to their church.[75]

As tyrants, merchants were predisposed toward violence. In his autobiography, Apollinarii Vasnetsov described a merchant with whom he and his
brother shared a train compartment as teenagers: "an unusually loud, big,
foul-mouthed and braggart merchant, owner of a ship . . . it seemed to me
that he tried to pick a fight with my brother, which I feared very much. Up
until that time I had never seen such a type of person, and he made an extremely negative impression on me." Shashkov recalled that a distant merchant relative beat his servants so brutally that he killed one. Unable to father a child, he didn't hesitate to kidnap one.[76]

Townspeople could be just as despicable as merchants. Seminary administrators believed that clergymen's sons who rented from townspeople risked
moral peril, and in 1891 the Holy Synod circulated an internal memo
warning that the inadequate, undisciplined, coarse upbringing that townspeople gave their sons made them unfit to study alongside clerical sons in

the bursa. Shashkov described the mother-in-law of a maternal aunt who married a townsman: "fat, greasy, always red-faced . . . she drank vodka heavily."[77]

The sins popovichi and clergymen associated with the urban estates were so heinous that some clergymen and popovichi questioned their national identity, just as they had done with the nobility. In 1904 a Church publicist published a book entitled *On Happiness and Philistinism,* in which he asserted that Russians "by their nature" are "not *meshchane.*" Because the word for townspeople (meshchane) in Russian is synonymous with philistines, this statement has a dual meaning. On the one hand, any individual belonging to this social estate group was not Russian. On the other hand, any individual who behaved like a philistine could not be Russian. Meshchanstvo (philistinism), which first began to be employed as a cultural concept in the early nineteenth century, connoted a certain type of uncultured, depraved behavior associated with excessive attachment to material objects, coarseness, and self-interest—precisely the types of traits that the clergy and their families attributed to the social estate group bearing the same name. These traits were also commonly identified with Jews, Tatars, and Armenians who lived in the Russian empire, who were not coincidently employed mainly in commerce and classified as townspeople. This overlap between representations of Russian townspeople and widely despised national minority groups further contested the national identity of these ethnic Russians. "Philistine" traits were also associated with real foreigners. In a 1917 publication one popovich recalled his brother's attitude toward the German people, among whom he lived during a scholarly research stay in Germany: "Despite his respect for German scholarship, my brother shared the Slavic antagonism toward the German character . . . he was unpleasantly surprised by the greediness of the German peasants, their pedantic nature, as well as their excessive attachment to external property, to their furniture, etc."[78] Disenfranchised from the ruling noble class, the generally pious and non-Western-oriented merchants and townspeople could have constituted a threat to popovichi's claims of hegemony over Russia's "national" culture, particularly once their educational levels increased. But popovichi and their fathers managed to strip them of any power by questioning the legitimacy of their national identity. And by reserving the right to decide who qualified for Russian national identity, they further enhanced their sense of leadership.

Whereas clergymen and popovichi depicted nobles as haughty, they usually represented townspeople, and especially pious merchants, as being respectful toward the clergy, if not their sons.[79] The urban estates therefore incited their wrath not because of their treatment of the clergy (as was the case in part with the nobility), but purely because of the sins inherent in their profession. These sins meant that the urban estates did not embody a culture that was worth contesting. Despite the purely physical threat, the clergy and their sons felt infinitely superior to the urban estates. The nobility, on the other hand, represented a distinct, Westernized culture, a culture that they had to carefully battle with words. This juxtaposition is evident in the autobiographical descriptions by popovichi and clergymen of the feuds between seminarians and secular estates. In the run-down neighborhoods where seminarians boarded, fistfights frequently broke out between townsmen's sons and clerical boys during their long walk home late at night from the bursa. Memoirists recalled how both groups incited each other; they would taunt the townsmen's sons by yelling out *kozly* (a derogatory name for townspeople, meaning "goats") when they walked by their houses, while townsmen's sons would often ambush popovichi with cries of "beat the *kut'ia!*" (derogatory slang for clergy). Although gymnasium students and seminarians also hurled verbal insults at one another, memoirists rarely recalled fistfights with gymnasium students. Even the names they called gymnasium students were tamer; they did not revert to zoological categories but made up derogatory names based on the color of the students' uniforms.[80]

As was the case with nobles, redemption was also possible for individual members of the urban estates who rejected everything their origins implied. "Good" merchants and townspeople—who forsake "trade and profit" for an education, for example, or give away all their wealth to charity—surface regularly in the memoir literature and in the writings of Church publicists.[81] Yet the essentialist features that distinguished the urban estates from nobles made redemption difficult for even the best townsman or merchant to achieve. In his 1883 novel *Pribalovskie milliony* Mamin-Sibiriak portrayed the son of an industrialist consumed by guilt over what generations of his family had done to their workers. He endeavored to regain ownership of the family factory so that he could reimburse these workers. Despite his admirable actions, however, Mamin-Sibiriak's hero was never able to completely overcome his social origins, for he was a "person who carries in his blood a difficult inheritance." The clergy was also capable of such prejudice. When a rare priest who had been born a townsman was investigated by the Church at the turn of the century for allegedly beating his wife, the dean of his parish depicted him as a typical philistine: despite earnestly trying to change, he would always remain stingy, coarse, and money-grubbing, frequently overcharging his peasant parishioners. He portrayed the townsman-turned-priest's miserliness as a passion that consumed and controlled him.[82] Redemption was possible, but for those whose social origins were particularly sinful, and who were devoid of redeeming features such as erudition, it involved an uphill battle of proving innocence, even in the absence of guilt.

In a seminal article at the turn of the century, Ivanov-Razumnik, a prominent self-professed spokesman for the intelligentsia, defined the intelligentsia first and foremost as anti-philistine. Merchants, as philistines, were consequently not invited to cooperate with political parties that considered themselves part of the intelligentsia. Anti-philistinism, along with antipathy toward market relations and the urban estates, was deeply rooted in noble as well as clerical culture. Although many of the traits nobles and clergymen associated with the merchantry and townspeople overlapped, some were mutually exclusive, demonstrating that one cultural tradition did not simply assimilate the other. Noble disdain for the urban estates' association with work, for example, was not shared by the clergy. These dual cultural origins of anti-philistinism explain why it became so entrenched in Russian culture and why in 1917 it emerged as perhaps the single idea that united all political parties, from nationalist black hundreds, to aristocratic monarchists, to socialists, communists, and liberal constitutionalists.[83]

Anti-philistinism was one of numerous abstract sins and virtues that popovichi, and to a lesser extent clergymen, personified through the prism of entire social estate groups. A person's merits and defects were not individualized in popovichi's narratives. Popovichi did not tend to subscribe to the liberal notion of equality. They did not believe that others were like them, though in some cases, others could become like them. But rather than drawing only on the German philosophical and Western socialist doctrines that influenced noble intelligenty—in which the individual tended to be seen as self-abnegating in communion with some absolute—popovichi, as we have seen, also drew on an inherent contradiction in the prescriptive clerical literature. They espoused a degree of social egalitarianism while still imagining society arranged hierarchically. This classification of people into groups devoid of individual variation has traditionally been regarded as premodern, but it has also been identified as a feature of the modern age, as a means of bringing order to the chaos of modernity with the assistance of the new sciences of the eighteenth and nineteenth centuries.[84] Popovichi were thus able to reconcile the teachings of their clerical heritage with the new secular ideas they adopted while retaining their native estate's evolving social bias.

For both clergymen and popovichi, secular society was riddled with serious quandaries. For most clergymen, the inequalities of the temporal world were to be reconciled in the afterlife. For popovichi, any secularization of religious hierarchies resembled a familiar component of modern politics, class struggle. Regardless of their politics, they tended to conceive of society as divided into the haves and the have-nots. By rejecting abstract principles of the public sphere, such as the market and the state, they also called for a renunciation of society as it was constituted. They were forging a new identity in a world they sought to save by refashioning it according to their formative environment. For the clerical world was as virtuous as the nobility and urban estates were sinful.

Prescriptive Norms for the Sacred Estate

In 1869 a new theological journal entitled *Handbook for Village Pastors* published the first of many articles on the importance of the home life of parish priests. The author explained that the moral characteristics of a pastor were most evident in his behavior in his own home, a holier sphere immune to deception. To this Church publicist, as it was and would continue to be to the Russian intelligentsia, there was no dichotomy between public and private: "One should not separate the public life of any person from his private, domestic life." Moreover, a pastor's home life served as an example of how family members should interact and how parents should raise their children. The home of a pastor was held up as a "small Church," an ideal that parishioners should strive to emulate, just as Protestant ministers' families had been employed as a model domestic hearth in Europe for centuries.[1]

The family in the broadest sense became increasingly important to Church publicists in the postreform era. Like Western European statist philosophers and Russian Slavophiles, jurists, bureaucrats, and reformers, Church publicists perceived the family as a microcosm of civil society, the foundation of the modern state. The family was the primal community to which individuals first and foremost belonged. It was not only acceptable but expected that believers would love their own family members more than their brothers in Christ. After all, one seminary textbook stated, even Christ had showed particular love for his immediate family. As the revolutionary movement spread and the autocratic government unsuccessfully sought to control the process of modernization through stillborn reforms and counter-reforms, it became evident to church circles that society was in crisis. For most Church publicists, infused with the spirit of moralism that permeated Russian theology in the second half of the nineteenth century, this crisis was at heart a moral one, and they argued that the primary means of solving it was to improve the morality of society's foundation, the family. But whereas for reform-minded secular jurists, part of the solution lay in abolishing the patriarchal family and transferring to the state the Church's authority over family in matters such as divorce, in the eyes of the Church hierarchy and publicists the family had been corrupted by Western-oriented secular morals, and this had happened because of the declining social influence of the Church.[2] Thus in order to strengthen society the Church needed to play a greater, not a lesser, role. The state had proven itself unable to avert crisis, and the Church hierarchy, once silenced, was freed by the Great Reforms to act and to assert its clergy as society's moral leaders. Because clergymen were both moral leaders *and* the only educated Russians who had preserved traditional Christian values, the clerical domestic hearth was to be a model for the rest of society.

Jose Casanova argues that sacramental religions posit a tripartite division of the universe: the heavenly sphere and, in contrast, "this world," which is divided into the religious world (the church) and the secular world proper. As inhabitants of the religious world, the clergy, imbued with priestly authority derived directly from God, embodied a morality inherently superior to that of the laity. They were the "religious virtuosi," the "spiritual aristocracy" whom Max Weber claimed was universal within any religion, a minority elite whose piety was distinct from the mass religion.[3] Since Russian Orthodox priests, unlike Catholic priests, married, a degree of their sacramental holiness was shared by their wives and their offspring, a transfer aided by the castelike nature of the clergy and the estate character of the bursa. Popovichi's sense of moral superiority over other social estate groups was fueled in part by the belief that they were born into the sacred estate, an idea advanced by Church publicists.

Dual complementary sets of ethics were conceived and enshrined in separate courses taught in theological seminaries beginning in 1840: moral theology, which prescribed general Christian etiquette; and pastoral theology, which established priestly ideals. By the 1860s the number of pastoral theology publications had increased tenfold.[4] Both sets of texts can be seen as an attempt to utilize the expansion of the clerical press to preserve traditions during a period of rapid transformation of society. Yet, if these instructions were merely recording traditions that everyone knew and followed, why did they need to be so meticulously described? The prescriptions they produced differed from the classic sixteenth-century *Domostroi*, the Christian rules for Russian households, which relied heavily on physical punishment, and which, despite its medieval date, is most often cited by contemporary historians as illustrative of the Church's attitudes toward family life. In encoding "traditional" instructions the Church was using modern methods to standardize and control what may have been traditional ideals, but in doing so they transformed these traditions by providing textual blueprints for modern self-fashioning. In the process they were not above using the Western ideas—particularly rationalism—they saw themselves as repudiating in order to restore the power over Russian society that they felt they had lost. While the general purpose of prescriptive texts designed for the clergy and laity was identical, their contents were markedly dissimilar.

Model Piety

In the 1860s the Church hierarchy set about reforming its pastorate and system of clerical education. In part, these reforms were a reaction to secular society's assault on the clerical estate. Bishops acknowledged that it was important for the church to obtain the support and respect of society, but they did not necessarily agree on the extent of the problems that plagued parish life, nor on who was to blame. If priests acted immorally, by, for example, haggling with parishioners over fees—and bishops argued that such behavior was never as egregious as secular writers claimed—their actions were the logical consequence of a pastorate starved for funds by the state and parishioners. If they drank, it was because of the disrespect and humiliation they endured at the hands of sinful nobles and ignorant peasants.[5] The crisis in the Church was a logical extension of a broader moral crisis afflicting state and society. The country sorely needed moral leadership, and the clergy were its organic leaders. Yet to lead Russia out of its quagmire, the Church needed to elevate priestly authority.

The first articles praising the eminence of the priesthood coincided with the birth of the pastoral care movement in the 1840s. These texts outlined three separate roles that a priest had to fulfill in his mission of leading parishioners to salvation: teach his flock, dispense the sacraments and perform the liturgy, and perform pastoral care. Ironically, the new emphasis on good deeds, which detracted from the exclusively sacramental nature of salvation, can be seen as increasing priestly authority; believers had to strive toward their own salvation, but without the guidance of a priest, their efforts would fail. And in an era when the temporal world was increasingly seen as salvageable, the priest's role was not only to prepare others for the afterlife, but to help them in this world as well. To do this, priests were encouraged to attend to the social and material needs of their parishioners, caring for their bodies as well as their souls. To fulfill the diverse roles now prescribed for clergymen, those who donned priestly robes had to devote every ounce of their strength and moment of their lives to the task. While the virtuous life for laypersons consisted of striving arduously toward perfection, pastors were required to be perfect, just as Christ was.[6]

Priests were described as the only beings who simultaneously inhabited both heaven and earth: like Christ, they belonged to heaven by origin but were rooted to the earth by their responsibilities. They were Christ's representatives on earth, left behind to continue his work and to serve as mediators between God and man. The churches where they served were literally heaven on earth, an earthly reproduction of a transcendent model; during their dispensing of the sacraments, priests were transformed into hosts through which the divine imparted grace. Priestly authority rendered priests superior to the rest of humanity. Lay professions required the use of only certain faculties, such as reason or memory; the clerical profession required the continual employment of each and every human faculty. Lay service professionals assisted others' earthly concerns; clergymen served others' eternal as well as temporal needs. Laymen spoke, thought, lived, and acted most of the time only for their own benefit; everything priests did was for the salvation or perdition of many others. If a priest did not succeed in delivering his flock to redemption, he forfeited his personal salvation.[7]

In elevating the priesthood, Church publicists drew on the new authority professions and science commanded. Unlike noblemen, who were not a professional class, priests possessed specialized knowledge and authority that validated their direction of the public and private lives of the laity. At the same time that doctors in Europe were being depicted as modern priests, priests were increasingly referred to in the clerical prescriptive literature with the term, commonplace in patristics and hymnology, "doctors of the soul."[8] This medical metaphor entailed inverting the secularization of the priesthood by secular professionals. Not disdaining secular professional discourse, Church publicists argued that a priest healed one's soul, while a doctor tended only to one's body. The primacy of the former was unequivocal.

Clergymen were reminded that because they had to serve as an example to others, their piety had to be "higher, purer and more perfect than the life of the laity." Priests were theoretically required to go to confession more than laypersons, and the types of questions they were asked during confession differed from those posed to the laity. While laymen were questioned about whether they had committed basic sins, priests were grilled primarily about their professional duties. They had to be more careful than laypersons to obey rules regarding fasting, and they were expected to pray more. As role models, priests were also directed to personify each of the good deeds the laity were to follow to attain salvation. In addition, clergymen were also supposed to exemplify holiness, admonition, firmness, and contemplation, qualities that were not required of laypersons. As opposed to Catholicism, where the pope is the arbiter of truth, in Eastern Orthodoxy, where only Christ is considered the head of the church, every ordained clergyman was also invested with the responsibility of upholding the dual meaning of truth (pravda and istina). Priests were guardians of truth, the manifestation of God's spirit, which was the ultimate authority and was embodied in the church's traditions.[9]

To attain moral perfection, clergymen, like all believers, were encouraged to pursue knowledge. But because clergymen were the spiritual leaders of their parishioners, their pursuit of knowledge was more vital.[10] One 1885 manual stated: "Indifference to learning and literary studies, aversion to mental labor, evasion of the pursuit of literature and scholarship of a theological character—is a degradation of the priestly rank and a contradiction of the concept connected to it of religious teacher."

Clergymen were expected to be well versed not only in religious literature but in secular subjects as well. This same manual went on to stress the value of secular learning for clergymen: "any serious scholarly work, even if it is connected with a specialty, which does not have an immediate connection to theology or to the priestly profession, can attest only to the intellectual maturity of the priest and to his striving toward spiritual self-perfection." Church publicists argued in part that priests had to improve their cultural level in order to elevate the authority of clergymen in parishioners' eyes. Secular learning could help priests bond with learned parishioners and woo them away from atheism.[11]

Among the secular subjects recommended in particular for study by clergymen were those classified as "hard" sciences, including history and the natural sciences. History appealed to the Church hierarchy for two reasons. First, Church hierarchs were increasingly interested in elevating tradition, the basis of authority in the Church, by associating religion with remembrances of the past.[12] Second, by arguing that the Church represented Russia's historical past, Church hierarchs legitimatized themselves as leaders of the national church in an era that saw the rapid growth of nationalism and increasing calls for religious tolerance and plurality.

A priest was required to be not only an assimilator of knowledge, but also a producer of scholarship. As the century progressed, clergymen were required to write some of their sermons and encouraged to keep confessional diaries. In these personal diaries they were to chart not only their own spiritual progress, but, in contrast to the Puritan practice of individual diary keeping, that of their parishioners. In part, this was a practical necessity born of the high illiteracy rates of Russian Orthodox parishioners. But it also underscores the greater authoritative power Orthodox priests, endowed with sacramental authority, had over their parishioners. These diaries were to serve as a daily mirror for clergymen's souls, providing a friend in times of need and an opportunity to identify existing imperfections and the means of correcting them. In keeping with the Church's disregard for any dichotomy between public and private, diaries were to chronicle a priest's parish work as well as his domestic life. They were instructed to note everything good and bad they had done each day, everything that had made an impression on them, and their feelings about the main events of the day. They were encouraged to read over the entire span of their diaries from time to time so that they could witness the depth of change in their morality and also find the traces of Divine providence in their actions.[13]

Clergymen's diaries thus served as a site for the construction of the self, a prerequisite for the development of modern Selfhood.

The praise of priests—and their valuation—reached such heights that some nineteenth-century Church publicists argued that priests were superior to both angels and the tsar. Although manuals reminded priests that they must be obedient to the divinely anointed tsar, given the tripartite division of the universe, the temporal realm that he ruled was still inferior to the spiritual sphere that the clergy led on earth. "There is no earthly power that is equal to the power of a clergyman," the author of one article on pastoral theology wrote in 1843. Another Church publicist, writing in 1860, declared: "A tsar can absolve from physical bonds; a priest can deliver souls from the power of the devil and from the bonds of sin . . . the tsar bears gold, a priest bears God."[14]

Priests were even exalted above monks, regarded in Byzantium and medieval Russia as the pinnacle status, and the group most often identified throughout history as the religious virtuosi. One Church publicist declared in 1873 that a monk's only goal was his own sanctification, whereas priests existed to sanctify others. Several others depicted monks as living individualistic, self-indulgent lives secluded from the dangers of the world. Priests, on the other hand, they argued, were forced to adopt a precarious middle path: to save their parishioners they had to live and act in the world while simultaneously avoiding it and not accepting its fallen state.[15]

Comparisons of monks and priests led some Church publicists, like their counterparts in the Protestant reformation, to question celibacy and defend the nuclear family as the ideal Christian community. Marriage, they argued, was the root of all societies, an unbreakable bond upon which all social relations were based, symbolic of the holy union of Christ and church. Marriage was a sacrament, and while married people were not physically chaste, they could attain spiritual chastity. Monks, one Church publicist noted in 1895, unfortunately often took for granted spiritual celibacy. More than one Church publicist noted that bishops in the early Christian church married. Monks had been seen as morally inferior to priests in the ancient Orthodox church, one priest argued in 1903, precisely because they were unmarried. The reason bishops were eventually required to remain celibate had nothing to do with the exaltation of virginity and everything to do with concern that their children would inherit Church wealth.[16] Because of the lesser influence of Augustine in Eastern Orthodoxy, sexual relations within marriage are not considered as sinful as they are in Catholicism. Consequently, several late-imperial Church publicists condemned abstinence within marriage without both partners' consent as impious and the elevation of virginity above marriage as a misunderstanding that arose from exposure to Western ideas.[17]

The most obvious proof that the Church did not elevate worldly marriage above otherworldly virginity was the fact that its priests married. Postreform Church publicists argued that marriage and family life were indispensable to the parish clergyman for three reasons. The first reason was practical: like nineteenth-century European medical doctors, they saw marriage as the means to contain "natural" sexuality. Second, only married priests could provide parishioners with a role model for conducting family life, and as leaders of their flock they confirmed the sanctity of marriage. Third, because the family was sacred, its love was capable of releasing priests from the spirit of the world, a world they were compelled to immerse themselves in to save their flock.[18]

As members of the model family, clergymen's wives and children were expected to adhere to the standard of model piety required of the clergy. They were instructed to be the first to enter the church prior to services and the last to leave. During services they were to teach others by their pious conduct, such as placing candles before icons and praying sincerely. Since a priest was the spiritual father of his parishioners, his wife and children were also their "elder" relatives. This model piety was not only prescribed in etiquette manuals, it was also encoded in Church law. For example, in contrast to laypersons, who were required to go to confession once a year, all of the members of a clergyman's family were obliged, at least in theory, to confess four times a year.[19] Although Church publicists mainly addressed the priestly rank, deacons were also ordained, and because even lowly unordained clergymen were members of the clerical estate, their behavior and that of their families reflected on the priesthood and were thus often implicitly addressed as well.

As an example to their parishioners, clergymen and their families had to lead a modest life in all aspects. Pastoral theology manuals emphasized that the clerical family should not indulge in overeating or extravagant clothing. The clerical family dwelling had to be in order, clean, convenient for prayer, tasteful, neither luxurious nor fashionable, and it was not to exceed five rooms in size. Just as it should not resemble the homes of the secular well-to-do, neither should it "be as ugly as a simple peasant hut." The clerical home, in keeping with the special mission of the clerical estate, had to be distinct from the dwellings of other social estate groups. Each room in a clergyman's home had to have an icon in it. The priest's study was to function as a home-church, where his family would gather to pray corporately.[20]

In running their households, clerical families always had to be careful to retain their humility. Manuals advised that "as a person required to be the example of Christian simplicity and industriousness," a priest should hire others only to do work that he and members of his family did not have the physical strength to complete. If he did hire servants, a priest could not treat them as secular persons treated theirs.[21]

Another reason servants should be employed only in a limited capacity was that, as outsiders, they could contaminate the clerical home with secular influences and expose its intimate life to pernicious gossip. Clerical children were therefore never to be tutored or minded by "outsiders." Isolating themselves from other social estate groups—who because of their secular status were inherently inferior—was one way to ensure the model piety of the clerical family. Clergymen were therefore recommended to fraternize closely only with other clergymen. By doing so, they avoided the danger of laypersons seducing them into humiliating their calling by engaging in secular leisure.[22]

In the case of the clergy, prohibitions on leisure were even stricter than for the laity. No moment of a clergyman's time could be wasted, for, in the words of one Church publicist writing in 1880, "the liability of a priest is so strict, his responsibilities are so multiple, that for him to waste his time on the activities of festive people is dangerous and sinful."[23] Yet because children needed enjoyment and families bonded through recreational activities, certain acceptable forms of recreation were allowed. One Church publicist described in 1885 the delicate balance between acceptable and unacceptable forms of socializing for the members of clerical families:

> The family of a priest may have friends, they are allowed to meet with their friends as much as they like; but it is indecent for the members of a priest's family to crave the entertainment of society. . . . We do not recommend the confinement of the members of a priest's family; that would be a violation of nature; during youth one needs to enjoy oneself. But not everyone needs to engage in that which society offers for leisure. There are many types of leisure, domestic and modest, in which the wife and children of priests may participate, which do not cast a shadow on the head of the household. . . .

The leisure that the author considered objectionable closely resembles the type of leisure characteristic of the Russian nobility: "secular leisure, in which cards are always ready, a merry society is always gathering, not knowing how to spend its time, very likely songs and music are heard, and often dances are held." There were three types of diversions acceptable for the clerical family, all of which served a utilitarian purpose by "encouraging the spirit." The first consisted of edifying domestic discussions (*besedy*) in which the entire clerical family, fellow clergymen, and well-minded parishioners participated. The second was spending time amidst nature, and the third was performing at home one of the "fine" arts, such as the reading of literature, singing, and music. Except for nature strolls, all of these activities were to take place within the shrouded environs of the clerical home, and all were collective, reflecting an emphasis on the family as community.[24]

Church publicists were aware that the expectations they placed on the clergy were high, and that they were incompatible with the realities of clerical daily life. Ironically, the highest glorification of the clergy by Church publicists occurred just as these very publicists were complaining for the first time openly about the material and ethical dilemmas that plagued the parish clergy. Yet this chasm between ideals and reality was seen by some as a useful challenge. "Reality is always far from the ideal," one publicist stated in 1895. Nevertheless, he continued, ideals are good for people because they bring light to human existence, drawing people toward them.[25]

To encourage their parishioners, clergy were required to epitomize what others should aspire toward, including overcoming tremendous obstacles.

Blessed Children

Buoyed by the inquisitiveness that marked the Great Reform era, the clerical and secular presses began in the 1860s to debate the validity of the castelike nature of the clerical estate. The majority of Church publicists condemned this practice, noting that there was no basis for it in canon law. It had even, one explained in 1877, been condemned by an ancient church council. Some Church publicists agreed with the secular press's assertion that clerical birthright was the main obstacle to reforming the clergy. It was responsible for the clergy's lowly position in society, they argued, and led the public to view clergymen as outsiders.[26] Yet in response to the sometimes shrill attacks in the secular press, a minority of Church publicists and clergymen defended clerical birthright. This contingent claimed that clerical sons were, like the apostles and saints, chosen by God. As one priest told the student body of Vladimir Seminary at the start of the 1887/8 academic year, "it is obvious that God himself directed you, by the location of your birth and upbringing, to study specifically in a clerical school." A number of Church publicists in the mid-nineteenth century compared the clergy to the biblical Levites. As Levites, one publicist argued in 1843, the clergy "should look at themselves as a specific class, completely different from ordinary mortal classes. God himself imparts such an understanding of their rank." The difference between ordinary Christians and their pastors was deemed comparable to the difference between Christians and non-Christians.[27] Even Church publicists who rejected this implication that the clergy was a separate race agreed that clerical traditions were preserved and imparted from one generation to the next. The key role nineteenth-century theologians assigned to domestic upbringing ensured that virtually all Church publicists, regardless of whether they believed it was nature or nurture that shaped a person, reached the same conclusion: only members of the sacred estate could produce future clergymen.

The Church's emphasis on the sanctity of the family was reiterated in the attention it devoted to the upbringing of children. The number of church-related articles and manuals on this topic skyrocketed when the clerical press expanded in the 1860s. In contrast to the institutional orientation that had characterized the post-Petrine state's attitude toward upbringing of elite males, these publications maintained that a good family was the best school for inculcating morality and that a domestic upbringing was indispensable and irreplaceable. The priority of Church publicists was first and foremost to tackle the subject of clerical upbringing. This was because the clergy in this respect, as in others, served as an example to the laity.[28] However, because of the uniqueness and vastly greater importance of the clerical profession, the upbringing of its children—particularly its sons, which most of the literature implicitly addressed under the guise of "children"—was not synonymous in content or consequence with that of lay children.

Writing in 1869, one Church publicist went so far as to argue that because clergymen were raising future priests, the upbringing of his children was a priest's most sacred duty. A clerical upbringing was to begin as soon as the child was conscious of his surroundings. By serving with their fathers at the altar and by assisting with paraliturgical rites during their preschool years and during school vacations, their distinctive upbringing would provide clerical sons with practical clerical training while instilling in them greater religious sensibility (*tserkovnost'*), piety, modesty, honesty, chastity, diligence, patience, and obedience than characterized children who received a secular upbringing and who were therefore less "soulful" than members of the clergy.[29]

Even most of those publicists who argued that membership in the clergy was a birthright agreed, however, that in addition to being chosen by God to be born into the clerical estate, a clergyman's son had to experience a *personal* calling to become ordained. The concept of vocational calling for secular professions dates back in Orthodox thinking at least as far back as Prokopovich's eighteenth-century sermons, and beginning in the late 1850s, Orthodox missionaries began for the first time to express a reluctance to enforce conversion, citing "freedom of conscience" and the need for individuals to choose their own religious creed. This emphasis on individual, as opposed to collective, calling regarding clergymen's sons appears to have first been voiced by Church publicists with the birth of the pastoral care movement in the 1840s.[30] In an 1861 manual that included specific guidelines for dispensing confession to seminary students, confessors were told to remind seminarians that they were called to be intermediaries between God and man, but were also told to try to dissuade those who only sought to support their families materially and those who led an impure life from entering the priesthood. Yet because only those individuals who received a clerical domestic upbringing were qualified to become priests, clergymen were encouraged, as late as the eve of World War I, to enroll their sons in seminaries in case they received a calling to become ordained. Otherwise, there wouldn't be enough candidates for the priesthood. In a speech given to seminary students in 1900, one bishop employed the image of ancient trees, stating that when such trees die, it is best to replace them with those trees that "from the moment they appeared in the world drank the juice of the ancient trees from which they originated." Addressing the minority of seminarians from secular social estates in the audience, the bishop told them to return to where they came from. Despite their seminary education, the fact that they had not received a clerical upbringing from birth disqualified them from the priesthood.[31]

Many bishops and Church publicists argued that individuals from secular social estates could not become clergymen because they did not possess either the proper disposition or the ability to martyr themselves. Given the low standard of living among the clergy, the Bishop of Kherson warned in the 1860s that it might be dangerous for the government if members of other estates became priests. The "clerical proletariat" is humble and meek, but other estates have developed expectations and a thirst for activity and have less ability to act practically or industriously. Describing the clerical milieu, he noted that "[by] its specific structure and character, these are people more or less not of this world."[32] Not surprisingly, Church hierarchs and publicists lashed out in particular against nobles becoming clergymen.

In part, secular schooling had spoiled boys from secular social estates for the priesthood. One bishop noted in 1861 that clergymen's sons who attended gymnasia became obstinate and unruly, while those who attended the bursa were humble, meek, and obedient. If secular schools ruined the characters of clerical boys, boys from secular estates who attended the bursa were nevertheless incapable of redeeming their characters through clerical education. In the testimonials (kharakteristiki) of Vladimir seminarians' character traits from the turn of the century, bursa administrators distinguished between students from the clerical and secular estates. Only seminarians from non-clerical estates were described as being more secular than church-oriented, and while plenty of clergymen's sons were described as possessing negative features, among students characterized as possessing entirely positive traits only secular-born seminarians were deemed "untrustworthy" or unqualified for clerical service. Because of their secular upbringing, secular-born seminarians were often accused of being a bad influence on clergymen's sons. On the other hand, seminary officials sometimes went to great lengths to protect clerical-born radical seminarians from government authorities, even to the point of destroying evidence such as atheistic and anti-autocratic literature. Their reasoning was that clergymen's sons were inherently redeemable.[33]

When writing about the natures of clerical and secular children, Church publicists came closest to making an argument about immutable differences that divided social estate groups. Although they rarely directly compared the two, the conceptions of the clerical and secular child, addressed separately in the dual moral and pastoral theological literature, were fundamentally distinct, akin to the church's tenet on differences between children born to Christian and non-Christian marriages. In manuals written about children in general, a puritanical view of the child's nature is presented. Proper upbringing is needed to change and control evil aspects of the child's temperament. By contrast, clerical children were conceived as inherently pure and a clerical upbringing was designed to protect their inborn good nature from outside contamination. A manual for clerical families in 1861, for example, stated: "a child is by nature sincere and easily speaks out; in him there can not be guile, hypocrisy, etc. . . . all these and similar traits are not bestowed by nature, but are acquired as a result of bad upbringing and living conditions."[34] The conception of the inherently good nature of children is analogous to the theories of Rousseau but is also in keeping with the Eastern Orthodox doctrine on original sin. In contrast to Western Christian teachings, infants are perceived as untainted by the transgression of personal sin. In Orthodox practice this translated into communion being given to infants from the time of their baptism onward, and their partaking of confession only when they reached the age of seven. Until age seven children were doctrinally viewed as unable to understand the difference between right and wrong, and hence sinless. Early church fathers had characterized young children as removed from the opportunity to sin because of their isolation from worldly affairs, their sexlessness, and the absence in them of passions of the soul, such as anger, grief, fear, pride, and inegalitarianism. The concept of children born into secular estates as inherently sinful was thus a departure from Orthodox doctrinal theology, a product of the movement to elevate the clerical estate, and by the turn of the century Church publicists began to return to theological teachings on uniform conceptions of Christian children.[35]

These conceptual differences regarding clerical and secular children are evident as well in church-related child-rearing instructions regarding reading. As was the case with directions to lay adults, clerical child-care manuals for the general population warned of the dangers of excessive reading. Child-rearing manuals for clerical families, on the other hand, stressed the positive aspects of reading. To read well was seen as the key to a child's success in school, and books were presented as his most influential teachers. Clerical parents were advised to expand their children's horizons and not restrict their reading materials only to religious literature. Because clerical sons were perceived as miniature versions of their fathers, the same types of secular books were recommended for them as were recommended for their fathers.[36]

Corporal punishment was also recommended in general child-rearing manuals written by Church publicists, but it was described in clerical child-rearing guides as morally harmful. Invoking fear of God and even the progressive notion of verbal reasoning were preferred methods of controlling clerical children. The purity that clerical children were perceived as embodying negated the need to exorcise internal demons. Anger was also portrayed as beneath a clergyman's dignity, and the specter of a pastor beating his children was anathema. On the other hand, clerical parents were warned never to spoil their children, but to provide a balance of strictness and affection. The type of parenting recommended for clerical children is reminiscent of Slavophile benevolent paternalism, which combined elements of the affectionate eighteenth-century European "good father," linked to the model of the modern self, with traditional patriarchal notions of unquestioned authority.[37]

Gendered Roles

Nowhere was the difference between the way Church publicists viewed the upbringing of clerical versus secular children clearer than in the roles they prescribed for mothers and fathers. Their gendered conceptions of

child-rearing, which, as we will see in subsequent chapters, popovichi interiorized and secularized, cemented the association of the clerical estate with
a distinctly Russian cultural tradition.

In his moral theology textbook, Khalkolivanov described families as patriarchal. The father serves as the single head and takes care of everyone's
needs. He is, in turn, obeyed by all. As was the case in a theologically prescribed hierarchical society, however, different members of the family, like
each estate, perform distinct roles. After all, the head of the family, like the
head of the state, cannot attend to all tasks himself, nor is his nature suited
to performing all tasks. In child-rearing manuals written for the laity,
Church publicists assigned supremacy to the mother in parenting. Mothers
were depicted as having natural access to their child's soul. They were instructed to be their children's first teachers regarding God and Christ and
to serve as an example in all spheres. These instructions were in keeping
with Victorian era European and Russian secular manuals, which assigned
mothers the dominant role in the lives of both their daughters *and* their
sons prior to age seven.[38]

By contrast, in clerical child-rearing manuals, it was the father who
reigned supreme; he was the primary keeper of the child's soul—particularly
the male child's soul. Unlike the lay father, the clerical father was not simply
father to his biological children; he was also father to his parishioners. It has
been argued that in early modern England following the Reformation the father inherited priestly power.[39] In the case of Orthodox priests, who were, unlike Catholic priests, both vessels of the divine *and* fathers, this power was
augmented by the nineteenth-century cult of the family. This enhancement
of power made it necessary for the clerical father to raise his sons, a task so
important that, unlike lay child-raising, it could not be left to women—even
women born and raised in the sacred estate. For while laymen and women
were perceived as possessing distinct gendered traits, their differences were
minimal compared with the gulf that separated clerical women and their ordained husbands.

Because the upbringing of lay children was less momentous and consuming, it could be assigned to a single parent. In the case of clerical sons,
upbringing was shared by both parents, according to clearly differentiated
duties. An 1861 manual contrasted the role of clerical parents, beginning
first with maternal responsibilities, which revolved around attending to the
physical needs of the child:

> The strict, vigilant concern of his mother for him, her tender love, with which
> she follows every movement of her child . . . with which she hurries to satisfy
> his desires, if she finds them good, and to replace them with others, if these
> desires turn out to be harmful for children—all this, of course, does not occur
> without the most beneficial effects on the child's soul. He becomes accus-
> tomed to looking at his mother as the being upon which he completely de-
> pends, to whom he owes his happiness. . . .

The clerical mother's love and attention, however, was balanced by the role of the father as the child's omnipotent mentor:

> On the other hand, the active participation by the father in the mother's affairs, his strict supervision of the child, accompanied often by observations, admonitions, incentives, and punishments, compels a child to see that each step of his is strictly watched, each movement of his is given one or another evaluation, and this brings him to the idea that every word, every hint and order of his father is for him an indispensable law, that his father is for him higher and more important than all others surrounding him, and that he obeys without contradiction, loves and respects his father as an unconditional duty.

To temper the strictness and authoritarianism that they were instructed to exercise in conducting their sons' upbringing, clerical fathers were reminded to remain mild and loving at all times.[40]

The primacy of the clerical father in raising his sons was formalized by his duty to administer personally his sons' extensive preschool education. Even literate mothers did not possess the liturgical authority to provide religious instruction, so if a boy's father had died, literate male members of the extended clerical family were to be assigned this responsibility. Before they enrolled in the bursa, clergymen's sons were expected to have learned to read Russian and Slavonic, to recite commonly used prayers, and to have mastered the foundations of Christian teachings and the first four fundamentals of mathematics.[41] Clergymen's active participation in their sons' upbringing was facilitated by the fact that there was little physical separation between their homes and workplaces. In contrast to peasant *otkhodniki* (migrant workers) and noble officers, who frequently traveled away from their families, and to bureaucrats and merchants, who spent most of their waking hours at their offices or shops, a clergyman's office, where he received parishioners, was located in his home, and his primary workplace, the church, was usually situated next-door.

Limiting clergywomen's care to their sons' material needs meant that they were essentially to continue in the home the gendered tasks they performed in the parish. Unlike nineteenth-century Western European and Russian noblewomen, parish clergywomen were not encouraged to remove themselves from the public sphere. By assuming many of the "secular" pastoral care responsibilities of their husbands, clergywomen could allow their husbands to focus on the more important task of performing the sacraments and providing religious instruction. Clergywomen were therefore associated more with the temporal, worldly sphere than their husbands.

Clergymen were warned of the dangers their wives posed: because clergywomen had greater responsibilities than secular women, they could also do more harm, and a bad clerical wife could destroy a priest and his parish. Church publicists bemoaned the fate of a clergyman saddled with a bad wife. These wives were distinguished by their lack of interest in parish affairs, by their overt concern with leisure and material objects, and by their gregariousness, intrusive curiosity, shrewishness, and maliciousness. They were depicted as having an adverse influence on their children and a bewitching effect on their husbands. They supposedly poisoned their husbands' good relations with parishioners by discouraging clerical philanthropy and demanding that their husbands charge more for the performance of religious rites. The line between "bad" and "good" wives was not always clear. Some bad wives were good housekeepers and exceptional mothers; their sin lay in their refusal to help their husbands with pastoral duties. Priests had to be on the lookout, however, since evil could lurk even within a "good" wife; because of the association of women with flesh, they were particularly susceptible to the devil's temptations. Indeed, the devil would try to infiltrate clerical families especially, since he envied the power of priests. Tempted by the devil, "good" wives were known to seduce their husbands before they performed the liturgy, a time when priests are forbidden to have sexual relations. No matter how much he loved and respected his wife, one 1869 article stated, a clergyman should never forget that she, "as a woman, in many matters can not equal a man." A clergyman was expected to spend time re-educating his wife.[42]

The association of clergywomen with the body and its passions is partially rooted in the modern Western binary cultural construction that distinguishes between women as natural, linked to the physical, expressed world, and men as cultural, representing reason and intellect. In the mid-nineteenth century this binary model was imported to Russia and was soon entrenched among learned Russians, including, seemingly, the educated clerical elite. In an instructive manual for seminarians on choosing a spouse, one clergyman wrote in 1860: "a woman lives by her heart; serious thought is a task that is beyond her strength . . . a man lives by his mind." At the same time, the differentiation of clerical wives into binary "good" and "bad" categories differs from these Western constructs. The clergy's association of its women with the public sphere negated elevating them as "domestic angels," as did pre-Petrine gender stereotypes, which lingered in both nineteenth-century clerical and peasant cultures.[43]

Intent on encoding an alternative educated Russian "national" tradition, Church publicists consciously created gender stereotypes distinctive to the clergy. They articulated this mission in their attacks on educated noblewomen. One sermon published in 1896 denounced noblewomen for being too interested in the "boisterous pleasures of the world" to raise their own children. Having handed their children over to foreigners to be reared, noble mothers failed to pass on to them "native feelings," which accounted for the indifference or hostility of nobles toward Orthodoxy. The reason estate schools for clergymen's daughters were first founded in 1843 was to produce educated clerical wives immune from the corruptive influence of noble girls and their secular, Westernized, privileged education. Since girls from secular estates could never be suitable brides for clergymen—noble girls would never be able to accustom themselves to the hardships of clerical daily life, and girls from the peasantry, merchantry, townspeople, and lower level bureaucracy did not share the clerical estate's culture, spirit, or lifestyle—these schools were open only to clergymen's daughters, who, it was hoped, would marry within their native estate. In addition, because training to be a good matushka had to begin, like the training of clergymen, at birth, clerical endogamy was rarely questioned, even when the estate structure of the clergy was being attacked. Whereas seminarians from other estates could compensate somewhat for their origins by receiving formal theological instruction at the bursa, so much of being a good matushka, one Church publicist argued, was learned at home, where generations of distinctive clerical traditions were inculcated by the clerical mother.[44]

As was the case in nineteenth-century Western Europe, the elevation of clerical family life was linked to the new emphasis on the importance of love in marriages. Concern over the role material concerns played in forging clerical marriages was repeatedly voiced by Church publicists and bishops in the second half of the nineteenth century. Clerical etiquette manuals emphasized that marriage was above all a matter of the heart. But whereas the Victorian love the Russian nobility emulated included romance, passion, sentimentality, and the relentless pursuit of happiness, the definition of clerical love marriages resembled the one proposed in sixteenth-century Protestant sermons. Love marriages were defined as spiritual intimacy, built on mutual help, harmony, respect, comfort, companionship, and shared devotion to the community formed by household and parish. Nineteenth-century Orthodox Church publicists argued that, without such love, priests would suffer greatly and turn to drink, since the majority of them lived in villages isolated from other educated people. To ensure the compatibility of clerical spouses, and to ensure that a matushka could perform her multiple duties, the "pure love" between them, however, had to be augmented by other factors, such as the wife's family background, and her possession of the "mental and moral requirements of a priest's wife."[45] For Church publicists, there was no contradiction between encouraging marriages based both on endogamy and on love. In their eyes, a clergyman could only truly love one of his own kind.

Compatibility of clerical spouses did not require identical natures and aptitude; in fact, it required just the opposite: they should complement each other by fulfilling the other's deficiencies. Clerical women, associated with the body, were ideal brides if they knew "housework down to its extreme details"; clerical men, associated with the mind, were ideal grooms if they were highly educated. The superiority of the male realm over the female was never questioned, yet neither was the necessity of both domains.[46] Two disparate individuals were transformed by the sacrament of marriage into one. It was this symmetry of mind and body that popovichi secularized and distorted. (See chapter 7.)

Fathers to Sons—

The Mamin Correspondence

Although less prolific than their secular sons, rank-and-file clergymen expressed their views in a wide variety of sources, including questionnaires, testimonials, petitions, autobiographies, diaries, and letters. Did clergymen interiorize clerical prescriptive norms? What were the values they preached to their adult secular sons? The answers to these questions lie in large part in familial correspondence, the single largest collection of the personal texts of rank-and-file parish clergymen that have been preserved in archives. The archive of the writer Dmitrii Mamin-Sibiriak is particularly rich in clerical personal texts. It contains numerous rarities among surviving clerical records, including the diaries of both his father and mother and the unpublished 1811 autobiography of a great-grandfather, one of the earliest examples of a parish priest's autobiography.

A minor populist writer in the pre-revolutionary period, Mamin-Sibiriak wrote critical portrayals of industrialists that eventually became a staple of the Soviet literary canon. Writing in 1940, a leading Soviet literary critic summed up Mamin-Sibiriak's reputation: "One does not need to chase after Aleksandr Nevskii or exhume 'The Igor Tale.' It is enough to open any book by Mamin, and our motherland will be open." Mamin-Sibiriak earned his hyphenated last name from his allegiance to his native Urals, his life-long residence and the setting for most of his fiction. His father, Narkiss Mamin (1827–1878), was a priest in a parish affiliated with a rural factory. Father Narkiss was a consultant on lightning for the Ural society of amateur scientists and read the conservative newspaper *Moskovskie vedomosti* regularly, copying quotations from poems it published as well as political and scientific articles he fancied. He also owned a library, and its contents included works on Russian history by Nikolai Kostomarov, a two-volume history of English civilization, an anatomical textbook, and a volume on the life of animals.[47] After Father Narkiss's death in 1878, twenty-six-year-old Dmitrii cared for his mother and younger siblings, even though at the time he was barely eking out a living by giving private lessons.

Four years before his death, Father Narkiss wrote to his son, then a student at Petersburg Veterinary Institute:

> But do not think, my sweet, that we live only by animal instincts, that we worry only about food, clothes, and sleep. We also are members of our small society, we sympathize with all of its needs, share its joys and sorrows. We do not separate ourselves from educated people. We would be prepared to work with them, to follow all the movements in the realm of enlightenment and progress, if only we had more free time and more means to live.

Father Narkiss's complaints about the hardships of clerical life were universally shared by rural clergymen, most of whom seethed with resentment

Father Narkiss Mamin with
Dmitrii and Dmitrii's younger
brother, 1868.

over their socio-economic situation. They viewed themselves as poor, and
even if a clergyman achieved prosperity in a parish in a capital city, the
memory of his impoverished childhood haunted him, and he continued to
perceive himself as destitute. Clergymen never presented themselves as eager for riches; the accumulation of wealth was repugnant to them. They argued that they themselves were more than willing to go without but could
not subject their families to such privations. Nor would parishioners allow
them to, for parishioners demanded that their clergy live in a respectable
manner. They were thus forced to waste precious time—which could have
been spent saving souls, engaging in pastoral care, pursuing self-knowledge,
or producing scholarship—earning extra money by working the fields.[48]

Clergymen saw themselves as victims. Paradoxically, this suffering ultimately redeemed them, rendered them, as one priest put it, "a type of martyr." Drawing on the genetic argument employed by some Church publicists, one priest wrote of a resilient, patient clerical nature, nurtured over
generations, that produced individuals tough enough to endure what clergymen suffered.[49]

Suffering was not their only means to redemption; holy work could also deliver them. One of the few aspects of their adult lives that clergymen did *not* complain about was performing their priestly and pastoral duties. For example, Father Narkiss noted in his 1851 diary the frequent early morning services he performed, but he never once objected to his rigorous liturgical schedule. Instead, he expressed eagerness to participate in the enlightening goals of the pastoral care movement. Announcing to his son that the Great Reforms had finally reached them, he euphorically wrote that "much is moving forward, toward progress." He was especially excited about a new school he was teaching in, which was a "very constructive endeavor," and about working with the local zemstvo to improve peasant hygiene. Their professional work was a source of joy for clergymen. In a letter to a fellow clergyman, one priest wrote in the 1890s: "In your last letter you bitterly complained about your fate. Everyone has their burden to bear. I find comfort only in work. . . ." Indeed, they lived to work; Ivan Tsvetkov's mother wrote him in 1887 that although his father was ill, he refused to retire, claiming that he would die without his work. Clergymen interiorized the precept that their professional mission was superior to that of lay professions, and some described themselves as vessels of the holy spirit placed on earth by God himself. In his diary published in 1871, one priest quoted the early church father John of Chrysostom that priests were higher than angels.[50]

The parish clergy also interiorized the belief, propagated by the pastoral care movement, of its superiority over the monastic clergy. They sometimes depicted not only bishops, but also simple monks, as selfish hypocrites. Since the eighteenth century priests had blamed the monastic hierarchy for their ills, accusing them of everything from enriching themselves at the expense of parish clergymen to abusing their subordinates in the same way that nobles had violated serfs. As was the case with nobles, clergymen argued that power had corrupted the episcopate.[51] In his 1851 diary, Father Narkiss expressed his fears about an upcoming visit from their bishop. When Ivan Tregubov (1858–1931), a leader in the Tolstoyian sectarian movement, considered becoming a monk, his widowed mother was horrified. Since her deceased husband could not counsel their son, Ivan's mother adopted the assertive parental role usually reserved for clerical fathers. Attempting to convince him to become a parish priest instead, Ivan's mother articulated the parish clergy's justification for considering themselves above monks:

> When you by your education and lifestyle discover yourself in the post of a rural priest, you can bring a great deal more assistance to the narod than if you lock yourself away in a monastery cell. The word of God gives greater preference to him who saves in the temporal world where there exists an entire abyss of temptation and all sorts of filth. Think, Vania, how many members of the simple folk there are in the world, who with pleasure would like to hear

good and wise words about the salvation of their souls. A priest has only to possess the desire to teach the narod in the Church of God, in school, and in private encounters—all this occurs as part of his official obligations. I advise you as your mother. And the savior himself said that he who teaches the narod will be admitted to heaven.[52]

The parish clergy, along with Church publicists who exalted them, ignored the fact that in the late nineteenth century Russian Orthodox monasticism became overwhelmingly female and communal (cenobitic) in structure, with convents increasingly engaging in the provision of social and educational services. Cenobitic nuns, who were also excluded from the Church hierarchy, did not fit their monastic stereotype of either the dictatorial bishop or the idiorythmic (non-communal) hermitic monk, sealed away from society. By virtue of the lofty place monasticism held in traditional Orthodox thinking, however, either type of monk or nun was competition to the parish clergy's assertion of themselves (shared by some Church publicists) as the new religious virtuosi, and according to at least one popovich church historian, it was precisely because bishops knew that learned priests were their main competition that they abused them. The one exception parish clergy consistently—but not vociferously—made concerned learned monks who were scholars or theologians. As pious Orthodox Christians who also exalted scholarship, they judged written works, particularly theology, by its content, not by its author, especially if the author was officially part of the clerical estate (as all monks were).[53]

Monasticism was also an anathema because it repudiated the foundation of the parish clergy: the family. In addition to their pastoral and priestly duties, the domestic hearth was the other realm the parish clergy dearly valued. In the words of one priest, writing in 1903: "I have never come across in any other social estate such feverous love—bordering on self-sacrifice —for one's family as I have found in the clergy, and that is why I always loved, and love now, this social estate." In their eyes, their professional and personal lives were intertwined, and they integrated this belief into the very structure of their autobiographies. In contrast to the autobiographies of Russian bureaucrats, who wrote little about their personal lives, clerical autobiographies focused as much on their private lives as on their professional achievements. They typically included considerable discussion of childhood, relations with parents and kin, courtship, marriage, family life, and the fates of adult children. Mamin-Sibiriak's great-grandfather, for example, who organized his brief autobiography around the important dates in his life, focused exclusively, with the exception of his education and ordination, on family milestones.[54] The clerical obituary genre followed the same structure. In these obituaries, clergymen whose marriages were not blessed with children were pitied as unfulfilled, and the deaths of children were considered so traumatic that they could drive a clergyman to an early grave. A rich family life was the pinnacle of achievement. One priest eulogized a colleague in 1891: "The deceased revered archpriest all his life thanked the creator for his domestic life." Father Narkiss was so devoted to his marriage that it appears the only time he felt compelled to keep a diary was for nine weeks in the summer of 1851, when his wife was absent visiting relatives. In his diary he poignantly described the emptiness, boredom, and pain he felt during this separation. He expressed doubt that he would survive without his wife and admitted weeping tears of sorrow.[55] This clerical cult of the family, along with the parish clergy's belief in the corrupting influence of power, explains why the parish clergy could exclude bishops— the overwhelming majority of whom were born into the clerical estate— from clerical culture. Bishops, like priests, were guardians of educated Orthodox culture. But once they were tonsured, they repudiated the family as an institution. They were thus no longer part of clerical culture, theologically informed by, but not synonymous with, Orthodox culture.

Like most clerical fathers, Father Narkiss corresponded frequently with his popovich son. Clergymen wrote to their sons about local parish affairs and kept them apprised of any news about family members. Clergymen also saw themselves as their sons' mentors in the secular world and regaled them with advice about their work and daily lives. They implored their sons to write to them about every aspect of their lives, awaited the post impatiently for replies, and reread their sons' letters over and over. Father Narkiss, for example, wrote to Dmitrii in 1874: "to repeat the same thing over and over maybe is boring, but for our peace of mind we very much need to know." The counsel they dispensed to their sons sometimes continued from the grave, in directives included in their wills. In his will one priest instructed his children "not to forget the poor" and to "instill in your children that God loves truth (pravda)."[56]

In his letters to his son, Father Narkiss urged him above all to devote all of his energy to the pursuit of a single professional goal. Although saddened and hurt to learn that his son's upcoming university exams would prevent him from coming home for the summer in 1874, Father Narkiss was proud that his son was sacrificing himself "in expectation of good consequences." A few months later, when his son, having been distracted from his exams by the student demonstrations he joined, learned that he had failed to take his exams in time and would have to spend an additional year at the Petersburg veterinary institute, his father reassured him: "only do not get depressed and with great, great determination and stubbornness strive toward your selected goal." Rather than chiding Dmitrii for wasting his time, Father Narkiss, who had previously tried to dissuade Dmitrii from attending student meetings, implicitly sided with him: "in our eyes you are that very same conscientious, honest toiler that you were earlier, only cruelly robbed of a joyous fate." In their fathers' eyes, popovichi could do no wrong. Like their fathers, they were martyrs. Because he knew his son was, in the clerical tradition, a "conscientious, honest toiler," Father Narkiss was also confident that Dmitrii would eventually succeed. In response to

Dmitrii Mamin-Sibiriak in the 1880s. (Courtesy of the Russian State Archive of Literature and Art, Moscow, f.316, op.1, d.155, l.1)

Dmitrii's query as to whether his parents had lost faith in him when he finally sat for his entrance examination and failed, his father replied that while they were upset, they would never lose faith in him for they knew in their hearts that he would eventually pass.[57]

Most clergymen did not view their secular sons as estranged from them, either emotionally or professionally. They were able to make direct connections between their own work and the professions their sons had chosen. Father Narkiss, for example, suggested that his son write stories about people based on the first-hand reports he had furnished him. Which, in fact, is what Dmitrii did, after peppering his father, whom he acknowledged was more of an expert than he on the history of their local region, with questions.[58]

Fathers' mentoring included cautioning their secular sons not to be seduced by attachment to material objects. In a letter, Father Narkiss applauded Dmitrii for having begun to write them chiefly about his studies. He expressed displeasure with his son's earlier letters, which spoke primarily about his "material circumstances," which interested his parents "considerably less." In that same letter Father Narkiss warned Dmitrii that young people were often careless with their money, and that he should be frugal at all times.[59]

Father Narkiss also warned his son about fraternizing in society, writing in 1874 that Dmitrii should evaluate potential friends' habits, tastes, and inclinations before deciding whether they were suitable companions.[60] Fully confident that his exceptional son could judge right from wrong, Father Narkiss left the decision in Dmitrii's hands, but he nonetheless felt obligated to warn him of the perilous temptations that lurked in secular society. His son had entered a society whose members were, for the most part, not the equals of his son, born into the sacred estate.

Dual Models of the Pastorate

Clerical prescriptive models were created by ordinary clergymen as well as Church publicists. The most prolific and widely read of these genres were obituaries of fellow clergymen. Although clerical obituaries published as leaflets and in theological journals were written primarily by prominent urban clergymen, rank-and-file rural clergy published obituaries in every edition of each diocesan newspaper. Before the first diocesan newspaper began publication in 1860, very few clerical obituaries were printed, and those that did appear were usually published eulogies from funeral services. The emergence of clerical obituaries, a biographical genre, was another manifestation of the development of the modern self in postreform Russia. As exercises in hagiography, obituaries provide an outline of what the author revered in the values he invokes when he praises the deceased. They further reveal the extent to which ordinary clergymen—the fathers of popovichi—modified and interiorized the prescriptive models we have examined in clerical textbooks, etiquette manuals, and collections of model sermons, rendering texts for modern Christian self-fashioning, as opposed to traditional Christian self-fashioning, which is purely imitative.[61] And because they were grounded in nineteenth-century clergymen's lives, they offered contemporary role models that other clerical prescriptive models—including saints' lives—could not.

Two dominant models of ideal parish clergymen emerge from many of these obituaries. They are distinguished by a number of distinct, but not always mutually exclusive, character traits and by different ways of relating to the world. The first is characterized by his complete devotion to spiritual matters, and he is therefore "otherworldly." The second is distinguished by his overt moralism and by his pursuit of secular scholarship; he is a "proto-intelligent."

The "otherworldly" clergyman is meek and modest, and the higher glory he seeks is not measured by worldly accomplishments. He does not like to speak about himself. In fact, he speaks rarely, but carefully. Each word he utters carries meaning. Jokes and empty words are foreign to him. He is exacting of himself, but incredibly tolerant of others' weaknesses. He is even-tempered, characterized by a gentle calmness and kindness. He never complains, even when unjustly persecuted. Sobriety is his trademark. He adores books but reads only theological texts, which his soul craves just as one's body requires food. Even when gravely ill, he serves the liturgy, in a voice often recalled as weak and quiet.[62]

The "proto-intelligent" clergyman is distinguished by his straightforwardness and by his commitment to speak the whole truth (pravda), regardless of the consequences. Extremely critical of himself, he also condemns the moral failings of others. He considers himself a pastor and is often complimented for his teaching and his dynamic sermons. His diligence knows no bounds; he is applauded for continuing to serve up until his death, despite a prolonged, painful illness, about which he never complained. His intelligence and erudition, manifested in the quality and quantity of his writings, are often praised.[63] Such immoderate industriousness and perfectionism is exemplified in the 1892 obituary of one priest, a Father Sergievskii: "His reading often lasted far into the night . . . he loved discussions, of a, how shall I put it, educated character—chiefly those in the realm of theology or history. In these discussions there appeared a particular, purely youthful, hunger for more and more education, a hunger for incessant progress in all-round education." His pursuit of knowledge, both theological and secular, was ceaseless. Believing his work to be deficient, Father Sergievskii was reluctant to publish a saint's life he was writing. He spent considerable time rewriting, striving for improvement with each draft.[64]

Nineteenth-century church historians traced the idea of dual hagiographical models to the sixteenth-century conflict between two groups of monks: the possessors and the non-possessors. The crux of their disagreement lay in their dissimilar stances toward the temporal world and bears some resemblance to the differences between otherworldly and proto-intelligent clergymen. The possessors attempted to change the world through almsgiving and education; the non-possessors attempted to surmount the world by withdrawing into prayer and contemplation. The possessors were renowned for their persecution of their opponents; the non-possessors preached forgiveness and tolerance. The Church condoned both types of clergymen: the leaders of the possessors and the non-possessors, Joseph of Volokamsk and Nil Sorskii, were both canonized. Encouraged by the growth of church history as a discipline, church historians uncovered these two opposing strains in the distant past, arguing that both still existed within the church in the late imperial period. Both were also represented in popular editions of saints' lives published in the nineteenth century, in the guise of the kenotic martyrs and apostolic princely warriors. These dual models can further be traced to the contradictory attitude toward the world first evident in early Christianity, a tension manifest in many religious traditions between participation in political-ecclesiastical activities versus a contemplative inner life of holiness.[65]

The social activism characteristic of the proto-intelligent and the possessors began to gain momentum with the advent of the pastoral care movement. At the same time, the withdrawal from the world characteristic of the otherworldly type and the non-possessors was represented by the revival of idiorythmic, or non-communal, monasticism at the end of the eighteenth century. This movement was exemplified by the Optina Hermitage and by the hermetic lifestyle of Serafim of Sarov. In opposition to "moralist" activists, Church publicists associated with this movement argued that salvation was achieved primarily through sacraments, not pastoral care.[66]

Despite the apparent differences between these two clerical archetypes, in actuality they were not binary models. They shared certain traits, and their seemingly divergent actions were often an application of the same values—those prescribed by the "model piety" expected from the clerical estate—onto different spheres. Postreform Church publicists noted this in seminary textbooks. Having presented Sorksii and Volokamsk as opposites, the author of a 1908 textbook stated that Volokamsk's "life is representative of the same asceticism as Saints Nil, but not of a contemplative, but a practical direction."[67] Since faith *and* good works were necessary for an individual to attain salvation, both means were encouraged by the Orthodox Church.

Both archetypes are commended for never complaining: the otherworldly clergyman never complains about worldly matters, while the proto-intelligent never complains about his internal pain. A chasm existed between the ideal and the empirical, so characteristic of religious dualism—for clergymen actually complained all the time. Existing reality did not conform to model piety values and was therefore tainted and should, in the eyes of parish clergymen, be altered, a sentiment their secular sons shared.[68]

Nineteenth-century Church publicists argued that only Christ had been capable of combining both clerical archetypes. The images of Christ they presented include all the traits associated with the otherworldly and proto-intelligent types. On the one hand, Christ is portrayed as the meek and humble kenotic ideal, who loved his enemies and died on the cross. On the other hand, Christ is presented as a social activist, preaching the gospel far and wide.[69] Since his successors were, unlike him, only human, they could not fulfill both of these roles simultaneously. Thus Christ's dual functions needed to be performed by two types of clergymen, and since each type was essential, they complemented, rather than contradicted, each other.

Both types are also reminiscent of the postreform intelligentsia ethos Semen Frank lambasted. The otherworldly clergyman epitomizes the intelligentsia's ascetic self-restraint, service to the collective good, and self-sacrifice; the proto-intelligent clergyman's single-minded vision, binary morality, steadfast belief in his moral leadership, and uncompromising stance are other traits associated by Frank with the intelligentsia. The intelligentsia ethos, professed by individuals across the political spectrum, was nebulous and broad enough to include both archetypes. And neither type correlated to a specific political orientation.

When popovichi turned their pens to the worth of their native social estate group, they interiorized these multiple clerical models along with the belief that the clergy, typified by their families, was the sacred estate. They assessed their clan not according to the moral theology texts by which they judged secular estates, but by employing the norms of model piety. But popovichi were not only using these texts to assess their forefathers; they also drew on them to judge themselves. In their eyes they were indeed blessed children. For popovichi—and even for their fathers—the world of the clerical childhood reconciled the dualism between "what is" and "what ought to be." Clerical childhoods were heaven on earth, a prototype for an ideal community that popovichi wished to use as a model for recasting secular society. Popovichi drew upon their former membership in the sacred estate—along with their claims to be both the narod and the intelligentsia—to argue that they were Russia's rightful leaders.

4

Clerical Childhood as Heaven on Earth

Popovichi created an alternative intelligentsia lineage in opposition to the Westernized noble intelligentsia, whom they portrayed as sinful foreigners diluting the Russian national customs the clergy shared with the peasantry. Subscribing to Rousseau's view that upbringing shapes character, popovichi drew specifically on the clerical childhood as a catalyst to construct the lineage of their Russian "national" intelligentsia. In describing their childhoods they glorified a sense of otherness, and they emphasized everything about their clerical upbringing that distinguished it from the nobility. Within this framework even seemingly mundane details of clerical family life were imbued with emancipatory meaning. Their childhood universe played a key role in popovichi's self-definition and in their mission in the secular world.

In response to the cult of the child, initiated in the eighteenth century and fueled by romanticism, nineteenth-century European autobiographers, Russians included, tended not only to devote a central place to their early years, but to employ them for political gain. In general, the formative years are recalled as one of two extremes: heavenly or hellish. Accounts of happy childhoods are common among autobiographers from the elite and propertied classes; unhappy accounts were penned by socialist workers, such as Maxim Gorkii, who sought to use youthful suffering to fuel accusations of social injustice. Yet in constructing the antithesis of the noble happy childhood, popovichi did not present their early years as miserable; like their noble peers, they often depicted them as Edenic. The words of the populist Dr. Savvatii Sychugov (1841–1902), who recalled his childhood as "holy," "sweet," "so happy, that even now it comes to mind involuntarily," are fairly standard among popovichi and clergymen. Yet as popovichi and clergymen both noted, their Edens were vastly dissimilar from the idyllic scenarios recalled by Sergei Aksakov, Leo Tolstoi, and other nobles, for whom childhood was typified by freedom, luxury, indulgence, and the attention of a myriad of servants. Rather, clergymen's sons saw it as shaped by prescriptive clerical values and by a close-knit, inseparable family. As one popovich, who interviewed dozens of clergymen and popovichi at the turn of the century for an ethnographic study of the mid-nineteenth-century clergy, concluded: "The distinguishing feature of the daily life of rural pastors . . . was domesticity, that is, the close unity of the members of the family and the close ties between them, based on mutual parental love."[1]

This second Russian genre of happy childhoods rooted in traditional, clerical culture constituted a counter-normative experience. Because of the cult of the child—which affected Church publicists as much as their secular counterparts—and because popovichi based their alternative intelligentsia culture on reconstructions of their clerical pasts, their childhoods were always on their minds. As one popovich wrote in 1906: "My childhood, which was spent under my parents' roof before my studies began, is especially memorable. It is almost seventy-five years since my birth, but my childhood is still so preserved in my memory with all its details, that it's as if it all occurred yesterday."[2]

Family is by its nature traditional in that it preserves its customs. The family is a powerful symbol of the past, and revolutionary change in Russia and the rest of Europe as well as the United States has been linked to individuals either breaking their ties to their families or altering the dominant patriarchal family structure. Conversely, the cult of the family is associated with eras of stability, including the rise of the authoritarian state in early modern Europe and Victorian Europe's "bourgeois" infatuation with the family as the perfect social unit. Popovichi were intent on overturning Russian secular society, but whose past were they trying to destroy? The "new men" of the 1860s—whom all popovichi came to represent—were indeed rebelling against the noble-dominated intelligentsia of the 1840s, but these men were not their fathers, a point one popovich literary critic made when reviewing *Fathers and Sons* in 1862.[3] Popovichi of all political persuasions were radical precisely because they were trying to replace the noble culture that had dominated Russian educated society with the traditional values of their clerical families. Many noble intellectuals, for whom rebelling against the men of the 1840s did mean rebelling against their fathers, were searching for new ideas, but popovichi's search led them back to their ancestral traditions. Instead of being understood psychologically, these concepts can be situated historically as parts of a broader text of cultural change.

Popovichi's veneration of their families often took conventional forms, such as compiling genealogies. Their genealogical research included listing famous clerical ancestors as well as tracing their priestly kin back a half dozen generations. In Russia, as elsewhere, genealogies were a highly developed and particularly aristocratic genre of family history commonly associated with wealthy nobles, who regularly published genealogical registers. Russian Orthodox clergymen, however, also composed unpublished family trees or engaged in genealogical research. One popovich, who, like others, inherited and preserved his father's papers, made specific references to his father's history of the family when compiling his own.[4] They saw themselves as continuing a clerical estate tradition, rather than an exclusively noble one.

As modern men who believed in their power to transform society, popovichi were interested above all in themselves. Genealogy linked them to a historical collective that was an extension of themselves. This collective, their families, empowered them, providing them with an identity separate from the noble intelligentsia. They were drawing upon one of the traditional functions of genealogies: to assist ambitious families to gain power in a genealogical battlefield between themselves and prominent families attempting to preserve their domination. The prescribed role of the clerical estate assured that abiding allegiance to their families was interwoven with symbolism. The Bolshevik Evgenii Preobrazhenskii (1886–1937), the main spokesman for economic opposition to Stalin in the 1920s, began to wear a cross his clerical mother gave him following his first arrest in 1906. Although he was an avowed atheist, he carried this cross with him throughout his entire life, and his son later suspected that he was wearing it when the NKVD arrested him in 1936. It was the only item of his possessions that was missing from the NKVD's official inventory.[5] While Preobrazhenskii's attachment to a family heirloom is fraught with meaning because of what that heirloom was, who he was, and who his parents were, it was nevertheless a private, covert act. The vast majority of popovichi, however, insisted on transmitting their knowledge about their childhoods, family members, and ancestors to the public for political gain.

Paradigms of Virtue

As viewed through the eyes of popovichi and their fathers, the clerical universe of their childhoods was the antithesis of the sinful worlds of the noble and urban commercial estates. As one popovich recalled at the turn of the century, their childhoods were not of this world. When recalling their early years, clergymen adopted the tone of the obituary genre and forgot their complaints about their adult professional experiences. Because the clerical home was heaven on earth, and because heaven is, by its nature, flawless and changeless, the representations of the clerical world by popovichi and clergymen are remarkably static, despite the inroads of change that marked the nineteenth century. Theirs was a restorative nostalgia, seeking to recover what they perceived to be an absolute truth.[6] The re-markably similar conventions of the childhood genres of popovichi and clergymen—as well as the similarity between their genres and the prescrip-tive clerical precepts of "model piety" examined in the previous chapter—indicates the degree to which popovichi continued to emulate the values of the clerical estate in the secular world. It also confirms the extent to which the clerical milieu, rather than the intelligentsia that they joined as adults, served as the formative influence for popovichi's collective self-definition. And since the ideals of model piety—utmost expressions of poverty, mod-esty, industriousness, piety, national identity, charity, and asceticism—included attributes for which Semen Frank castigated the postreform intel-ligentsia but were not generally esteemed by noble intelligenty, it was popovichi who made these values part of the ethos of the intelligentsia. Popovichi's interiorization of the concept of model piety—that the values of members of the clerical estate were distinct from those of the laity—was also key in allowing atheist popovichi to subsume religious values as cleri-cal estate values. It allowed them to discard religious dogma that believers embraced, while maintaining a clerical estate identity.

The clerical world described by clergymen and their secular sons was uniformly indigent. Despite the financial diversity among clergymen based on rank and geographic locale, the sons of urban priests and rural sacristans alike depicted their families as martyrs, victims trapped in an endless cycle of poverty. Even after one popovich's father, a priest, moved from a rural to an urban parish, his son, writing in 1906, noted no change in his family's standard of living: "poverty haunted and oppressed father." In some cases, popovichi went so far as to state that their families suffered *more* economic hardship than the peasantry. A populist radical, the son of a sacristan, claimed in 1903 that "we were extremely poor, and our diet was more im-poverished than that of the peasantry." In some cases, this frugality is por-trayed as elective. One rural popovich, writing in his unpublished autobi-ography in 1920s, claimed that even when the pantry was well stocked with the garden's harvest, it was considered indulgent not to eat decaying, older vegetables. Because members of the parish clergy were not ordinary believers, they were allowed to engage in voluntary poverty, characteristic of the ascetic feats of saints. Despite their parents' poverty, for example, nu-merous clergymen and popovichi recalled that their families never refused beggars money or a meal.[7]

Without glorifying their families' suffering, many popovichi expressed gratitude for having been taught the value of poverty at a formative age. In a letter to his sister, one popovich wrote in 1864: "I began to understand at a very early age the surrounding world and to see that there were two sacred companions of our family: poverty and honesty. . . . I am proud even today, and I undaunted look everyone in the eye and undaunted judge both words and characters that are not industrious." Poverty begot other cardinal values besides honesty, such as industriousness and humility. Describing a fellow popovich and theological seminary teacher, one popovich remarked half a century later: "[his childhood] was filled with endless deprivation, constant work, and bitter, but true humility before all people. Therefore the child-hood of the deceased was spent in a severe school, which inculcated in him love of work and that rare delicate humility which he was distinguished by in all of the days of his life."[8]

Regardless of how much they suffered materially, poverty did not rob popovichi and clergymen of a happy childhood. Material well-being was unimportant compared with the benefits reaped from family love and cleri-cal values. One popovich recalled in 1911: "From the external side—almost extreme poverty. My widowed mother had four young children. . . . But from the internal side—unrestricted and in its own way happy childhood.[9]

Descriptions of poverty are widespread in the autobiographies of Bolshe-viks but are not predominant among other revolutionaries and are largely absent from the personal narratives of non-revolutionary intelligenty who were not of clerical background. The vast majority of revolutionaries —including Bolsheviks—who were not of clerical background and were not the sons of workers or peasants claimed they became poor only after a fa-ther's death or a change of fortune. Their eventual poverty was therefore involuntary, undesirable, and unnatural. Loss of a fortune was frequently the result of a father's spending beyond his means on lavish consumption and hospitality.[10] And while noble-born Bolsheviks went out of their way to describe their families as disdainful of material objects, nobles and mer-chants unaffiliated with the revolutionary movement often bragged in their memoirs about their fathers' wealth, and the opulent furniture, elabo-rate dinners and gardens of their childhood universe.[11]

Piety, dismissed by radicals from secular estates as irrelevant to their fam-ilies and rarely mentioned in most childhood memoirs written by non-radi-cal intelligenty from secular estates, permeated popovichi's depictions of their early years. Like their fathers, they described clerical piety as more rig-orous and ascetic than lay piety. Several clerical sons recalled that their households followed Lent so strictly that no exceptions to the Lenten regime and to church attendance were made, even for gravely ill children. Families followed a strict routine of praying corporately before and after every activity. Children were taught to memorize prayers as soon as they could talk. Sergei Bulgakov summed up the distinctiveness of clerical piety: "My great wealth, my special blessing from God, lay not only in that I was born and raised under the blood of two churches . . . but in the family of an Orthodox priest, in the atmosphere of a home-church, as if our home it-self was a church."[12]

Just as the clerical family worshipped and engaged in parish duties com-munally, clergymen and popovichi emphasized that they functioned as a collective in the home and fields. By day sons plowed and weeded along-side their fathers. By night the entire family assembled. Fathers filled out clerical documents, while their wives and daughters sewed or spun yarn.[13]

Just as in an Orthodox monastery, the clerical family harmoniously blended a religious community with a labor unit. But unlike a monastic community, they provided a microcosm of a model society within the world.

Whereas most noble autobiographers recalled childhood as a time of endless frolicking, and nobles often ridiculed hard-working individuals, popovichi and clergymen recalled domestic chores engaged in physical labor as an integral part of childhood. They generally considered these chores a gift. A popovich who became a radical populist writer recalled the time he spent working in the fields with his father as the happiest moments in his life. The emphasis on the industriousness of their families was so great that clergymen's sons frequently omitted any reference to servants or hired laborers employed by their families. In fact, they cited examples of clerical family members working for peasants or nobles—a rare occurrence—more often than they mentioned hired laborers employed by clergymen. In keeping with prescribed clerical etiquette, when they did mention the presence of servants, they emphasized that the servant did not wait on their family but worked and ate alongside them. Aleksandr Sadov (1850–1930), a professor at Petersburg Theological Academy, emphasized in his 1913 autobiography that the hired labor in his parents' household was only temporary and did little to ease the burden of his parents: "she [mother] could not go to church, since all morning up till mass she toiled completing the housework. She toiled alone because my parents never had a servant, with the only exception being times when my mother was ill." Sadov explained that his father "always participated as much as he could" in the chores for which he hired peasant laborers.[14]

Unlike noble autobiographers, those popovichi who did grow up with peasant nannies did not present them as parental surrogates. In fact, they either downplayed their role or presented them as outsiders. A Bolshevik popovich referred to his nanny as "unpleasant Grunia" and accused her of stealing his possessions. Another popovich referred to his elderly nanny only in passing, merely citing her age. Mamin-Sibiriak, who kept in contact with his nanny as an adult, never mentioned her in his autobiographies.[15] Whereas for noble autobiographers peasant nannies represented a link to the broad populist ideals of religious feeling, nature, and national identity, popovichi associated these attributes with their families.

As prescribed, the clerical family functioned as a self-contained unit. The definition of family employed by clergymen and popovichi was narrow and restricted, confined, with the occasional exception of grandparents, to the nuclear family. Aware that all other Russian social estate groups lived in extended, non-nuclear families, popovichi and their fathers chose to emphasize their distinctive domestic configuration. Although they had affiliated themselves with many aspects of peasant traditional culture and manual agricultural labor, when it came to family life, they presented themselves as vanguards of change. The clerical family bonded not only during chores and prayer, but also during leisure. The boundary between leisure and work was often not clearly demarcated. Clergymen and popovichi remembered singing religious and secular songs both when guests were visiting and also when members of the family performed their domestic chores together in the evenings, figuratively transforming the clerical home into an Orthodox church, where the liturgy is sung collectively. As prescribed by model piety, clerical families tended to refrain from socializing with laypersons. One popovich recalled that his relatives feared "strangers [*chuzhie*]" Clergymen's sons often cited their siblings as their only or closest childhood friends. They formed a self-sufficient pack, who lived, as one popovich put it, "harmoniously and lovingly."[16]

The other forms of leisure described by memoirists generally conform to the edifying activities of communal respite after labor recommended in the didactic literature. They cite in particular enlightening discussions (*besedy*) and reading aloud by the father or by one of the sons to the rest of the family. The secular forms of Western "high" culture that fill the pages of noble memoirs are not only largely absent from the memoirs of clergymen and popovichi, they are, in some cases, repudiated. Sergei Bulgakov recalled: "we had nothing in our childhood from the 'cultural' sphere: no music, no art. . . ." Outdoor recreational activities were also frequently cited by popovichi and clergymen. Such activities included stargazing, swimming, fishing, and mushroom hunting. In these descriptions, love of nature and the countryside were a source of family bonding, spiritual communion, and love of *rodina* (homeland). Rather than associating nature with freedom, as noble memoirists did, popovichi and clergymen frequently recalled outdoor activities as family outings. Apollinarii Vasnetsov remembered his entire family strolling through the woods on spring evenings: "love of nature, that is, being in love with nature, keenness of observation, was inculcated in me by my father from my earliest childhood." In emigration Metropolitan Evlogii (1868–1948) summed up the spiritual component of exposure to nature in his childhood: "Our Russian nature had no less of a profound effect on my child's consciousness than the church or everyday life [*byt*]. An inexpressible feeling of the charms of spaciousness, the fields, the meadows . . . agitated and gladdened my soul."[17]

Other clergymen's sons also specified the specifically *Russian* element of their childhood space by referring to their native villages as *rodina*. Like the German term "*heimat*," by the nineteenth-century "*rodina*" simultaneously denoted both one's birthplace and the nation as motherland. The abstract concept of the nation could therefore be understood through the concrete experience of one's local environs, fusing local and national identities into a patriotism that was both personal and collective. Noble memories of childhood focused primarily on their private country estates, but for popovichi and clergymen their childhoods, like the canvases of postreform Russian landscape painters intent on creating a Russian national identity, took place in a generic Russia, surrounded by the churches, rivers, fields, mountains, and trees that dotted its landscape far and wide. This association of

The Clerical Family Portrait: Aleksandr Nikitskii with his parents and siblings, Novgorod province, 1860s. (Courtesy of the Archive of the Academy of Sciences, St. Petersburg division, f.84, op.1, d.61, l.15)

love of *rodina* with love of nature is evident in the eulogy by a seminary teacher of his former teacher, a fellow popovich: "You instilled in us a feeling of attachment to *rodina*, to her nature." Recreation spent outdoors was yet further confirmation, along with kinship to the narod and suffusion in the Orthodox faith and clerical values, of the way Russian national identity was embodied in the clerical estate. For regardless of their political and professional differences, popovichi and priests alike were prone to discussing themselves and their kind as "purely" or "completely" Russian. In this vein, Sergei Bulgakov could even describe alcoholism—a vice that plagued his ancestors, his father, and his two brothers—as "the Russian weakness."[18]

Batiushka —

Two Types of Clerical Fathers

In contrast to noblemen's autobiographies, in which beloved servants and indulgent mothers are typically juxtaposed to absent fathers, it is the patriarchal figure who dominates popovichi's and clergymen's depictions of their happy childhoods and whom they often acknowledge as the most important influence in their lives. In keeping with clerical etiquette manuals, they credited their fathers with assuming the principal role in raising them, a perception that is accentuated by their descriptions of their fathers as the ones who administered their preschool education. In one case, a popovich never even mentioned his mother in his autobiography. In the obituary of his father that he wrote in 1905, one popovich, a zemstvo doctor, addressed the deceased:

> before me stands the unforgettable, dear memories of my sweet childhood, which was so affectionately, so sincerely, warmed by your love, by your concern, your participation. And before me also stand the memories of my early youth, when you, not only by means of your paternal authority, but also with your mind and heart, directed my youthful, indefinite deeds; when you directed my first vacillating steps onto the foundation of a conscientious life with your experienced hand.

Popovichi expressed love for their fathers in slightly different ways. One thanked God above all for being his father's son. Another explained that his father provided him with an example of how to live every step of his life, including how to die. Still another had his family picture photographed in front of his father's portrait.[19]

The revered patriarch is just as likely to be present in the autobiographies of radical popovichi. In 1932 the Bolshevik Aleksandr Voronskii (1884–1943) recalled his childhood thoughts: "I believe Father; he is for me a higher being. He knows everything. I will never be his equal." This homage to patriarchy, though absent from the autobiographies of French revolutionaries and non-clerical-born Russian radicals who belonged to populist revolutionary parties, is present in the autobiographies of numerous Bolsheviks from all social estate backgrounds.[20] This shift toward parental reverence coincides with the rise of authoritarianism in Russian radical parties, but it was a consistent theme in popovichi autobiographies stretching back to their inception. And whereas Bolsheviks from non-clerical backgrounds tended to praise both of their parents and present them as pro-revolutionary and irreligious oppositionalists to tradition, popovichi expressed admiration for their fathers in particular and described them as steeped in clerical culture. Because their mothers were barred from dispensing sacraments, their fathers were the most prominent symbols of the clerical estate and its traditions.

The esteem in which popovichi held their fathers was inseparable from their profession. One Bolshevik memoirist recalled in his 1960s autobiography: "My family, and most of all my father, influenced me. He was a sincerely religious person." The term *"batiushka,"* which they used to address their fathers, has a dual meaning. It is both a colloquial name for fathers and also the familiar name that parishioners use to address their priest. Their fathers were always priests as well as fathers in their eyes. Because of his authority and his closeness to God, such a father's affection was particularly potent. One popovich, in his aptly titled 1899 autobiography "In the Family of a Priest," described this power: "Batiushka blesses me. I kiss his hand, and he, tenderly stroked me on the shoulder . . . and I sleep that night sweetly, sweetly."[21]

Clergymen's sons' narratives of their fathers mirrored the prescriptive clerical literature not only in subject matter but also in form and content. They generally portrayed their fathers as conforming to either the prescriptive proto-intelligent or the otherworldly model. In part this was because the clerical press institutionalized the identification of the father as a role model by soliciting clergymen's obituaries written by their sons, including those who had left the estate, thus allowing some popovichi to have a hand in crafting the prescriptive clerical literature. But because they were seeking to ally themselves with their native estate, and thus present their fathers as ideal clergymen, they consciously chose clerical models. Because they are archetypes, the presentations of their fathers by popovichi often masked the particularities of their individual experiences. Yet despite the element of "hagiographical depersonalization" they employed, the topoi that supplied them with idealized guidelines of behavior were also flexible narrative ingredients that allowed for interpretation and individualization.[22] The lives and autobiographical narratives of Sergei Elpat'evskii, who described his father as the otherworldly type of clergyman devoted completely to spiritual matters, and Ivan Orlovskii, who described his father as a proto-intelligent distinguished by his greater involvement in temporal affairs, are each representative of many others, and they illustrate how popovichi could personalize these models.

Dr. Sergei Elpat'evskii, first arrested for revolutionary activities during his university years in the 1870s, served as a zemstvo doctor in several provinces and participated actively in the 1891 famine relief effort. He also served as the editor of a prominent liberal-populist journal, *Russkoe bogastvo,* and in 1906 became a founding member and co-leader of the Labor party (*Trud*). He ended his career working as a doctor in the Kremlin hospital after the Bolshevik revolution. He wrote his memoirs in the 1920s, and the first edition of his memoirs of his adult life was published in 1929 (his childhood memoirs, which closely resemble a speech he gave at the fiftieth anniversary of his father's ordination in 1897, have never been published).[23] The quintessential intelligent, Elpat'evskii counted the renowned writers Leo Tolstoi, Anton Chekhov, and Maxim Gorkii among his friends. He died of natural causes in 1933 at the age of seventy-nine.

Elpat'evskii reported that his father, born into the priesthood, had initially wanted to embark on a secular career. After his two brothers both became monks, however, the senior Elpat'evskii obeyed his mother's wishes by entering the priesthood and ensuring that his father's parish seat remained in the family. While the typical "otherworldly" father characteristically did not yearn for a secular career, Elpat'evskii's description of his father's subsequent obedience and serene resignation to his fate conforms to the common pattern. Once he was ordained, the senior Elpat'evskii devoted himself wholeheartedly to the clerical profession and broke with all remnants of secular life. This was symbolized by his selling of his beloved flute. Although he was a married priest, he emulated many ascetic ideals, exercising the self-restraint for which the intelligentsia was also renowned. For example, he exceeded the norms of temperance by completely abstaining from drinking alcohol. His stoicism and commitment to self-sacrifice was a core component of the ethos of the intelligentsia, which Elpat'evskii himself defined in a 1905 treatise: "in their social behavior [they] act not in the name of narrow, personal, group, professional, or class interests, but in the name of the interests of the country in general, the narod in general."[24]

The piety of the otherworldly father was often characterized by his exclusive devotion to liturgy, prayer, and the rite of confession. His was an exclusive commitment to spirituality. After his family purchased a kerosene lamp, for example, the senior Elpat'evskii spent each evening reading theological journals. He rarely read secular literature, and when he did, he preferred Russian historical and romantic novels filled with descriptions of natural beauty that evoked spirituality and patriotism, and he was profoundly affected by what he read. Elpat'evskii described his father as "a deeply religious man in the old Russian manner (modest and quiet) . . . he was hostile to the new political path upon which [Konstantin] Pobedonostsev's intrigue drove the Russian clergy." Meek and modest, he disliked the flamboyant priest Ioann of Kronstadt, who was linked to the ultranationalist Black Hundred movement. The senior Elpat'evskii was embittered by the state's directive that priests must report anti-autocratic statements uttered

Sergei Elpat'evskii at the height of his professional prominence. (Courtesy of the Institute of Russian Literature, St. Petersburg)

during confession. In his mind, the law of God was clearly superior to the law of the state, and the sanctity of confession should not be violated. On the other hand, he lived in fear of such an incident because, being obedient, he would report the confessor to the authorities, even though he believed that it was not his place to judge others or take sides. Although Elpat'evskii did not share his father's antipathy toward political involvement, he did emulate his aversion toward nationalist sentiment by vociferously defending the rights of minority groups in his publicist and fictional writings.[25]

Since the otherworldly type of father was socially passive, he was averse to initiating change. The senior Elpat'evskii, despite his family's poverty, charged his parishioners only meager sums for the ceremonies he performed. His son defended him by recalling that when his father was asked why he refrained from charging what other priests did, he replied that one could not change the "old order." The father suffered as a result of his inability to change; his son recalled that one enduring memory of childhood was of his unhappy father laboring night and day in the fields to feed his family.[26]

Another reason Elpat'evskii's father would not increase his fees was his affinity for his peasant parishioners. He had known many of them since childhood, and they rewarded his loyalty with ample gifts of eggs and free agricultural labor. Such depictions of harmonious relations with peasant parishioners are commonplace in the autobiographies of popovichi. In contrast to noble radicals, who sometimes described their fathers as brutal serf-owners, Elpat'evskii and other popovichi radicals who grew up in the prereform period did not implicate their fathers in the serf system. Even if radical popovichi agreed that religion entailed exploitation of the peasantry, they did not provide any examples of this exploitation from their past.[27] They presented their fathers as exceptions to the rule, a topos that a number of other popovichi, including those who portrayed proto-intelligent fathers, employed in different contexts (e.g., learnedness, ethics, artistic talents) to demonstrate that their fathers stood out from other priests. Although a few noble radicals emphasized that their fathers advocated emancipation and later assisted the peasantry as arbitrators of the peace, their fathers were "repentant noblemen" who were atoning for their sins, rather than life-long servants of the people.[28]

The portrait of his father written by Ivan Orlovskii in an obituary published in 1905 conforms to the second type of father, the proto-intelligent. An ethnographer of his native Smolensk province, Ivan Orlovskii was employed as a teacher at a women's diocesan school. His politics were nationalist monarchist, and he was affiliated with the center-right Octobrist party.

Ivan's father was a rural priest, but his library contained over 1,500 volumes, and only half of them were religious titles. His son recalled: "He had a passionate love of books and reading." He also kept a diary and wrote a lengthy chronicle of the history of his village. He expressed a preference for the "hard" sciences, those based on tangible data and rationality: "He also loved science, and in his office, besides books, one could also catch sight of a telescope and home-made instruments—a Leyden jar, barometers and various forecasters of the weather, mechanical devices." His learnedness was so advanced that it "allowed him to feel equal to, and sometimes even superior to, many rural landowners." The historical figure he most revered was Peter the Great.[29] Orlovskii shared his father's predilection for rational scholarship: as a member of the Smolensk archival commission and the Moscow archeological society, he was known for the conscien-

Ivan Orlovskii at age 24. (A.V. Zhirkevich, *Ivan Ivanovich Orlovskii,* 1909)

tiousness and thoroughness of his data collecting, a skill he used when writing works such as the Smolensk city museum catalogue.

Orlovskii's father's intellectual interests did not preclude piety. Rather, he approached religion with the same inquisitiveness and zeal that he devoted to science: "He was a sincere and firm believer. . . . He loved to read and discuss theological questions, many of which actively interested and worried him." His interest in theological debates and his enthusiasm for questioning doctrines were functions of the assertive morality: "Independence and steadfastness of views, with no fear of being known as an eccentric; honesty and straightforwardness, connected to a sincere aversion to any hypocrisy and deception, exaltation, and artificiality." Because of this moralism, Orlovskii's father was incapable of silencing his views, even if they led him to contradict his superiors. Eventually he was denounced and relocated to another parish by the consistory; he was devastated by this admonishment, since he was convinced that he knew better than others. His health worsened because of the strain, although he hid any frailty.[30]

Ivan inherited his father's intolerance, sense of self-righteousness, and tendency to condemn others, all of which were traits Frank used to criticize the intelligentsia. He was a rabid antisemite who blamed Jews for the woes suffered in Smolensk during the 1905 revolution. According to his biographer, a close personal friend, Ivan's motto was "Russia above all for Russians" and "being called a 'Black Hundred' was something he usually took pride in."[31]

The senior Orlovskii was a perfectionist who was as demanding of others as he was of himself. Although a forgiving man who was always moved by the sight of tears, he was quick-tempered and could be irritable "to the point of rudeness." The proto-intelligent father treated his children more severely than did the otherworldly father. Orlovskii described the awe his father's domestic upbringing inspired in him:

> Reasonable severity, discipline, religiosity and churchliness (*tserkovnost'*), development of the mind and heart—these were the fundamentals of his upbringing of his children. . . . This strictness did not hamper him from expressing love and concern for his children. However, his love for his children never brought Father Ioann to the point of spoiling them. He was implacable not only to improper behavior, but also to trepidations of the soul, and he did not hesitate to offend one's pride in order to correct a deviation from righteous truth (pravda). As a result, a conscious respect developed toward him, similar to worship.[32]

Although physical punishment of some kind was common in the clerical household as late as the early twentieth century, overt physical domestic abuse of clerical children appears to have been rare enough for individual cases to have been given serious attention by Church officials in the postreform period.[33] Nevertheless, numerous popovichi and clergymen claimed that corporal punishment was completely absent from their home life, often because their fathers were too pure to inflict pain. Those popovichi and clergymen who did admit that they suffered domestic violence sometimes portrayed it as innocuous, or as justified by their inability to excel at their preschool studies. Kliuchevskii even defended the infamous *Domostroi*, arguing that medieval parents had chastised out of love, not out of a desire to injure, and that corporal punishment was offset by the peace immanent in a known order of things. A number of popovichi did describe brutal domestic violence inflicted by their demanding, often drunken, proto-intelligent fathers, yet they too tended to excuse the abuse by citing their fathers' extraordinariness and by claiming they had been impaired by external hardships and limitations. The radical writer Shashkov, for example, described his scholarly father as a "true artist," who, in addition to his duties as a priest, was the choir director of the town cathedral. He played a variety of instruments and composed music; his musical gifts were known as far as Moscow. Shashkov excused his father's brutal beatings of choirboys by emphasizing his talent, his perfectionism, and the travails he had endured as a schoolboy. He asserted that his father was worthy of being an opera singer but was confined by his profession. Shashkov further excused incidents when his father would disappear for days on end only to come home drunk and tyrannize his family: "How could one not drink living that incredibly boring and monotonous life?"[34] Proto-intelligent fathers were very different martyrs than otherworldly fathers, but to their sons, they were martyrs all the same.

Like the otherworldly father, the proto-intelligent father was also popular among his parishioners, albeit for different reasons. The senior Orlovskii was "beloved by the gentry for his intelligence and sociability, by the peasantry for his order (*poriadok*), strictness, responsiveness, and good service." His parishioners appreciated his wry sense of humor as well. He was also respected because he punished sinners and displayed an "ability to sympathize actively." Somewhat prosperous, he donated all of his money to charitable organizations and institutions, a fact he modestly hid, and which was discovered only after his death. He was committed to pastoral care, exemplified not only in the material assistance he provided parishioners but in his efforts to enlighten them through sermons and instruction in the school he ran in his own home.[35] Orlovskii displayed the intelligentsia's characteristic social activism by carrying on his father's commitment to serving the masses: he founded a voluntary fire brigade and opened a library in his home village. His efforts did not reward him materially. Like his father, he left his heirs penniless when he died at the age of forty in 1909. Following his death, Orlovskii's large family was saved from destitution by the material assistance donated by his many friends among the local clergy.

Orlovskii recalled that his father also worshipped his own father, "who was reminiscent of him in many aspects." Although popovichi and clergymen focused on their nuclear family, some included portraits of their grandparents. They used the same typology they employed to describe their fathers and portrayed their grandfathers as the same type of priest—otherworldly or proto-intelligent—their fathers were.[36] Their grandfathers served as transmitters of a clerical tradition, a tradition that Elpat'evskii among others, at the beginning of their autobiographies, describe as virtually unchanged over the past two centuries.[37]

Elpat'evskii and Orlovskii both consciously and selectively modeled their narratives to correspond to specific clerical archetypes. The senior Elpat'evskii was in actuality a member of the Imperial Geographic Society and a schoolteacher, secular roles that his son never mentioned and that conform more to the proto-intelligent type. In turn, the senior Orlovskii was described by a family friend as an exemplar of an old-school "meek and modest" Russian priest, the opposite of the type of priest portrayed by his son. Neither popovich appears to have chosen to describe his father as resembling himself: Elpat'evskii's radicalism appears most reminiscent of the assertive moralism of the proto-intelligent father; the conservative clerical schoolteacher Orlovskii seems on the surface most akin to the otherworldly father. Yet they did not simply invert models to portray their fathers as their opposites. A general survey of popovichi's portraits of their fathers reveals that they employed archetypes interchangeably: the particular political affiliation of popovichi did not dictate which kind of father they portrayed in their autobiographies.[38] Instead, they personalized models while still adhering to them. The populist writer Elpat'evskii identified with the notion of his father as a romantic. He depicted his "otherworldly" father as completely committed to his clerical duties, but he also presented his father as too otherworldly for the institutional church, rendering his father a rebel of conscience. The ethnographer Orlovskii chose to describe his father as a rational scientist who shared his son's scholarly interests. Because of the turbulent revolutionary era in which he lived, Orlovskii's conservative monarchism pitted him against many of his fellow countrymen. He saw himself engaged in a moral battle, similar to the one in which he depicted his father as embroiled. Because popovichi entered a world different from the one their fathers inhabited, and because they were modern men intent on choosing their destinies, they refashioned these models to accommodate their new lives. The multiplicity of models within the prescriptive clerical literature and the different ways in which individuals could interpret each model provided popovichi with a wide variety of ways to interpret their clerical heritage. This variance explains why popovichi tended as a group to affiliate themselves with their clerical pasts, while individual popovichi did not gravitate toward any one particular political orientation or secular profession.

The two types of fathers popovichi and clergymen described were both patriarchal, conforming to a prototype of masculinity. Mamin-Sibiriak described his father as entirely masculine: "everywhere father appeared in the halo of his calm, manly love." The masculine archetype in the modern age has been linked to the embodiment of nationality, and for popovichi and clergymen, their fathers were a personal incarnation of the "Russianness" that they associated with clerical lifestyle.[39] Both types of fathers were consumed by devotion to a single idea, by a grave sense of moral mission uncolored by emotions, and by an unceasing commitment to self-improvement and contempt for material gain. They were the antithesis of the excessive materialism, languidity, and sentimental emotionalism that popovichi and clergymen alike associated with the nobility and noble autobiographers themselves attributed to their happy childhoods. The reverence that popovichi and clergymen displayed for their fathers demonstrates their unconditional respect for both clerical values and the authority these values represented.

Matushka—

The Clerical Mother

The degree of popovichi's attachment to patriarchy and what it signified is particularly evident in their portraits of their mothers. Although popovichi and clergymen portrayed both parents as adhering to the values of industriousness and piety, when discussing their parents separately they tended to present them according to clerical gender models. In keeping with prescriptive manuals, they expressed a preference for the traits they associated with their fathers. Popovichi and clergymen further allied themselves with this institutionalized patriarchy by professing greater affinity for their grandfathers over their grandmothers.[40] Two types of mothers emerge from these narratives, contrasted against either the "otherworldly" or "proto-intelligent" archetypal father.

Clergymen's sons often presented their parents as binary opposites. In his autobiography published in 1916, Dr. Sychugov recalled that his mother "possessed a strong, practical mind, not inclined toward idealism, and an iron will. In contrast to my father, who would not have thought twice about giving away the shirt off his back to a needy person, mother was quite miserly." This juxtaposition is just as likely to be found in clergymen's autobiographies. Metropolitan Evlogii noted:

> By nature merry, cheerful, social, he possessed a kind soul, meek and poetic; he loved singing, music, poetry . . . he often cited selections from pre-Pushkin poets. . . . I loved my father very much; he was a sweet, kind man . . . my mother, Serafima Aleksandrovna, was by nature more serious than my father, although she was abnormally morbid, rather nervous, possessing a tendency toward melancholy, toward suspiciousness.

The above quotes are illustrative of the type of mother who dominates popovichi's autobiographical narratives. In contrast to the otherworldly father, she is depicted as willful, excessively practical, materialistic, uninterested in intellectual topics, and in some cases, even despotic. Several popovichi recalled being beaten at the hands of such mothers.[41]

The second type of mother is contrasted to the proto-intelligent father. Illiterate and prone to excessive displays of emotion, she is acquiescent and overindulgent. One popovich who depicted his mother according to this type recalled that she was so kind that she made him throw any fish or crabs he caught back into the water. She was a more compassionate and patient teacher than his father but was unable to assume full-time responsibility for his preschool studies because she ran the household without the assistance of a servant and was always nursing an infant.[42] This type of mother was beloved by popovichi and defiantly their mother of preference. Nevertheless, they did not present her as a viable role model.

Although they rejected their mothers as their true role models, clergymen and popovichi treated them with compassion. They argued that their mothers had been emotionally hardened by the physical tribulations of their lives. Aleksei Dmitrievskii (1856–1931), a professor at Petersburg Theological Academy, explained in 1913 that his mother's strong, sharp personality, typified by its willfulness and miserliness, stemmed from having been forced her entire life to fight for every morsel. Yet it was his mother, he noted, who fought to improve the family's material situation, engaging in any honest work she could find, including winter fishing and sewing. Many popovichi and clergymen acknowledged that if it had not been for their mothers' practical natures, their families would have perished. In keeping with the teachings of clerical manuals, they recalled their mothers as deeply concerned with their sons' physical well-being. One popovich re-called that when he was studying in the seminary, his mother, despite her poor health, would travel a great distance several times a year to bring him food packages. The fact that clerical mothers, unlike noble mothers, breast-fed their children, was highlighted by many popovichi, from Blagosvetlov, whose quote opened this book, to the first autobiography written by a popovich. By the mid-nineteenth century the act of breast-feeding was cel-ebrated in Russian society as a symbol of maternal devotion, self-sacrifice, and natural, civic duty, a fashion popovichi openly exploited. Yet while Eu-ropean workers presented mothers who saved their families from complete destitution as heroic alternatives to deadbeat fathers, because popovichi and clergymen placed lesser value on material needs, they did not credit their mothers' actions as principal in their upbringing.[43]

Nevertheless, family life required the participation of both parents. In-deed, fathers and mothers are portrayed as complements whose contrasting characteristics balanced and fulfilled each other, and the marriages of their parents usually resonate in their autobiographies as happy. They did not, how-ever, question the moral superiority of the male type over the female. One popovich recalled in 1904 that his father had a great deal of moral influence on his mother, and therefore family relations were always harmonious.[44]

When embodied in females, even positive clerical values such as industri-ousness and piety could be distorted. Some popovichi described their mothers as so preoccupied with work that they were unable to think about any other concerns. Others were careful to distinguish between their parents' religiosity. While they associated their fathers with informed, educated piety, they portrayed their mothers as possessing a blind faith, typified by an absence of any doubts or questions and an obsession with the external regulations of church life, such as fasting.[45] The rejection of the mother as a role model, along with the renunciation of traits associated with her, signals a conscious embracing of masculinity over femininity. Their fathers' mas-culinity represented the spiritual values of the heavenly realm; the femi-ninity associated with their mothers represented the mundane, physical concerns of this world, embodied in the flesh. The body was indispensa-ble, and although it was not inherently adverse to its opposite, the soul, it was inferior. The body was associated with material needs and unre-strained emotions, which the clergy and popovichi also identified with the Westernized nobility, the antithesis of the clerical tradition.

Exceptions—

A Case Study in Memory

Idealization of childhood, of a long-lost paradise that can never be re-captured, is a standard trope in modern autobiographies. The late Imperial Russian genre of the happy gentry childhood has been attributed to post-emancipation nostalgia for life on prereform estates. Popovichi were also inspired to idealize their past by a sense of loss after leaving their native estate and facing an often hostile secular society. Alienated in adult surroundings, popovichi turned their childhoods into a function of adulthood, a means to assert their own identity. In the words of Roy Pascal, "memory can be trusted because autobiography is not just reconstruction of the past, but interpretation. . . . It is a judgment on the past within the framework of the present, a document in the case as well as a sentence."[46] Their experiences after they left the clerical estate made them into a different type of men than their brothers who stayed behind in the clergy.

The popovich Andrei Filonov (1831–1908) published two versions of his autobiography of childhood: the first in 1864 at the age of thirty-three; the second in 1890 when he was fifty-nine. They present completely different visions of his childhood, particularly in the representations of his father and his mother. Filonov's autobiographies offer a glimpse into the role of memory in popovichi's constructions of the past. The majority of autobiographers write their life stories near the end of their lives, and popovichi were no exception: they tended not to write their memoirs of childhood as young men, and most did not write, much less publish, multiple versions of their memoirs. Unfortunately, Filonov wrote next to nothing about his adult life, nor did he include an introduction to his later text. It is therefore impossible to confirm decisively whether he grew despondent in the secular world and as a result underwent a shift in his perception of childhood. The little that he did write, however, suggests that this was indeed the case. Filonov's about-face may be quite unusual; the social prejudice popovichi faced was experienced throughout their lives, and letters, petitions, family obituaries, and the few autobiographies that other popovichi wrote when they were young men testify that many regarded their childhoods as idyllic even in their youths. On the other hand, those few popovichi who wrote countertypes to the happy clerical childhood did so in autobiographical novels written when they were still young men. The fact that they were writing fiction may explain their deviation, but their youth may also have been a factor.[47] Filonov's case does demonstrate how one popovich over time adopted a more traditional view of his past, one that not coincidentally conforms to the clerical prescriptive literature.

Andrei Filonov was born into a rural sacristan's family in Smolensk province in 1831 and received his education at the local seminary and the Pedagogical Institute in Petersburg. During the course of his career in education, he taught Latin and Russian language and literature at a variety of secondary schools, including the prestigious Smol'nyi Institute for women in Petersburg and the Naval Cadet Corps, began publishing scholarly articles on pedagogy in 1856, and went on to write several widely used textbooks. In 1873 he became a permanent member of an educational commission on popular reading and an inspector of gymnasia. In 1883 he assumed the position of director of a male gymnasium.

In his first autobiography, Filonov inverted the conventional depictions of exemplary fathers and imperfect mothers. His father had no redeeming features, and he was capable of unspeakable cruelty: "My older brother, who is now a total cripple, was born with crippled legs and one leg shorter than the other. But how my father would beat him, I can't even describe it. It was horrible! We all lived for the moment father would leave the house for work. . . . The nicknames our father gave us all stemmed from some sort of physical handicap or birthmark we had." He depicted his mother, on the other hand, as intensely pious and otherworldly: "she was not a woman, she was an angel." Unlike the materialistic mothers often described by other popovichi, Filonov's mother had only two dresses to her name. She was beloved by their neighbors for her pristine character. Because she was the daughter of a wealthy priest and thus unable to weave the family's clothing, his father beat her. He terrorized her to the point where she would "simply shake from head to foot, like a leaf."[48] The thirty-three-year-old Filonov clearly favored his mother over his father.

After he had spent an additional twenty-six years in secular society, Filonov's view of his mother and father changed radically. In the second version of his autobiography, his father and mother adhered closely to clerical prototypes. In contrast to his unequivocal love for his mother in his first autobiography, in the second version the figure of his beloved father dominates. He had earlier devoted virtually no attention to his father's clerical service; now he depicted his father as an exemplary sacristan:

> my father was characterized by a pious appearance; he had a wonderful voice and sang beautifully in Church. . . . My father's behavior was extremely modest. He never drank. Parishioners loved father. . . . Father was an industrious man, he worked until his face was covered in sweat, until his strength was completely depleted. . . . My father was an extremely wise man, even though he had never gone to school. He rationally thought things through.

The father who terrorized his wife has vanished. Now he is an exemplary husband: "Father loved mother so very much. When she was ill he took care of her with such tenderness. He would carry her himself from the bed when she was so ill she couldn't stand. He washed her himself." His parenting skills had also improved dramatically: "father loved us children . . . he did everything he could to take care of us and educate us." If he did raise a hand to his children, it was justified, and it arose from his fierce loyalty to his beloved wife: "He made sure we all listened to mother's orders and would punish us harshly if we didn't listen to her." In his second version he emphasized his mother's illiteracy and her materialism. She now appeared as well-dressed and in control of the family finances, which, he hinted, she mismanaged out of greed: "he [his father] gave mother all of his earnings and often would forget about how much he had given her even though his sacristan's salary was tiny."

Filonov offered a few hints as to why clerical patriarchy became more important to him as he grew older. He published his first autobiography under his original last name, which is not a clearly discernable clerical surname. He then published two later autobiographies under the pseudonym "Borisoglebskii," the name of his native village as well as a combination of the names of two of Russia's most prominent medieval saints. Toward the end of his life he wished to affiliate himself more openly with his past and his Orthodox heritage, both of which were intrinsically connected with his former membership in the clerical estate. Whereas he did not refer to his adult self in his first autobiography, in his second autobiography, which was also devoted exclusively to childhood, he interjected his adult self once to espouse his piety: "Even now the temple of God draws me toward itself." Apart from this statement, the last glimpse the reader has through his eyes is of his arrival in Petersburg in 1851 to begin his higher educational studies. He arrived from distant Smolensk by foot, after a protracted and agonizing trip, which he chronicled in a third memoir. He alluded to his holy mission in the secular world by stating that he would never have made it without the intervention of God. He ended this memoir and his second autobiography by emphasizing a familiar theme in popovichi's narratives, that of his impoverishment and otherness in this new society, symbolized by the single ruble in his pocket and the torn shoes in which he first appeared in the dazzling capital city.[49]

Self-fashioning, or modern self-fashioning to be more precise, implies choice. To be a modern self an individual must at least believe that he is in control of the construction of his identity. This raises the question of exceptions to the genre. If all popovichi fashioned themselves according to their clerical past, were they engaging in self-fashioning? First, there are exceptions. Filonov's earlier autobiography, many fictional popovichi autobiographies, and a couple of autobiographies written in the Soviet period, including one written in 1924 at the request of Soviet employers by a young popovich seeking work as an insurance agent, all unequivocally reject the father as a role model. The author of the 1924 autobiography, like the young Filonov, inverted the traditional genre, presenting his father as an immoral, cruel hypocrite and his mother as a progressive atheist. This case could be construed as the result of coercion; yet another popovichi writing his required autobiography in the same year for the same firm managed to denounce his past without mentioning any specifics or implicating family members.[50]

Second, not all popovichi wrote autobiographies. While some popovichi's autobiographies were solicited, in the imperial period, at least, the authors had a choice about whether to comply. For choosing to spend a considerable time mulling over their past, they had to have a purpose, which was to announce to the public that they were affiliating themselves with their clerical past. Those who chose not to write their autobiographies made a statement with their silence. That silence is difficult to interpret, but it is a likely indicator that at least some popovichi were indifferent to their past. Testimony by a few of the popovichi who wrote autobiographies confirms this speculation. Elpat'evskii, for example, poked fun at a popovich who, in the postreform period, became ennobled and attended his first noble assemblies and gave "a seminarians' speech" about the role and meaning of the nobility in Russia, often repeating "We, nobles, should . . ." This popovich, meanwhile, was hardly accepted by the local nobility; to become ennobled, he had swindled countless nobles to enrich himself. Another popovich claimed that some popovichi in the prereform period hid their social origins.[51] Popovichi could choose whether or not to try to assimilate into the society they entered, and some who chose to assimilate apparently turned their backs on their past.

Third, within their heritage, popovichi had two different archetypes to choose from. As modern men they did not try to identically replicate their role models; rather, once they made the choice, they could personalize their model and make it their own. Finally, popovichi believed they could choose to reject all or part of their clerical heritage, as the testimony from their own pens in the above examples attests. They knew other popovichi who rejected their pasts, just as they knew many of their noble peers and colleagues had. And they consciously made an entire series of choices, from whether to leave the clergy, to what profession to enter or political movement to join, to whom if anyone they should marry. (See chapters 6 and 7.) They struggled with most of these choices precisely because they knew they had options. And the only choice they all shared was to leave the clerical estate, and even that decision was understood as an individual choice.

Self-Portraits of Saintly Children

Popovichi's portrayals of their beloved fathers are fused with depictions of the most important person in their autobiographies of childhood: themselves. They painted themselves in similar hues to their role models, attributing the model piety and extraordinariness that characterized their fathers to themselves as children. This sense of internal otherness, of innately possessing sacred knowledge or instinctive morality, has been traced to the autobiographies of elite Bolsheviks and prominent women populists who were not of clerical origin.[52] However, popovichi of all political persuasions, along with many clergymen, described themselves as this type of child. Although the reasons popovichi depicted themselves as different from other children varied or overlapped, most popovichi were united by a sense that they were extraordinary children.

Depictions of themselves as boy geniuses are common in the autobiographies of popovichi and clergymen. One popovich bragged that when quizzed along with his cousins, he alone was able to correctly answer his grandfather's questions. Their intelligence and ideal behavior was often rewarded by special attention from their parents. Another popovich, writing in 1860, recalled that he and his father would share a bed, where they would talk throughout the night about intellectual and philosophical topics.[53] He was such an extraordinary child his father treated him as his equal.

In some cases, this unusualness manifested itself in less desirable ways, such as in a childhood plagued by illness. Some popovichi and clergymen recalled standing out from other children because they stuttered or sleep-walked. Others described near-death experiences. One popovich, writing in 1900 and referring to himself in the third person, described the advantages he garnered in return for his sickly constitution and brush with death: "the spiritual nature of Ia.I. even in childhood was better and stronger than his physical nature. From his early years he turned out to have a passion for studying, a gift for comprehension, wit, and an extraordinary memory."[54] The spiritual was infinitely superior to the material, rendering weaknesses of the body a blessing for the soul.

A more acutely tuned soul often manifested itself in heightened concern for others, melancholy, or over-sensitivity. Nikolai Dobroliubov's description of himself is replicated in numerous other autobiographies by popovichi: "I was of a very kind and impressionable nature. I used to weep bitterly when I heard of some misfortune, I suffered at the sight of another's suffering. I remember that I could not sleep at night, I lost my appetite and could do nothing when anyone was sick at home."[55]

A solemn character rendered many young popovichi devoid of any desire to play games. Other popovichi who acknowledged playing childhood games often modified circumstances in order to present these games not as leisure activities but as ways to introduce traditional clerical values. The children in his family, one conservative popovich explained in the 1890s, were rarely given manufactured toys. Instead, they created their toys with their own hands: "With hand-made toys the child is completely immersed in creative activity. Here he for the first time applies his existence to the purpose of activity, of work." While since the days of the Decembrists members of the radical intelligentsia had also been depicting themselves as too serious to engage in childhood games, this topos can once again be found among popovichi of all political persuasions.[56]

Those who did describe playing games as children sometimes traced their perceived entitlement to leadership back to their domination of play-time. The Bolshevik Voronskii explained in 1932: "If I could not run the show, I refused to play. This occurred, however, rarely—my cousins, sisters, and coevals eagerly joined my crew. Adults considered me the ring-leader. I had no patience for objections and demanded absolute obedience." Similar is Sergei Bulgakov's description in emigration of his relationship with his brothers: "I regarded all of them (I mean those older than me) condescendingly, and they acknowledged my superiority." The distinct leadership role of the clerical estate—and their integral link to it—was asserted by other popovichi in their descriptions of "playing church," which included adopting the guise of their fathers and performing a mock liturgy at home with their siblings.[57]

Popovichi—including those who were prominent Bolsheviks—further distinguished themselves from intelligenty of secular backgrounds by attesting to their unquestioning religious belief and complete adherence to the Orthodox Church's teachings in childhood. The event of attending church is recalled by popovichi as one they deeply loved. Many popovichi described the great sorrow they felt as children if they were too ill to attend church services or if during Lent their parents did not wake them for one of the multiple daily services. Assisting their fathers in church—a privilege reserved for their native estate—was recalled as a joyous and much anticipated event. The unpleasant aspects of accompanying their fathers to bless parishioners' homes, such as haggling with parishioners or being plied with alcohol, which some Church officials argued children should not witness, were rarely mentioned by popovichi, including those active in the revolutionary movement. Many popovichi further emphasized their distinctive role as Russia's future spiritual leaders by discussing the traditional ceremony during which the beginning of a clergyman's son's preschool instruction was marked by prayer in front of icons brought from the parish church for the occasion.[58] By contrast, both radical and non-radical sons of educated professionals and nobles often described themselves as rejecting religion at an early age. One Bolshevik from the nobility claimed he engaged in iconoclastic acts as a small child, despite his parents' fervent faith. On the other hand, by the early twentieth century, when popovichi had made their formative contribution to the ethos of the intelligentsia, numerous new intelligenty from lower class estates also began to describe themselves as pious in childhood.[59]

Evgenii Zamiatin (1884–1937), an urban priest's son and author of the classic early Soviet anti-utopian novel *We,* summed up his precocious early childhood: "Already at four years old I was reading. My childhood—spent almost without friends: my friends were books."[60] The ability to read at an abnormally early age, being deeply affected by the books they read, and reading every title they could get their hands on are all standard topoi in the autobiographies of intelligenty, regardless of their social estate background or political leanings. Forming individual interpretation by reading to oneself is also commonly associated with the advent of the modern self. There are, however, several differences that distinguish the function of reading in the autobiographies of popovichi and, in particular, their noble foes.

In their responses to a question posed in the early twentieth century by the compiler of a collection of autobiographical narratives of postreform Russian writers, noble respondents stated that as children they read mainly foreign works. By contrast, popovichi, incomparably less prepared than their noble peers to read Western European languages, cited mainly Russian-language texts. The Russian fictional works they most frequently mentioned included books by contemporary giants such as Gogol, together with minor early nineteenth-century historical novelists such as Mikhail Zagoskin. Their choice of Russian authors who wrote about Russian themes, while born in part out of practicality, was also a sign of their overt patriotism (fluent in Latin, they could have, after all, chosen to read classical works). In his response to a 1912 questionnaire, one Vologda seminarian stated: "My favorite writer is Turgenev because all of his works in the complete sense of the word are Russian." Another stated that he liked novels that "tell about the life of the Russian people and not some other kind."[61]

Smitten by a fervent sense of national identity, popovichi recalled that in addition to Russian historical fiction, heavily laden with romanticism, works on Russian history were their preferred reading choice in childhood. Most popovichi cited *History of the Russian State* by Nikolai Karamzin as their favorite book. While conservative intelligenty from secular estates also recalled reading Karamzin's work with enthusiasm, popovichi's interest in Karamzin's particularly nationalistic rendering of Russian history cut across political lines.[62] Popovichi read the kinds of books their fathers read, books endorsed by clerical prescriptive norms. They presented their passion for reading in childhood as part of the clerical tradition rather than the heritage of the intelligentsia they joined as adults.

The seriousness that popovichi generally attributed to themselves as children also characterized the types of books they read and the way they read them. Elpat'evskii claimed he never laughed as a child because, as opposed to Western European literature, there is little lightheartedness and glee in Russian literature. The vast majority of Vologda seminarians surveyed chose to read classic belles-lettres in their free time, rather than such popular literature as detective or adventure stories, and 20 percent preferred "serious" literature, defined as religious or scholarly books. Children's literature, frequently cited by noble autobiographers, is absent from popovichi's reading lists, in part because until the early twentieth century the only children's literature widely published in Russia were foreign works such as German fairy tales and the stories of Jules Verne.[63] The child who turns to books for escape into flights of fantasy, common among nobles, is thus an anomaly among popovichi.

Popovichi not only claimed to have read serious books, they also described the determined and solemn way that they read them. Popovichi adhered to the Orthodox belief that knowledge is a means toward salvation. The seriousness with which *bursaki* approached reading is evident in an1856 entry in the seminary diary of Fedor Giliarov (1841–1895), who went on to become a conservative teacher: "I don't want to read empty, good-humored stories. I have begun to occupy myself more with . . . the reading of useful books." Because of its utilitarian function, popovichi argued that the reading of books should be approached in a somber, orderly fashion. Elpat'evskii complained that students: "read unsystematically without any guidance." The extensive lists of every book read during their student years compiled by popovichi as diverse as the church historian Sergei Smirnov (1870–1916) and the radical publicist Dobroliubov demonstrate this desire to systematize their reading of literature.[64]

Popovichi attributed to themselves a veneration for the written word similar to that reserved for sacred texts. Many popovichi emphasized that because it was more difficult for them to obtain books as youngsters, books were dearer to them than to nobles. They recalled reading books over and over until they had learned them by heart. One radical popovich, writing in 1921, recalled the approach he and his fellow seminarians took to reading: "to ensure that the reading of a book, its contents, and the ideas which it contained evoked a response in the mind and heart of the reader, it was essential that the reader carefully concentrated on every phrase of the book, that he carefully read the book."[65]

Popovichi also expressed a preference for literal-minded content. They seldom mentioned reading poetry as children. Nikita Giliarov-Platonov (1824–1887), the editor of the conservative newspaper *Sovremennye izvestiia,* acknowledged in 1886 that he had never had the patience or the taste for verse. He also disliked lyrical passages in fiction on the grounds that they marred the narrative. Describing himself in childhood he wrote: "My soul demanded an objective representation." A Vologda seminarian also expressed his preference for realism in literature, stating that in his favorite works "I feel that everything written there is truth (pravda)."[66] Popovichi, like other intelligenty, turned to a life of the mind, but for popovichi of all political orientations it was a mind that combined the realism characteristic of the radical intelligentsia with the romantic nationalism coined by the Slavophiles.

Since they were pious youngsters, popovichi naturally read religious literature. Not coincidentally, the one Western title several of them recalled reading was *Robinson Crusoe,* which was available in Russian translation early on; Crusoe undergoes a powerful religious conversion through intense reading of the Bible and suffering. Crusoe shared another trait with saints' lives, the explicitly religious literature popovichi recalled reading, that would characterize popovichi as adults: they were all individuals who ultimately succeeded in overcoming adversity. One Vologda seminarian summed up his interest in the saints' lives genre: "Since early childhood I have been completely smitten by the idea of suffering." Elpat'evskii recounted the saints' suffering that inspired him as a child: "I immersed myself for days in accounts of the torment of the first Christians in Rome, in the Lives of Russian saints who had withdrawn into the woods to save themselves from sinful life or had been killed while preaching Christian faith to pagans. . . ." Saints served as role models to Elpat'evskii, and their travails inspired his interest in downtrodden peoples. His reading of saints' lives also shaped Elpat'evskii's extraordinary sensitivity and the way he reacted to books generally. He was unable to distance himself from what he read: "Books deeply agitated me, they agitated my soul to the point of physical pain. . . . And then there were the tears which usually flowed, when the plot turned to suffering and torture. My heart pounded and it became difficult to breathe." Elpat'evskii's tears were undoubtedly also provoked by the late eighteenth century European cult of sensibility, which affected all educated nineteenth century Russians, but the source of popovichi's tears was qualitatively different. For example, a writer who was not from the clergy also recalled, in a 1911 publication, weeping over what he read as a child—but he wept because he was moved by the beauty of the language, not because of empathy or moral outrage.[67]

Although many liberal, conservative, and radical intelligenty from secular estates also recalled reading saints' lives as youngsters, they do not appear to have made a claim that it had shaped their characters. Popovichi were able to draw on saints' lives as a part of the clerical tradition they used to fashion themselves. One popovich bragged in 1904 that he was related to saints. Another recalled in 1860 that his father used to tell him interchangeably about events in biblical and Russian history, interspersing tales from his own life among these histories: "he told me many similar incidents, either from the history of our native land, or from his own individual life." His reaction to his father's stories was always the same: his heart swelled with patriotic pride and pounded vicariously from the suffering and grief endured, and from the fact that the story of his own family, representatives of Russia and of the Orthodox Church, was directly connected to the national and Christian narratives.[68] By exalting the importance of saints, popovichi were exalting their own significance.

Popovichi further venerated themselves by describing their childhoods as conforming to those of Russian saints. Russian saints generally have one of two types of childhood. Either the saint is born to virtuous parents and from birth exhibits signs of his saintliness, or he is born to an average family and displays extraordinariness only after an act occurs in late childhood that completely alters him. Popovichi, born into the sacred estate, chose the first model. Such saints were, like popovichi, distinguished in early childhood by their extraordinariness, which manifested itself in a number of ways: learning to read as toddlers; shunning childhood games; scholarliness; precocious spirituality, meekness, humility, obedience, or piety; sickliness; excessive abstinence and disdain for material objects.[69]

In the saints' lives genre, the parents, particularly the fathers, of this first type of saint are themselves often portrayed as saintly. Several popovichi and clergymen attributed to their fathers the same childhood distinctiveness that characterized themselves. One popovich explained in 1904: "As a boy, my father differed from all the rest because of his modesty and what appeared visually to be a weak frame." His father was further differentiated from others by a scar on his forehead, the result of a horseback riding accident in childhood.[70] Popovichi's saintliness, then, was genetic.

Dobroliubov, on the eve of his death in 1861, wrote his eldest sister: "I wander about the world a ship; I am alien to everyone, no one knows me, no one loves me. . . . If I said something about my parents, about my childhood, about my mother, no one would understand me. . . . To tell you the truth, since Mamma's death I have not had a single joyful day." Another popovich radical, Nikolai Tregubov (1855–1927), suffered tremendously from the fact that he and his siblings lived in various parts of Russia, far from their widowed mother. In 1902, at the age of forty-seven, he wrote his brother: "And I become still sadder when I look at Mama's life and the lives of all of us. We grew up, received our education and departed into different directions. And we suffer and Mama suffers. Our entire family is reminiscent of a broken nest." Still another radical popovich explained in his 1892 prison diary the value his parents' letters had assumed: "I read them greedily, greedily, as I had never read earlier, it seems, my most cherished letters." The revolutionary collective has been identified as a replication of the family unit.[71] But in the case of popovichi, the family they sought to recreate was based on their clerical past, and their association with the revolutionary movement, comprised of individuals from different estates, did not satisfy their familial desires.

Popovichi defined the components of their heavenly childhoods in contrast to the ideals of their noble rivals. Their ideal of a model clerical childhood has all the markings of the "model piety" that clerical etiquette texts prescribed for clerical children and their families. In their eyes, the clerical world was as different from the realm that secular estates inhabited as heaven was from earth. Separate from birth, they saw themselves as Christ-like, entering the secular world from heaven. They perceived themselves as superior to the offspring of other estates, as an example for others to emulate, much like a saint. They drew upon clerical archetypes they personalized through their fathers' biographies as codes of ethics with which to fashion themselves and transform secular society into the world of their childhoods.

On their journey from the heavenly world of their childhoods to secular society, however, popovichi had to make an important stop in a transitory realm. This realm, the dreaded and mythical bursa, or clerical boarding school, would later prove essential in their justification for voluntarily leaving the clerical estate. Enrollment in the bursa would signal an abrupt end to their happy childhood and provide them with the opportunity for saintly martyrdom.

Martyrdom, Moral Superiority, and a Bursa Education

"A seminarian is someone very peculiar, distinct,

and perhaps even the only one of his kind."

—1896 diary entry of Dmitrii Zelenin (1878–1954),

popovich and future ethnographer

At around the age of nine, a clergyman's son's idyllic childhood abruptly ended when he began his formal ecclesiastical education in the bursa by enrolling in a primary-level church school. In the words of one popovich, "from that time on another life began."[1] With the exception of the minority of clergymen's sons who lived in one of the three or four towns per province where church schools were located, students boarded at the bursa until the conclusion of their secondary education at a seminary ten to twelve years later. The bursa experience elicited a dramatic response from popovichi and clergymen, who wrote more about this aspect of their lives than any other.

Unlike autobiographies of clerical childhood, recollections of the bursa were often written in response to a single text that established a conventional genre of bursa memoirs. In 1862 Nikolai Pomialovskii (1835–1863) published his pseudo-autobiography *Seminary Sketches* (*Ocherki bursy*), the first account of the bursa written by a popovich. Pomialovskii portrayed a school whose academic program consisted exclusively of rote memorization, where bursaki lived amidst squalid poverty, barely subsisting on starvation rations. Students were not educated in Pomialovskii's bursa; they were only beaten and tortured at the hands of cruel teachers, corrupt administrators, and over-age bullies. He depicted a training place for future clerics devoid of any spirituality, a system intended to encourage morality that instead spawned depravity and corrupted the souls of its inhabitants. *Ocherki bursy* shocked its secular readers, the vast majority of whom had never been behind the walls of a bursa. In his review of the book, the celebrated nineteenth-century critic Dmitrii Pisarev compared it with Dostoevskii's *Notes from the House of the Dead,* concluding that the horror of the bursa far exceeded that of the prison camp Dostoevskii described.[2]

The response of secular society to *Ocherki bursy* was muted, however, in comparison with the reaction from former seminarians. Virtually all postreform bursaki attested to reading it either as children or as adults. References to the book can be found in an anonymous seminarian's diary kept in the 1860s, in an 1873 underground Vladimir Seminary journal, in the demands of the national Union of Seminarians in 1905, and in the responses of Vologda seminarians to a 1912 questionnaire. The vast majority of bursa memoirists maintained that their experience, while similar in many respects, was less extreme than Pomialovskii's. One popovich, writing in 1909, criticized Pomialovskii for misleading readers by focusing exclusively on the primary level of clerical education in church schools, which was infinitely worse in terms of punishment and pedagogy than clerical secondary education, which took place in the seminary; he argued that many bursaki transferred the bitterness they accumulated in the church school to the seminary, even if their experiences in the seminary were positive. A few popovichi did state that their experience was identical to that described by Pomialovskii. Dr. Sychugov even claimed that his own ordeal in a prereform provincial bursa, "from which it was a long way up to God and a long way off from the Tsar," was worse than what Pomialovskii experienced at his privileged St. Petersburg bursa. Still others employed *Ocherki bursy* as a point of reference, explaining throughout their text which aspects of "Pomialovskii's bursa" existed or were absent from their experience, particularly if they, unlike Pomialovskii, attended the improved postreform bursa. This approach was also utilized by several bursaki who refuted Pomialovskii's portrayal, seeing it as fodder for the anti-clerical secular press.[3]

Most popovichi—including radicals—were extremely ambivalent about their bursa experience over the course of the imperial period; a few professed genuine love for the institution, many others pure hatred. Yet popovichi tended to construct a remarkably similar, distinct, enigmatic bursa universe, permeated by values that, they argued, shaped them as a group. The bursa served as a stepping stone, both chronologically and figuratively, between the clerical home and the temporal world they entered as adults, and the degree of affinity or antipathy they expressed toward the bursa reflected the extent to which they associated it with either their idyllic childhoods or their disillusionment with secular society. Their clerical schooling was the single most important event in the lives of popovichi, and it was an institutional experience that they shared as a group. The collective solidarity popovichi expressed toward each other was thus rooted not only in their common clerical origins and childhoods, but also in their collective bursa experience. They employed the terms "popovich" and "seminarian" interchangeably, and the bursa experience—as well as the experience of joining their individual story to the collective story begun by Pomialovskii—cemented their group identity. In the words of Zolotarev, writing in 1946: "every one of my seminary friends bore in him his school tradition. . . . Consciously or unconsciously their heads and their hearts were stamped with distinguishing and unmistakable characteristic traits, which seminarians born in the south and north, west and east of our country carried in themselves."[4]

Sharing this unique experience allowed them to intensify their bond with individual popovichi they had never met. In a letter to a seminary friend following Dobroliubov's death in 1861, the future Kadet party member Kliuchevskii wrote: "This loss is the kind that causes one to grieve deeply in one's soul . . . as a person he was a seminarian." The liberal Kliuchevskii's affinity for the radical Dobroliubov is not surprising: many popovichi emphasized that they felt an affinity for other seminarians regardless of political affiliation. Even the Bolshevik Lepeshinskii described in his 1921 memoirs his fellow popovich and onetime acquaintance Aleksei Peshekhonov (1867–1933), a populist who was a minister of the provisional government and a persecuted foe of the Bolsheviks, as a "seminarian by education," a smart, diplomatic man, a proper, deft polemicist.[5]

As an estate school the bursa also forged a sense of continuity between popovichi's forefathers' lives and their own. Unlike nobles, who as late as the early nineteenth century were often still educated exclusively at home, since Peter the Great's reign all male members of the clergy had been required to attend the bursa. As Mamin-Sibiriak wrote, "After all, our fathers, grandfathers, great-grandfathers, and great-great-grandfathers went through all this too." In their autobiographies popovichi and clergymen alike wrote that some of their first preschool memories were graphic horror stories told by relatives about corporal punishment in the bursa.[6] So integral was the bursa experience to their families' tradition that even those few clergymen's sons who never attended the bursa felt an affinity for bursaki. One such popovich, a revolutionary who wrote his autobiography in the 1920s, recalled a group of seminarians he befriended during his final years studying at a gymnasium who became his closest friends: "Among my new friends I found like-minded persons and from that moment on I did not feel lonely." Since bursa tuition was free for clergymen's sons, a secular education was seldom an option, except for very wealthy clerical families. It was not uncommon, however, for clergymen's sons to enroll in secular schools for a year or two. In such cases, they either attended a zemstvo or parish school before being sent away to board at the bursa or completed their secondary studies at a gymnasium. Such popovichi nevertheless continued to draw on their bursa experience as the main source of their identity. Despite the fact that he graduated from a gymnasium after attending the bursa, in his 1866 university diary Ivan Tsvetkov referred to himself throughout as a "bursak": "As a man and as a bursak. . . ."[7]

The bursa was the institution through which popovichi's collective memory was interwoven. It became their museum, a site of memory that they revisited not only figuratively but literally. By the late imperial period seminary alumni associations sprang up throughout Russia. Popovichi employed in varied professions living in the same cities joined local branches. Numerous popovichi and clergymen went to emotional reunions held at the seminaries they had attended, in some cases traveling great distances. Even Ilarii Shadrin (b. 1879), author of an updated version of Pomialovskii's exposé, was dismayed when he was unable to attend his tenth and twentieth seminary reunions. In 1914 he sent a letter to be read at his twentieth reunion, explaining his absence and apologizing to any of his schoolmates who might have been offended by his novel. He explained, just as Pomialovskii had, that he had not meant to attack the clergy; rather he hoped to help his own kind by shocking society into reforming clerical schools. In old age some popovichi scheduled informal gatherings with friends from their bursa years. A Bolshevik popovich described a meeting with his seminary friends in 1952; they sat around singing church songs for hours. Despite the portrait of suffering that alumni painted of bursa life, some popovichi even chose voluntarily to educate their sons at the bursa, including those who had sufficient funds to send them to a gymnasium.[8]

Being labeled a seminarian might have been pejorative in secular society, but for most popovichi it was a source of pride, which explains their desire to share their ordeal with the public. In spite of—or precisely because of—the scars inflicted on them in the bursa, the experience served as yet another source of their moral superiority over their noble-born foes, and bursaki often contrasted the bursa to the gymnasium, the educational institution most nobles attended by the mid-century. For like workers in industrial England, their sense of solidarity was borne from a combination of martyrdom and class hatred. In their eyes, the bursa reinforced clerical prescriptive values, although ironically most popovichi claimed it was the antithesis of their heavenly childhoods. It served as a principal source of the activism, masculinity, and collectivism that defined their understanding of modern selfhood. One Bolshevik popovich recalled in 1925: "I love to think about the seminary and am thankful to it that in spite of the strict, monastic order it educated revolutionaries and ascetics." Dr. Sychugov, writing in the late imperial period, noted that although he would never idealize the bursa, he was thankful to it his whole life for instilling in him patience and "iron energy in the attainment of set goals." Some were destroyed morally by the bursa, he argued, but those who survived emerged saved.[9]

What was this universe like? How—and why—did popovichi simultaneously condemn certain aspects of it while embracing the whole? To understand why the bursa elicited such a dramatic and symbolic response from memoirists, the actual structure of a bursa education must first be examined—for Western and Soviet historians' view of the bursa as a substandard academic institution resembling Pomialovskii's *Ocherki bursy* (which until very recently was the only Russian memoir of seminary life translated into English and well-known enough in Soviet Russia to have been made into a Russian language film in 1989) is erroneous.[10] The bursa offered an alternative, but not inferior, education to that provided in secular schools.

The School behind the Stories

Everything about a bursa education—the curriculum, pedagogy, material conditions, length of study, social life, and regulations—differed significantly from education in gymnasia, where mainly noble boys studied, and the Realschulen, the technical secondary schools that served raznochintsy and sons of other secular estates who could afford an education. Even after the clerical estate was partially dismantled in the 1860s, the bursa remained an estate school whose utilitarian mission was to prepare students for the priesthood. Between 1867 and 1886 only 3,441 students from nonclergy families enrolled in the bursa, and the majority of them remained there for only a few years in order to receive an inexpensive education. The parish clergy, fearful that a massive influx of non-clerical students would overwhelm the already overcrowded bursas and leave their children without an affordable education, continued to view the bursa—which they were responsible for funding—as an estate school. With the exceptions of Siberian and south-western dioceses, which suffered a chronic shortage of clergymen, the Church subsequently established quotas that limited the enrollment of nonclergy students to no more than 10 percent, an all-time high that was not reached until the turn of the century.[11]

The fundamentals of a bursa education remained relatively consistent throughout the nineteenth century, although there were repeated attempts to reform the curriculum, with the aim of making it either more academic or more practical. Thus in 1814 and 1867 a more academically minded program was enacted, while in 1840 and 1884 reform moved in the direction of practicality. Most of the numerous subjects taught in the seminary fit into the same three forms of two-year courses that the six-year program of the seminary had traditionally been divided into: philology, philosophy, and theology. In addition to these three main fields, a seminary education consistently emphasized two other subjects within the humanities: history and the classics. Combined with the six-year church school course of study, a full bursa education was two years longer than the gymnasium program.

As might be expected, the most striking difference between the curriculum of the bursa and those of the gymnasium and Realschule lay in the teaching of religion. While *Zakon Bozhii,* a catechism course that covered the Old and New testaments, the commandments, prayers, and explanations of the liturgy and symbols of the faith, was an obligatory subject in all Russian secular schools, it was the only religious subject taught in them.[12] By contrast, the curriculum of the church school throughout the century included catechism, the order of church services, biblical history, and church singing. The full range of theological courses taught during the full seminary course in 1840 included moral, dogmatic, and pastoral theology, scripture, a course on liturgical books, homiletics, Canonical law, patristics, a course on priestly duties, the writings of Russian Church Fathers, the writings of Latin and Greek Church Fathers, and the New Testament. In 1867 many of these courses were consolidated, and theology was confined to the last two years of study. In 1884, however, theology was reintroduced into the first four years of seminary study and a course on polemical theology was added.

The seminary's religious curriculum also included pragmatic courses to prepare students to attend to parishioners' minds and bodies. Courses on medicine, agriculture, and history of sciences were taught between 1840 and 1867, and in 1867 pedagogy, which included teaching in practice schools, was added. In addition, Eastern languages and other Slavic languages, designed to further missionary activity, were taught at certain regional seminaries as electives.[13]

Practical courses were tempered by the weighty emphasis on idealistic philosophy in the seminary curriculum. As established by the seminary reform of 1814, philosophy, which was almost entirely absent from the program of nineteenth-century Russian secular schools, included the study of logic, metaphysics, ontology, cosmology, moral philosophy, pneumatology, natural theology, and philosophical history. Some of these courses were later combined, but the curriculum consistently included the reading of the works of major classical and Western philosophical thinkers.

Idealistic philosophy was considered important for seminarians to study; mathematics and the natural sciences were not. Apart from physics, none of the sciences offered in the Realschule were part of the bursa curriculum. The postreform gymnasium also suffered from scant attention to the natural sciences, but it boasted a hearty mathematics program, especially before 1871.

The study of modern Western languages was also deemed largely irrelevant for seminarians. From 1814 to 1840 and again from 1867 to 1884, seminarians were required to study either French or German, but during other years the study of either language was optional, and few seminarians, at least in Vladimir, chose to enroll. By contrast, both French and German were required in the gymnasium and Realschule. The methodology of the teaching of Western languages also differed; in the bursa attention was given almost exclusively to reading and translation, while the spoken language was neglected.[14]

In place of modern Western languages, the bursa curriculum traditionally focused heavily on classical languages. Prior to 1840, Latin was the language of instruction in most seminary classes, and students wrote their philosophy compositions in Latin. Between 1840 and 1883 Latin and ancient Greek continued to be taught each year, and Hebrew was required in the last two forms until 1867. These languages were not taught in Realschulen, and Latin and Greek did not play a major role in the gymnasium curriculum until 1871. The teaching of Western culture was thus not absent from the seminary, but the Western subjects seminarians were taught—classical languages, literature, and philosophy, along with modern Western philosophy—differed significantly from the Western civilization taught in Russian secular schools.

There was a far greater emphasis on Russian national culture in the bursa. In addition to Russian Church history, which was always an integral part of the bursa curriculum, a separate course in Russian history was taught at the seminary and church school between 1840 and 1867. Although the study of Russian history was combined with general history in 1867, the focus of students' historical studies remained centered on Russia, as they had before 1840. Modern Western writers were consistently absent from the bursa philology program, which after 1867 shifted its focus from a concentration on classical authors to an exclusive coverage of major Russian authors. In 1884, the amount of time allotted in the seminary program to Russian philology, the history of Russian literature, and Russian history was increased. Neither Russian Church history nor a separate course in Russian history or literature were ever taught in gymnasia or Realschulen.[15]

The pedagogy employed in the bursa, particularly on the primary level of the church school, also differed from that of the gymnasium; it relied considerably more on rote memorization. Thus teachers often spent the entire class period quizzing students as to whether they knew the assigned text by heart. Rote memorization declined after being denounced during the church school reforms of the 1860s, but it continued to be employed by some individual teachers, and it endured in the postreform bursa under the guise of repetition, which was widely employed.[16]

The almost exclusive reliance on rote learning and repetition in the church school was mitigated by the use in the seminary of composition writing to instill critical thinking. The result was that while students at the church school possessed a primarily mechanical knowledge of texts, seminarians were often able to discuss seriously what they had learned. Unlike gymnasium students, who were rarely required to write compositions, seminarians in every form had to write compositions for almost every subject they studied, in addition to practice sermons they wrote during their last two years of study. In the prereform period, students frequently wrote as many as forty-five a year; in the postreform period, up to eighteen; these essays were often as long as forty pages. Topics assigned were sophisticated and scholarly for secondary school students. At Vladimir Seminary in 1887 they included, among others, "The moral freedom of man and its relation to incentive and execution of moral law," "The degrees of strength and clarity of consciousness, and the definition of so-called unconscious psychological phenomena," and "How did the influence of Byzantium manifest itself in medieval Russian literature?" Teachers worked closely with individual students on the plan of their compositions. They corrected essays carefully, occasionally writing several pages of comments. Seminarians were harshly graded if they did not employ the newest literature, if their writing style was uneven, or if they used repeated set phrases. Seminary libraries possessed a wide array of primary texts seminarians could use when researching their compositions, such as philosophical and theological treatises and statistical and ethnographic materials.[17]

In addition to critical thinking and intensive writing, the seminary program was also more scholastic, abstract, and theoretical than the gymnasium program. Although the various reforms of the nineteenth century attempted to make seminary subjects more practical and comprehensible to young students, they were not entirely successful. One of the most frequent complaints made by auditors and bishops was that courses were taught either on too advanced a level or too quickly for students to comprehend. Unlike church school teachers, seminary teachers were almost always graduates of one of the elite theological academies, and many were often prominent scholars in their respective fields. Paid less than their gymnasium counterparts and usually married with families to support, they were intellectuals devoted to their disciplines rather than career teachers. The tendency to teach by lecturing can also be attributed to the lesser pedagogical training that bursa, as opposed to secular, instructors received, and to the greater overcrowding of classes in these chronically underfunded schools.[18]

In contrast to the students in Pomialovskii's anarchic bursa, seminarians who hoped to graduate studied a great deal in an attempt to keep up with this demanding academic program. The 1856 bursa diary of one popovich, who was later employed as a provincial bureaucrat, referred to hours spent studying lectures and writing compositions every day. He worked late into the night and was exhausted when he finally went to sleep, often clutching a book in his hand. On many occasions he went to bed at eleven in the evening only to arise at two in the morning to begin studying again. The bursa course was notoriously hard to complete. In the case of one church school, only about one of every three students who enrolled in the 1860s graduated. Among those who did graduate, admission from the church school to the seminary was not automatic. Students had to take rigorous examinations designed to weed out a large number of applicants. Attrition was less severe among those who were admitted to the seminary, though in the case of at least Vladimir Seminary, approximately one-third were expelled in the second half of the nineteenth century for poor academic performance. In the postreform period the grades of all bursa students were regularly published in diocesan newspapers for the entire clerical community to see and compare. An entry from the bursa diary of another popovich, a future teacher, also written in 1856, captures the preoccupation of seminarians with their academic success: "I can't get the examinations on Monday and Tuesday out of my head. . . . It seems I not only pray to God about this, but I also give beggars money because of this, and if I am not able to pass these exams then what will happen?"[19]

Bursaki were assisted in structuring their studies efficiently by published instructions, enforced by bursa administrators, dictating virtually every moment of their lives. For example, six days a week students at one church school in 1861 were required to rise at six in the morning. From seven to eight they dressed and said their prayers, and from eight to nine they prepared their lessons and walked to class. From nine to one they had classes. From one to three they had dinner and rested. From three to five, more classes; from five to six they rested. From six to nine they did their homework. From nine to eleven they had supper, rested, did their housework, said their prayers, and prepared for bed. In addition, every Wednesday and Friday bursaki attended church, as they did during all extra holiday and Lenten services. Given the extremely regimented nature of bursa life it is not surprising that the rector of one seminary referred to the bursa in an 1879 speech he gave to his students as "our monastery."[20]

Components of monastic rule were consciously incorporated into seminary regulations designed in the 1860s. Like monks, bursaki were isolated as much as possible from the outside world, including their families. They were allowed to travel home only for vacations, and these occurred only three times a year: at Christmas, Easter, and for the summer recess. Each lasted two to six weeks, and whether or not a bursak could go home for every vacation depended on how far his family lived from school and on whether his parents could arrange for his transportation. It was a serious offense for a boy to remain in his parents' home during the school year. The only exception was in times of grave illness. Bursaki were allowed visits from their parents at their apartments or dormitory rooms, but these visits were to be kept short and infrequent and were forbidden during the hours allocated for studying.[21]

To bursa administrators, many of whom were monks, educating Russia's pastorate was too important a task to allow parents, even those born into the sacred estate, to interfere. Here the church shared the modern idea that children were better off raised in an institution by professionals. And unlike the gymnasium, the bursa—like the English public school—was an agent of moral as well as academic education. The Church hierarchy argued that the autonomy of the family had to be violated in favor of a systematized and regulated upbringing that the Church fully controlled. Bishops, who, after all, had rejected family life when they took their monastic vows, apparently had little faith that the clerical family was living up to its lofty prescriptive norms. Bishops, along with, ironically, some of the same Church publicists who praised the pastorate, complained that bursaki did not study enough at home, learned ill manners, and failed to attend church regularly. The influence of mothers was particularly suspect. One pastoral theology manual claimed that bad clerical wives destroyed clerical sons, and the only solution was to send their sons away to school as soon as possible.[22] At the all-male institution of the bursa, these boys were protected from feminine wiles.

By educating bursaki in seclusion, bursa administrators also attempted to completely remove them from contact with secular persons. Students who lived in dormitories were not allowed to leave school grounds without a chaperon or permission. Those who rented apartments had more freedom; they were usually allowed to go into town during certain daytime hours, as long as they recorded the times they left and returned. They were, however, forbidden to visit places where they could come into contact with outsiders, such as restaurants, theaters, and town gardens. Administrators were intent on sequestering bursaki from secular culture within the bursa as well. In 1871 the Synod, arguing that exposure to secular culture was harmful and that students were being distracted from their studies, forbade the staging of literary-musical evenings and concerts that had traditionally been held in the bursa. Staging amateur theatrical productions in the bursa was forbidden throughout the century as unsuitable for future pastors.[23] The Church hierarchy sought to preserve bursaki during their formative years so that they would be distinct—and thus purer—from the population they would eventually serve and lead.

Despite the administration's goal, numerous bursaki came into regular contact with secular individuals who served as their landlords. Ideally, all students were supposed to live in bursa dormitories; however, the Church was never able to secure funds to build enough dormitories to accommodate the entire student body. Until the schools were disbanded in 1917, a substantial number of students continued to rent rooms in privately owned apartments. To maintain a sense of community and also for reasons of economy, bursaki rented rooms in groups. In Vladimir, as was probably the case in other Central Russian provinces, the majority were usually able to rent from clerical families, but a sizeable minority had to be housed in the homes of townspeople or bureaucrats.[24]

Boarding in homes provided many bursaki with their only exposure to women. The families they rented from were usually headed by elderly widows who needed the extra income. The only other possibilities for contact with the female sex were interacting with the wives and daughters of teachers if they were invited to their homes, tutoring girls to earn extra money, and attending parties, if granted official permission, on church holidays, such as Mardi Gras, at the homes of local bursa friends or relatives. Groomed in an insular world, where boys of nine were treated roughly the same as young men in their early twenties, bursaki missed many of the

Petersburg seminarians and staff, circa 1910. (Courtesy of the Central State Archive of Cine-, Photo-, and Phono-Documents, St. Petersburg)

usual social, sexual, and developmental milestones of youth and adolescence. Social traits such as politeness and amiability, which secular school administrators praised in student testimonials, were not encouraged by bursa officials, who instead emphasized moral traits such as strength of will and character, conscientiousness, a sense of shame, and repentance.[25] In contrast, their noble peers were taught dancing and drawing, including the sketching of nude models.

The financial constraints that prevented the building of adequate dormitory space also consistently rendered the material conditions of bursaki's daily lives substandard to those in the gymnasium. Official reports throughout the postreform period include descriptions of school buildings as decrepit and filthy, bedclothes as slovenly, air as foul and frigid, furniture as tattered and scarce, and students as underfed and unwell. Their diet was at times so inadequate that hunger drove some bursaki to commit theft.[26]

The Church hierarchy's insistence on institutionalizing bursaki, even without sufficient dormitory space, also stemmed from Orthodox theological doctrine on sin and age. Once they turned seven, even clerical children could be corrupted, and strict punishment was needed to expel bad influences from their souls. Although severely punishing small children—at least clerical children—was objectionable and condemned by the Church, punishing school-age children was necessary, and parents could not always be trusted to put aside their love and adequately discipline their offspring.

Throughout the imperial period, expulsion was the penalty for serious offenses in the bursa. Prior to the reforms of the 1860s, the main form of punishment for minor misbehavior in the bursa was flogging. These beatings were so severe that a few students died as a result of them. In 1868, after vigorous debate, the Synod banned physical punishment in the bursa. But flogging did not cease, particularly in church schools, until well into the 1870s, and even after the practice declined, other punishments remained an integral part of bursa life. Penalties for petty misdeeds during the late imperial period included being made to stand still or on one's knees for up to several hours, loss of a meal, or imprisonment in the punishment cell. Punishment in Russian gymnasia was also strict, but it was not as severe, frequent, widespread, or varied as in the bursa. Corporal punishment was employed in the gymnasium only between 1828 and 1839 and was used only on students in the first three grades. Moreover, punishment in the gymnasium was not a ritual of public humiliation. In the prereform period, bursaki were almost invariably flogged in front of their fellow students, and in cases of serious crimes, in front of the whole school. In the postreform period, students who were required to stand on their knees in the cafeteria did so as fellow students ate their meals and watched. Punishment was thus not a private, individual experience, but a public spectacle.[27]

In 1905 another Pomialovskii, Ivan (1845–1916), a popovich archeologist employed as a university professor, wrote a report for the office of the Minister of Church Affairs on the academic qualifications of seminarians to enter universities. He summarized the differences between the educational

programs in the gymnasium and seminary and argued that the most positive aspects of the seminary program lay in its distinctive traditions. He
highlighted the seminarians' ability to research independently, the development of their theoretical dialectical capabilities, and their industriousness, all
attributes commonly associated with the modern self. Pomialovskii, like other
popovichi, concluded that a seminary education was superior to gymnasium
instruction.[28] Pomialovskii articulated the distinctiveness of the alternative culture the clergy and their sons epitomized. The abstract, demanding, and idealistic education offered in the bursa was foreign to those schooled in secular institutions, as was the harsh material deprivation and social isolation. And it
was specifically this distinctiveness—even its most negative aspects—that
popovichi employed in their autobiographies of bursa life to argue that they
were the rightful moral leaders of society.

Ascetic Feats

As constructed by popovichi and clergymen, the bursa tradition was one
of intense suffering that rendered all of its victims martyrs. In some cases,
being beaten is the only point about their bursa education that autobiographers recount.[29] Although memoirists who attended the bursa in the postreform period generally acknowledge the decline of flogging, other methods
of physical punishment are cited, such as teachers pulling students by the
hair and beating them with fists or vines. The extent to which corporal
punishment remained a part of the bursak identity is evident in a complaint issued by the Union of Seminarians in 1905 about ear-pulling.[30] Even
after reform, the experience of physical suffering remained the crucible of
bursaki's collective identity.

At times, the descriptions border on the fantastic. One popovich born in
1845 recalled in 1909 that many of the students in his bursa were bald,
having had their hair torn out by the roots by teachers. The public spectacle of the act served both to martyr the punished boy and to bond him
with the peers who witnessed his pain. Like the sufferings of a persecuted
sect, it both defined and cemented the community.[31]

Memoirists described the punishment they bore as the torture of inno-
cents. They occasionally mentioned the reasons why students were punished—these ranged from omitting a single word in a memorized text to
missing a note in singing class—but more often they stressed that punishment was arbitrary. There was no logic to bursa terror. One popovich recalled in 1864: "we were flogged for any reason—for the fact that we sat
quietly and for the fact that we sat noisily. Sometimes we were simply
beaten for no reason at all."[32] Punishment is portrayed as egalitarian: everyone suffered. Every student was punished at some point, no matter how
hard he studied or how much his parents bribed teachers.[33]

These beatings rendered seminarians the ultimate ascetics. Some memoirists described themselves as having borne their pain stoically. One
popovich, writing in 1938, recalled that after the choir director beat him

Petersburg seminarians in their classroom, circa 1910. (Courtesy of the Central State Archive of Cine-, Photo-, and Phono-Documents, St. Petersburg)

on the head with a bow, he hid his pain from his fellow students, despite his festering wound. As one priest wrote in 1890, "we were epic heroes (*bo-gatyri*), we patiently endured everything."[34] By enduring the bursa experience, popovichi saw themselves as partaking in the agony of Christ. The suffering they individually endured would move them collectively to the head of the line on the final judgment day.

Since they believed that the pain they suffered brought them closer to salvation, they also believed that it transformed them into exceptional human beings. In 1900 a deacon described the invincible strength students derived from this constant pain: "Our nature became capable, with the passing of time, of accustoming itself to any disagreeable situation." Attempting to explain the bursa to his noble biographer, Ivan Tsvetkov wrote: "it was a more difficult life than that of a convict." They were real men, exemplifying the virtues of Christian manliness, including physical strength and courage.[35]

Ascetic feats were also required in order to endure bursa poverty. Popovichi described the shocking destitution of the bursa as visible in the very structure of its buildings. The historian Afanasii Shchapov (1830–1876) wrote: "Imagine a stony bursa, already built in the second half of the last century. Dark cells, suffocating with stench—rooms with a Paleozoic layer of mud on the floor, with cracks, through which not only rats, but also cats are able to climb in." Popovichi recalled that in the wintertime, students sat in unheated classrooms after they had walked, sparsely clothed and often bootless, from their lodgings, which were sometimes located on the opposite side of the town. The health of students was constantly endangered by their poor diet as well as by the cold. One popovich claimed that starvation drove some boys to barter sexual favors to other students for a crust of bread. The quality of the food was recalled as dubious; Professor Petr Kazanskii (1812–1878) of Moscow Theological Academy claimed that rats and mice were occasionally found in his kasha and soup. Under these appalling conditions, popovichi portrayed themselves as joining together in solidarity. One recalled in 1906 having spent his evenings huddled with twelve other boys studying "by the weak light of a single flickering tallow candle shared by all."[36]

Popovichi often accused the bursa administration of fostering these horrific living conditions. They argued that the poor diet of students was a result of the theft of food or funds by bursa administrators.[37] Living conditions, particularly the quality and quantity of food, often sparked seminarian unrest.[38] They valued the material deprivation of their childhoods, since it was imbued with the clerical values of poverty and humility. But impoverishment in the bursa was unacceptable; it was not an ideal, or even a necessity, but an avoidable torment inflicted by the greedy on innocent children. The suffering they endured was therefore not idealized, as the privations of their childhood were, but it was glorified as a testament to their superiority and moral and physical strength. Physical suffering fluently transmuted into tales of holy martyrdom reminiscent of the early Christian martyrs portrayed in saints' lives.

Since their noble peers had not enjoyed the bursa experience, they were inferior. Comparing their suffering to the luxurious holiday they imagined gymnasium life to be was standard fare in bursa narratives. In particular, bursaki bitterly compared the lesser punishment to which gymnasium students were subjected with the torments they themselves had suffered. One priest recalled in 1911 the hatred he harbored toward the "well groomed, squeaky clean, cheerful gymnasium students, mama's boys with rolls behind their cheeks." Popovichi's bursa suffering was yet another source of their superiority as populists. One popovich recalled in his 1916 autobiography a public exchange between two populists, one a popovich and the other a nobleman, in which the former explained why popovichi alone could understand the peasantry, and subsequently why they deserved leadership of any populist group:

> But then you, Bogdanovich, did not have to study in a poverty-stricken school, because you are a nobleman from Pskov province, and I, for example, am the son of a sacristan from Perm province . . . yes, and the majority assembled

here are the bursa poor and I will prove that to you right now. Let's take Kostylev, he is an Arkhangel'sk bursak, Vorontsov is a Saratov bursak, Starostin a Vologda bursak, Morozov a Viatka bursak.[39]

Bursaki were aware that memoirists writing about the gymnasium did not tell tales of martyrdom. All these memoirists had to complain about was separation from their families, the boredom of some classes, and the relative strictness imposed on them after having run free on their estates during their preschool years. Indeed, some gymnasium memoirists had only good memories of the institution. Popovichi trumpeted their physical martyrdom to secular readers precisely because it was the antithesis of the gymnasium genre. Why else did so many popovichi focus in their bursa memoirs on their years in the church school, which by their own accounts was more violent and crude than the seminary? Describing their pain was a strategy employed to demonstrate to secular readers how tough they were. The general tone of their letters home to their parents from the bursa, for example, reveal a degree of normalcy missing from most bursa memoirs. Some popovichi even attributed the desire to use their bursa experience to themselves as youngsters. According to the ethnographer Mikhail Fenomenov's unpublished 1927 autobiography, "Already when I was a student I recalled my life in the church school with acute bitterness, and I even planned on narrating it."[40]

Popovichi's torment in the bursa distinguished them as a group from their noble peers, and the bursa experience became a collective trauma—as is common in the modern age—that was the founding myth of their collective identity.[41] Former bursaki were envious of those who had escaped this torment, but they were also proud of their own triumph. Their interpretation of the bursa performed a transfigurative function, wresting victory from defeat. The bursa may have harmed their bodies, but it made their souls stronger. Like Christ, whom torture could not destroy, their spirits, nurtured during their saintly domestic childhoods, could not be broken.

Heaven versus Hell

In their autobiographies popovichi and clergymen usually presented the bursa as the antithesis of their childhoods. Home represented heaven; school symbolized hell, exemplified by a Bolshevik popovich in his 1921 memoir:

> The first impressions of childhood from the countryside and its surrounding nature left in many of our impressionable young souls profound and ineffaceable vestiges. Our kind family, the simple rural life, unrefined people, muted rural poverty, meek distress and quiet joys, the river, yellowing cornfields, the unimaginable expanse of the fields and sky—these were our first impressions. Surrounded by our native atmosphere, fostered by the love of our kin, we lived a free life, not experiencing any feeling of fear or embarrassment before

others. . . . When we arrived at school and then days, weeks, months, and years of study dragged on—reality drew us other, dreary pictures. In place of kind and attentive parents we saw and had contact with ignorant, backward, and stern people—our educators and teachers. In place of our former confidence in ourselves, honesty, and other moral qualities and temperament, there crept into our souls feelings of distrust toward those surrounding us, shyness, fear, and suppressed anger.[42]

Departing from home for the bursa is described as a wrenching experience, and part of the rage bursaki vented against the bursa resulted from the homesickness they suffered. One popovich recalled in 1915: "The departure for town, where I had never been before, and the separation from my family were very difficult and painful for me. I was so close to my family and I received such loving kindness from them that this loss seemed terrible to me and I cried a great deal, just as my mother and sisters did."[43]

Memoirists relied on daydreams about their families to survive. As one priest wrote in his 1911 autobiography, "we read the letters which we received from home over and over . . . my brother and I reconciled ourselves to our fate only because there, far away, was something sweet and dear, which shone like the sun." In the case of the clergy and its secular sons, school never became the surrogate family that it was for many noble intelligenty. Even those who rented rooms never described their hosts as parental figures. Indeed, many recounted the abuse and prejudice they endured in the homes of secular landlords.[44]

Parental visits and vacations home are universally recalled as the happiest times in the lives of bursaki. One popovich, whose family had to travel only three hours to the bursa, recalled in 1913: "Batiushka visited us fairly often . . . words cannot describe the joy his appearances brought us." One of the main demands of bursaki was to be able to see more of their families. For example, in 1905 Ekaterinoslav seminarians protested for the right to be allowed to travel home to see their families during Mardi Gras and the first week of Great Lent. In Mamin-Sibiriak's memoirs bursaki resemble prisoners waiting out their sentence: "Every day in the evening each one with great joy crossed off one day from his life. If one could only survive until Christmas—our dreams did not go beyond that. . . . Time remained our most terrifying enemy." Noble memoirists also recalled vacations as the highlight of their school years, but unlike bursaki, they contrasted imprisonment in the city (where schools were located) to domestic idylls on their country estates. It was the countryside, rather than their families, for which they tended to yearn.[45]

Vacations replenished depleted clerical values. Metropolitan Evlogii claimed in emigration that each visit home eradicated the damage the bursa had incurred: "In the environment of a sound, pious regime everything alien that had stuck to me during the winter at the seminary, quickly shed from me, and I returned to the innocent, living faith of my childhood."

Even without vacations, the purity of their childhoods ultimately triumphed over the evil of the bursa, as their early childhoods at home served as invincible armor that protected them from bursa depravity. One popovich wrote in 1910: "People who had a solid character and had been directed on the right path since childhood became tempered in the environment and did not yield to the influence of the terrible surroundings."[46]

By contrasting home to the bursa, bursaki dissociated their families from their negative feelings about school. In their narratives they were careful not to implicate the parish clergy in their condemnation of the bursa, and they believed they would not have suffered as much if their parents could have played a role in running the schools. Thus one of the resolutions passed in 1905 by the all-Russian Union of Seminarians was a demand that elected parental representatives become voting members of the bursa administrative board. Bursaki never blamed their parents for sending them to the bursa; rather, because their attendance there was mandated by the state and a formal education was the only means to a profession, they expressed gratitude to their parents for selflessly enduring material hardships to pay their room and board. One popovich, referring to himself in the third person, described his indebtedness in an autobiography written in the early 1890s: "with tears in his eyes, Ia.I. always recalled his father and mother, having given themselves, and all that they had, to educate and bring up their children."[47]

Bursaki succeeded in dissociating the parish clergy from the bursa by directing all of the blame for their suffering toward monastic administrators. Bursaki portrayed their abuse as a continuation of the age-old rivalry between the ruling celibate monks and the disempowered parish clergymen. One of the demands of rioting Tula seminarians in 1905 was that monks be prohibited from becoming rectors and that future rectors be elected by the local clergy, not by the Synod. This charge against monastic administrators had been leveled a half century earlier by Pomialovskii, who wrote: "It's a wonder that these childless monks did not punish children for loving their parents." In their autobiographies and adult correspondence popovichi painted monks—excepting, as their parents did, most monks who were theologians—in the same dark hues their parents had employed, attributing to them corruption, greed, careerism, pride, laziness, and despotism. According to one popovich employed as a theological academy professor, they were "generals in cassocks." When another popovich wrote his parents in 1835 disparaging the other tenants of his apartment house for their acquisitiveness, he ended his tirade by adding: "to say nothing of the fact that the proprietor of the house is a monk."[48] By shifting the culpability for the brutality of the bursa system entirely to monks, popovichi established a lifelong pattern of not implicating the parish clergy in wrongdoing. The existence of dual clergies allowed them to bifurcate the clerical world into two domains: that of the eternal, sacred realm of their holy childhoods and saintly fathers; and that of the temporal, corrupt institution, epitomized by monks and the demonic bursa. This bifurcation made it possible for them to continue to adhere to clerical values, even if they rejected other aspects of their heritage.

Legitimate and Illegitimate Authority

Clerical brothers who attended the bursa at the same time shared living quarters, so although they were separated from their parents, many popovichi nevertheless found a substitute for their revered fathers in the person of their older brothers. Given the large size of clerical families, most popovichi thus remained physically connected to their family unit until they left the clerical estate.

Brothers are portrayed as protectors, but also as authority figures who enforced clerical values such as industriousness and studiousness, which the bursa curriculum also promoted. Bursaki hungrily accepted their brothers' authority over them. It was legitimate authority, in the Weberian sense, because, like their fathers' love, it combined strictness with affection. In 1844 the older brother of Professor Nikolai Subbotin (1827–1905), having recently graduated from the seminary, quizzed Nikolai, still a seminarian, during their correspondence: "are there many students from your form who have managed to become top students or are you the only one? I implore you to write me about each one of your assignments. It is extremely interesting for me." Besides driving him to succeed, Nikolai's brother also expressed his love: "[uncle wrote me] that you missed me in Shuia, that you were so glad to receive my letter from here that you took it with you to Vladimir. Reading that passage in uncle's letter, I mentally kissed you, and reading that passage I almost openly cried, I don't know myself from what. It seems, out of love for you."[49] In their relationships with their brothers, bursaki re-created the patriarchy of the clerical home.

Whereas brothers and fathers were legitimate authority figures, bursa teachers and administrators were not. The absence of any benevolence in these individuals nullified the validity of their authority. In their descriptions of the beatings and punishments they endured, popovichi and clergymen often singled out a particular individual who abused them, usually portraying him as a sadistic, larger than life monster. A priest's description of a particular teacher, published in a diocesan gazette in 1891, is typical: "His teeth were bared, and they chattered as if he wanted to eat his victim." Tambov seminarians, in an underground seminary journal produced in 1908, drew caricatures of bursa administrators as literal devils.[50] A few bursaki claimed that homosexual teachers preyed on good-looking students, exchanging intercourse for exemptions from flogging.[51]

When confronted with such illegitimate authority figures, many bursaki chose to rebel, despite the harsh consequences. Student unrest in the bursa, which began at an earlier date and was fiercer and more prevalent than in any other Russian educational institution, had always existed, but it began in earnest in the 1860s.[52] It gradually increased throughout the century, gaining powerful momentum in the 1890s and peaking in 1905. The breaching of bursa authority was not necessarily politically motivated; although the increase in unrest in the late nineteenth century was sparked by revolutionary literature and ideas, individual acts of insolence toward officials and defiance of bursa regulations were consistent throughout the century. Smoking and drinking, for example, were always widespread, far more so than in gymnasia. Students talked back to teachers, and sometimes yelled at them for no particular reason. Impertinence was not merely the result of adolescent rebellion; even preteen students at the church school were cited for answering their teachers rudely.[53]

Students also retaliated with violence. During an uprising at Smolensk Seminary in 1894 the army had to quell rioting after the police were unsuccessful. Teachers and administrators were lucky if they suffered only broken apartment windows during uprisings; seminarians not infrequently did bodily harm as well. By the 1890s, numerous murders or attempted murders of bursa administrators were committed by students. This violence became so acute in 1905 that the rector of Vitebsk seminary believed rumors that students had bought sixty-five revolvers and were going to kill the entire bursa administration.[54]

Yet alongside the "demonic" teacher is another stock character—the "good" teacher—the opposite of the monster described above. "Good" teachers never beat bursaki. Instead, they invited favored students to their homes as guests. A few even secretly introduced popovichi to radical ideas. Bursaki described these teachers as sharp intellects, a marked contrast to their colleagues, whom they mocked as "semi-philistines," "untalented," "completely stupid." Some memoirists emphasized the existence of a lone sympathetic teacher. They described these angelic teachers with the qualified affection that typified parent-child relations in the clerical home. The portrait one popovich painted in 1891 of his favorite bursa teacher is reminiscent of memoirists' beloved fathers:

> About him one could say that he was both feared and loved. Not a single student, even one of the regular favorites, would have dreamed of causing any kind of ruckus which would have been unpleasant for Gavriil Ivanovich. This wasn't so much because of fear of punishment, but rather because in relation to him, acting up was considered an inappropriate action which would not have met with any support from others.[55]

Whereas clergymen were more likely to emphasize their favorite teachers as friendly peers, popovichi's adoration knew no bounds. Referring to his favorite teacher in his seminary diary, Dobroliubov commented: "I attached myself to him like a dog and was ready to do anything for him and not think of the consequences." He viewed this man as his savior:

that righteous, courageous, good, and completely intelligent man would keep me from all kinds of vileness! The thought of his qualities always excited lofty feelings and intentions of imitation in me. With new strength, new energy, I undertook tasks and seemingly my mind was becoming clearer and my patience grew and my whole being was revived and uplifted. A kind of holy excitement developed in me and supported me in my endeavors.

When he learned that his idol was moving to a different city, he was crushed: "I would like to burst into tears, to smash my soul, to throw myself around his neck, to kiss his hand, to fall at his feet . . . why shouldn't I be unhappy, if my soul loves nothing in this world besides another, the soul that it can't have?" Popovichi who became revolutionaries were not the only ones prone to such reverence. Professor Subbotin's brother wrote him in another letter from the theological academy regarding his former teacher, who now taught Subbotin: "Love, love him! Any intelligent and kind student cannot possibly not love him."[56] Unlike clergymen, popovichi tended to invest their favorite teachers with divine qualities. These teachers proved that individuals as modern selves could make a difference, even in the hellish world of the bursa.

Yet in the search for angelic teachers to serve as role models, bursaki were sometimes disappointed. The frustration that arose from trying to transform teachers into surrogate fathers is evident in the suicide note a seminarian named Vladimir Sobolev wrote in 1897:

> if you were like us, perhaps, and not always detaching yourselves by callous, dry formality, you would attempt to get to know your pupils better, you would be able outside of class to have domestic discussions with them (since there is nothing to do at home), to instruct them about an intelligent, honest life, to give them advice about what they should do, read, how they should live their life and much more that is also lofty and righteous. My God! If we saw you as kind, humane teachers how we would deeply and sincerely esteem you! What benefit such humane relations would bring to our downtrodden brother-seminarian, what benefit your kind words would engender, falling upon young, unspoiled hearts.

The bursa was a bridge between popovichi's holy childhoods and the corrupt temporal world they needed to save. Trapped in this purgatory, favorite teachers, no matter how angelic, could not compete with students' fathers. In numerous memoirs, these teachers were ultimately destroyed by the bursa, driven to incapacitating alcoholism or to nervous breakdowns.[57]

Bursaki constructed a universe embroiled in a Manichaean struggle between good and evil. Describing his teachers, one popovich wrote in 1899: "some were gentle angels and others were evil demons." Descriptions of the relative merits and deficiencies of an individual teacher are rare: they were either horrible monsters or unblemished saints. Popovichi displayed a dual attitude toward authority both before and after they left the bursa. Illegitimate authority, in the persons of "demonic" teachers and monastic bursa administrators, were to be collectively resisted at all costs. At the same time, legitimate authority, represented by "angelic" teachers, brothers, and fathers, were to be followed and even revered. There was no room for compromise. Their anti-authoritarian authoritarianism is similar to attitudes toward authority, paternalism, and hierarchy among early twentieth-century Russian workers. Among autobiographies written by former gymnasium students, however, only Bolsheviks tended to attest to a similar degree of anti-authoritarianism, and any discussions of popular and unpopular gymnasium teachers are comparatively mild.[58]

Yet in popovichi's depictions of legitimate authority, even their "angelic" teachers were suspect. Popovichi did not depict themselves as blind followers. The figure of the teacher appeared in two guises, "demonic" and "angelic," but there existed only one figure for the beloved father and brother. No one could fully replace their family, the repository of clerical values. Their ultimate disillusionment with "angelic" teachers left them with one choice of legitimate authority in the outside world: themselves.

Inegalitarian Egalitarianism

Teachers and administrators were not the only official authority figures in the bursa. Under this highly regimented system, students had to have a leader present at all times. Since teachers did not live with students, an elaborate system of student teachers' aides (*starshie*) was constructed to assist the administration in enforcing authority. Some starshie supervised students in their apartments or dormitories, others monitored their behavior in church, still others quizzed students during class. Starshie were usually recruited from among the ranks of the top pupils. They were required to report any abnormal behavior to the inspector. Although technically not allowed to administer punishment themselves, in the prereform bursa it was common practice for starshie to beat students, either on their own initiative or at the request of teachers who preferred to use student "executioners" rather than dirty their own hands. The *starshii* system was theoretically abolished in 1868 as an obstacle to comradely relations among students. Despite this prohibition, however, starshie continued to be appointed in the bursa, sometimes in a limited capacity and often under other titles.[59]

Bursaki did not view starshie as legitimate authority figures. Appointed by the dreaded bursa administration, starshie instead inspired both hatred and fear. Bursaki recalled that some starshie continued to administer beatings long after teachers had ceased to flog students. Because of their superior academic success, starshie were conceited and viewed their fellow students as inferior. Bursaki who did not serve as starshie described them in much the same way they depicted the "demonic" teacher. The popovich Aleksandrovskii recalled in his 1893 obituary of his seminary friend, the writer Karonin:

> I remember well the scenes of wild torture of students by these starshie. A drunken starshii, whose eyes, despite their youth, were already red and pulsating with blood, ordered about ten students onto their knees. He rolled up the sleeves of his shirt, and began, for no reason, to beat them on the cheeks. . . . But in addition to drunken fierceness, among the starshie there existed those who practiced this cruelty for the sake of enjoyment.[60]

Starshie were not the only students who exercised power. All students, at some point in their studies, possessed power in the bursa hierarchical structure; memoirists described a bursa custom in which new students were beaten in a ritualistic fashion. To protect themselves, newcomers endeavored to befriend an older student or join a gang. Professor Kazanskii recalled that younger students were treated as slaves by older students, forced to wait on them in the dormitory and forbidden to speak or move around the room in their presence. The rigidity of this hierarchy is illustrated by Kazanskii's likening of the status of new bursa students to that of untouchables in Indian society.[61] Bursaki described themselves as indoctrinated by this system, which, like any authoritarian structure, compromised its victims by inducing all of them at some point to take part in maintaining its unjust social order.

Many bursaki admitted that they interiorized notions of inequality inherent in the stratification of parish clergy ranks. When boys entered the bursa, they informally inherited the status of their fathers, and along with it, the animosity between priests, deacons, and sacristans. Recalling why he did not like another student, the publicist Giliarov-Platonov wrote in 1886: "he was the son of a sacristan and a sacristan is '*ty*' [informal 'thou'] for a priest and a deacon." The fact that seminarians addressed each other, regardless of background, as "*ty*" (thou) was difficult for Giliarov-Platonov.[62]

Just as popovichi applied a bipolar moral juxtapositioning to their teachers and administrators, they divided students according to typologies of good and evil. In their categorizations of seminarians, popovichi often divided students into either two or three types. The two main types were diametrically opposed, and both remained in the clergy. One type included idealistic spiritually inclined students, who were innately good, abstained from drinking and card playing, and tended to be studious. They tutored lazy and remedial students to save them from being beaten in class. This honorable type is represented in bursaki memoirs by the stock character of the "saintly friend." Like the "beloved teacher" who often met a bad end, these unusual friends were apt to die immediately after graduation. The antithesis of the "saintly friend" was the immoral seminarian who didn't attend class, drank in taverns, and played billiards. Having entered the priesthood despite his wicked ways, this type swindled to obtain the best possible parish for the least amount of work. Popovichi either did not include themselves in this typology, or they classified themselves as a third, moderate group posed between the moral and immoral types. The traits they tended to assign to themselves included industriousness and intellectual independence.[63] Unlike the "saintly friends," who were destroyed by the bursa, popovichi saw themselves as survivors.

Alongside the many stratifications bursaki described, they contradictorily insisted that bursaki were a united community. Reading their personal texts, the reader is suddenly jarred to find authors emphasizing the *tovarishchestvo* (comradeship) that rendered every bursak worthy of their friendship and provided some compensation for the harshness of bursa life. Having recently graduated from the seminary, Kliuchevskii wrote a seminary friend in 1861:

> Farewell, joyful seminary life! But no! Still for a long time that life will ring inside me with its most sonorous chords! After all, you must admit that there are many, very many pleasant, melodious sounds in that life, since it is the life that surrounded our first dear youth, even though there was also much in that life that was thorny and rough. But regardless, there was in it one blessing, one rare, comforting phenomenon—tovarishchestvo, sincerity between students.

Another popovich claimed that when an epidemic of typhoid broke out in his seminary, the affected students recovered, not because of the seminary doctor and his medication, but because their seminary comrades sat day and night by the sick, willing to risk their lives to attend to them. Still another considered tovarishchestvo important enough to devote one of the five chapters of his 1895 bursa memoir exclusively to it.[64]

To highlight the idea of the bursa collective, memoirists tended not to focus on friendships between individuals. Instead, they defined friendship as a harmonious, tightly knit community of individuals who functioned as a single unit. Seminary tovarishchestvo replicated the clerical family. In 1886 one popovich described this familial relationship: "What kind of relations existed between peers, or in general between students? The most amiable, the most patriarchal. We had one heart and one soul: there wasn't any notion of individual possessions, everything was collective. Students who were better off cheerfully shared with their poor comrades. Hence everyone was satisfied and cheerful."[65]

Commitment to the collective led some popovichi who served as starshie to stress that they refused to beat fellow students. Despite their hatred of them, many bursaki described starshie as themselves subject to abuse from their superiors. If a starshii refused to mete out discipline he himself was punished; if he passed a student who later failed under examination by the teacher he was beaten and sent to the back of the class.[66] No matter where a bursak stood in the hierarchy, he was always subject to discipline from his superiors. This institutionalized brutality joined all bursa students as a community of victims.

Bursaki recalled recreational rituals that bonded the members of the collective. Even the most horrific memoir accounts of the bursa usually contain some happy memories of leisure time. In the prereform bursa there were certain days in May when classes were canceled and students and teachers strolled about in the town or spent the day playing games outdoors. In the midst of a brutal account of bursa life published by a radical popovich in 1903 the reader is suddenly jolted by a description of the emancipatory power of these May days: "But even in the midst of this joyless gloom there occurred truly happy days, when we were resurrected from the dead. This was during leisure in the month of May . . . these recreational days have remained as one of my happiest memories of childhood."[67] Bursaki who attended the postreform bursa often described gathering in one another's rooms with a guitar to sing for hours and enjoy their comrades' company.[68]

Popovichi recalled with loathing attempts to destroy the bursa collective. Informers were either beaten or shunned, and stealing from other students was considered a sin. Bursaki complained in their autobiographies and during uprisings about the "spy system" the bursa administration attempted to instill among students.[69] In their narratives they celebrated not the individualism of rebelling against the collective, but trying to conform.

Bursaki considered themselves collective victims of social injustice. Professor Evgenii Golubinskii (1834–1912), who attended the prereform bursa, recalled the extent to which seminarians viewed the administration as their oppressors: "We, the students, served to some extent as the serfs of the supervisor and the teachers."[70] Like inmates in a prison camp, bursaki constructed a society that was internally divided but presented itself as equally united in its interactions with outsiders, united in a war of "us against them."

Bursa students actively demonstrated their collective loyalty by rebelling primarily either due to injustice toward individual fellow bursaki, or to improve the lot of bursaki everywhere. There were incidents of collaboration —establishing radical *kruzhki* (informal study groups), for example—between bursaki and gymnasium students from the late nineteenth century on. But the main goal of the uprising of bursa students in 1905 was based on uniting bursa students nationwide into a "Union of Seminarians," which they accomplished by establishing branches in every seminary. In fact, there were incidents in 1905 in which bursaki spurned invitations to strike with secular-school students. In turn, while demands and proclamations issued by bursaki in 1905 included a few references to universal freedom for all Russian students, the overwhelming thrust of their protest was aimed at solving problems that related directly to bursaki and to bursaki alone. As was stated in one of their proclamations, "The goal of our movement should be the reform of the clerical estate." This insular interest in themselves is also reflected in the content of late nineteenth-century underground bursa journals, whose articles were devoted mainly to the problems of seminarians, the parish clergy, and seminary life.[71]

When seminarians did turn to outsiders to assist them, they usually sought help from former bursaki who had left the clergy. Seminarians striking in Tula after the 1905 revolution declared: "Let us follow the example of our older brothers, who are studying now in the universities. After all, they have not forgotten us. . . ." Seminary graduates who had achieved prominence in the secular world in the early and mid-nineteenth century, such as the statesman Mikhail Speranskii (1772–1839), Dobroliubov, and Chernyshevskii, meanwhile, were revered by popovichi during their bursa years as members of their own kind who had left their mark on secular society.[72]

Those bursaki who did join political factions while at the bursa interacted freely with adherents of different ideologies, remaining, above all, bursaki. For example, Petersburg Seminary in 1906 had a *kruzhok* devoted to anarchism, another dedicated to social revolution, and another that adhered to social democracy. All three kruzhki shared the same library. All of the various Russian political factions existed in the bursa, and many bursaki who displayed an interest in politics did not pledge allegiance to any single group. A search of a Vladimir seminarian's room in 1906 revealed that he had in his possession Tolstoi's *The Great Sin,* works by members of the Kadet party, and literature of the Black Hundred movement.[73]

One reason bursaki embraced each other was that they believed their heritage was so distinctive that only one of their own could understand and love them. Popovichi construed this distinctiveness as a source of their superiority, but they were also willing to admit that they paid a price for being outcasts. In his obituary of Karonin, Aleksandrovskii explained:

> There was no place for him to learn delicate, refined manners, and therefore all of his movements were coarse and awkward. There was no place for him to develop his aesthetic side either. He was prohibited from even showing his nose in the theater or in any public places. . . . In this manner, the bursak of that period, situated outside of any society, other than that of his comrades, became inhuman and isolated.[74]

They were fit only for the company of each other, and this bonded them eternally.

Clergymen rarely presented this idealized depiction of the bursa collective, nor did they tend as much to typologize students. After leaving the clerical estate, popovichi clung to their peer group from their native estate. Having entered the unfamiliar and unreceptive world of secular society, all popovichi experienced similar problems, yet they experienced these problems as isolated individuals. In response to their lack of membership in a social group in secular society, popovichi looked back to the community they had experienced at the bursa. This community was not, however, entirely egalitarian. Modeled along the lines of the clerical family and the Church's conception of society, it was organic yet hierarchically systematized. Popovichi judged their peers harshly. This contradiction between viewing their community as typified by both solidarity and inequality is evident in Sobolev's 1897 suicide note. On one hand he stated that when he was kept back a year, "each student deeply sympathized with my undeserved grief." On the other hand, he repeatedly claimed that the majority of seminarians stood far below him in terms of their intellectual abilities.[75] Just as they accepted only those forms of authority they deemed legitimate, bursaki did not embrace all of the inegalitarianism in the bursa. Patriarchal relations, present in the clerical home, were just. Abusive treatment of subordinates, however, was the unfortunate result of temporal power, which they viewed as a corrupting, systemic force. They were inegalitarian egalitarians, intent on replacing the temporal hierarchy with their own.

Piety and Deconversion Narratives

In keeping with the rigorous supervision of bursaki inside and outside of the classroom, their religious activities and demeanor were strictly enforced. Students who broke the routine of religious life were punished harshly. In fact, no other aspect of students' behavior came under such intense scrutiny.

Bishops' and auditors' reports confirm that the majority of bursaki participated in religious rituals with great enthusiasm and solemnity. Many volunteered to attend extra services and receive communion more frequently than required. Many expressed reverent piety by bowing down to the ground during prayers. Some took the initiative to intensify their religious experience; in 1877, for example, the students at Vladimir Seminary requested of their own accord to have the icon of Saint Kirill brought to the seminary hall so they could venerate it more often.[76]

Popovichi generally ascribed to themselves in the bursa, at least initially, the same degree of piety they had at home. One revolutionary, writing in the 1920s, recalled that when he studied at the bursa, "I was a completely religious boy . . . I very much loved several church services." Another popovich, the law professor Aleksandr Kistiakovskii (1833–1885), described how at the bursa he excelled the norms of piety, abstaining completely from food one day each week and traveling on his own initiative to services at a saint's relic held at four in the morning. Still another popovich, who later became a bureaucrat, repeatedly appealed to God in his 1856 diary for assistance and inner peace. Each night before he went to sleep, this diarist would say a special prayer to himself after he was already in bed. He would then cross himself and fall into a deep and pleasant sleep until morning.[77] As a direct tie to their domestic upbringing, religion soothed popovichi like a lullaby.

Although faith was standard, by the late imperial period it was not universal among bursaki. In the 1870s, Church officials began to note a small number of students who were either late to, absent from, or misbehaving during services or prayers. The incidents began to increase in the 1890s.[78]

Participation in breaking religious regulations was not, however, necessarily a declaration of atheism. Besides being ordinary youthful misconduct, these infractions were sometimes acts of religious dissent. Some bursaki believed that coerced religious behavior was not genuine, a point their moral theology textbooks emphasized. In the petitions submitted by striking seminarians in 1905, bursaki repeatedly objected to mandatory church attendance and prayers, which they alleged had "a demoralizing effect on the religious upbringing of students." At Ekaterinoslav Seminary in 1886, a student cited religious voluntarism as the reason for refusing to get on his knees during church services: "prayer is a free matter; I am not able to pray by coercion."[79]

Religion was a part of both bursa and domestic clerical life. When taken to its extreme, the juxtaposition popovichi often made between home and school necessitated that the two worlds be seen as completely autonomous. Hence just as there were two types of clergy, monastic and parish, there were, for some popovichi, two types of piety. In 1912 the brother of one popovich recalled how his brother, as an adult, experienced this distinction:

> The sincere faith, deep piety, and purity of soul and life of S.S. suffered a trying ordeal during the Liberation Movement. It was as if he ceased to regard the 'clerical dignitaries' of the Church, as he called them, with the trust and love he had previously felt. This was because he saw that they sometimes did not stand on the side of the true Church of Christ. . . . However, he continued to love to pray in his native rural church.[80]

True faith was connected with popovichi's sacred childhoods, nourished by the clerical family. A corrupted, coerced piety was associated with the institution of the Church, symbolized by the bursa.

The majority of popovichi appear to have remained practicing Orthodox believers throughout their lives, recording in their diaries and correspondence expressions of faith in the power of prayer and confession, references to God and to scripture, or mentioning regular attendance at church services.[81] Significantly, those popovichi who did become atheists stated that they did so either after leaving the clergy or at the bursa, and not in the clerical home. One popovich recalled in his 1929 autobiography, published in 1969: "The seminary drove me, like many others, to lose my faith in God." Rather than presenting atheism as the correct way of thinking, some popovichi thus depicted it as the fallen state they were reduced to after the degradation of the bursa. Deconversion is yet another sin the bursa committed. In an 1862 letter to a friend, Nikolai Pomialovskii described how religious he was as a child and wrote that, after he lost his faith, "My conscience tortured me and I grieved over the loss of the heavenly kingdom." Atheism was a source of lamentation at least in part because it signaled the loss of a precious piece of the childhood world they had left behind. And in a few cases, radical popovichi, inspired by a hardship or tragedy in their lives, abandoned their atheism as adults and returned to the faith of their idealized childhoods.[82]

For those popovichi who became atheists at the seminary, their faith in religion usually dissipated only as a result of transference of their religious

belief into faith in another universal principle, such as Marxism or naturalism, which was particularly in vogue among late imperial seminarians. Like
sacred truth, they appealed to some bursaki as another all-encompassing
blueprint for the future. This transfer of faith meant that the loss of their
religious belief was fairly effortless. One popovich recalled in 1921 that after becoming a Marxist at the age of seventeen, "The religious feeling,
which had been so fierce in me as a child, evaporated. Interestingly, the
break for me occurred painlessly, although it did not happen at once." The
cessation of their religious faith meant not the rejection of their native religious ways of thought, but a reorientation toward the new absolute cosmology they embraced. The scientist Ivan Pavlov, who like many other
popovichi atheists lamented the loss of his childhood piety, explained to
Nikolai Bukharin in 1931 that it was not Marxism but science that was his
religion: "I am inspired by a different faith, faith in science, which is imbued into all nooks of human nature and teaches man to seek true happiness not only for himself, but without fail for others as well." Significantly,
Pavlov continued to attend Easter and Christmas services until the end of
his life in 1936. He explained to a colleague that he did so because celebrat-
ing the holidays reminded him of his happy childhood.[83]

Naturalism and Marxism were not the only secular ideas that appealed
to seminarians. In the petitions that bursaki submitted during seminary
unrest in 1905, seminarians repeatedly demanded greater access to secular
culture, including adding dancing to the bursa curriculum and allowing
unrestricted access to the theater, concerts, and public lectures. In the nineteenth century some attended professional theater performances and performed plays covertly at the bursa, risking expulsion. One popovich in
1915 recalled longingly absorbing secular culture from afar: "On holidays
we loved to go to the town garden and listen to music and watch the urban
residents dance under the open pavilion."[84]

Seminarians' interest in secular subjects did not, however, preclude their
remaining pious. The case of the sacristan's son Florentin Troitskii who
played a major role in an uprising at Vladimir Seminary in 1894 illustrates
that atheism was not universal among the very bursa radicals who demanded greater access to secular culture. During interrogation Troitskii
claimed that his life's dream was to be tonsured a monk and serve the
Church as a missionary. An investigation into the library records of the
seminary revealed that Troitskii had only borrowed books on religious subjects. The straight As he had earned in liturgy class further attested to his
keen interest in religion.[85]

Whereas the bursa administration, dominated by monks, believed clerical and secular culture were antithetical, many bursaki believed that the
two could be combined—as popovichi would do once they left the clergy—
without tainting the integrity of the former. For example, in addition to demanding further access to secular culture, the Union of Seminarians in
1905 also appealed for greater attention and time to be given to readings

from the New Testament and that access to theological journals be improved. In their appeals to their fellow seminarians they invoked the name of Christ to compel them to join their revolt.[86]

For those popovichi who became radicals, their politics were sometimes motivated by their theological education. Dr. Tsezorevskii, born in 1834, recalled in his 1907 autobiography published in a clerical journal how seminary teachers had taught them that pravda (truth-as-justice) should be one of their central values: "Pravda, that is, concern for the immense group of poor people, who as a result of their constrained economic and legal position do not have the strength nor the time to participate in the works of society toward the goal of equal rights."[87] These teachings also affected bursaki who did not join the radical movement. In emigration Metropolitan Evlogii described how a seminary education inculcated in him and in others populist leanings: "The narod provoked deep pity in me. I worried that it would disappear into filth, darkness, and poverty. This mood was shared by other seminarians." For those popovichi who joined the populist movement, atheism was not a requirement; they could fuse their religious piety with faith in radical ideologies. While Russian populists have usually been portrayed as atheists, the conversion of several Jewish populists to Orthodoxy to bring them closer to the Russian peasantry, the observance of Orthodox rites by some popovichi populists in prison, and the reading of Orthodox texts by non-popovichi populists, make this assumption questionable. Russian populists were, after all, heavily influenced by early nineteenth-century French utopian and Western Christian socialists, who sought to found a new Christianity in which workers were their saviors.[88]

Aided by their bifurcation of the clerical world, those popovichi who did forsake their religious beliefs did not reject the clerical values that were instilled in them as children. Describing an atheist seminarian named Siniavin, one popovich in a 1906 publication recalled how Siniavin's atheism was tolerated until Siniavin, the son of a bureaucrat, turned against the parish clergy:

> However, he was forgiven for everything, until matters turned to the clergy. When Siniavin cursed the clerical estate and *kamchatochniki* [the class dunces], the students passionately arose to the defense of their parents. "How can it be, that they curse our parents in that manner. . . . We will not tolerate that." In general, Siniavin accumulated many enemies even among his new friends.[89]

Regardless of the nature of their piety in the bursa, popovichi did not reject or question the clerical values that were a link both to their childhoods and to their identity as former members of the clerical estate. Religious faith and clerical values were thus not inseparable, and clerical values could exist outside of sacred space.

Self-Reliant Men

By consciously making the choices of whether to stay religious and what to believe in, popovichi were acting as modern selves. As we have seen, they also expressed their modern selfhood by transforming themselves from victims into martyrs. Their organized anti-authoritarianism can also be seen as part of the process of developing this sense of self, as can their decision to define their community. A final aspect of the modern self exhibited in popovichi's bursa narratives is the claim to be self-educated, self-made men.

Like many memoirists from Russian secular estate groups who attended secular schools, many popovichi denied that the erudition they acquired during their school years was the result of their formal education. In 1927, for example, one popovich recalled: "We became used to the idea that everything that school gave us was completely unnecessary, and that it was possible to receive real knowledge only outside of school by means of self-education." Even some popovichi and clergymen who did not condemn the bursa experience shared this sentiment. The one aspect of their formal education that former bursaki did acknowledge had affected them was composition writing, the part of the bursa curriculum that more than any other allowed individual expression and required independent thinking, and a pedagogy conspicuously absent from the gymnasium program.[90]

According to bursaki, self-education was far more significant in the bursa than it was in the gymnasium, rendering their education, along with composition writing, superior to that of their secular peers. Describing his seminary experience, the scientist Ivan Pavlov recalled that "there existed what was so lacking in the lamentable structure of Tolstoi's gymnasium . . . the opportunity to pursue individual intellectual inclinations."[91] Memoirists also argued that since reading was one of the only forms of leisure allowed by the bursa administration, bursaki had little choice but to spend their free time reading. Popovichi portrayed themselves as more intensely devoted to the single-minded pursuit of the ideals of scholarship and self-perfection than gymnasium students. In order to argue that bursaki studied purely because of their love of knowledge, one popovich who became a gymnasium teacher went so far as to claim, in his 1900 autobiography, that the bursa administration paid absolutely no attention to students' academic performance in the prereform bursa. Unlike gymnasium students, bursaki therefore did not study to receive high marks. While this is a case of a popovich distorting the facts to fit his agenda, it is true that seminarians were openly encouraged by the Church hierarchy to engage in self-education "in the Evangelical spirit." Kruzhki were officially sanctioned by the bursa administration as late as 1908, despite the role they had played in the 1905 seminary uprisings and in the Russian revolutionary movement in general. In turn, one major difference between kruzhki in secular and clerical schools was the exclusively radical character of the study circles in the former; in the seminary, some kruzhki were completely apolitical.[92]

In his obituary of Pomialovskii, the popovich ethnographer Nikolai Blagoveshchenskii (1837–1889) wrote that "Pomialovskii was the main savior of himself." Blagoveshchenskii attributed what he perceived as Pomialovskii's incredible resourcefulness and strength in large part to his bursa experience. Because Pomialovskii was so opposed to the bursa system, he developed an uncanny degree of skepticism and a sharp, analytical, critical mind to protect himself against its influence. The bursa had forced him to look deeply inside his soul, and this "constant inspection of his impressions saved him." Unlike his secular born peers in educated society, Blagoveshchenskii concluded, Pomialovskii had no help from anyone. He had to do everything himself.

Popovichi sought their estate identity not only among family, but also, as in the case of Blagoveshchenskii, among fellow clergymen's sons. Despite their condemnation of much of their bursa experience, popovichi actually idealized certain aspects of bursa life, such as comradeship, leisure, patriarchy, paternalism, self-education, and ironically, their suffering. The notion of the seminarian collective runs through their reminiscences. During their adult lives in secular society they looked back on the bursa in order to forge a sense of affiliation with their own kind. They were proud of their education, and they drew on its particularities as a source of superiority over their secular peers.

In a way analogous to Church publicists' conception of society as divided into sinful and virtuous social estates, popovichi portrayed the bursa universe as populated by groups invariably opposed to one another. In the secular world, as seen in Chapter 2, they relied on this model to ally themselves against outsiders. Popovichi portrayed themselves as having learned in the bursa how to escape from their surroundings when confronted with a hostile environment. They drew upon religious dualism to bifurcate their parents, teachers, and peers, as well as to juxtapose the "heaven" of home to the "hell" of school. In their eyes, they were soldiers in a battle between good and evil that embroiled the world. Once they left the bursa, the battle lines would shift beyond the borders of the clerical estate. At the end of his brief life, Blagoveshchenskii noted, Pomialovskii grew disillusioned and realized that secular society was also a bursa.[93] But popovichi first had to consciously make the choice, as modern selves, not to follow in their beloved fathers' footsteps.

Holy Exodus

Leaving the Clergy

On the first page of his 1882 autobiography an anonymous priest objected to the secular press's assertion that all clergymen's sons were desperate to leave the clergy because they perceived it to be a despicable estate. He was more than willing to admit that the parish clergy had its share of problems; indeed, his entire autobiography is devoted to the trials and tribulations of the priesthood. But as an insider he understood that popovichi's decision to leave the clergy was much more complicated than an overt rejection of their heritage. Many scholars have logically concluded that the dearth of candidates for clerical positions in various European countries in the nineteenth century was a sign of secularization or dechristianization.[1] But popovichi did not repudiate the clerical traditions of the Russian Orthodox Church. How they managed paradoxically to see themselves as leaving the clergy in order to preserve clerical traditions and impose them on secular society—the very opposite of traditional secularization theory and dechristianization—is the subject of this chapter. Not only popovichi, but their parents, many Church publicists, and some members of the Church hierarchy also agreed that popovichi were continuing, rather than rejecting, clerical traditions.

Opening the Gates

Once they left the bursa, seminarians were faced with the prospect of beginning their professional careers. For those who chose not to become clergymen, the options available to them changed over time, but for most of the imperial period some kind of restriction existed regarding the types of higher educational institutions they could enter, and, to a lesser extent, the types of jobs they could take. Before discussing popovichi's reasons for their departure from the clerical estate and the clerical reaction to their decision, the quantitative dynamics of their departure, their evolving legal status, and the opportunities available to them in secular society must be examined.

The first legal restrictions on clergymen's sons entering secular society date back to the eighteenth century. To compel reluctant clergymen to send their sons off to study in the bursa, the Petrine state imposed minimum educational requirements for clerical positions. In 1732, it also forbade clergymen's sons from filling positions such as clerkships, which had for centuries provided homeschooled clergymen's sons with secular employment. When the state needed literate manpower, however, as it did in 1779, these laws were rescinded. Yet in the early nineteenth century, when the state became concerned about the number of clergymen's sons who were attaining noble estate status by ascending the Table of Ranks, a restriction was added: the only members of the clerical estate who could hold civil service positions were ordained clergymen's sons who had graduated in the top tier of their seminary class. The state was even more concerned about popovichi infiltrating the higher echelons of the military, long a bastion of the noble ruling class. Popovichi were therefore barred from becoming officers until 1826, and several of the higher educational institutions that trained officers and bureaucrats, such as the School of Jurisprudence and Military Academies, did not grant admission to seminarians until the Great Reforms. Enrolling in the three non-noble secular estates—the merchantry, peasantry, and townspeople—held no appeal, since the peasantry and townspeople paid the dreaded poll tax and merchants were also subject to a special tax. Given demographic pressure, the lack of a sufficient number of desirable jobs outside of the clergy fueled chronic clerical underemployment. In 1832, the new imperial law code allotted seminarians six months to find employment before they became part of the poll-tax population. More onerous still, the government's periodic response to unemployment was to draft thousands of unemployed clerical sons en masse to serve twenty-five-year terms in the army.[2]

Prior to 1869 all popovichi had to receive permission to be released from the clerical domain by ecclesiastical authorities. They rarely denied such requests if the popovich in question had already been admitted to a higher educational institution or had secured secular employment. If a seminarian sought employment as a teacher in any level of the clerical educational system, or as a clerk or administrator in the clerical bureaucracy, he remained in the clerical domain although he was no longer a member of the clerical estate, and thus did not need to seek a release. At Vladimir Seminary, one of forty-eight seminaries open in Russia in 1850, between 14 and 29 percent of graduates consistently left the clerical estate (but not necessarily the clerical domain) during the first half of the nineteenth century (see table 1). Exit in the prereform period was frequent enough that virtually all clerical families had a relative, either immediate or distant, who had left both the estate and the domain. Dobroliubov, for example, had both paternal and maternal uncles who were secular civil servants.

In the prereform period popovichi who sought secular higher education tended to enroll in pedagogical institutes and specialized medical schools. These schools offered less expensive tuition, more readily available financial aid, and easier entrance examinations—an important criterion for seminarians given the differences between bursa and gymnasium curricula. Moreover, because nobles preferred not to study in these less prestigious institutions, these schools frequently recruited popovichi, offering them fellowships and stipends, and in some cases even paying their travel expenses. In 1855, popovichi constituted 46 percent of the students at Petersburg Pedagogical Institute. By contrast, in 1848 popovichi comprised only 268 (6.9%) of all Russian university students.[3]

In 1863 a new law was passed that made it significantly easier for seminarians to enroll in universities: if they completed two-thirds of the seminary course, their entrance examinations were waived. Many popovichi took advantage of this opportunity, and the number of them enrolled in universities rose to 388 (9.5% of the university student body) in 1865–1866.[4] By 1866 the percentage of the graduating class of Vladimir seminarians who left the clerical estate, including those who left the fourth class that year to enter universities, had jumped to 32 percent.

In 1869, as part of Great Reform legislation, all clergymen's sons were granted, retroactive to the year of their birth, a privileged secular status that exempted them from the poll-tax population. Sons of ordained clergymen became "hereditary honorable citizens," which meant they enjoyed the same rights as the sons of personal (as opposed to hereditary) nobles; sacristans' sons became "personal honorable citizens," a slightly lower status that could not be passed on to their children. Popovichi responded to the opportunities their newfound secular status provided. As Table 1 illustrates, in 1870, 40 percent of graduating seminarians at Vladimir Seminary chose secular education or employment; by 1878 this number had risen to 69 percent. That year 1,810 clergymen's sons (34.5% of the total student body) were enrolled at Russian universities versus 2,273 nobles (43%).[5]

Once Dmitrii Tolstoi, as minister of education, issued his edict in 1879 requiring seminarians to pass final examinations at a gymnasium or a Realschule before admittance to most secular higher educational institutions, the number of seminarians entering universities, and secular professions in general, immediately plummeted, just as Tolstoi had hoped (see Table 1). In 1888, popovichi comprised only 9 percent of the Russian university student

Table 1—Vladimir Seminarians by Profession, 1814–1894

Year	Total	Clerical	Secular	Other[*]
1814	137	85%	14%	1%
1822	222	76%	19%	5%
1830	260	68%	25%	7%
1838	376	76%	14%	10%
1846	437	57%	29%	14%
1854	354	70%	21%	9%
1862	264	77%	16%	7%
1870	233	52%	40%	8%
1878	297	30%	69%	1%
1886	292	74%	24%	2%
1894	303	63%	35%	2%

Source: Calculated from *IVDS*, 1–336.
* Unknown; died immediately after graduation; or unemployed.

body. Because of the differences between the curricula of secular and clerical schools, the required examinations presented a formidable barrier to seminarians. However, they soon began to enroll in large numbers in select institutions. Seminarians were allowed to enroll without obtaining secular secondary school diplomas or taking entrance exams in Warsaw University beginning in 1886, and in Iur'ev University in 1897, to increase the "Russian" element in the two universities in nonethnic Russian regions, and the same waiver always existed for seminarians applying to Tomsk University, newly opened in 1888. The number of popovichi entering secular professions subsequently rose again (see table 1). In 1905, restrictions were lifting on seminarians entering any university, only to be renewed again regarding the established Russian universities in 1908. In 1909, 82 percent of the students at Warsaw University were former seminarians.[6] Restrictions thus did not prevent most seminarians who wanted to receive a higher secular education from doing so, but they did serve to further solidify popovichi's sense of martyrdom and their collective experience, creating, in effect, their own estate-based universities.

Throughout the reform period, the Holy Synod actively campaigned for a privileged secular legal status for clergymen's sons. Once they attained this status, the Church hierarchy maintained, their fear of becoming part of the poll-tax population would be alleviated, and those who were either unqualified for or uninterested in clerical service would leave the clerical estate. The hierarchs' desire for disinclined clergymen's sons not to enter the priesthood implicitly advocated the concept of calling. The departure of those who were not called would subsequently improve the quality of clerical candidates and reduce the excessive number of unemployed seminarians.[7] But when clergymen's sons' legal status was changed in 1869, the clerical hierarchy was not prepared for the mass exodus that followed. Bishops in some dioceses soon found themselves faced with a shortage of qualified candidates for the priesthood. Surprisingly, the majority of bishops and Church publicists did not support Tolstoi's 1879 edict. In their eyes, popovichi were performing a type of clerical service in the secular world.

Cultural Ambassadors

Relieving demographic pressures is not the only explanation for the Church's support of the exodus of popovichi from the clerical estate. Their flight also coincided with the growth of the pastoral care movement. To many Church hierarchs and publicists, popovichi were the most extreme manifestation of their attempt to serve and engage society. Not all Church hierarchs and publicists approved of popovichi's secular mission. The minority who disapproved were often the same sectors within the Church that were opposed to the pastoral care movement.

In 1883 an unsigned memorandum, most likely written by Pobedonostsev, was circulated by the Holy Synod. It accused popovichi of being the Church's enemies and of severing all ties with their native estate. In turn, a number of Church publicists cast a shadow over their motivations for leaving the clergy by accusing them of seeking primarily to improve their material and social position. A few saw popovichi as representative of a dissident sector within the priesthood itself; in the 1860s one bishop asserted that the fathers of some seminarians who left the clergy were priests who hated their profession and were envious of other social estate groups.[8]

Some Church publicists argued that it was a misfortune that the clergy was losing "the best and the brightest" of its sons to secular professions. A few Church officials retorted that only enemies of the Church would trumpet the news that obtuse seminarians were choosing ordination. One seminary rector boasted in 1878 that God had provided the clergy with a limitless reserve of serious, able, and moral sons to staff both clerical and secular positions. Most agreed that the way to stem the tide was to reform the clergy and make it a more desirable profession. However, in 1905 Tomsk Seminary attempted forcibly to halt the deluge by asking permission from the Synod to punish the parents of seminarians who chose secular careers by transferring them to less desirable parishes. Their request was denied, and the Synod reaffirmed that seminarians had every right to choose their own vocation.[9]

Church publicists, priests, and officials directly attacked the 1879 decree as unjust and biased. One seminary rector told his pupils that it was blatantly wrong to close the doors of educational institutions to someone simply because of his social origins. In the clergy's eyes, the decree was yet another example of their victimization at the hands of the state and society. One priest complained in 1882 that popovichi attempting to enter universities were more discriminated against than any other group in Russia, including peasants, Jews, German "colonists," and Tatars. Rather than blaming radical popovichi, or suggesting that only popovichi engaged in illicit activity be the targets of the ban, the clerical press ridiculed the state's decree by repeatedly publishing statistics demonstrating that former seminarians excelled in their university studies over their peers.[10]

Overshadowing concerns about the mass exodus, most Church publicists gloated over the professional achievements of popovichi by publishing bibliographies of their works and quantitative studies of their representations in secular professions. An 1865 defense of the bursa bragged that former seminarians were serving society in every way imaginable, "and they carry themselves with honor and dignity."[11] Many Church publicists and officials celebrated popovichi's success as their own.

Sectors of the Church hierarchy took pride in popovichi because they were conceived of as an integral part of its temporal mission. Addressing his seminary students, one rector noted in 1878 that even though he had complained about the exodus of seminarians from the clergy, he did not perceive popovichi as abandoning their native traditions: "I do not rush to call their flight simply an abandonment of faith and Church." The state also needed good and moral people to serve it, he added, and secular professions could become an extension of their fathers' clerical vocation: "Serving faith and your true government, and bringing use to society, you will be of a real use to the church, being well connected societal people, although you may not be employed in an official capacity by the church."[12]

Because they were secular "missionaries" saving society, popovichi had to be cautious and selfless in their choice of a secular career. In a pastoral theology manual published for seminarians in 1860, one priest wrote: "I pity anyone who chooses a particular profession only in order to possess the means of his livelihood. He will never be satisfied with his position. He will not be able to fill the emptiness in his heart with anything. Boredom and some kind of vague gnawing will torment him. His end will be horrible because he will realize that he was a useless and superfluous component of society."[13]

In the eyes of Church publicists and hierarchs, some secular professions epitomized this mission of saving society more than others. Because teaching was part of priestly duties, the pedagogical vocation came the closest to replicating clerical service. As one bishop put it when releasing a popovich from the clerical estate in the prereform period: "Teaching youth is a lofty, even, one could say, holy calling." A bureaucratic career, despite Church publicists' emphasis on popovichi serving the fatherland, was at the bottom of the list. They associated the bureaucracy with corruption and abuse of power and preferred to have popovichi serve the citizens of the fatherland directly rather than through noble-dominated state institutions.[14]

Popovichi could also serve as bridges between the clerical and secular worlds in a more subtle way. As a rule Church publicists were highly critical of fictional portrayals of the clergy, but they generally accepted popovichi's depictions, even if they were less than flattering. If the author was one of their own kind, then his view as an insider was valid. After all, the clerical press published clergymen's complaints about clerical conditions. Only outsiders—and few Church publicists considered popovichi outsiders—meant harm when they raised the issue of clerical shortcomings. They applauded popovichi's effort to provide a glimpse into what they felt was, for outsiders, a foreign world, but a world that nonetheless secular readers would benefit from venturing into vicariously.[15]

Popovichi were also deemed useful agents of cultural Russification. The national identity of popovichi, unlike that of the secularized and Westernized nobility, was not suspect. In the words of the bishops on the clerical estate reform committee that met in the 1860s, they were "completely Russian, without any foreign tinge in their tribe." Particularly in southwest Russia, where a Catholic Polish nobility reigned, bishops were eager as early as the 1860s to employ popovichi as a "middle estate," staffing secular professions. These bishops invoked the examples of England, Germany, and Holland, noting that in those countries sons of clergymen constituted a large percentage of artists, scholars, writers, technicians, bureaucrats, traders, and statesmen.[16]

The role that Church officials envisioned for popovichi as the Church's ambassadors to society was encoded in certain Synodal legal provisions. Until 1917 the Synod continued to stipulate popovichi as part of the clerical estate. The names, ages, professions, and residences of all adult children of clergymen, for example, were required to be recorded in parish service records. The Church did not classify anyone who had a clerical grandfather, brother, or uncle as "inososlovnye" (persons from other estates), entitling them to receive a tuition-free bursa education at the expense of the parish clergy. Adult children of clergymen, regardless of their professions, were forbidden to marry anyone outside of the Orthodox faith throughout the nineteenth century.[17]

A local church-related study of the parish clergy published in 1897 noted that the large number of seminarians who had left for universities had led to a healthy degree of secularization and liberalization within the clergy. This had occurred, the study noted, because popovichi continued throughout their adult lives to have close contact with their families.[18] Popovichi were a product of the pastoral care movement but were also a catalyst for modernization and reform of the clerical world. They were seen in some church circles not as an Orthodox rebuttal to modernity, but as a constructive response. The Church's influence on society could only increase as the boundaries between secular and religious became less clearly demarcated.

Parental Approval

Church publicists promoted the concept of vocational calling, but with one important proviso: that popovichi receive their parents' blessing. Individuals were first and foremost members of families. Obedience to one's parents, even as adults, was a cardinal virtue.[19] For those popovichi who wished to leave the seminary before graduation—either to enroll in another educational institution or to begin employment—parental permission, and thus parental approval, was required.

Popovichi who discussed this topic in their autobiographies uniformly recounted that their parents, particularly their fathers, ultimately blessed, and in a few cases enthusiastically supported, their decision to leave the estate. This claim is corroborated by familial correspondence. A number of popovichi who were part of the postreform mass exodus noted that a change in clerical parents' attitudes occurred when parish service reforms were passed in the 1860s. Prior to the 1867 law forbidding the inheritance of clerical positions, parents who did not have a daughter whose husband could eventually take over the father's seat wanted one of their sons to become ordained so that the older generation could remain in their home. This was why Elpat'evskii's father became a priest. The 1869 law prohibiting the ordination of seminary graduates under the age of thirty, designed to produce more mature priests, also encouraged clerical parents to consent, since many ordained clergymen did not want their sons to be forced to serve temporarily as lowly sacristans. Writing at the turn of the century, one popovich recalled: "From the mid 1860s on fathers did not exert pressure. Out of caution they advised their sons only to complete the full course of the seminary, so as not to lose the right to enter the priesthood, and regarding the future they said: 'It is more apparent to you.'"[20]

Popovichi claimed that entering a secular profession was not perceived as heretical by clerical parents. Many popovichi recalled being told stories in childhood about legendary secularly employed relatives. In particular, clerical families instilled in their children an awe for relatives who had become scholars. In some cases popovichi explained that their fathers actually encouraged them to leave. Disgusted by their powerlessness before the monastic hierarchy, the disrespect some parishioners showed them, and their inability to correctly perform pastoral duties in the absence of adequate salaries, some clergymen wanted to spare their sons the moral hardship they had suffered. By enrolling their sons directly into a gymnasium instead of the bursa, a minority of priests closed the door to the clerical profession for their sons. Since only wealthy parents could afford the cost of tuition, the number of parents who wanted to send their sons to gymnasia was probably higher than those who actually attended. Mamin-Sibiriak claimed that his father wept when he realized he could not afford to send his sons to a gymnasium. Numerous clergymen in the postreform period who petitioned to withdraw their sons from the bursa and enroll them in secular schools stated that they did so to ensure their sons more vocational choices upon graduation.[21]

Providing their sons with choices was increasingly important to clerical parents for two reasons. First, popovichi in the postreform period were the first clerical generation allowed to freely select a profession. Choice hadn't been a major issue earlier because fewer possibilities existed. Second, Church publicists from the mid-century on increasingly emphasized the importance of vocational choice. The quality of the priesthood was now linked to candidates for ordination experiencing a calling from God. Conversely, God could also call clergymen's sons to enter a secular profession.

In his letters to his son written in 1874, Father Narkiss Mamin expressed confidence in his son's independent decision-making abilities. He advised him to earn extra money "so that upon graduation from the academy you can freely choose your place of employment." Like the sacristan father of Aleksandr Smirnov—who flatly refused to give his son advice when he agonized over whether he should enroll in a university: ". . . as to what you should do, that will be God's decision. We are all in the hands of God"—Father Narkiss believed that God would speak to his son directly through divine inspiration. Clerical parents remained confident that God would direct their sons, especially if their sons continued to adhere to the tenets of the Orthodox Church. As another priest in 1907 wrote his son, studying at an institute in Petersburg: "if in addition to everything you write us about your life, you also pray to God and go to church, then it means that everything is splendid with you."[22]

A few popovichi portrayed themselves as carrying out their fathers' youthful dreams. For one popovich, his father's vicarious living through his sons was so momentous that reference to it was the only comment he wrote on the cover of the diary his father kept in the 1890s: "He completed only the church school. He constantly heard from his colleagues about how he had not graduated from the seminary. Therefore, he strove emphatically to give his children an education. He did not advise them to enter into the ecclesiastical domain. . . . He gave me and my brother a secular higher education."[23]

Having their sons receive as advanced an education as possible usually outweighed any desire clergymen had to see their sons ordained. The esteem of the parish clergy for education is evident in the 1938 autobiography of the teacher Georgii Solomin (1867–1941). He recalled the head priest in his father's parish telling his father, a sacristan, that he was a fool. Solomin's father answered that bigger fools existed. When the priest asked him to name one, Solomin's father replied: "Your brother-in-law, the sacristan Sinetskii. He has three sons, and they all became shepherds. I have five sons, and I transformed them all into people!" Solomin noted: "Evidently, this subject was a sore spot for the archpriest, for he fell silent." Educated individuals—defined by graduation from at least a secondary school—were so revered that the code word for them was "people."[24]

The extent to which the parish clergy perceived the attainment of a higher education and professional accomplishment—even in secular careers—as the fulfillment of the clerical ideal is also illustrated by the 1905 obituary of a clergyman written by a fellow priest. Describing the sons of the deceased, all but one of whom left the clergy, the author wrote:

> The revered archpriest took all measures to assure that he brought his children up according to the discipline and instruction of the Lord. Thanks to his efforts, they all brought joy and comfort to their parents when they grew up. All of the sons of the revered archpriest completed studies in higher educational institutions, and at the present time successfully prosper and occupy extremely visible positions in their professional careers.

Most clergymen appear to have preferred that their sons receive a higher education at a theological academy, but since only a minority of theological academy graduates went on to become ordained, this preference did not rule out their sons' leaving the clerical estate upon graduation.[25] And if their sons could not or did not want to attend one of the four elite theological academies, the vast majority of clerical parents settled for a secular higher education.

Like most parents, clergymen wanted their sons to have a better life. Upward as well as outward mobility partially explains why sons of priests were much more likely to leave the clergy than sons of sacristans. A sacristan's son, popovichi and clergymen explained, could make his father proud by becoming a priest; the most a priest's son could do if he remained in the clergy was to replicate his father's success.[26] Outward or upward mobility did not, however, entail the rejection of one's origins implicit in theories of social mobility. Sons could take their fathers' careers a step further, becoming better educated and imposing clerical values on new spheres.

Having their adult children live within close geographic proximity to their parents often outweighed any preference about employment. One clergyman wrote his son in 1835: "my sincere blessing of any job, wherever you like and wherever possible, only not too far away, about that we implore you."[27] Ensuring continuity of clerical traditions, which could be cemented through education, conscientious vocational choice, and most importantly, close family ties, was the primary concern of clerical parents.

Most popovichi who discussed parental approval in their autobiographies emphasized that they would not have left the clergy without their parents' permission. Some altered their plans—for example, graduating from the seminary before enrolling in a university—in order to receive their parents' blessing.[28] Their acquiescence to their parents' wishes is corroborated by letters, such as Nikolai Dobroliubov's 1853 correspondence with his father. That year, the year before he was to enter the sixth and final year of the seminary course, Nikolai and his father had petitioned for Nikolai to enter Petersburg Theological Academy. Permission was granted, and Nikolai passed the exams for the final year of the seminary course and left for Petersburg in the summer of 1853. Nikolai, uninspired by his seminary studies, had long wanted to enroll in a university, but his father, who fully supported his son's decision to seek a higher education, feared that the tuition was beyond his means. Nikolai agreed to attend the academy because it was considered the most intellectually rigorous of the theological academies and because its location in Petersburg would facilitate his contact with literary publicists. Once he arrived in Petersburg, however, Nikolai met fellow seminarians who were sitting for the entrance examinations to Petersburg Pedagogical Institute. Pressed for time by the institute's impending application deadline, Nikolai wrote his parents informing them of his change of heart, and enrolled in the Pedagogical Institute before he received his parents' reply. Before Nikolai left Nizhnii-Novgorod, Father Aleksandr had suggested in passing that if Nikolai did not pass the academy entrance examinations, he could try and enroll in the Pedagogical Institute. Yet confused by his son's seemingly impetuous decision, and fearful that the bishop would disapprove of his son's breach of their original request, Father Aleksandr initially expressed dismay. Nikolai responded to his father's indignation by apologizing profusely, explaining his decision in great detail, and offering immediately to withdraw from the institute. As was the case with other popovichi, Nikolai unequivocally stated that he would never act without his parents' blessing. In his reply, Father Aleksandr gave his blessing, reassured his now frantic son, and attributed his last-minute decision to Divine Providence.[29] Their parents' approval assured that popovichi did not have to break with their past.

If a parent objected to a popovich's departure, the mother was usually singled out as the culprit, as in the case of one popovich whose father died when he was a bursa student. Since his father died before the 1867 parish reform, he recalled that his mother insisted he immediately occupy his father's position as a sacristan to support them. The bishop refused to allow his mother to withdraw him from the bursa, arguing that he too was the son of a sacristan, and his mother had also wanted him to end his studies prematurely. She should not interfere with God's wishes, he lectured the mother, for God might intend for her son to become a priest or occupy an even loftier position. Significantly, this popovich remembered his father begging him on his deathbed not to become a sacristan. It was his mother, not his father, who tried to hinder his path.[30]

In saints' lives mothers are also more likely to oppose their children's calling. Both saints and popovichi left their parents' homes to embark on radically different courses, but many more saints encountered parental resistance. They were often forced to wait years to receive parental permission, and in some cases actually disobeyed their parents and left without their permission.[31] Unlike the saints in saints' lives—the majority of whom were monks—popovichi were family oriented throughout their lives. Their departure did not signal a withdrawal from the world, epitomized by the family unit, but full entrance into it.

Besides expressing concern about the uncertainties of secular employment for their unordained sons, the only other preference some clerical parents voiced was their belief that as priests, their sons would have greater access to God and would be able to intercede through prayer on their behalf. Writing in 1903, one priest recalled his father saying, "I want my sons to become priests and to remember me before the altar of God. This will be the best reward for me." By the turn of the century a few articles in the clerical press appeared complaining that generational strife, which had torn apart noble families for decades, was now dividing clerical families. Interestingly, besides the cases of some popovichi who became professional revolutionaries, familial strife is completely absent from popovichi's autobiographies. They did tackle the subject in their fiction, which presents a less static, timeless clerical world. But even in these fictional accounts, despite their disagreements, the older and younger generations are able to reconcile. In a 1906 short story by a popovich writer about clerical family life, for example, the father and sons have heated political arguments that last half the night. Nevertheless, they always part on good terms, and the monarchist father is eventually swayed by his sons' liberalism.[32]

Even among revolutionaries, familial contact, if not harmony, appears to have been preserved. A few popovichi revolutionaries emphasized their parents' utter lack of interest in temporal affairs and partisan politics in order to explain why their radical affiliations did not affect their relationship. If radical popovichi discussed their parents' reaction to their political beliefs, most emphasized that their parents were frightened that radicalism would endanger their sons' souls. Others recalled worrying at the time of their conversion to radicalism that they would alienate their parents. Preobrazhenskii stated that the reason he was reluctant to become a revolutionary was his fear that this step would entail "a break with my family." In fact, the break did not occur until he and his father were both arrested in 1936 on unrelated charges. He continued to visit his parents in the 1920s and '30s, even after his father had been "dekulakized" twice. Several radical popovichi acknowledged feelings of guilt, saying that the knowledge of their father's disapproval pained them greatly. Konstantin Ostroviantov (1892–1969), a Bolshevik who wrote his autobiography shortly before he died, described how devastated he was by his father's grief when he delivered an anti-religious speech in his home town following the October revolution: "For the first time in my life I saw my father crying. My heart was gripped by a sharp pain . . . I silently kissed his hand and left, in order not to see the great sadness of my father." Afterward his father told him that he would always pray for his soul.[33] By including the detail of kissing his father's hand, the ultimate symbol of the deference of parishioners to their priest, this atheist popovich continued to bow to—and fuse—clerical and religious traditions a half-century after the Bolshevik revolution. Because the vast majority of clerical parents did not disown their sons or disrupt their relationship with them over political differences, popovichi of all political persuasions were able to retain select aspects of their heritage.

Popovichi knew that their fathers, like the Church hierarchy, were proud of their accomplishments in the secular world. The Soviet dissident writer Varlam Shalamov (1907–1982), author of *Kolyma Tales,* which stands alongside *The Gulag Archipelago* as one of the most famous memoirs of gulag life, recalled in his autobiography that his father, a priest, believed fate had ordained that the parish clergy and its offspring should rule Russia. His father dismissed ascetic monks as incapable of this mission because they, unlike the parish clergy, did not live amongst the narod. Because popovichi were raised alongside the narod, only they possessed the closeness and knowledge of the people required to be Russia's rulers. If he heard of a work of fiction, Shalamov's father always asked if the author was from the clergy. He often boasted about popovichi, reciting the names of those who were famous surgeons, agronomists, scholars, professors, orators, economists, and writers. He hoped that popovichi would remain closely tied to their native estate, providing the clerical estate with the opportunity to grow rich from their ideas. And, like Church publicists of the late imperial period, he thought the strong, large clerical family could serve as an exemplar on which to model Russian society.[34] Rather than hindering their departure for secular society, many clergy imparted to their sons the idea that they, the natural-born leaders of the intelligentsia, should go into the world to save Russia.

Reasons for Departure

While some popovichi in both the pre- and postreform periods, primarily those who did not complete their education, left the clergy because they were unable to secure ordained positions, most popovichi graduated at or near the top of their seminary class and therefore could have had their choice of clerical appointments. In turn, popovichi autobiographers generally presented their departure from the clergy as a matter of voluntary choice. A few mentioned some external motivating factor—such as their refusal to serve as a lowly sacristan before becoming ordained—but they did not cite any one factor as a single influence.[35] Instead, they usually specified one or a combination of ethical reasons that justified their exodus within the parameters of moral discourse.

In describing their reasons for departing from the clergy many popovichi depicted a clerical world that bore little resemblance to the idyllic world of their childhoods. The myriad of grievances of parish clergymen about their adult lives suddenly surface in popovichi's personal narratives.

This discrepancy appears despite popovichi's general assertion that clerical life changed little over the course of the nineteenth century. Like their fathers' narratives, popovichi's narratives of childhood and adult life clash. While they portrayed their family's experience as Edenic, they were willing to make harsh judgments about the life of the generic clergyman that would have awaited them.

One of the criticisms voiced by many popovichi was that the process a clergyman endured to obtain a clerical position was morally offensive. They cited the widespread use of bribery, the custom of obligatory marriage prior to ordination, and unethical practices such as a seminarian's marrying a girl in order to obtain her father's parish seat. Many of these popovichi stated that their unwillingness to marry under these circumstances was the primary reason for their departure. In a letter to his sister Masha written in the 1850s, the popovich writer Levitov explained that he was leaving the clergy because marrying in order to become ordained would prevent him from fulfilling his primary goal, helping his family:

> I will work and I will, at least, know that my efforts will not be wasted as they were in the seminary and that these efforts will establish the future of my parents and the future of my dear Alioysha and Masha. . . . I am leaving so that I will have the opportunity to marry my sister off to a suitable man, and so that, if God allows, my father and mother will find in my wife an admirable creature, who would respect them, and in addition to that, would love them, which will never happen if I become a priest because the wives of priests are never able to tolerate their in-laws. Therefore understand me, my family, understand my noble goal, my brotherly love toward all of you.[36]

Many popovichi also mentioned their objections to clerical poverty, although they emphasized that they did not leave the clergy to seek affluence. In fact, popovichi rejected a clerical career, which, although certainly not lucrative, would have provided them with the minimum of room and board, to risk the unknown, which offered no guarantees of financial security. Rather, they explained that they deplored that clergymen were forced to farm, and thereby neglect their parish duties, in order to feed their families. They wanted to be able to devote themselves wholeheartedly to their professional goals. In addition, if they had entered the priesthood they would have risked compromising themselves morally by having to haggle with peasants over contributions for ceremonies they performed. Tikhonov, a political conservative, considered in his autobiography published in 1912 that his work as a schoolteacher was a more virtuous form of service to the people than the priesthood. A teacher, after all, did not depend on "extorting the last crumb of bread from poor people" to subsidize his livelihood.[37]

Some popovichi explained that they chose not to enter the priesthood because certain Russian Orthodox Church teachings would have forced them to compromise their ideals. The contemporary Church's obligations to the autocracy were seen in particular as morally objectionable. Ivan Tregubov explained to his mother in 1887 why he could not become a priest:

> You advise me to become a priest. . . . A priest often has to do that which the word of God forbids. For example, the word of God forbids one to take an oath. It states: "do not take an oath at all." But a priest is required sometimes to be sworn in where one is commanded to take oaths. The word of God forbids one to curse and command, to bless those who curse, and to pray to defeat the enemy. But a priest sometimes must pronounce an anathema, that is a curse, and must pray that God will help us defeat our enemies. And there is a lot, a great deal which the word of God forbids and which a priest must do. Where is the path to salvation for a priest? How can I become a priest after this? Won't I then lose the possibility of salvation?

Tregubov, who had flirted with the revolutionary movement before becoming a Tolstoyian, believed that by leaving the Orthodox Church, he could save not only himself, but also Russia. If he became a priest, he would be powerless to fight to overturn the policies of the Church and autocracy, which he considered immoral and detrimental to the future of his country.[38]

The driving force behind their criticisms of clerical reality was a rigid adherence to Christian ethics. Popovichi frequently argued that the realities of parish life made it virtually impossible to realize clerical ideals. Like their fathers, they blamed all of the problems of clerical life on external factors, be it the state, the monastic hierarchy, or parishioners. They implied that if clerical reality had been different, they might have remained in the clergy. One popovich, a conservative, described this chasm between clerical reality and ideals in his 1886 autobiography when he recalled his decision to leave the clergy: "Of all professions, the clerical profession is the falsest, although in theory the most ethical. It is false precisely because it is so ethical. A soldier, peasant, merchant, doctor, professor—each one is what he appears to be. He serves, ploughs, trades, heals, teaches. But a pastor, as defined by Pastoral Theology, and a batiushka in reality—these are two different beings. The former is a container, a shell, a husk, an appearance, a mechanism without a soul."[39]

Some popovichi refused to become clergymen precisely because they felt they could not live up to this high ideal. In an open letter to fellow seminarians written in 1905, striking seminarians wrote: "We are made into pastors. We, who are coarse, wild, broken, hostilely disposed toward people, toward society, children of darkness." Filonov recalled in 1890 his thoughts about becoming a priest upon graduation from the seminary: "'What kind of a priest am I?' I thought to myself. 'I love to drink, I love to entertain Orthodox folk with various stories, whims, and concerts.'" Professor Kazanskii noted in 1879 that he had not received what he considered the necessary pastoral preparation at the seminary to become a priest. Another popovich cited in 1929 his loss of faith as the primary reason for his departure; the concept of an atheist priest was repugnant to him.[40] These popovichi regarded themselves as too rooted in the temporal world to act as intermediaries between God and man.

Only the mythologized batiushka figure was capable of attaining popovichi's lofty ideal of the priesthood. One popovich recalled in his 1830 autobiography that although he possessed some of his father's attributes, he did not inherit the entirety of his father's ideal Christian character.[41] Neither did the priesthood as a profession. Having presented their fathers as extraordinary priests, some popovichi made an ethical distinction between "good" and "bad" priests similar to the typology they employed when categorizing seminarians in their bursa memoirs. "Bad" priests embodied everything that popovichi sought to escape by leaving the clergy—lack of faith, careerism, corruption, greed, and debauchery. "Good" priests, on the other hand, were pious, industrious, temperate, and studious—qualities that their fathers symbolized. The same Ivan Orlovskii who idealized his "proto-intelligent" father and espoused reactionary political convictions wrote to his biographer in 1909: "In general, I am always prepared to passionately defend the clerical estate and clerical day-to-day life [byt], but *popy* [a derogatory term for priests] are extremely offensive to me."[42] Yet even "bad" priests were largely seen as victims of an institutional system that corrupted them, rather than as villains. In turn, "good" priests were martyrs. To avoid being hapless victims or martyrs and actually implement clerical ideals, popovichi had to enter secular professions.

Nevertheless, because popovichi embraced the clerical ideal of moral leadership, some made the decision to leave tentatively. In a letter to a former seminarian written in 1877, one seminarian asked for advice about whether he should become a priest or attempt to receive a higher education. "If only you knew my heartfelt doubts," he added.[43]

Not all popovichi presented their decision to leave the clergy as motivated by condemnation of some aspect of the clerical world. The idealism that many popovichi displayed in their criticisms of clerical reality was also demonstrated by a second group who explained that they left in order to receive a higher education. Subscribing to the clerical belief in education as one of the means to facilitate self-perfection, they recalled being preoccupied not so much by the desire to forsake the clergy as by a single-minded yearning to continue their studies. Professor Kistiakovskii claimed in 1895 that he sought a secular higher education only after he was unable to enroll in one of the prestigious theological academies. He wrote a friend on the eve of commencing his studies: "All the same, I really would like to [enroll in a theological academy]. Well, I will try at least to enroll in a university. My father is not in a position to subsidize my studies at a university, but I will without fail enroll. I will be a servant, a slave to whoever will give me a corner and a piece of bread in Kiev, who will shelter me and keep me warm." Another popovich wrote in 1856 that his desire to seek knowledge existed as an autonomous, uncontrollable force that directed the course of his life: "When I graduated from the seminary a pastor's career and quiet family life lay ahead for me. But in my heart the thirst for knowledge seethed. I wanted to study. And this desire arose in me early on. It did not depend on me. As a result, I decided to leave the clerical estate and go to Petersburg University."[44]

Other popovichi, on the other hand, knew exactly what type of knowledge they sought. Having mastered the theological subjects of the seminary, they wished to progress to new secular fields of knowledge. Their longing to study certain secular subjects in depth led them to the university, which, one popovich recalled in 1906, "for us literally represented the promised land . . . the kingdom of ideas such as fraternity, equality, freedom, and pravda." The suicide attempt by Sobolev, whose 1897 note was discussed in the previous chapter, was made when he realized he would not be able to pursue a university education. In his note he wrote: "My noble, passionate desire to study, to receive an education at a higher educational institution in my beloved natural science department, has remained unresolved, unrealized, forever destroyed." Seminarians protested any restrictions imposed on their admittance to higher educational institutions in the late imperial period, and the main complaint they expressed in petitions during the mass rebellion of seminarians throughout Russia in 1905 was their restricted access to these schools.[45]

Regardless of whether they condemned any aspects of clerical life, popovichi generally cited matters of conscience as a reason for their departure. The significant role that popovichi awarded their consciences is evident in an 1866 diary entry written by Ivan Tsvetkov shortly after his decision to leave the clergy: "In my opinion, it is necessary to think, speak and act such, as *my* own mind, *my* own conscience tells me." None of them supported the notion of obligatory clerical service for clergymen's sons. They believed that an individual should be ordained only if he experienced a calling, and if he did not experience this calling, he should leave the clerical estate. An open letter addressed to the intelligentsia in 1905 by striking seminarians addresses the consequences of not allowing clergymen to receive a calling: "A caste needs a product. The product is manufactured in clerical schools. It is here that the reason for the destruction of the clergy may be found."[46] By refusing to serve in the clergy because they lacked an inner call, popovichi demonstrated their respect for both the traditional profession of their forefathers and the new clerical concept of calling.

Popovichi provided three sets of reasons for their departure from the clergy: the chasm between clerical reality and ideals, the desire to obtain a higher education, and the lack of a clerical calling. The specific traits that they described as informing their decision to leave the clerical estate—disdain for the pursuit of material profit, single-minded pursuit of a goal, moralism, abhorrence of corruption, idealism, commitment to self-improvement and respect for scholarship—were also attributes of both the "otherworldly" and the "proto-intelligent" fathers. Although some of these explanations may be rationalizations, popovichi's need to employ such justifications demonstrates that their departure from the clergy did not entail a spiritual break.

Although they retained clerical traditions, their departure was also a sign of the onset of modern selfhood. Popovichi individually chose their own professions in the context of the new and varied choices that their modernizing society offered.[47] Since they did not portray their departure from the clergy as an abandonment of clerical traditions, how did they explain this seeming contradiction of the implementation of clerical ideals in the rapidly changing secular world?

Service Vocations

In a letter to his brother written in 1916, Professor Dmitrievskii demonstrated the extent to which popovichi had internalized the notion of calling for all professions: "It is offensive and difficult to hear about a person who enters a profession not out of calling, but for the sake of a piece of bread." Mamin-Sibiriak wrote his parents in 1872 that choosing a profession was the single most important choice he would make in his life. Writing his brother nearly ten years later, he recalled that a fashionable phrase from his seminary youth was "a job that suits your soul." By entering secular professions in order to implement their clerical ideals, popovichi were thus exhibiting, in the words of Max Weber, "the valuation of the fulfillment of duty in worldly affairs as the highest form which the moral activity of the individual could assume. This it was which inevitably gave everyday worldly activity a religious significance."[48] There are two important differences, however, between the conceptions of vocational calling in late Imperial Russian Orthodoxy and in Weber's Protestant society. First, because of the notion of model piety, members of the clerical estate, as opposed to all Puritans, were the only individuals truly expected to spend each waking moment implementing "good deeds." Second, whereas Protestantism, in Weber's analysis, interpreted divine calling to one's profession as signifying that financial success in one's job was a sign of God blessing one personally, popovichi equated secular calling with self-sacrifice and the duty to serve others.

All of the professions popovichi entered in large numbers were quintessential service professions. Service to the people lay at the heart of the Russian intelligentsia's mission. Noble intelligenty who entered the helping professions, however, shifted their forefathers' military or bureaucratic tradition of service to the state, to service to the people. Popovichi, on the other hand, were able to argue that they were attending to the people's needs just as their forefathers had for generations. Nobles' service to the state also rarely entailed the lifelong commitment that clerical service did.

One historian of the Russian nobility has argued that noble intelligenty in the late nineteenth century had a more patronizing attitude toward service to the people than other members of the intelligentsia.[49] The professions popovichi entered in the largest numbers—education and medicine—were also occupations that many clergymen engaged in, whether as parish teachers or as medics. They were also, consequently, professions nobles had traditionally shunned. Noble professionals might share popovichi's devotion to improving the plight of the peasantry, but they could not claim that they were following in the footsteps of their serf-owning fathers. By entering particular service professions, popovichi were thus able to reconcile their desire to continue clerical traditions with their intelligentsia mission.

The single most popular secular profession among Vladimir seminarians throughout the nineteenth century was education. Popovichi constituted 26 percent of secular secondary schoolteachers and 39 percent of secular primary schoolteachers in the mid-century. Their contribution to education remained steady. In 1880, 32.4 percent of the teachers in secular primary and secondary schools in Russia were from the clergy.[50]

Many popovichi who became teachers perceived themselves as emulating their fathers. One popovich recalled in 1917 the link between the teaching profession he and his brother chose and his father's employment: "He was an outstanding pedagogue. In the church school he was considered one of the best teachers. . . . Without a doubt, my brother and I inherited from our father a proclivity toward pedagogy." For the minority of popovichi in the postreform period whose fathers did not teach in a formal classroom, their fathers still served as a prototype of how to educate the people. One popovich who became a teacher described in 1901 his father's impact on his decision to devote his life to teaching:

> Concerning the question of influences on me during the above mentioned period of my life, the most beneficial influence on the entire turn and character of my intimate sympathies and social convictions, retained for my entire life and guiding the direction of my further social-pedagogical activity, turned out to be the influence of my father, a modest rural priest. He inspired me, both by his personal example and by his kind convictions, love and respect for the peasantry as 'our provider.' I was also undoubtedly inspired by the close contact I had with the peasant world in my early childhood. This contact implanted in my soul good seeds and pure memories, which were subsequently strengthened in me by the thought, inspired by my father, about the necessity and obligation to serve our narod in the sphere of its enlightenment and education.

His words literally parrot Church publicists when he refers to the "holy pedagogical mission."[51]

Other popovichi combined this commitment to enlightening the people with the clerical mission of pursuing knowledge by becoming professors in higher educational institutions. Popovichi comprised 23 percent of professors in 1839, 17 percent in 1875, and 21 percent in 1904. Nobles had largely shunned the professoriate in the prereform period, because until 1863 professors' salaries were quite paltry. Popovichi thus played a major role as the founding fathers of Russian academia: twenty of the thirty-one Russians who taught at Moscow University prior to 1800 were former seminarians.[52]

Popovichi sometimes drew on their clerical background to explain why they chose to enter specific branches of scholarship. In an unpublished Soviet-era autobiography, the sacristan's son and ethnographer Dmitrii Zelenin explained that he was raised in a remote rural village amidst his peasantlike clerical relatives: "folkloric sayings and anecdotes surrounded me from earliest childhood. All of this had its impact later on when I chose my scholarly specialization."[53]

Popovichi's heightened sense of Russian national identity also fueled their prominence in the field of Russian history. They comprised the majority of students enrolled in historical-philology departments in 1875–1876, and in 1880 all the professors in the history department at Odessa University were popovichi. They also dominated the historical-philological department at Kazan University during 1840–1904, as well as Kazan University's Russian history department. Significantly, few popovichi taught in Kazan's world history department, where the majority of professors were of noble origin.[54] Limited exposure to modern Western European culture, the prominence of Russian history in the bursa curriculum, the parish clergy's traditional role as collectors and cultivators of local history and the messianism of national churches within Eastern Orthodoxy all contributed to popovichi's preference for the history of their native land. The study of Russian history was yet another direct service to the people, who comprised the nation, rather than to the state.

The medical profession presented popovichi with the opportunity to serve the people directly while drawing on science as a form of knowledge. Thus they entered the medical profession in large numbers throughout the imperial period, and medicine was the second most popular secular profession among graduates of Vladimir Seminary over the course of the nineteenth century. Popovichi comprised 30 percent of all doctors in 1840; between 1856 and 1864 they constituted 23.3 percent of all doctors in government institutions. In 1880, 43 percent of the medical students at Khar'kov University were popovichi. The social stigma the nobility attached to working with one's hands deterred nobles from studying medicine, even after the Great Reforms. The particular appeal of the medical profession to popovichi, as opposed to individuals from other non-noble social estate groups, is particularly evident in a comparison, based on social origin, of the career patterns of seminarians who graduated from Voronezh Seminary, which traditionally had a high number of nonclergy students. Between 1774 and 1908, one out of four popovichi who studied at Voronezh Seminary became doctors, as opposed to one out of ten *inososlovnye* Voronezh seminarians.[55]

Popovichi doctors in the second half of the nineteenth century gravitated toward service in the countryside as part of the new "service" institution of the zemstvo. In his 1903 biography, one popovich, whose two brothers also served as zemstvo professionals, traced his decision to serve the people as a doctor to his clerical childhood: "We all early in childhood became accustomed to love the simple peasant. We completely consciously devoted ourselves to zemstvo work, hoping, as far as possible, to bring assistance to the simple man." Many other popovichi who became doctors expressed similar sentiments. Others saw their medical service as a direct continuation of their forefathers' profession. Dr. Sychugov explained that whereas his father and grandfather had served the local peasants as priests, he gave up his private practice and returned to his native region to serve them as a zemstvo doctor.[56] By choosing the medical profession, popovichi complemented their fathers' attendance to the spirituality of the people by attending to their physical needs.

The zemstvo employed other professionals such as statisticians, and popovichi entered this profession in large numbers. A popovich employed as a zemstvo statistician explained in a letter to his brother that service lay at the heart of his profession: "To serve people, situated in communication with them—this is a great delight! . . . Regarding my spiritual interests, statistics presents itself in the capacity of service to life and people." Popovichi who entered more unusual professions also tended to explain their decision as motivated by an ethic of service to the nation. The artist Viktor Vasnetsov (1848–1926) wrote a friend in 1897: "he is happy who can plant and develop at least a small seed of good and beauty in his native land."[57]

Popovichi's contribution to the bureaucracy was also significant: they constituted over 17 percent of early nineteenth-century officials, and 20 percent of mid-nineteenth-century officials. But working in the bureaucracy —at any level—was not the first choice of seminary graduates throughout the nineteenth-century, and they entered it in large numbers only during years when they had the least number of other career choices, either before the Great Reforms or after the restrictive Counter-Reforms. A steady fodder for the lowest level of the bureaucracy were "unsuccessful" popovichi who had been unable to complete their bursa studies and had no other choice for employment. By the mid-nineteenth century it became difficult for clergymen's sons who had not at least attended the seminary to obtain clerical positions, even as a sacristan, deacon, or monk. But their legal status and literacy ensured that few, including those who did not manage to complete their primary education, ever became manual laborers.[58] Indeed, popovich who served as lifelong civil servants often explained in their autobiographies that they did not enter the bureaucracy by choice. When they were given a choice, such as what department to study in at universities, they consistently favored the faculties of history, medicine, and science over law, the department that appealed most to noblemen and from which most state officials graduated. Popovichi's association of the former—and not the latter—with social service is evident in Elpat'evskii's characterization of gentry sons who pursued careers in law as having inherited from their fathers' indifference to peasant distress.[59]

There were several reasons why popovichi did not regard service as a clerk or civil servant highly. First, such professions did not directly serve the people. Second, popovichi perceived the civil service as a lucrative profession, accessible to those individuals who possessed connections—that is, nobles. The bureaucracy was a frightening, foreign world that they sensed would never accept them. And since popovichi did not consider material gain to be an acceptable objective, the promise of wealth did not attract them. Lastly, popovichi, like Church publicists, unanimously depicted the bureaucratic system as corrupt, and hence corrupting. Civil servants were forced to take bribes, which adulterated their souls, and grovel, something the sons of the sacred estate were far too proud to endure.[60] In his autobiography published in 1870 one popovich recalled why he did not enter the bureaucracy: "I understood, that without protection it would be difficult for one of us to land a position in government service, and even if he was lucky enough to get a position, it would not be wise to put oneself on such a path, which would lead one to dust and ruin." Both popovichi and parish clergymen recounted horror stories of popovichi employed in the bureaucracy who fell into the depths of alcohol and corruption.[61]

Even more than a bureaucratic career, a career in commerce was considered totally unacceptable by clerical parents and largely shunned by popovichi. Bureaucrats at least served their state, but traders served no one besides themselves. Moreover, the Church hierarchy argued that engaging in commerce ill-suited the pristine character of clergymen's sons—implying that they would fail at business ventures. Yet the rare popovich who became a businessman could justify his profession according to the clerical service ethic. The stockbroker Ivan Tsvetkov, for example, explained in 1909 that his career choice had been motivated by his desire to destroy Russia's poverty and improve the living standards of its people. He believed he could accomplish this by working in these new banks, which provided Russia with the infrastructure for advanced industrial development by offering inexpensive and widely available credit to capitalists. Describing his decision he wrote that "it was already time for me to start life itself, it was time to do something for society," and he contrasted himself to those who sat around doing nothing but enriching themselves in bureaucratic posts. Unlike them, he longed to be useful and active. Ivan eventually used the wealth he acquired to serve Russia in a different fashion: he bequeathed his unique collection of Russian drawings to his nation by giving his house-museum to the city of Moscow.[62]

Popovichi's interest in service careers paralleled the parish clergy's increased activities in these spheres. The latter reflected a new modernized definition of clerical service as devoted to healing the bodies of the population in addition to their souls. Yet unlike the archetype of the "otherworldly" father, popovichi were not content to place their trust in God's will and accept worldly imperfections. Like the "proto-intelligent" father, popovichi believed that their values had to be implemented in the apostolic tradition. But unlike the proto-intelligent model, popovichi felt the need to leave the clergy to act. They were more inclined toward critical thinking than their brothers who remained in the clergy, more willing to take the initiative to change the imperfections of the world. Many popovichi ironically saw entering secular professions as the best means of realizing their ideal of clerical service. By leaving the clergy they sought to break the cycles of dependency that they saw as plaguing the parish clergy. In the more independent climate of the secular professions they believed they would have the opportunity to follow their own consciences and to serve others. Like late Imperial Russian Jews, popovichi expressed a preference for self-employment, or at least jobs unlike the civil service, which allowed them the freedom to act as modern selves. In the 1920s, Elpat'evskii described his choice of profession:

> I vividly recall what was in my soul when I enrolled in the university. There were two motives: the first was a ceaseless, voracious striving toward freedom, toward independence. I chose the department of medicine because there wouldn't be any authorities over me and I would be able to live wherever I wanted, even with those African or American Negroes. I would be needed and useful everywhere. Secondly, in order to conquer the land of darkness, troubled and indefinable. All the same, I felt a fervent pull regarding my personal participation in the dispersal of this land of darkness.[63]

Popovichi presented their entrance into intelligentsia professions and movements as a continuous narrative and as a natural progression from their clerical heritage. They interpreted leaving the clergy as a way to retain their values, and they aspired to realize the ideal of clerical service in the secular world. Their desire was to administer to the needs of the population just as their forefathers had for generations. While in the first decades of the nineteenth century clerical service to the people had primarily been defined in ecclesiastical terms of worship and prayer, in the increasingly more complex society of late Imperial Russia these needs were defined more broadly. The professions popovichi chose to enter have traditionally been defined as distinctive to the intelligentsia, but, in the minds of popovichi and the pastoral care–minded clergy, they were seen as an extension of the clerical profession.

Although popovichi were wedded to continuing clerical traditions, they took advantage of the new opportunities modernization afforded them and acted as modern men, choosing their own professions. Like Weber's Protestants, they transformed and extended monastic asceticism to daily life in the temporal world. Nineteenth-century parish clergymen viewed themselves as competing with the monastic ideal, and as "activist-ascetic" virtuosi they transmitted this ideal to parish life, thereby rejecting the monastic conception of a separation of religious and secular spheres. Popovichi, in turn, inherited this "spiritual aristocracy" from their fathers. But unlike their fathers, they were not content to simply bridge the religious and secular. Like monks, they made the individual choice to leave their formative community behind. And to some extent they were like cenobitic monks and the warrior saints of Byzantium, represented in the Russian tradition by Alexander Nevskii, who wished to bring the church into the world instead of adapting the church to the world, a goal the leaders of the Reformation as well as medieval Franciscans shared in the Christian West.[64] Popovichi, like their fathers, viewed their own salvation as intrinsically tied to their success as moral leaders, making them responsible for the world in a way secular men in Russia had not previously been.

In their attempt to meld clerical and secular worlds, popovichi faced an uphill challenge. They sought to overcome religious dualism and transform an unfamiliar, and often hostile, world into a realm as heavenly as their childhoods, offering the intelligentsia in the process a new source for its commitment to utopian collectivism. Elpat'evskii described his youthful intentions: "a vague dream about a future, when there will be no oppression or persecution, when there will be no violence and torture."[65] To create the world Elpat'evskii described was the daunting task popovichi faced.

The Search for Secular Salvation

In 1899 the popovich Lebedev, an independent farmer living in his native village, fell under suspicion of political impropriety. In a written confession to the police, he explained that he had his own personal conception of salvation, which entailed enlightening the people and doing good deeds.[1] Many popovichi, even those who retained belief in heaven, similarly sought a secular, temporal form of salvation, and they chose to redefine both the clerical salvation mission and the priestly concept of moral leadership by focusing on transforming aspects of the earthly sphere. Their modern conception of agency displaced religion from the central role: believers determined how God fit into their plans rather than trying to understand how they fit into God's plan; unbelievers substituted themselves, science, or the collective for the divine. What linked salvation-minded popovichi was the role they elected for themselves, their single-mindedness, their disregard for boundaries between public and private, and their sense that they were bringing clerical values to the secular world.

The intelligentsia's self-conception as the saviors of Russia has a long history, from Bakunin's 1836 declaration of "raising the earth to the heavens" to the poet Konstantin Bal'mont's 1903 statement that "the idea of creating human happiness on the earth is still dear to me today."[2] Single-mindedness of will and commitment to self-sacrifice, however, have more commonly been associated solely with the quintessential revolutionary. After all, they had been depicted as ideal traits in such classic creeds of postreform Russian radicalism as Sergei Nechaev's *Revolutionary Catechism*. But it was this prototype, the same one Semen Frank lambasted as the populist-minded postreform intelligent, that popovichi, regardless of political affiliation or generation, embraced as their own.

There is an active messianic element inherent in romanticism, a movement imported by Russian intelligenty from Western Europe. But Russian Orthodox clergymen and Church publicists also espoused a service ethic, which bound self-perfection to saving Russia. Romanticism itself, of course, was deeply influenced by Christianity. The existence of these same messianic strains in Russian Orthodox discourse—particularly in clerical prescriptive texts—allowed popovichi to associate their search for secular salvation with their native estate's traditions.

Diaries—

The Secular Confessional

Autobiography implies a search for salvation as the autobiographer attempts to give meaning to his life.[3] In their autobiographical narratives, popovichi explained their salvation mission in secular society, but it was in their diaries that they nurtured and articulated the leadership role that they, as offspring of the sacred estate and modern selves, would play in this mission.

In the late eighteenth century diary keeping became normative for educated Russians. Early diaries often recorded only external events, but writing about the self became an integral part of the genre by the mid-nineteenth century. The intelligent of the 1830s and 1840s cultivated a cult of the "inner man," expressed in the myriad self-revelations in Herzen's diaries and in the correspondence of Bakunin, among others. This new fashion has been attributed to Western influences of self-analysis, reflected in the fervent popularity of Rousseau's *Confessions*. In the nineteenth century diaries became a secular form of confession among French Catholics, motivated by the sense of loss and dislocation brought about by the onslaught of modernity. Russian literary scholars, in turn, have also referred to nineteenth-century Russian diaries as secular confessionals.[4]

In the Orthodox faith confessions have traditionally been an oral exchange between priest and parishioners inside the sanctity of the church walls, recorded in writing only in cases of physical necessity. By the late imperial period, however, the onset of modernity and the pastoral care movement challenged this tenet of the institutional Church. On the one hand, the charismatic priest Ioann of Kronstadt, who attained national celebrity status, received thousands of letters, many of which amounted to written confessions, from believers he had never met. Priests, through the confessional diaries they were enouraged to keep, served as their own personal confessors; this spurred some members of the clerical estate to send written confessions to clergymen relatives.[5]

Many popovichi kept diaries, and the majority of those who did began writing them in the last years of their seminary studies, and most continued only for several years. The ethnographer Dmitrii Zelenin was encouraged to begin his diary by one of his seminary teachers. Zelenin explicitly associated the intense degree to which he engaged in self-examination with the atmosphere fostered in the seminary. He feared that once he left the seminary, his introspection would slacken.[6] Indeed, he only kept a diary from 1895, three years before he completed the seminary, until 1902. Popovichi were trained before they left the clergy to employ diaries to groom themselves, a hallmark of modern selfhood, to save society.

Many diaries are begun at a turning point in an individual's life, when events force a reconfiguration of identity. For popovichi, the time when they chose to leave the clergy—their last few years in the seminary— marked this break, and it is not surprising that this period coincided with their formative adolescent years. They sought to construct a new identity in their diaries, weaving themselves into the messianic mission of both clerical tradition and that of the intelligentsia they were joining.

Popovichi referred to their diary entries as their confessions, as the popovich revolutionary Mikhail Novorusskii (1861–1925) explained in his 1892 prison diary: "Holy week. . . . Here is another day of Easter. Something flutters in my breast at the consideration of that word, that thought. . . . However, my diary will be set up so as not to ignore my inner life. From time to time, now and then, I want to confess, to be cured before someone. . . . It is necessary to carry out this analysis in order to get rid of former mistakes and sins."[7]

As confessions, these diaries served as tools for self-definition and self-improvement to prepare the diarists for their mission. In the first pages of his 1895 diary, the future Moscow Theological Academy Professor Sergei Smirnov reflected on its purpose: "I wish to grow accustomed to keeping an eye on him who is more important than anyone or anything—that is, myself. I want to know myself, to look after and know myself in order to improve myself." Zelenin asks himself "who am I?" throughout his diary. The future bureaucrat Petr Smirnov (b. 1833) confessed in his 1856 diary that he was unable to recognize himself in the mirror. The man he saw and the man he thought he was were incompatible: "What is this lack of character? When on earth will I resemble a person?" Petr proceeds to discover "what makes a person a person." He decides his soul is weak and unaccomplished and that he suffers from "hunger of the mind." In order to become a person he must constantly watch himself, since the "formation of character" according to "moral principles" is the key to his transformation. He quizzes himself: "Have I become completely conscious of all that I should be conscious of and should know?"[8]

Popovichi also express the same self-loathing that is characteristic of the Russian intelligentsia diary genre. Sergei Smirnov explains that his quest for self-improvement is vitally necessary because he is riddled with imperfections. The next line of his diary reads, "Lord, how I am displeased with myself! I am a vague, unfixed, an unfinished creature." Smirnov despised himself because he perceived himself to be an ordinary man, incapable of great feats: "But I do not desire to turn my notes into my personal diary. In the first place, I do not wish to do this because who needs my ordinary personality?" By believing that he *should* be an extraordinary person, Smirnov began to depart from the Christian humility and renunciation he concurrently expressed in his diary. But rather than move, in a linear direction, toward salvation, a standard topos in any religious self-narrative, Smirnov explained that he was digressing, not progressing. In another passage he alludes to the transformation that had occurred: "I now respect myself so little, I so little value that which should be and was once dear to me." Sergei did not, however, cease his pursuit of inner moral perfection. Six months after he began his diary he complained, as other popovichi did, that he had not worked hard enough on himself. Zelenin's anguish about the loss of faith in himself was so great, he considered suicide. Yet he too refused to abandon his self-scrutiny: "I have a choice between happiness and mental work, self-perfection, and I am leaning more toward the last."[9]

Like other popovichi, Sergei Smirnov and Zelenin viewed their former selves, the selves of their childhood, as superior to their present state. Born into the sacred estate, popovichi generally believed that they were "saved" at birth and remained blessed while under the supervision of their saintly fathers. Their autobiographical narratives, therefore, tend to lack the element of conversion and struggle commonplace in religious autobiographies as the saved self recounts the journey to its present state of grace.[10] A popovich may feel estranged from his former self, he never loses sight of it.

Their innate "saved" self rendered popovichi's self-loathing tamer than that of intelligenty from other estate groups. Even though he didn't recognize himself in the mirror as a "person," Petr Smirnov never questioned his ability to become one: "I have been given talents, feelings, ideas, in a word, I have been bestowed with all that is necessary to be a person." Unlike the pious Slavophile Kireevskii, popovichi did not consider their diaries a selfish, unchristian endeavor. Their selves were well worth the attention they lavished on them, and they rarely neglected their diaries for long spells. Zelenin, for example, expressed guilt when he failed to write in his diary for five days, and, like other popovichi, he always found something worth recording. Like Petr Smirnov, he was confident that his diary would enable him to master himself because he was a special self: "Is it necessary to work on your character, to change it. To the extent it is possible. Yes, of course it is possible! And especially for me!"[11]

Popovichi shared the dual contradictory elements of self-affirmation and self-condemnation that characterized the realists of the 1860s; however, their self-affirmation was stronger than other realists, as they were able to draw on their native estate's traditions for their self-respect. As Dobroliubov asserted in a 1855 diary entry, "I am as if purposely chosen by fate for the great purpose of revolution! . . . The son of a priest, raised in the strict rules of the Christian faith and morality, born in the center of Russia, having spent my first years in close contact with the simple and middle classes of society." And while the realists' self-condemnation stemmed from their realization that the task ahead of them was so immense that it was unattainable, popovichi began to think that whatever tasks they set for themselves were surmountable if they returned to their true selves.[12]

In fact, when they compared themselves to others, popovichi typically ceased any self-castigation and explicitly portrayed themselves as extraordinary individuals. Ivan Tsvetkov wrote in his diary in 1866:

> It seems to me that if I had not been ruined to the point of near death in that diabolical seminary, but had developed correctly both morally as well as physically, that I would have been God only knows who, simply a remarkable man among Russians. And now, despite all the damage done to me, I can find among my comrades, either from the seminary or from the gymnasium, not a single person who possesses more vigorous analysis or a stronger character.

Dr. Sychugov took Tsvetkov's immodesty a step further: "For a long time the peasants have been saying that I do not live like other people live, but rather that I live in a godly manner."[13] They believed they were morally superior, a trait Semen Frank denounced the postreform intelligent for.

Popovichi's diaries are often organized around units of time, including meticulous records of what they did during every single hour of every day.[14] Their lives, like the rigid bursa regime, had to be structured carefully since every moment of every day was crucial in their quest for self-perfection. Popovichi strove to perfect themselves to achieve their own salvation, and, in keeping with both the clerical and intelligentsia mission, to save others. The first was a prerequisite to fulfilling the second, as one popovich explained in his turn-of-the-century autobiography: "make myself a person first, and then think about others." In his diary, Zelenin referred to the abnormality of contemporary society. The definition of happiness he articulated in his diary expressed a desire to rectify these deficiencies: "happiness does not lie in emotional pleasures, which appear in the most varied ways, but in correcting the unhappiness of those close to you." Otherwise, he said, "I will always think of myself as a hypocrite, a failure." To ready himself for his mission, Zelenin drew up a blueprint of the ideal teacher whom he could model himself upon before serving as a church school teacher in 1898. This desire to save the world was even voiced by a popovich whose 1850s diary was held up by a priest in 1880 as a model of the ascetic practices of fasting, praying, and worshipping in church. Employed as a teacher in a gymnasium, he also engaged in self-analysis, so that in part he could fulfill "my duty to take part in the fate of my fatherland."[15] The modern clerical self embodied by popovichi differed from the traditional clerical self; popovichi, empowered by self-confession, believed that the clerical self alone was able and required to transform the temporal world.

In his diary, Zelenin displayed his fascination with major non-clerical Russian thinkers of the day, such as Dostoevskii and Tolstoi. Yet it was the early Christians that he identified as his role model. He admired their high morality, self-sacrifice, and, first and foremost, their devotion to a single ideal. If all lived according to the rules of the early church, Zelenin concluded, society would be saved. According to him, this was not only possible, but a clear vision of the future: "our ideal, the ideal of Christianity, is not at all behind us, but lies ahead." He would save himself and society through devotion to the single ideal of scholarship, which he literally referred to as "my salvation."[16]

Not all popovichi secularized salvation in the same way. Some shared Zelenin's choice of their professions as a vehicle to achieve secular salvation; others sought it in political or personal realms. In some cases the ideal they sought changed over the course of their lives. Generally, however, they did not seek more than one ideal simultaneously, since the pursuit of their particular ideal of salvation was all-consuming and single-minded. In their pursuit of secular salvation they sought to transform the sphere of their influence into a heaven on earth, thereby secularizing clerical models.

Salvation in the Professional Sphere

Unlike the stereotypical noble-born sloth immortalized in Goncharov's *Oblomov*, postreform intelligenty increasingly fashioned themselves as hardworking. One noble intelligent remarked at the turn of the century that the main interest in his life was work, "but not in terms of its external, but in terms of its inner aspects." Another expressed guilt in his 1903 autobiography for his laziness during his student years. A worker intelligent concluded his 1920s autobiography by declaring his joy that at the age of seventy he was still extremely productive.[17]

By contrast, the older generation of popovichi already valued industriousness in their prereform narratives, as did popovichi throughout the nineteenth century in narratives written before they left the clergy. Unlike intelligenty from other estates, popovichi were able to link their work ethic directly to their estate heritage. For example, after remarking that his father believed that work was more important than socializing, one popovich declared in 1906, "I believe that he was entirely correct." Popovichi portrayed themselves as imbued with the same industriousness they had attributed to their saintly fathers, a trait for which Russian saints and clergymen were praised. Yet because clergymen could not devote themselves wholeheartedly to their professional ideal due to their many duties and financial constraints, popovichi left the clergy in part precisely so that they could achieve their fathers' ideal. As they secularized the salvation mission, they redefined sacrality and work. Work became sacred in a way it had not been before in secular society; popovichi often referred to their workplace, be it a laboratory or a university, as a "temple."[18] For many popovichi, their professional activities were now their salvation.

Because it could be a source of salvation, popovichi did not begrudge their labor; rather, it was a source of immense gratification, even joy. As Ivan Tsvetkov wrote his nephew in 1910, "a person is constructed so that only work can impart happiness to him." Popovichi often found that work served as a source of comfort during a crisis. For example, when the writer Blagosvetlov lost his job as a teacher and was unemployed and penniless for nine months, he explained in his 1856 official statement to his former employer that he turned to work: "amongst the constant spiritual anxieties and apprehensions about the unknown future, I shut myself in the quiet of the office and sought activity." Nevertheless, popovichi did not depict work as easy. Ivan Tsvetkov portrayed himself in his 1909 autobiography as a saintly martyr, who worked eighteen hours a day even when he was in poor health.[19] Self-sacrifice, a key element of the salvation process, was necessary to achieve happiness.

Popovichi also emulated the prescriptive clerical genre and developed the intelligentsia self by condemning recreational activities that detracted from work. Describing his years as a medical student, one popovich wrote in 1893: "I had no friends; the means for leisure were even less. Moreover, I had no inclination toward it." Professor Ivan Pomialovskii referred in his 1870 diary to the few hours of the week when he was not working, reading, or attending church, as meaningless: "I did nothing." Leisure, which played such an important role in defining the rituals of noble identity, was condemned as selfish since it served no goal other than pleasure.[20] Like Frank's intelligent, they were utilitarians to their very core.

Some popovichi took this denial of pleasure to an extreme, finding fulfillment of their personal needs only in their work. Professor Dmitrievskii was married in 1899 but remained unable or unwilling to consummate the union; his wife eventually divorced him. In a letter to his wife written in the early 1900s he described how his romantic passion was satisfied by his work: "Scholarship [*Nauka*] is the most charming of the women in the world. It is so affectionate, so tender to me, that with its embrace it takes care of all the afflictions and misfortunes of life." Numerous other non-radical and radical popovichi never married, instead choosing a life of celibacy outside of monasticism, a life Orthodox publicists preached was reserved for only the chosen few. Several radicals from other social estate groups described themselves as having done the same, but such a sacrificing of one's personal life by non-popovichi who were not radicals was rare.[21] This decision by some popovichi not to marry was another break with their clerical past, since all parish priests were obligated to marry prior to ordination.

Often, once popovichi established a particular pursuit as the source of their salvation, they devoted themselves to it zealously, declaring that they had forsaken interest in unrelated pursuits. If they were in the midst of pursuing a single-minded goal, such as education or work, many popovichi claimed that they could not allow themselves to entertain the thought of marriage, even when they felt themselves to be in love. One radical popovich, on the other hand, recalled that during his years as a student at Petersburg Medical Academy he purposely disavowed any political yearnings in order to devote himself purely to his studies. Only when he left the academy did he turn to politics, which he embraced as the new purpose of his life by becoming a full-time revolutionary. Popovichi were so single-minded that it was impossible for them to pursue two goals at once—even, in some cases, a personal and a professional life—since this would force them to divide their fervor. A number of popovichi scientists, in turn, specifically ignored the precept of political activism held sacred by the intelligentsia, including their fellow scientists from other estates. They maintained that their professional enthusiasm eclipsed any interest in politics.[22]

Popovichi often portrayed the pursuit of professional goals as utterly consuming. Professor Mikhail Koialovich (1828–1891), a prominent historian of the Uniate confession, described in 1856 his attitude toward his scholarly work: "I thought the entire year only about the Uniate, I breathed it, dreamed about it when I slept. It became my most beloved pursuit, the best food for my mind."[23] It was this zealousness that characterized the postreform intelligent Semen Frank admonished.

When they failed, or perceived that they had failed, to achieve perfection in their work, they felt anguish. They had failed their mission and therefore had fallen from grace. The conservative bureaucrat Tikhonov, whose first employment was as a teacher, recalled the tremendous torment he endured after he taught his first class: "I felt that I had done something terribly bad, something along the lines of a crime. My soul became so troubled, I was embarrassed and ashamed. Tears were ready to gush from my eyes. I grievously conceded that I had not at all executed in the class what should have been done." In the seminarian Sobolev's 1897 suicide note, he expressed self-loathing over his inability to attain the ideal of his life and attend the university: "I still feel sufficiently filthy. What is it that allows me to end my life so easily, to once and for all sever the tie to my dreams and ideals? My ideal! You poor thing, the goal of my unattractive, refuse of a life—now you will remain undigested and regurgitated!"[24]

When they were not able to concentrate fully on their work, as was the case temporarily for Sergei Smirnov, they often expressed agony. Smirnov noted in his diary: "Perhaps my academic torment has abandoned me for a time. So I live the life of an orphan. It does not cast questions, does not irritate my head, does not agitate my blood. It's terrible, just terrible."[25] They could not live without their goal because their entire sense of self, their very salvation, lay in its pursuit.

Salvation in the Political Sphere

Clergymen were largely restricted from entering the political arena. For their sons, however, political activism became a second sphere in which to seek secular salvation. Popovichi who became politically active expressed the same consummate devotion to politics that distinguished other popovichi's attitude toward work. The popovich populist revolutionary Aleksei Teplov (1852–1920), for example, explained in 1917 what his political activity meant to him: "The ideal of happiness for the common folk, based on the principles of socialism, and more importantly on love of the folk, this ideal became the basis of my life."[26]

Popovichi's anti-authoritarianism, their antipathy toward compromising what they believed to be absolutes, their cohesive sense of identity based on their clerical childhoods and schooling, and their allegiance to the nation above all were manifested in their general aversion toward joining political parties, a trend that priests also exhibited. Elpat'evskii contrasted these traits in 1926 to the congeniality and submissiveness of the quintessential nobleman in his description of his friend Mamin-Sibiriak: "It was dangerous to offend Mamin. He could answer harshly; he was not a man of the salons. He was a populist in the best and the simplest sense of the word, but he did not belong to a party, he could not confine himself to any party shackles." Many other popovichi, along with some non-popovichi, described their decision not to join a party in the same words.[27] Popovichi's dogmatic steadfastness to their individual convictions was also a central trait of Frank's postreform intelligent.

Popovichi embraced traditional, rural values, which explains why it was as populists that they made their most significant contribution to the revolutionary movement. As table 2 demonstrates, the participation of popovichi in radical movements culminated at the height of the populist movement in the 1870s, when they constituted 20–25 percent of all radicals. Yet once populists began to form political parties in earnest, popovichi's involvement with the movement dipped. Between 1905 and 1907 only one out of thirty-seven members of the Central Committee of the Social Revolutionary Party, the heirs of the populist movement, was a popovich. Their contribution to other newly formed Russian political parties was just as insignificant; only 0.4 percent of Bolsheviks who joined before 1917 were popovichi, and of the Central Committee members of parties whose social origin was recorded, there was only one popovich among forty-six Social Democrats (1898–1910); two popovichi out of fifty-nine Bolsheviks (1903–1918) and only a handful of popovichi were on the Central Committees of liberal, centrist, and far-right parties, such as the Kadets, Octobrists, and Union of Russian People.[28]

Popovichi were so sure of the correctness of their convictions, and the fallaciousness of their peers, that one popovich explained in his 1905 autobiography his lack of membership in a political party as a negation of

Table 2—Popovichi in the Revolutionary Movement

Years	Total	Total with origin*	Sons of clergy	Went to Seminary†	Popov'ny
1850s	954	308	2.8%	0.3%	0
1860s	1,356	567	12.5%	5.5%	0.4%
1870s	6,956	2,765	18.5%	4%	2.3%
1880s	6,532	4,041	10.7%	1.2%	1.2%
1880–1904	2,530	1,065	3.4%	1.1%	0.6%

Source: Calculated from *Deiatelia revoliutsionnogo dvizheniia*, vols. 1–3, 5 in ten parts, Moscow, 1927–1934; and unpublished vols. 1–25 in the State Historical Library in Moscow (GPIB) and OR RGB, f.520, k.55, d.1–2. Based on individuals arrested, searched, or monitored by the Russian government. Data through the 1870s are complete. Data for the 1880s include individuals whose last names began with the letters A-Z, I-P, S, Shch, E. Data for the Social democrats (1880–1904) include individuals whose last names began with the letters A-Gm.

* Percentages that follow are based on the total of individuals whose social origin is recorded.

† Since a small percentage of seminarians were not clergymen's sons, seminarians without their social origin recorded have been listed separately.

everyone around him: "all the time I remained in the deepest recesses of my soul a nonparty person (*bezpartiinyi*), all the time I skeptically and critically related to everything that my colleagues did." As disharmonious as their approach to politics was, popovichi understood their aversion to political parties as a rejection of particularism in favor of the universalistic. Adhering to an organic ideal of Russia similar to the church's metaphor of the body of society, they were willing to oppose anyone else's leadership of Russia by asserting that such leadership—unlike their own—would divide the country. One popovich, for example, explained in 1917 that his late brother ultimately joined the Kadets, not because he wanted to take sides in the struggle between Russian political parties, but because he thought the Kadets were the party most dedicated to uniting Russia. Like the Tsar, many popovichi endeavored, as did their fathers, to remain "above politics" (*nadpartiinost'*), a concept that became a mantra of the intelligentsia in the early twentieth century, even after political parties were legalized in 1906.[29] Their concept of a single, unified, political viewpoint was a modernization and secularization of the power of the pastorate.

Pravda (truth-as-justice) was heralded by both the postreform radical populist intelligentsia and the Bolsheviks, so much so that it became the name of the main Soviet newspaper. Popovichi of all generations and political orientations, however, including those who were not politically active, emphasized their commitment to this conception of truth, which was inculcated in them by their bursa teachers and Church publicists. In 1836 one popovich bureaucrat wrote his brother: "let pravda and honor be your leaders!" Ivan Tsvetkov's rejection of the revolutionary movement did not deter him from writing his brother in the 1860s: "something evil overcomes me and I don't want to write any more. Indeed, if only so-called *pravda-spravedlivost'* existed." Professor Nikolai Glubokovskii (1863–1937), a monarchist, eulogized his brother on the eve of World War I by referring to social justice: "He maintained an unshakable faith in the triumph of pravda and fought for it."[30] Popovichi did not have to advocate overthrowing the Tsarist government to desire to serve as warriors correcting injustices and thereby perfecting the earthy realm.

As warriors, popovichi were also committed to living the life of "ascetic self-restraint" Semen Frank assailed. The ascetic tradition was dedicated to denying the world; popovichi, buoyed by reform-minded Church publicists, secularized this tradition by entering the world and rejecting its present incarnation. The revolutionary Nikolai Tregubov compiled a list of personal commandments in 1917 that reflects this secularized asceticism, rooted in Orthodox tradition. His list included: "do not engage in sexual activity, do not have thoughts about sex, do not fall in love, do engage in physical labor, do not eat certain foods, go to sleep early, do not smoke, do exercise." But Tregubov, who subsequently reconverted to Christianity, associated his ascetic self-denial with Christian mysticism as well as a commitment to rational care of the self associated with modernity. His list of commandments also included: "elevate and preserve your spirit from error" and "always reason and act in accordance with logic."[31]

In their asceticism, radical popovichi were able to draw on prototypes created not only by Church publicists, but also by their fellow popovichi. Preobrazhenskii's description of his life in the revolutionary underground in 1905, for example, emulates Rakhmetoff, the ascetic hero of Chernyshevskii's *What Is to Be Done?*, who slept on a bed of nails: "Because of the absence of a bed in my room I slept on the floor on top of two newspapers. I ate only salami and bread, spending not more than twenty kopecks a day, and each evening I walked by foot to Bezhintsa and back, so that I covered eighteen versts."[32]

Many popovichi portrayed themselves as above material concerns, particularly in relation to their fellow citizens. The conservative bureaucrat Tikhonov recalled in his 1912 autobiography his dislike of his fellow teachers during his initial employment as a schoolteacher:

> All the same, a rapprochement between me and them did not follow. They were all distinguished by too much pragmatism, and they possessed too little love toward school affairs and toward poetry in general. As it now appears to

me in recollection, they were all of the American primary schoolteacher sort. Outside of school he is simply a citizen, concerned with earning himself a better piece of bread.

Their greed was so alien to Tikhonov that he resorted to comparing them to foreigners. For his part, Tikhonov portrayed himself as more than willing to forego physical comfort. After being reproached for his modest financial position during his employment as a schoolteacher, "I said to myself, that if the unpleasantries of a teacher's rank are limited only to the inability to carouse, I am prepared to remain a teacher forever and I intend never to conceal from people that I do not have enough to eat or drink." Tikhonov, who subsequently earned a substantial amount of money as a bureaucrat, was critical of his wealth, noting at the end of his life that, although he was fifty times richer than his father ever was, his father nevertheless lived a happier life.[33]

Popovichi's disdain for material consumption and accumulation did not, however, prevent any of them, regardless of their political sentiments, from portraying themselves as the deprived, living at the mercy of the wealthy. Their poverty had been a source of superiority in their bursa memoirs; in their narratives of life in secular society, it continued to be not only a source of martyrdom, but also a source of resentment. Some complained in their autobiographies about being aware of how badly dressed they were in comparison with others. The fact that they often had to live in debt at different points in their adult lives angered them. Regardless of their relative poverty at the height of whatever professional success they achieved, they, like their fathers, tended to regard their financial status as paltry in comparison with the wealth of others.[34] They blamed this contradiction between their preoccupation with financial matters and their asceticism on secular society, whose inequities forced them to concern themselves with the material.

Radical popovichi, those most likely to have abandoned their religious faith, described their political convictions as a complete system of belief, and several of them even directly linked their politics with the salvation mission by characterizing the Russian revolutionary movement as religious. Looking back in the 1920s, Elpat'evskii described Russian radicalism as "religious, not in the sense of a particular religion, but in the sense of the stamp religiosity imposes on a person . . . nothing seizes a person and permeates him so thoroughly, his behavior, his daily life, all of his life, as religion does." He referred to revolutionaries as apostles and martyrs, reminiscent of the first Christians the non-political popovich Zelenin sought to emulate.[35] Radical popovichi were not the only Russian revolutionaries to describe their politics as a religion. Herzen described his youthful conversion to radicalism as "a religion of a different sort that took hold of my soul." Vera Figner explained that Christian ideals "are implanted in all of us, consciously or unconsciously, from our cradles." Elpat'evskii's characterization of the Russian revolutionary movement as religious departed from that of his radical peers from other estates, however, when he added a nationalistic element. He contrasted French and Russian revolutionaries, noting that Russian radicals were characterized more by strict personal morality and an ascetic lifestyle. That popovichi brought a secularized religious morality to the revolutionary movement was apparent to their contemporaries from other estates. In her reminiscences of the radical movement of the 1860s, written at the turn of the century, Elizaveta Vodovozova described the revolutionary fervor of the raznochintsy as substantially different than the radicalism of noble youths: "imbued with an ardent faith, rather than wholesale negation. . . . They passionately believed that it was possible to accomplish all of these benefits in the very near future."[36] And, this fervor, expressed in their asceticism, steadfastness of convictions, and commitment to pravda, was shared by popovichi regardless of political beliefs. Rooted as it was in their heritage, this fervor could also be applied to different spheres, including the personal.

Salvation in the Personal Sphere

As Russian intellectual historians have long noted, love and relationships with women took on greater significance for Russian intelligenty of the 1830s and 1840s than for their contemporary peers in Western Europe. Traditionally, the cultural sources of this phenomenon have been identified as German romanticism, French Christian socialism, and Hegelian idealism. It has been argued that even after the decline of romanticism, the Russian intelligentsia continued to imbue the personal with universal meaning, infusing their private lives with political significance. One's personal love for a single woman was intrinsically connected to the liberation of humanity; love activated a man, enabling him to save society. Idealization of women, symbols of the heart of society, was the perfect means to this end, and sectors of the intelligentsia voiced it by granting central importance to the question of women's rights, even in a country where few people, male or female, had any rights at all.[37]

It was the realm of love, already highly politicized by the prereform intelligentsia, that served as the third sphere in which many popovichi temporarily sought salvation. They offered a new twist on the idealization of private life, one that permanently altered the postreform intelligentsia's perception of morality, individuality, femininity, and leadership. Popovichi shared the prereform noble intelligentsia's idealization of love and marriage. But, for most of them, the idealization of love and marriage did not entail the idealization of women. Love was less a means of rescuing humanity than a means of achieving their own personal salvation. Saving themselves ultimately would save society, but this deliverance would require society—and the women they loved—to submit to popovichi, not the other way around. Attempting to spurn any values—including some of those associated with love and marriage—that they perceived to be noble and Westernized, they turned to clerical love as a model. But this clerical love had to be secularized, since the prescriptive model called for marital symmetry, for two beings to be joined in a singular organic identity. Popovichi, on the other hand, sought to transform their partners from subject to object. Their secularization of clerical love was also the result of differences in circumstances. For their fathers, although prescribed to seek love, were seldom able to find it, at least initially, since prior to their ordination they often had to marry brides whom they hardly knew. And, for their fathers, salvation, in any case, was to be enjoyed only in heaven.

Romantic love is an integral part of the modern self. Historians of Europe and the United States have argued that romantic love became invested with religious significance in the nineteenth century. It became a new salvation, either because of the individualism inherent in Protestantism's central focus on the direct interaction between an individual soul and God, whereby a desacralization of consciousness allowed the relationship between man and woman to be substituted for that of God and believer, or, in the case of Catholicism, the disorientation brought about by modernity, which compelled individuals to seek out a trusted confidant in a changing, unfamiliar world steeped in individuation.[38] Popovichi's secularization of love, then, was part of a trend in modern Western culture. But their identity as members of the sacred estate shaped the particular way in which they expressed their secularized attitudes toward love not only in their marriages but in their friendships as well.

The unhappy romances that crop up in Victorian novels are absent from the clerical model. Either love existed in a clerical marriage or it did not; its absence was regretted, but the emotion of love itself was not marked by pain or drama. For popovichi, the loss of the ideal of love could destroy them. The same Pomialovskii who inaugurated the bursa genre died at the age of twenty-eight after the noble parents of the girl he loved refused to let her marry him and married her off to someone else instead. On the eve of his death in 1862, he wrote a friend: "I loved her for five years, for five years I thought only about her and breathed her, prayed for her." As long as Pomialovskii had had hopes of her love he had controlled the alcoholism to which he now abandoned himself.[39] Pomialovskii's narrative of love reads like a romantic novel, yet he was a quintessential realist, a new man of the 1860s. The zeal and single-mindedness that Pomialovskii and numerous other popovichi displayed in their private lives—virtually identical to the manner in which other popovichi sought political and professional ideals—was rooted not only in romanticism, but in their particular secularization of the salvation mission.

Many popovichi who loved a woman tended to perceive her as a remote object. In the diary he kept while he was at the seminary in 1856, Fedor Giliarov, who was later employed as a gymnasium teacher, records falling in love with a girl he glimpsed in church. He finds out everything he can about her and proceeds to arise at five in the morning each week to be sure to secure a place in church where he will have a good view of her. Although he can imagine nothing more blissful than receiving her hand in marriage, he is completely pessimistic about the possibility of attaining her love. He doubts that she will ever pay attention to him or that her parents would consider him as suitable: "Well, and what is that point of going on about that which *can not be.* They will marry her off to some piggish merchant, who will not know her worth. And I am supposed to simply hide, to be silent and not show my face." At one point, he thinks it would be splendid if she married his relative, since then he would have frequent opportunities to see her. Giliarov never considers disclosing his feelings to the object of his devotion: "However, I do not want her to notice my love for her. I want to love her so that no one besides myself knows about it, even her." In fact, he never even makes her acquaintance.[40]

Numerous other popovichi who actually met the object of their idealization also refrained from declaring their love. The bureaucrat Petr Smirnov recorded in his 1856 seminary diary a walk he took with the girl he loved: "it was already dark. Together we went to the garden and strolled for a long time. We spoke . . . about the ideals of the soul, about what we liked and what we loved . . . I wanted to say, that you [thou] are my ideal—but my heart became confused and protested against this." Some popovichi described themselves as hesitating so long to declare their love that they lost their beloved to another suitor. Others were plagued by indecision and never mustered the courage to propose.[41] Having lost the object of their desire, many popovichi then took the extreme step of choosing to remain bachelors for their entire lives.

Most popovichi claimed that self-consciousness was not the only reason for their hesitancy. Some depicted themselves as unwilling to settle for a union with a woman who fell short of their ideal of a marriage partner. Arranged marriages were abhorrent to them; they would settle only for true love with the woman of their dreams.[42] Because they defined love as a complete fusion of souls, their definition of love elicited the expectation of a total harmony of viewpoint. Unsure he could achieve this, Ivan Tsvetkov rationalized his decision not to marry his beloved in his 1866 diary: "I was ready to marry her. But at the same time I thought: will she be a complete helper to me in all of my matters and senses? Will she agree to endure together with me all the labors, unpleasantries, and hardships that may await me in life? In a word, will she be my loyal ally and friend in every respect?"[43]

Popovichi tended to conceive of love not as a symmetry of two individuals, but rather as the complete surrender of one individual to another. Imbued by their innate sense of superiority, they expected the women they loved to submit entirely to them, a rejection of the concept of the inherent worth of each individual that is part of Christian doctrine. Professor Dmitrievskii, who never consummated his marriage, might appear to have managed to preserve his wife as his ideal, but he attempted nevertheless to instruct her in how she should live her life. He became enraged when she did not follow his instructions. He continually chided her for her "frivolity." On the eve of World War I, when she finally fell in love with another man, after resisting for over a decade her husband's and doctor's orders to take a lover to relieve a nervous condition, she found herself pregnant. Dmitrievskii exercised the ultimate moral authority over her by refusing to grant her the divorce she needed to marry the father of her child. He was perfectly willing to allow her to replace him with another husband, he wrote her, as long as *he* judged the groom a suitable mate for her.[44]

Many popovichi evaluated potential mates by their degree of submissiveness. One conservative explained his decision to annul his engagement in his 1923 autobiography: "This fiancée was a not particularly beautiful girl, but not ugly, very intelligent and superbly educated. But I noticed that she had a very imperious character and that she had a tendency to keep her husband under her thumb." No matter how much popovichi desired to seek salvation in love, weakness toward the opposite sex was never an option. A friend summed up in 1893 the attitude of the popovich populist writer Karonin toward women:

> In general, he ridiculed, or shall we say slighted, weakness toward the female sex. Regarding the "female question," about which he read a great deal of literature, he devised a particular, completely perfected, ideal, which none of the young ladies with whom he was acquainted fulfilled. Despite all of his cordiality in relations, it seems that he ignored women who did not fit the ideal he constructed. If he later married, then I am convinced that his beloved conformed to his conception of a pure woman.[45]

Women were required to fit their ideal; popovichi were not apt to consider modifying themselves to appeal to women. Their aversion to any notion of compromising their convictions in political affairs spilled over into their personal lives. A woman was just as difficult to commit to as a political party.

Indeed, women were even more suspect than political parties. Unlike their noble peers, popovichi did not place women on a pedestal. Even a popovich such as Dobroliubov, who despite never marrying idealized women in his professional writings, expressed misogynist sentiments in his diary. At sixteen Dobroliubov fell in love with a twelve-year-old girl. Although she was still a child, he described her as manipulative, as possessing "a woman's cunning" that he feared. In his 1832 autobiography, the bureaucrat Aleksandr Orlov launches into an indictment against women: "I did not worship the ignorance of the female sex and I still to this day am surprised that voluptuaries delight in the art of their insidiousness. . . . I have seen everything in them except humanity!" He then recalls his nighttime trysts with peasant girls, from which he would awaken completely disenchanted and jaded: "the ideal of beauty deceived me. I wanted to love romantically, but romances should stay in one's head. . . . To tell the truth, I never wanted to marry."[46] Women, imbued with the material (in the guise of their beauty), were unworthy of being pursued by some popovichi as their single ideal.

In some cases, popovichi refused to marry because they did not want to consummate their marriage vows. Numerous memoirists report being deeply affected by their reading of Tolstoi's *Kreitserova sonata*, despite the Church's objections to the novel's condemnation of sexual activity within marriage. Some of the noble-born idealists of the 1830s, including Nikolai Stankevich and Bakunin, also never married, fearing that the ideal of love would be ruined by physical contact with the material. In the case of popovichi, however, their puritanicalism stemmed less from fear of defiling the object of their idealization; rather, they dreaded being infected by contact with a lesser being. Fedor Giliarov didn't want his beloved to know about his love, because his feelings were a part of his dialogue with himself. Contact—in his case of any type—would lead to a loss of self. Sex has been identified as particularly problematic in utopian fantasies, which are in essence sealed to keep out imperfections, and in the case of popovichi the utopia was their all-important selves.[47]

Popovichi accepted the prescriptive clerical view of women as potential seductresses. Most popovichi described themselves as possessing puritanical views of sex. The Bolshevik Voronskii, for example, wrote that after his cousin explained the facts of life to him by describing how he had been seduced by his teenage peasant nanny, he cried hysterically. He was repulsed by what he had heard and lost his respect for adult society. At the opposite end of the political spectrum, the bureaucrat Tikhonov recalled that he was disgusted by the lovers kept by many of the students in the Forestry Academy he had attended as a youth. As was the case with Voronskii, it was the women and not the men involved who repulsed him. The clothes, manners, and jargon of these women horrified him. Professor Dmitrii Rostislavov, in his 1877 memoirs, describing his childhood in the 1810s, actually made a direct reference to these clerical prescriptive gender models: "I felt awkward and uncomfortable around women and girls. Could it be that my mind was influenced by ascetic ideas that women were temptresses?"[48]

Popovichi were also inclined to conceive of women as prone to possess the other traits of the "bad" wife of prescriptive clerical literature. In one of his bursa compositions, for example, the archaeologist Aleksandr Nikitskii (1859–1921) wrote: "Women especially, having been freed by Peter the Great from sequestering, strove for luxury." In an article published in an underground Vladimir Seminary journal in 1873, the author concluded that women were better off living in the East where some were kept in harems: "They are much happier than European women, who suffer from agitated passions, ambition and envy."[49]

Whereas noble intelligenty described the physical attributes of the women they loved in great detail, few popovichi dwelled on the appearance of their beloveds. When popovichi did write about external beauty, they generally did not accept the aristocratic ideal of feminine charm. European, or "modern" women were the object of seminarians' scorn, and renunciation of them was one more way to attack the Westernized nobility. In 1906 one popovich recalled a girl who smoked, read, and argued: "We embodied in her our conception of a 'modern' girl, and we related to her derisively. We found her unattractive." Another referred in 1913 to a girl as attractive because she did not flirt like other women, because she was "simple and natural, like Mother Nature herself."[50] Popovichi criticized most women for precisely the same reasons they attacked the nobility: they associated both with attachment to material objects and sentimentalism.

Popovichi's general rejection of femininity, which their noble peers embraced, can be explained by their wholesale adoption of a masculine ideal steeped in the virtues of Christian manliness. They had, after all, chosen their patriarchal fathers as their role models. But their portrayal of courage during their bursa ordeal, the will-power and self-control they saw themselves as embodying in their asceticism, and the heroism they saw in their commitment to an impersonal cause, are also all traits associated with modern masculinity.[51] In their minds, the clerical model they embodied was exclusively male. Unlike their fathers, who understood the necessity of both genders, popovichi attempted a radical synthesis of the two that entailed the surrender of the feminine half. As warriors attempting to transform the temporal sphere (with the clerical world occupying a higher position in the tripartite division of the universe), they needed to distinguish themselves from all that was traditionally associated with that sphere. Misogyny, rather than love, tended to activate them. They were willing to acknowledge a role, albeit secondary, for the feminine (their mothers) in the clerical world, but that world, unlike the temporal, was perfect. There was no role for women in their vision of society. Building heaven on earth entailed identifying and removing sin, an act that led to the disjunction between the balance of binary constructs, of sacred and temporal, that characterized their fathers' worldview.

Some romantics of the 1830s experienced a somewhat similar crisis over what they perceived to be a gulf between their ideal of love and their inability to achieve it; but they blamed themselves—not the women—for the failure. The radical intelligentsia of the next generation saw private life as insignificant compared to their public mission. In his diary, the anarchist Prince Petr Kropotkin never even mentioned his wife. In an 1862 entry he stated: "In general, I was not created for women and women not for me." The post-1905 intelligentsia has been portrayed as making private life public, just as an identifiable misogyny was emerging among the worker Bolsheviks who joined its ranks.[52] By contrast, over the course of the century, popovichi who chose to have an intimate life tended to try to force their private lives to follow the same criteria they and other popovichi applied to their public lives. Those who did not seek a private life did not view intimacy as insignificant; on the contrary, it was so significant that it could not be pursued simultaneously with a professional or political goal. Popovichi sought in the nineteenth century, albeit unsuccessfully, to collapse the dichotomy between public and private. While the intelligentsia's conception of private life wavered, the popovichi's commitment to it—along with their attack on femininity—did not.

The marital difficulties the Tregubov brothers endured provide a case study of what could happen when popovichi actually married and consummated their marriages. The three brothers had different professional and political affiliations (political radicalism, like professional success, did not tend to run in particular families): Ivan was a leader of the Tolstoyian sectarian movement; Nikolai, a zemstvo statistician and onetime member of the Social Democrat party, appears to have been a victim of early Soviet terror; Anasii (b. 1863) was an engineer unaffiliated with any political movement, who worked in the ministry of trade in Baku in the 1920s before becoming a professor. But their relationships with women followed similar patterns and resembled the travails of numerous other popovichi.

On the eve of his marriage, Nikolai Tregubov expressed great hope in a letter to his brother Ivan:

> I have constantly suffered directly from a deficiency of close, open, friendly relations with a certain person, with whom I would be able to share all, all of my thoughts and ideas. . . . I know this teacher now for two years already. Given the nature of her sympathies and opinions, she is suitable for me. . . . She will be a very close friend and sincere comrade. And that moral loneliness has been simply killing me. I am afraid that I could go out of my mind from yearning.

Once he married, however, Nikolai soon found that his wife did not meet his high expectations. He accused her of not following his orders, of opposing him, of not loving him. To punish her for her disloyalty, Nikolai beat her and forbade her to speak. His misogyny stemmed in part from his anger over not being able to realize his ideal. Yet unlike the Victorians, who blamed mismatched partners for a failed marriage, Nikolai took the modernist approach by actually questioning marriage as an institution. In fact, he took the modernist view a step further, questioning the existence of romantic love. Love, he wrote his brother, was not only "nonsense" and an "illusion," it was also by its nature selfish: "only egoists engage in love, people with narrow, small mental worlds." He even reasoned that it was wrong to love one's child and not love the children of others.[53] Nikolai completely repudiated the particularism inherent in the personal sphere for the universalism of revolutionary brotherhood.

Nikolai's younger brother Anasii's failed marriage also illustrates the rejection of individual happiness in favor of service to a collective good. Moreover, it reveals the immoderation many popovichi displayed in their pursuit of love and the radical way they could replace one conception of salvation with another. As a student, Anasii fell in love with a young girl named Zhenia, the daughter of one of his gymnasium teachers, who was himself a popovich. In a letter to his brother Ivan written after his marriage, Anasii admitted that their courtship had consumed him entirely:

> However, I treated the love I felt as serious and decided "if I am going to love, than I am going to love honestly, that is, I will love only Zhenia, I will preserve myself and even my kindness for her alone." The stronger love overpowered me, the more I tried to show Zhenia that I loved her . . . the more I avoided contact with other women, not allowing myself even a single smile, a word, a handshake, and in the end, I even shunned other women, even if they were old ladies . . . (all this was extreme, provoked by Zhenia's insistence, as you will see later, but this excessiveness was also in my character).

Numerous other popovichi shared Anasii's conception of love as an insidious force in their descriptions of falling in love as paramount to literally losing their minds.[54]

When Anasii enrolled in Moscow University the couple married. Several months later, however, Anasii insisted on divorcing his pregnant teenage wife. In a letter to Ivan, he explained his sudden decision by denouncing the selfishness of individual pleasure and by redefining his salvation as embodied in scholarship:

> You wrote me earnestly requesting that I live together with my wife. You wrote that one's wife should be more precious than scholarship. About that you and I are of completely different opinions. It is not scholarship, but rather humanity, which scholarship serves, that is incomparably more precious and important than one's wife, who is only a single person as opposed to an entire people [narod]. I place more value on the opinion of all people than of single individuals . . . for me scholarship does not consist of some kind of merry entertainment or seasoning for life's banquet, as you want to say. In scholarship I see a source, a key to the truth of the puzzle of life, and therefore it is closer to me than a wife.

A popovich like Anasii who did not seek to transform Russia politically could still perceive himself as serving the universalistic principle of the nation through his profession.

Anasii expressed no remorse. He demonized Zhenia, describing her as evil and violent. She personified all of the traits of the "bad" wife described in prescriptive clerical literature. He portrayed himself as a victim, manipulated by Zhenia to the point where he lost control and was unable to break away from the spell she had cast upon him. He only pitied himself. What grieved him the most was the fact that this personal turmoil interrupted his work, the new source of his salvation: "I myself desire nothing else besides scholarship . . . now, under the influence of all of this I do not have the strength to work, which is terribly difficult for me." Anasii was perplexed that he was not the object of compassion. After all, he had exchanged the "false" ideal of his romance with Zhenia for the "true" ideal of scholarship. He wrote Ivan:

> This is all very hard for me, Vania, very hard. Not because some sort of sin tortures my soul, but because no matter how hard I tried, no matter how much I concerned myself so that everything I did was kind, one never receives a just trial concerning one's actions. . . . Not one word is uttered about your humane virtues and about your finest traits and wishes, even though they are completely virtuous.[55]

Whereas Nikolai forsook love for revolution only after he could not realize his idealized version of marriage, Anasii replaced love with scholarship because he believed the latter was the true key to salvation. Here an individual, Zhenia, was sacrificed for the greater good. The end justified the means.

Ivan, who chided both his brothers for their marital difficulties, never married. In an 1899 letter to his widowed mother, Ivan likened himself to Christ, who too had not married. Near the end of his life, in the 1920s, however, Ivan finally became engaged. He soon experienced some of the drama his brothers had endured. After his fiancée told him in a letter that "You and I possess a different spirit," Ivan refused to speak to her for three years. He could not bear the thought of a lack of agreement between lovers. After they reunited, Ivan rationalized that his love for his fiancée was "divinely-summoned love," which is higher than common passion between a man and a woman. His fiancée conformed to his universalistic ideal of love, since he saw God in her eyes.[56]

Some of the friendships that popovichi initiated in the secular world also followed the pattern of the Tregubovs' relationships with women. Popovichi tended to befriend individuals they revered. Describing one friend, the bureaucrat Tikhonov stated: "if he set a particular goal for himself, he achieved it no matter what." When someone did fulfill the ideal to which popovichi adhered, their admiration knew no bounds. Tikhonov recalled: "I became such good friends with Boris Stanislavovich that I began to imitate him in everything: the way he played the guitar and sang . . . his punctuation of several words, his habit of ridiculing everything." Dr. Krylov, born in 1841, remarked in 1893 that he considered one person he knew "almost as a God, although he was only the teacher of a gymnasium."[57]

Friends could become so important that they served as the momentary ideal of a popovich's life. In the full romantic tradition of friendship as a form of love, Ivan Pozdnev, born in 1886 long after romanticism had waned, addressed his best friend in his prison diary he kept in the early 1900s:

> Most importantly, I have been left completely alone. I don't have that close being, comrade and friend, whom I passionately, honestly and tenderly love and respect and to whom I confided my secrets and the issues which trouble

my agitated soul . . . I dream about those days which were so joyous for me, when we were together, when we walked arm and arm, discussing and laughing loudly! I sincerely believe and hope that we will again be together, that we will live, as it is called, one life.[58]

Just as in their romantic liaisons with women, however, the friends popovichi revered sometimes fell short of the ideal they constructed of them. Popovichi often grew disillusioned when they witnessed the imperfections of their idols on a day-to-day basis. Tikhonov, for example, stopped being friends with Boris Stanislavovich after Boris was implicated in a scandalous romance. This extreme vacillation could affect their relations with all with whom popovichi came into contact. Aleksandr Dianin, for example, initially welcomed servants into his home and praised their work, even adopting them as surrogate family members; however, he quickly became disillusioned with their work. Retainers were either fired or forced to quit after he cursed them as unfit and wicked. His wife protested that he sought an ideal servant, just as he sought an ideal wife.[59]

As they had in their bursa recollections of their teachers and classmates, popovichi either worshipped or spurned others as adults. Their saintly fathers were role models not only of what they should be, but also of what other people should emulate. The uncompromising attitude some popovichi adopted toward their wives and friends is indicative of their bipolar morality. They saw individuals as either good or evil, a characteristic for which Frank castigated the postreform intelligentsia. Their willingness to make the determination between good and evil is in striking contrast to their fathers, who ideally left judgment to God. Since popovichi conceived of a secularized understanding of salvation, final judgment on earth was not only feasible but even necessary. This salvation, with its exclusive role for human agency, also required them to do the saving. To deliver others from sin or danger, they needed to judge them, and their clerical birthright rendered them uniquely qualified to do so.

Popovichi who sought secular salvation in the personal sphere, however, were more easily disappointed than those who sought it in political and professional realms. In part this stemmed from their embrace of public service and their conception of personal happiness outside of the common good as selfish. They attempted to collapse private and public but became frustrated by their inability to achieve complete submission. The personal sphere forced them to deal concretely with other individuals, rather than allowing them to lose themselves in the abstractions of work or politics. Popovichi, despite their general reputation as raznochintsy realists, were idealists in their repudiation of the material. Regardless of whether popovichi sought secular salvation in personal, political, or professional spheres, they were frustrated in their quests. No matter how much they achieved in their professions, popovichi always demanded more from themselves, and politics without compromise was an unrealistic endeavor.

Just as individuals were not perfect, the temporal world could never become heaven on earth. Like all utopian fantasies, the missions popovichi undertook failed.

1917 and Beyond:
Professor Dmitrii Zelenin and the Fate of Popovichi's Ethos

In 1918 children of clergymen were disenfranchised along with their parents: they were denied state employment, ration cards, and admittance to educational institutions. Some popovichi who had not received their higher education before the revolution ended up as manual laborers. Rehabilitation was, however, theoretically possible for popovichi. If they publicly repudiated their fathers by denouncing them (in a newspaper announcement, for example), they could at least apply to universities. In some cases priests, desperate for their children to receive a higher education, proved that such actions were, in their eyes, meaningless, by accompanying their reluctant children to Soviet administration offices and standing by until they denounced them in writing. If ordained clergymen's children engaged in work deemed socially useful by the regime and were not financially dependent on their parents after 1918, they were not disenfranchised.[60]

Of the popovichi who had established their careers before the revolution, those who were theological academy professors or had been politically active were particularly vulnerable to arrest, especially when the Soviet regime became more repressive under Stalin. With the closing of the theological academies and seminaries immediately after the October Revolution, former professors also faced employment discrimination and were denied their pensions. Despite the difficulties pious and/or anti-Soviet popovichi faced after the October Revolution, like their fathers and ordained brothers, few of them appear to have emigrated. Viktor Vasnetsov's émigré son, a mathematician who returned to his roots by becoming a priest in 1932, recalled that his father replied to foreign friends who urged him to emigrate "that he was born in Russia, had served for her his whole life, and wanted to die in his motherland."[61] An old man at the time of the revolution, Vasnetsov, along with many popovichi who were pioneers from the heyday of populism, died peaceful deaths in early Soviet Russia, often writing their memoirs in their final years.

Among the younger generation of popovichi who had established successful careers outside the clerical domain before the revolution and were never politically active, some were actually able to continue their professional activities relatively unmolested. Many were academics. The ethnographer Dmitrii Zelenin, whose long life (1878–1954) spans both the late imperial and Soviet periods, is illustrative of this professional continuity between regimes. Kirill Chistov, one of the most prominent ethnographers

The artist Viktor Vasnetsov in 1885.

of the late Soviet period, wrote of Zelenin in 1979: "he was a living incarnation between the best traditions of Russian academia of the nineteenth century and academia of the Soviet period." Zelenin's biography and professional legacy provide a key as to what happened to the salvation ethos of
popovichi and their alternative intelligentsia culture during the Soviet period. His biography also allows for an examination of how a career pattern
embodied the modern self—used in this book to redefine the intelligentsia—and how a popovich was able throughout his adult life to adhere
to popovichi's collective values.[62]

In typical popovich fashion, Zelenin was incredibly prolific and highly
accomplished in his profession. He published 306 articles and books within
his lifetime, beginning with his first monograph in 1903, when he was

twenty-five. By 1904, the year he graduated from university, he had authored eighty-eight publications, including book reviews. Four of his early articles were on topics related to popovichi, including a historical study of the church school where he studied and an article in a national journal on what he referred to as "seminarians' dialect." Zelenin had begun ethnographic work as a seminary student, when he was recruited, along with other seminarians, to gather material for the famed nationwide Tenishev ethnographic survey of the Russian peasantry.[63] Shortly thereafter he began to engage in ethnographic work during summers in his native province of Viatka for the Russian Geographic Society, and in 1901 he was awarded the silver medal of the society; in 1902 he was decorated with its gold medal.

Like numerous other pre-revolutionary popovichi who reached national prominence in their fields, Zelenin encountered resistance along the way due to his uppitiness, zeal, and his non-conventional way of thinking. Like them, he never let it deter him. In an unpublished Soviet-era autobiography, he attributed the difficult time he had enrolling in graduate school in part to his professors being envious of the medals he earned at such a young age. At Iur'ev University, in present-day Estonia, where Zelenin studied as an undergraduate due to its lenient admittance policy regarding popovichi in the late imperial period, politics and ethnicity divided the faculty, and Zelenin's admission to graduate school there was opposed by both the German professors and the conservative Russian professors. Because ethnography was not yet its own discipline, and because there was no tradition of studying folklore at Iur'ev, Zelenin had been a maverick, independently developing his own methodology, which many professors did not accept as valid. There was disagreement as to which faculty he should enroll in; a professor of comparative linguistics finally agreed to mentor him. The controversy Zelenin faced in graduate school was replicated in the reviews his early work received. Because he was a pioneer of the ethnological direction in folklore and linguistics in both Russia and Europe, his publications received a great deal of attention—not all complimentary—in the press. The regional Russian folktales he published in 1914 and 1915 were, by contrast, well received by reviewers, but like popovichi publicists before him, he was praised for his incredible industriousness and for his passion and knowledge of his subject, and was criticized for his "unaesthetic" literary style.[64]

From 1916 to 1925 Zelenin was employed as a professor of Russian language and literature in Khar'kov. In 1918, he was awarded a professorship at the more prestigious Kazan University, but because of the dangers of traveling during the civil war years, he was not able to move to Kazan. His correspondence from 1917, when he was still living in Petrograd, with his future colleagues in Khar'kov reveals that the questionable prestige of Khar'kov University was not Zelenin's only concern: despite the fact that Khar'kov was a largely Russian-speaking city in Eastern Ukraine, Zelenin expressed concern about being forced to give his lectures in Ukrainian and about Ukrainian chauvinism.[65] His fears were never realized, but they do illustrate how Zelenin, like other popovichi, were more comfortable immersed in their own culture.

In 1925 Zelenin was brought to Leningrad and appointed Professor of Ethnography of Eastern Slavic Peoples, a post he held until his death in 1954. The same year he arrived in Leningrad he was elected *chlen-korrespondent* (corresponding member) of the Academy of the Sciences, an honor rare for someone so young. From 1917 until after his death, his books were published in or translated into Russian, German, French, and English. He was a member of more than thirty Soviet and international scholarly associations and commissions. During World War II he was evacuated from Leningrad to Samarkand, and by all accounts he worked the entire time. He was only once briefly arrested, despite the fact that his profession suffered several debilitating purges in the 1930s.[66] In 1945 he received a gold medal from the Academy of Sciences.

Zelenin was not a Marxist, which explains in part how he escaped the purges. In the pre-revolutionary period he never sympathized with the revolutionary movement, referring at the time to the 1905 revolution as a *smuta* (sedition). Politics appear not to have interested him very much; he didn't write about political topics in either his pre-revolutionary personal texts or his published works. Like popovichi scientists, his devotion to his scholarly work was all-encompassing. In the midst of the turmoil that engulfed Russia between the February and October revolutions in 1917, Zelenin did not choose sides; he defended his doctoral dissertation at Moscow University. His greatest concern during the civil war years appears to have been that his beloved library was not with him in Khar'kov but was divided between Kazan, his family in Viatka, and his old apartment in Petrograd: "A tragic situation for a scholar" he wrote a friend and colleague. The only hint of his political orientation during the Soviet period comes from a project he conducted during the civil war in Khar'kov, when he collected a wide variety of political *chastushki* (limericks), some of which he published in 1925 in a German journal. According to a post-Soviet scholar who has read all his research notes for this project, he was sympathetic to the anti-Soviet limericks.[67]

Zelenin first came under attack when he quarreled with the Marxist historian Mikhail Pokrovskii over the origins of the Russian people. Pokrovskii accused him in 1927 of Great Russian chauvinism based on Zelenin's 1925 book, published in German in Germany, on the traditional everyday culture of Eastern Slavic peasants. The book achieved international renown, but by the mid-1920s studying such a specific people, particularly Russians, in a modern period, was considered politically incorrect. One positive review of the book was published, interestingly, in Soviet Russia by a fellow popovich, even though the author was a Marxist. By 1929 non-Marxist ethnographers came under fierce attack, including Zelenin. In 1930 he was identified as a representative of the right wing of Soviet ethnographers, a group that was accused of having not adopted a single new approach to ethnography in the thirteen years since the October Revolution. But in 1932 the primary target of academic purges shifted to Marxist scholars themselves, as Marxists engaged in fierce infighting over the correct ideological line. It thus became more dangerous to be a Marxist than a non-political old-school academic, and those non-Marxists who had survived the earlier purge largely escaped the particularly bloody purge of ethnographers in 1937. During the turbulent 1930s, most of the older generation of ethnographers to which Zelenin belonged either fell silent or tried to become Marxist.[68]

Given Zelenin's pursuit of secular salvation in his work, he did not remain silent. He published by adopting a certain degree of the Marxist methodology and terminology that was fashionable at the time and by shifting the focus of his research. He temporarily stopped publishing on Russian and other Eastern Slavic peasants, and as ethnographic fieldwork was replaced in the Soviet Union by the study of "primitive communist formations," Zelenin began to write about prehistory, material structures, and non-Slavic peoples in the contemporary Soviet Union. In an article he published in 1938 about the peoples of the extreme North, he claimed: "October and Leninist-Stalinist nationality policies have opened for them the complete possibility of a cultural, prosperous, joyful and happy life."[69]

Yet in 1930, at the height of the persecution of old non-Marxists ethnographers, Zelenin managed to study his—and many other popovichi's—favorite theme, Russian peasants, while earning favor with the communist state by organizing a seminar at Leningrad University devoted to the study of collective farms. This was the single politically correct act cited in his 1955 obituary, yet Zelenin's motivations could be interpreted as anti-collectivization, as a last-chance effort to record peasant life before it was destroyed forever.[70]

Once Russian culture and ethnicity was resurrected as a politically correct subject during and after World War II, Zelenin published a few articles on medieval Russian customs and attempted, to no avail, to publish in Russian his colossal 1927 masterpiece on Russian and Eastern Slavic peasants. He never stopped collecting new material for the Russian edition, even during the turbulent 1930s. And while Zelenin could be seen as trying to toe the party line in the 1930s, his contemporaries never accepted him as a Marxist; he was lambasted by reviewers for idealism and for being a "bourgeois scholar." The editor of his 1936 book on the cult of fire among native peoples in Siberia—a work considered worthy enough by French scholars that it was published in French translation in 1952—even stated in its preface that Zelenin's work was not Marxist, but praised its wealth of factual material.[71]

Dmitrii Zelenin in his later years. (Unknown artist)

The insincerity of Zelenin's conversion to belief in Communism is also attested to by the fact that he never abandoned his Orthodox faith. Icons hung in a secluded part of his Leningrad apartment to which he never allowed anyone access. His letters from his niece, with whom he corresponded from 1921 to 1947, are filled with congratulations on religious holidays, discussion of theological literature, and reference to regular attendance of church services by Zelenin's sister.[72]

Like so many of his fellow popovichi, Zelenin never married. His former student Nina Gagen-Torn referred to the two rooms in a building in the geographic institute that he lived in from 1925 until his death in 1954 not as an apartment, but as a "museum depository." The light was barely visible through the windows, blocked as they were by cases and boxes, filled to the brim with his collections of peasant clothes, footwear, and work tools from his native Volga region. The walls of Zelenin's apartment were also crammed with bookcases, and by the end of his life it was barely possible to move about. He died there in 1954 of a brain hemorrhage, hunched over his desk working, a pen in his hand.[73] Because he lived alone and had, as he had his entire life, only limited social contact with a few academic colleagues, rumors circulated that his corpse was not found until suspicious neighbors investigated his apartment several weeks later.

Zelenin's collections of Russian peasants' everyday artifacts constitute the most tangible part of his legacy. After his death, his niece gave the items to the Museum of Anthropology and Ethnography in Petersburg, and Zelenin remains the museum's main contributor for the Soviet period.[74]

His scholarly works constitute another part of his legacy. The studies he published before the late 1920s are considered classics and almost all were republished in the 1990s (including the first Russian edition, in 1991, of *Russische Volkskunde*). Writing in 1979, Chistov stated that Zelenin's works were the most widely read by Soviet ethnographers for the periods he wrote on. Marxist theory was then beginning to wane in Soviet Russia, and Chistov praised Zelenin for rejecting "the drive to force conclusions (and even more publish them) before finding the necessary facts." The materials Zelenin collected and never published, many of which were closed to scholars during the Soviet period, are also being published or used by post-Soviet scholars as primary sources. One post-Soviet scholar has suggested what view should be taken of the works Zelenin published during the 1930s: his quasi-Marxist approach is useless, but the material he collected is invaluable (ironically, this is the same conclusion the authors of his 1954 obituary reached). Like the first wave of Russian émigrés, who saw themselves as both contributing to and preserving aspects of Russian culture unwelcome in the Soviet Union until the day they could be integrated into their homeland, Zelenin has in essence done the same, informed by a clearly populist-minded understanding of Russian national culture.[75]

Lenin had no children, and, as popular lore has it, he used to say that the Soviet Union was his child. In this case, Russian academia was Zelenin's child. Memoirs of his former students show that they remember him as being incredibly accessible to them, showering them with attention and care, exuding enthusiasm about their studies, and always remaining responsible about his obligations to them. His students emphasized that he educated several generations of Soviet ethnographers and placed them in positions throughout the country, particularly in the postwar period after the profession had been devastated by the purges. According to Chistov, every Soviet ethnographer, even if they never studied with Zelenin, heard his lectures and considered him one of their most influential teachers.[76]

Unlike his clergyman father, Zelenin therefore passed on his ethos not to his children, but to his students. The traits his former students praised in their biographical sketches of him are the same traits associated with popovichi and many clergymen in the pre-revolutionary period. Gagen-Torn recalled Zelenin's seriousness of purpose: "we were amazed by his academic tone: he was exacting, brisk, demanding. Carefully organized work replaced humor and romance in his lectures." Another former student wrote that Zelenin's industriousness, erudition, thoroughness, and moralism were symbolized by the fact that he worked until his final hour. Still another former student lauded his single-mindedness and asceticism: "Nothing else existed for him except for interests, events, facts that were one way or another tied to scholarship. Teaching and scholarship—that was his entire life. He never had a family. The need for comfort was completely foreign to him." The same student emphasized Zelenin's activism and moralism by commending him for always having worked without a secretary or assistants: "He never used another's labor."[77] With the exception of his 1955 obituary, all of the biographical sketches of Zelenin published in the Soviet Union after his death directly related these traits to his clerical origins and education. In her 1979 biography of him, Gagen-Torn, referring to *Russische Volkskunde,* wrote: "organic love for the Russian people completely runs through it. He himself came from the narod, like a tree comes from the ground." Others told of his poor childhood in a large sacristan's family; they emphasized that his upbringing and education were imbued with a strong work ethic, that his clerical father was the harbinger of education in the village, and that his interest in the peasantry had sprung from having grown up surrounded by authentic peasants, completely cut off from the outside world. His Soviet biographers accepted the widespread pre-revolutionary conception of popovichi as an integral part of the narod.[78]

After 1917, the alternative intelligentsia ethos that popovichi represented remained in Soviet Russia, preserved in large part by a profession to which popovichi had always made a major contribution—academia. The values academics from all social backgrounds were praised for in their obituaries and *Festschrifts* from the 1970s, a generation after Zelenin's death, bear an eerie resemblance to the secular salvation mission that Zelenin's biographers praised, and to the ethos of popovichi described in this book. They are lauded for their single-mindedness, for being principled and disciplined, for working until their final hour.[79] Obituaries of academics from the first years of the twenty-first century, two generations after Zelenin's death, reveal an even more striking similarity to the popovichi ethos. Academics in post-Soviet Russia have been hit harder than most by the economic upheaval that accompanied the abrupt transfer from Communism to capitalism. Most have resisted retraining themselves and, despite dismal salaries, remain steadfastly devoted to their work. Like popovichi, they often see themselves as martyrs representing a cultural tradition that is threatened. And because of the lifting of censorship, deceased academics are now praised for traits many Soviet academics would undoubtedly have liked to have been more free to exercise, and which popovichi were renowned for: independence, fearlessness, honesty, bravery, originality, critical-mindedness, and opposition to hypocrisy and compromise. Since politics no longer matter—in fact, being above politics is once again fashionable—scholarship can now be depicted as the sole meaning of the deceased's life. An ascetic element is present in these hagiographical portraits: the deceased are no longer simply hard workers, they are now modest and passionate.[80] Could it be that Zelenin and his brother popovichi passed on their ethos—albeit altered, just as they had altered their fathers' values, and disguised officially as the worldview not of priests' sons but of the democratic "raznochintsy" intelligentsia—not only to their students, but to Russian academia at large?

Apart from cultural institutions such as the Moscow Circus, the Bolshoi Ballet, and the Mariinskii Theater, the Russian Orthodox Church and the Academy of Sciences (including the university system and various academic societies and institutes) are the only pre-revolutionary institutions that have continuously functioned—though often under duress and in altered form—throughout the Soviet period until the present day. To the general population of post-Soviet Russia, these two institutions represent a link to a past many are in the process of rediscovering and reevaluating as they forge a new national identity. While contemporary Russians can draw on their rich and universally renowned artistic heritage as a source of pride, many of those who want to fully understand their ancestors have been turning to pre-revolutionary scholarly publications, many of which are widely available in massive reprinted editions, and to the resurgent Church, which, in an era and region rife with nationalism and ethnic tension, advertises itself as the repository of Russian national identity. Popovichi like Zelenin provided a living bridge in the Soviet period between the Church and the Academy of Sciences, just as they had bridged clerical traditions and secular society before 1917.

Zelenin did not have children; this was not the case for all popovichi. Popovichi's descendants in Russia today are fully conscious and proud of their heritage. In his autobiography written shortly before he died in 1989, Andrei Sakharov wrote that his popovich grandfather, a liberal lawyer who worked to abolish the death penalty, served as his inspiration. With the collapse of Communism, progeny of pre-revolutionary clerical families have begun actively researching their past, and some have published collections of family papers that survived the Stalinist terror. But just as Zelenin passed his ethos on to his students, contemporary Russians need not be part of a clerical family to feel that popovichi represent their heritage. The ethos of popovichi has thus become truly modern, accessible to non-kin. When I began to research this project, the word "popovich" was no longer part of the Russian language. Now, in post-Soviet Russia, the term is used, and popovichi as a collective entity are beginning to emerge as a valid field of study, particularly among young scholars in the Russian provinces.[81] Just as descendants of popovichi compile genealogies to re-create their families, the aim of much of this research is on tracing the post-revolutionary fates of popovichi, along with their fathers. Still in the preliminary stages, these studies have yet to tackle the problem of reconstructing the ethos of the pre-revolutionary clerical estate. Instead of focusing on the uniqueness of this small, isolated group, the authors of these studies present the clergy as the most persecuted social estate group, as a key to understanding the Soviet tragedy, which they feel all Soviet citizens shared. In 2004 a provincial Russian scholar published in a small journal the findings of her decade-long oral history project on the fates of local pre-revolutionary clergy, in which she interviewed their surviving children and grandchildren. In it she refers to rural priests as "intelligenty-peasants" who were representative of the various strata of the population. Echoing the idealistic representations of popovichi enthusiasts in the late imperial period, she claims that priests are the ideal representatives of the nation. Their children were part of a second mass exodus from the clergy, one that, unlike that of the 1860s, was forced. She concludes by suggesting that their children became vessels of cultural continuity through their service to education, a sphere popovichi like Zelenin contributed to both before and after the revolution, and one of the few successes—achieving universal literacy within a few decades—of the Soviet experiment: "In the era of 'the great break' of the 1930s rural priests were annihilated along with their best parishioners. Having destroyed the church, Soviet power in many ways destroyed spiritual life in the countryside. But the worthy life of the parents was not in vain. The majority of children of priests became teachers, continuing the spiritual mentoring of their fathers."[82] How Russians will define that spiritual mentoring, and what it will sow, remains to be seen.

Conclusion

This book has focused on an alternative educated Russian culture that defined itself in opposition to the culture of the noble intelligentsia. Anti-aristocratic to its core, the popovichi intelligentsia was united by its identification with a Russian national culture. Its members were imbued with a sense of social egalitarianism that rendered them hostile, or at the very least ambivalent, toward accumulated wealth and capitalist enterprise. Their mission was to serve the collective good; the concept of individual interest was repugnant to them. They valued self-sacrifice and devoted themselves to trying to save the nation, whether through political activity, scholarship, cultural endeavors, social activism, or science. Industriousness, thrift, and modesty were among their values. Yet at the same time, popovichi were not egalitarians; although they wanted to reconstitute the existing society, they continued to conceive of it as structured by hierarchies. Most importantly, they viewed themselves as the nation's only leaders, and subsequently they were loath to compromise. Unlike most of their noble peers, who derived their identity from a perception of themselves as civilized, cultured, and Western-oriented, popovichi viewed their legitimacy as derived from "Russianness" and morality. They tended to judge others according to a binary juxtapositioning of good and evil. Their moralism also dictated that they be just as exacting of themselves as of others, in private as well as in public. This moralism, the heart of popovichi's sense of self, led to a cultural revolution in late Imperial Russia, manifested in a shift in the ethos of the postreform intelligentsia.

As did other educated Russians, popovichi read the works of Western thinkers and writers. Yet because they sought to fashion themselves as the antithesis of their noble foes, they drew primarily on clerical prescriptive models. In particular, they drew on the newfound moralism that permeated the reformation-like pastoral care movement. The ideals of the nineteenth-century parish clergy that have been discussed in this book are the polar opposite of the anti-clerical stereotypes that have dominated the historiography. Although they are often portrayed as lazy, greedy, drunken, and illiterate, clergymen in fact revered industriousness, "worldly" asceticism, and learnedness, and were disdainful of material acquisition or consumption. A chasm existed—one they readily acknowledged—between their lofty Christian virtues and the reality of their daily struggle to support their families, but even if they engaged in frowned-upon behavior, clergymen did not alter what they valued. They interiorized the archetypes in clerical texts and passed them on to their sons. Popovichi's dedication to good deeds, such as social service, made these secular men the outermost extension of the pastoral care movement, which encouraged priests to work toward improving social conditions. They also inherited from their fathers a specific professional outlook, which the nobility, who were not a professional class, lacked. Popovichi were taught that they were imbued with "model piety" and Russian national identity and that these traits made them uniquely qualified to be the nation's leaders.

Popovichi remained a distinct subgroup of the intelligentsia, but they also exerted a powerful influence on the character of other intelligenty. Two factors contributed to the acceptance of popovichi as role models. First, individuals from non-noble secular social estate groups who joined the intelligentsia at the turn of the century shared a number of popovichi's values, including their anti-aristocratic stance. Second, popovichi entered the intelligentsia in large numbers at a time when some noble intelligenty were particularly receptive to new morals. Yet the seemingly smooth integration of popovichi into secular professions and movements would not have been possible if the ethos of the noble intelligentsia was as antithetical to popovichi's value-system as popovichi themselves depicted it to be. The union of the two groups was possible because both types brought from their native estate a strong service tradition, and because many of the Western ideas that noble intelligenty used to fashion themselves—such as romanticism—were also steeped in Christianity. Unlike nobles, however, popovichi were conscious of the fact that they were drawing on religious, or at least clerical, traditions, and, most significantly, they perceived those traditions as rooted in Russian national culture. They saw themselves as relatively immune to Western influences, and in an age of increasing nationalism, this empowered them. It also provided a continuity of morals and ideas over generations. Particular Western ideas fell in and out of fashion in Russia, whereas clerical models, at least in the period covered in this book, were relatively stable. Popovichi thus became and remained a particular type of realists (*realisty*) with traits associated with both romanticism and realism.

Unlike nineteenth-century Russian nobles, popovichi were not particularly preoccupied with Russia's relationship to the West. Russian nobles defined themselves vis à vis Western Europe, and the question of Russia's relationship to Europe has been assumed to be one of the major issues, if not *the* major issue, that occupied the Russian intelligentsia. Conversely, popovichi defined themselves and their nation in juxtaposition to the nobility. Russia's nobles could be seen as representatives of Western culture, and, in fact, popovichi did see them as such. But it is significant that popovichi viewed their nation's primary competition, and its primary dilemma, as internal rather than external. While this paradigm might be seen as a harbinger of the purging of "internal enemies" under Stalin, it can also be interpreted as an alternative to the messianic nationalism and anxiety about Western Europe long associated with Russian culture and politics. Unlike the Westernizers or Slavophiles, popovichi didn't believe Russia was any better or any worse than Western European nations. They patriotically believed that Russia was as distinct a nation as all other nations. In his study of his fellow popovichi, Zolotarev came to the conclusion that popovichi were not a uniquely Russian phenomenon. He argued that in other countries, clergymen's sons were the bearers of their national culture; he cited the contributions of Protestant ministers' sons such as Nietzsche and Schelling to German culture. It was popovichi, rather than pan-European Westernized nobles, Zolotarev argued, who placed Russia on the stage of world culture, rendering Russia the equal of any other nation. A noble-born colleague of Ivan Pavlov's, who argued in emigration that to understand Pavlov's character "one must take into consideration Pavlov's clerical origin. . . . Pavlov was of pure Russian extraction," shared Zolotarev's view and summed up what he perceived as the difference between the abnormal relationship his noble brethren had with the West, and Pavlov's healthy attitude:

> Pavlov did not go to extremes in his admiration of the West like those who considered anything Western better than its Russian counterpart; neither was he a Slavophile who believed in the special virtues of the Russian soul and longed to proselytize the West. Pavlov was a Russian patriot in the best sense of the word, that is, he believed that Russia, like many other nations, had contributed much to the world and that she would once again contribute something of her own, something original and precious, to the general sum of world culture.[1]

Popovichi's retention of a clerical identity raises serious questions about the binary opposition of traditional to modern. First, popovichi's values, and even those of their clerical fathers, were drawn from both traditional and modern ways of thinking. Second, popovichi were "modern" in that they were self-reliant agents of their own destiny. Their decision to self-identify with their native estate is as much a testament to the emergence of a class structure as it is a sign of the failure of the Russian social estate system to modernize. The larger spectrum of choices available to popovichi is to some degree emblematic of all Russians in the postreform period—with the exception of the nobility, which had earlier enjoyed some freedom. As individuals popovichi also made the ethical choices, associated with the modern age, about which political movement or party to join, which profession to enter, and which woman to marry if they chose to marry. Shunning the institutional constraints of the Church, they chose to mediate individually either directly with God or, if they were atheists, with their consciences, to decide the best means of attaining clerical ideals. Finally, they chose not to assimilate into the dominant culture they entered. If popovichi embodied a modern sense of self, however, it was not a secular or autonomous self. The sense of self that emerges from their narratives was inseparable from an understanding of community based on kinship ties and hereditary privilege. The purpose of their lives was some form of collective salvation. Because the models they created were based on traditional Orthodox ideals, they appropriated the unity of public and private, self and community, that characterizes Christianity. Even if tradition itself is seen as a modern concept invented by nineteenth-century intellectuals in response to the anxieties caused by modernity—which played no small part in popovichi's decision to model themselves on a lost past—these clerical models provided continuity to the oldest of narratives, that of the Bible.[2] Popovichi demonstrate how modern "backward" Russia actually was in the late imperial period, while also illustrating how modern, educated, seemingly secular individuals could define themselves simultaneously in traditional and modern terms. Neither the concept of modernity nor the process of modernization had to be, or has to be, accompanied by the "privatization" and decline of religion.

Yet in fashioning themselves on clerical models that were not designed for secular, modern society, popovichi invariably transmuted them. This is most aptly demonstrated by their decision to enact some version of heaven on earth. As has been noted recently by a historian of the Soviet terror, the building of heaven on earth entails the nearing of the eschatological horizon, negating the distinction between the unenlightenment of fleshly temptation and willful evil as morality is reduced to a simple good/evil dipole and the possibility of violence becomes imminent.[3] No matter how much historians of Imperial Russia may seek to avoid the teleological approach to explaining Soviet authoritarianism, one is nevertheless left without adequate explanations of why such unprecedented violence occurred. Popovichi's ethos can be linked to the potential for violence beyond their radical utopianism. The convergence of popovichi's high ideals and lowly reality, their tendency to see individuals as members of essentialist groups, their dogmatic refusal to entertain compromise, their hatred of the noble ruling class, the absence of any traces of guilt in their attitude toward the peasant masses, their unequivocal belief in the legitimacy of their self-appointed leadership, their sense of superiority over and distinctiveness from the rest of the population, and the authoritarianism inherent in their reverence of patriarchal figures—which is so blatantly absent from the landscape of 1789 France—can all be seen as forerunners to the tragedy that began in 1917.[4] The juxtapositioning of two opposing intelligentsias as early as the nineteenth century also helps explain why some members of the common people could be so anti-intelligentsia in 1917, perceiving the intelligentsia as bourgeois and Western, while at the same time following the leadership of intelligenty who were socialists.[5] It also helps explain how the Soviet government, which recognized the intelligentsia as a class in 1936, could seek to retain the "democratic" (raznochintsy) strain of the pre-revolutionary intelligentsia heritage while rejecting the legacy of the "Oblomovs," the noble intelligentsia.

The fact that the ethos described in this book—aspects of which were previously associated only with the radical intelligentsia—was not limited to radical popovichi also indicates why many Russian intellectuals who did not support the Bolsheviks were able to acquiesce to some of the regime's policies and goals. In the case of non-political popovichi, this included dissociating themselves from politics by immersing themselves in their own activist, but non-political, ideals. Moreover, the overarching values that popovichi tended to adhere to intersected with explicitly formulated political boundaries and contributed to a specific anti-materialist and anti-pluralist genre of discourse. But while these values bring to mind certain clichés about Russian culture, when examined within their cultural context, these values were actually much more complicated, contradictory, and similar to Western European principles than such clichés would suggest.

The link between popovichi and Soviet authoritarianism, albeit for different reasons, has been made by scholars. Inspired by the émigré philosopher Nikolai Berdiaev, a colleague of Semen Frank's who argued that popovichi converted their ancestral faith into belief in Communism, scholars have contended that there is an inherent connection between Orthodoxy and Communism that lies at the root of alleged Russian exceptionalism. Although many of these scholars do not directly implicate popovichi, adherence to their general thesis assumes that any argument about popovichi's affiliation with their clerical heritage is a study of the Russian origins of Bolshevism.[6]

There are several major flaws in this theory about the Orthodox roots of Communism. In the first place, the distinctions between Eastern Orthodoxy and Catholicism are in fact less significant than the doctrinal differences that separate Catholicism and Protestantism.[7] Orthodoxy is a mainstream Christian religion, and there is nothing specific to Eastern Orthodoxy that would encourage belief in Communism any more than belief in any other Christian faith would. Universalistic religions always contain values that are at variance with this world, and a revolutionary element is inherent in Christianity, which is grounded in the millenarianism of the New Testament's depiction of God descending to earth to transform the temporal world. The tenets of Christian doctrine remain relatively undisputed, but because the moral level of theology is open to interpretation, the social activist element of Christianity has been accentuated in different countries at different times. Christian socialism is a predominantly modern Western movement, and the translation of scriptural prophecy to revolutionary action has been a recurrent phenomenon in Europe. Clergymen served as bearers of activist ideals in all the major revolutions of the Western world, including, most recently, in the appearance of Liberation Theology in Latin America. Any connection between Orthodoxy and revolution is thus, in addition to the emergence of a modern selfhood, an example of the similarities, rather than the differences, between Russian and Western historical developments. Some of the other links we have noted between potential violence and popovichi's alternative culture, such as class struggle, inegalitarianism, and stereotyping, are also an integral part of modern politics rather than specific to Russia, just as the enlightenment idea of progress has been linked to both Western democracy and Stalinism.[8]

On the other hand, the particularities of the Imperial Russian social and political structure affected the temporalization of religious values in Russia. The castelike nature of the Russian parish clergy, coupled with its requisite obedience to the state and its predominant otherworldly orientation, ensured that it was its secularly employed sons who served as agents of this literal transferal of the pastorate. Russia lacked the clashes between church and state that propelled many of the countries to her west toward change. The fact that popovichi—even those who were atheists—served as bearers of modernity could not but affect the nature of modern politics in Russia.

Yet despite this social element unique to Imperial Russia, there was no casual connection between popovichi's contribution to the intelligentsia ethos and an illiberal revolution. In fact, only a minority of popovichi became revolutionaries. A common set of moral and activist values motivated individual popovichi to choose a realm—be it society, knowledge, the state, the church hierarchy, or their spouses—to restructure. Popovichi recognized the liberal distinction between public and private, but they generally did not accept its legitimacy. Instead, they sought to collapse public and private into one, an urge Hannah Arendt identified as the modern predicament. Popovichi's mission helped prepare Russia for revolution, but just as the temporalization of religious values in Europe led to a variety of revolutions, this revolution would not have been Communist or violent without a convergence of other factors unrelated to popovichi. Just as religious denominations like Methodism have historically inspired individuals toward conservatism, radicalism, or liberalism, individual popovichi interpreted their secularized religious mission differently.[9] And popovichi's clerical heritage provided them with a multiplicity of models that could be applied in different ways while adhering to the same value system. All revolutions employ the language of good and evil, and the cultural revolution of the self that popovichi generated might have ended in February 1917. After all, the February revolution, when people of all classes chose their own destiny through their actions in Petrograd, at the front, and in the countryside, represents the spirit of the active modern self more than the events of the following October. For some of the minority of popovichi who lost their religious belief, the February revolution did not go far enough. These popovichi—some of whom were Bolshevik Party members—were only the most extreme manifestation of a general modern trend toward secular utopianism, which led, in other countries besides Russia, to a manifestation of authoritarian designs.

Glossary

batiushka—Father; familiar name parishioners use to address their priest

bursa—Collective term for both primary and secondary levels of ecclesiastical education, at the church school and seminary

bursak (pl. *bursaki*)— A student at the *bursa*

byt—Everyday life

desiatin—A land measure that equals 2.7 acres

intelligent (pl. *intelligenty*)—An individual who considered himself a member of the intelligentsia

istina—Truth in the sense of verity; compare *pravda*

kruzhok (pl. *kruzhki*)—Independent study circle

kuteinik—A derogatory slang word for members of the clerical estate in pre-revolutionary Russia. It also connotates boisterous. *Kuteinik* is derived from *kut'ia,* the grain used to prepare a food eaten after funerals and occasionally on holidays

matushka—Mother; name parishioners use to address a priest's wife

meshchanstvo—Townspeople; philistinism

narod—The common people; masses; folk. Usually refers to the peasantry

obshchestvo—Society; specifically educated society or noble, high society

popovich (pl. *popovichi*)—Orthodox clergymen's son (or sons), employed in a secular profession

popov'na (pl. *popov'ny*)—Orthodox clergymen's daughter(s)

pravda—Truth. In Old Russian its extended meanings included justice, right, and law; compare *istina*

raznochintsy—People of various ranks. General legal term for individuals who did not belong to a social estate group

Realschule (pl. *Realschulen*)—Technical secondary school

starshie—Student deputies (literally, elders) in the bursa

tovarishchestvo—Comradeship

treby—Voluntary contributions the clergy received directly from parishioners for ceremonies performed, such as weddings, funerals, and baptisms

zemstvo (pl. *zemstva*)—Limited local self-government instituted by the Great Reforms of the 1860s

Appendix

Data on Identifiable Popovichis' Personal Texts

Name	Born	Profession*	Genre†	Date‡	Birthplace
Akinfiev, I.Ia.	1851	Botanist	A-c (P)	1901	Stavropol'sk
Alandskii, S.I.			A (P)	1883	
Al'bov, M.N.	1851	Writer	A-c (P)	1888	Petersburg
Al'bov, N.M.	1866	Botanist	D (P)	1896	Nizhegorod
Aleksandrov, A.I.		Prof. Univ.	L, P (U)	1903	Kazan
Aleksandrovskii	1853		A (P)	1893	Samara
Almazov	1829	Bureaucrat	A (U)	1886	Smolensk
Ametistov, I.A.	1845	Rev. (R)	C (U)	1870	Khar'kov
Amfiteatrov, A.V.	1862	Writer (R)	A (U/P)	1903, 1930s	Kaluga
Anastasiev, A.I.	1852	Pedagogue	A-c (P)	1901	Simbirsk
Andrevskii, A.A.	1845	Teacher, Gym.	A-c (P)	1889	Kiev
Antonovich, M.A.	1835	Writer	A (U§), A-c (P)	1880s–90s	Khar'kov
Apollov, A.I.	1864	Tolstoyian	L (U)	1876–78	Kostroma
Ardashev, P.N.	1865	Prof. History	A-c (P)	1903	Viatka
Arkhangel'skii, S.F.	1873	Teacher, Sem.	O (P)	1906	Vladimir
B—v, A.	1831	Singer	A (P)	1884	Petersburg
Babin, N.	1858	Bureaucrat	A (P)	1895	Perm

Name	Born	Profession*	Genre†	Date‡	Birthplace
Barshev, Ia.I.	1807	Prof. Law	A-c (P)	1890	Moscow
Barsov, A.V.	1843	Teacher	A (P)	1900	Petersburg
Barsov, E.V.	1835	Ethnographer	A-c (P)	1885	Novgorod
Barsov, N.I.	1839	Prof. PDA	A-c (P)	1887	Petersburg
Bazarov, A.I.	1845	Chemist	A-c (P)	1887	Germany
Beliaev	1890	Prof. Tech	A (P)	1923	Vladimir
Beliunin, E.	1869	Rev. (R)	L (U)	1892	Vladimir
Belokurov, N.A.	1860		L (U)	1893	Moscow
Belokurov, S.A.	1862	Archivist	D, A (U)	1882, 1886	Moscow
Berdnikov, I.S.	1839	Prof. Univ.	A-c (P)	1890	Viatka
Berezhkov, M.N.	1850	Prof. Univ.	A-c (P)	1900	Vladimir
Berezskii, P.K.	1842	Doctor	A-c (P)	1893	Pskov
Bezsonov, P.A.	1828	Prof. Univ.	A-c (P)	1879	
Biriukov, N.A.	1862	Teacher, Sem.	A (P)	1912	Tolob'sk
Biriukov, V.P.	1888	Ethnographer	A (P)	1929	Perm
Blagosvetlov, G.E.	1824	Publicist (R)	C (U)	1856	Stavropol
Blagoveshchenskii, N.A.	1837	Ethnographer	F, A-c (P)	1865, 1889	Petersburg
Blagoveshchenskii, N.M.	1821	Philologist	A-c (P)	1891	Petersburg
Bogoslavskii	1875	Rev. (R)	A (P)	1921	Vladimir
Bogoslavskii, G.K.	1847	Bureaucrat	A (P)	1915	Chernigov
Bolotov, V.V.	1853	Prof. PDA (M)	L (U)	1906	Tver
Brilliantov, A.I.	1867	Prof. PDA	L, A (U)	1894, 1904, 1908, 1923	Vologda
Brilliantov, I.I.	1869	Historian	L (U)	1894–98	Vologda
Bronzov, A.A.	1858	Prof. PDA	A (P)	1908	Novgorod

Name	Born	Profession*	Genre†	Date‡	Birthplace
Brovkovich, I.	1840	Bureaucrat	O (P)	1891	Mogilov
Bulgakov, Sergei	1871	Prof. Econ.	A (P)	1930s	Orel
Bulgakovskii, D.G.	1845	Ethnographer	A (U)	1913	Orlovsk
Bunin, A.A.	1833	Pedagogue	A (P)	1904	Voronezh
Chernavskii, M.M.	1855	Librarian (SR)	A-c (P)	1925	Smolensk
Chernyshevskii, N.G.	1828	Publicist (R)	D (P) L, A (U§)	1848–53, 1855–62, 1863	Saratov
Dianin, A.P.	1851	Scientist	L (U)	1891–96	Vladimir
Dmitrievskii, A.A.	1856	Prof. PDA (M)	A, L (U)	1896–1912, 1914–16	Astrakhan
Dmitrievskii, A.S.	1897	Clerk	A (U)	1922	Vladimir
Dobrokhotov, D.N.	1852	Lawyer	A-c (P)	1913	Riazan
Dobroklonskii, A.P.	1856	Historian	A (P)	1938	Moscow
Dobrolenskii, F.L.	1825	Teacher, Sem.	A (P)	1904	
Dobroliubov, N.A.	1835	Publicist (R)	D, L (P)	1855, 1853–61	N. Novgorod
Dobroliubov, V.A.	1849	Businessman	A (P)	1901	N. Novgorod
Dobroliubov, V.I.	1831	Bureaucrat	L (P)	1853–60	N. Novgorod
Dobronravov, I.M.		Writer	F (P)	1903–06	
Dobronravov, L.M.	1887	Writer/Clerk	F, L (P)	1913–14	Kishinev
Dobrynin, Gavriil	1752	Bureaucrat	A (P)	1823	Belgorod
Drozdov, M.A.	1860		O (P)	1900	Riazan
Dubasov, I.I.	1843	Archaeologist	A (P)	1884	Tambov
Eleonskii [Milovskii]	1861	Teacher, Sem.	F (P)	1895–1911	Nizhegorod
Eliseev, G.Z.	1821	Journalist (R)	L, A (U§)	1861, 1880s	Tomsk
Elpat'evskii, S.Ia.	1854	Doctor (R)	A (P/U)	1920s	Vladimir

Name	Born	Profession*	Genre[†]	Date[‡]	Birthplace
Fenomenov, M.Ia.	1883	Ethnographer (SD)	A (U)	1927	Orel
Filonov, A.G.	1831	Teacher, Gym.	A (P)	1864, 1890, 1903	Smolensk
Galabutskii, I.A.	1865	Dir. School	A (P)	1902	Odessa
Gedeonovskii, A.V.	1859	Rev. (SR)	A-c (P)	1925	Orel
Giliarov, F.A.	1841	Teacher, Gym.	D, A (U/P)	1856, 1904	Moscow
Giliarov-Platonov, N.P.	1824	Publicist	D, L (U) A (P)	1859, 1870, 1886	Moscow
Gloriantov, V.I.	1830	Bureaucrat	A (P)	1906	
Glubokovskii, M.N.	1865	Doctor	C, L (U)	1881, 1901–03	Vologda
Glubokovskii, N.N.	1863	Prof. MDA	O (U)	1900s	Vologda
Golubinskii, E.E.	1834	Prof. MDA	A (P)	1923	Kostroma
Greznov, Evgenii	1830	Doctor	A (P)	1903	Vologda
Grigor'ev, I.G.	1738	Bureaucrat	A (P)	1802	Suzdal
Gruzinskii, A.E.	1858	Philologist	L (U)	1897–1914	Moscow
Gur'ev, Mikhail	1845		A (P)	1909	
Ivanenko	1860s		N (U)	1884	Poltava
Ivanovskii, V.S.	1853	Doctor (R)	A (U)	1897	Tula
Izmailov, A.A.	1873	Writer	F, A (P)	1903, 1911	Petersburg
Izmailov, F.F.	1798	Teacher, Sem.	A, (P)	1870	
Karonin, N.E.	1853	Writer (R)	L (U)	1879	Samara
Karzhanskii, N.S.	1879	Journalist (SD)	A (U)	1938	Smolensk
Kazanskii, P.S.	1812	Prof. MDA	A (P)	1879	
Khitrov, A.		Teacher, Sem.	A (P)	1891	Moscow
Kistiakovskii, A.F.	1833	Prof. Law	A (P)	1895	Chernigov

Name	Born	Profession*	Genre†	Date‡	Birthplace
Kliuchar', S.N.	1894	Clerk	A-c (U)	1924	Vladimir
Kliuchevskii, V.O.	1841	Prof. History	L (P)	1860s	Penza
Kniazev, N.	1855		O (P)	1891	Iaroslavl
Koialovich, M.I.	1828	Prof. PDA	L (P)	1856	Grodno
Kolchin, M.A.	1855	Doctor (R)	A-c (P)	1887	Arkhangel'sk
Krasnoperov, I.M.	1838	Statistician (R)	A (P/U§)	1903, 1929	Viatka
Kriukovskii, V.Ia.	1852		A (P)	1910	Tambov
Krylov, V.P.	1841	Doctor	A-c (P)	1893	Iaroslavl
Kudriavtsev, V.D.	1828	Prof. MDA	D (U)	1861–91	
Kulzhinskii, I.G.	1803	Teacher	A-c (P)	1859	Chernigov
Lavrovskii, V.	1874		C (U)	1894	Tver
Lavrskii, K.V.	1844	Statistician	A (U)	1905	Nizhegorod
Lazurskii, V.F.	1872	Philologist	A (P)	1917	Poltava
Lebedev, A.P.	1845	Prof. MDA	A (P)	1907	
Lebedev, S.N.	1875	Farmer (R)	C (U)	1899	Vladimir
Lepeshinskii, P.N.	1868	Rev. (SD)	A, A-c (P)	1921, 1925	Mogilev
Levitov, A.I.	1835	Writer (R)	L, F (P)	1850s, 1853	Tambov
Levkoev, I.G.	1862	Prof. Sem.	A (P)	1912	Vladimir
Liubavskii, M.K.	1860	Historian (M)	A (U)	1928	Riazan
Livanov, F.V.		Bureaucrat	F (P)	1877	Saratov
Luppov, P.V.	1867	Bureaucrat	A (P)	1913	Viatka
Malein, I.M.	1834	Teacher	A (P)	1910	Tver
Malinin, D.I.	1882	Rev. (SD)	A (P)	1921	Kaluga
Malov, S.E.	1880	Ethnographer	A, L (U)	1914–45	Kazan
Mamin-Sibiak, D.N.	1852	Writer (R)	L, A (U§/P)	1872–1912, 1894	Perm

Name	Born	Profession*	Genre†	Date‡	Birthplace
Nadezhdin, N.I.	1804	Ethnographer	A (P)	1841	Riazan
Neskovskii, M.	1843	Publicist	A (P)	1896	Polotsk
Nikitskii, A.V.	1859	Archaeologist	D (U)	1883–85	Novgorod
Nikolaevskii, Boris	1887	Rev. (SD)	I (P)	1960s	Ufa
Novorusskii, M.V.	1861	Rev. (R)	D, A (U)	1887–92, 1919	Novgorod
Orlov, A.A.	1791	Bureaucrat	A (P)	1832	Tobol'sk
Orlov, D.I.	1853	Doctor	A-c (P)	1903	Kaluga
Orlov, N.A.		Doctor	O (P)	1905	Vladimir
Orlovskii, I.I.	1869	Ethnographer	O (P)	1905	Smolensk
Ostrovitianov, K.V.	1892	Rev. (SD)	A (P)	1960s	Tambov
Ovchinnikov, E.M.	1847	Doctor	A-c (P)	1906	Viatka
Ovchinnikov, M.P.	1844	Rev. (R)	A (P)	1916	
Pavlov, I.P.	1849	Scientist	A-c (P), L (U§)	1917, 1936	Riazan
Pavlovich, M.	1850	Schoolteacher	O (P)	1905	Volynsk
Pavlovskii, A.D.	1857	Prof. Univ.	A-c (P)	1906	Iaroslavl
Peshekhonov, A.V.	1867	Statistician (R)	A-c (P)	1913	Tver
Pevnitskii, V.	1852	Prof. KDA	A (P)	1911	
Pokrovskii, N.V.	1848	Archaeologist	A (P)	1909	Kostroma
Polisadov, G.A.	1836	Teacher	A (P)	1860, 1915	Vladimir
Pomialovskii, I.V.	1845	Prof.	D (U)	1870	Petersburg
Pomialovskii, N.G.	1835	Writer	F (P), L (P/U§)	1859–63	Petersburg
Popov, M.R.	1851	Rev. (R)	A (P)	1900s	Ekaterinoslav
Potapenko, I.N.	1856	Writer	A-c (P)	1911	Kherson
Pozdnev, Ivan	1886	Clerk (R)	D, L (U)	1889–1920s	

Name	Born	Profession*	Genre[†]	Date[‡]	Birthplace
Preobrazhenskii, E.A.	1886	Rev. (SD)	A-c (P)	1925	Orel
Pribylev, A.V.	1857	Doctor (SR)	A-c (P)	1925	Perm
Raskol'nikov, F.F.	1892	Diplomat (SD)	A-c (U[§])	1913, 1923	Petersburg
Rostislavov, D.I.	1809	Prof. PDA	A (U[§])	1877	Riazan
Rozanov, N.P.	1857	Teacher, Sem.	A (U/U[§])	1920s, 1930s	Moscow
Sadov, A.I.	1850	Prof. PDA	A (P)	1913	Nizhegorod
Sadovskii, E.T.	1881	Teacher	A-c (U)	1927	Kiev
Semenov, P.V.	1874	Bureaucrat	A (P)	1913	
Serebrennikov, A.P.	1880	Pedagogue	L, A (U)	1890s, 1940	Perm
Shadrin, I.G.	1870	Writer (R)	A (P)	1915	Vologda
Shalamov, V.	1907	Writer	A (P)	1970s	Vologda
Shashkov, S.	1841	Writer (R)	A (P)	1882	Siberia
Shchapov, A.P.	1830	Historian (R)	A (P)	1863	Irkutsk
Shestakov, P.D.	1826	Teacher, Gym.	A-c (P)	1887	Kaluga
Shmakov, S.	1860s		L (U)	1877	Arkhangel'sk
Sidorenko, E.M.	1862	Rev. (SR)	A-c (P)	1926	Tavrich
Skvortsov, A.A.	1883	Soldier	L (U)	1905	Orlov
Smirnov, A.V.	1854	Doctor (L)	F (U), L (U) A-c (P)	1879, 1879–99, 1897	Vladimir
Smirnov, A.V.	1872	Statistician (R)	L (U)	1900s	Vladimir
Smirnov, Ia.V.	1808	Teacher, Gym.	D (P)	1850s	Vladimir
Smirnov, K.V.	1856	Clerk	L (U)	1877–78	Vladimir
Smirnov, P.A.	1833	Bureaucrat	D (U)	1853	Kaluga
Smirnov, S.I.	1870	Prof. MDA	D, A (U)	1895, 1900, 1903, 1900s	Vladimir
Snezhnevskii, V.I.	1861	Archivist (R)	A (P)	1908	Kostroma

Name	Born	Profession*	Genre†	Date‡	Birthplace
Sobolev, V.	1870		N (U)	1897	Khar'kov
Sokol'skii, S.	1870s		N (U)	1887	Valdimir
Solomin, G.K.	1867	Teacher	A (U)	1938	Orel
Solov'ev, N.I.	1850	Bureaucrat	A (P)	1899	Vladimir
Solov'ev, N.M.	1867	Teacher, bursa	A-c (U)	1921	Vladimir
Solov'ev, S.M.	1820	Prof. Univ.	A (P)	1879	Moscow
Strakhov, N.N.	1828	Lit. critic	A-c (P)	1891	Khar'kov
Subbotin, N.I.	1827	Prof. PDA	L (U/P), D (U) A (P)	1845–75, 1881, 1899	Vladimir
Sychugov, S.I.	1841	Doctor	A (U§/P)	1890s	Viatka
Tankov, A.A.	1856	Teacher, Gym.	A (P)	1904	Kursk
Teplov, A.L.	1852	Revolutionary	L (U), A (U§)	1905–09, 1917	Penza
Tikhomirov, A.A.	1876	Teacher (SD)	A-c (U)	1925	Vladimir
Tikhomirov, D.I.	1844	Pedagogue	A (P)	1901	Kostroma
Tikhonov, V.A.	1847	Bureaucrat	A (P)	1912	Ukraine
Tikhonravov, M.V.	1820	Teacher, Sem.	L (P)	1850	Vladimir
Tregubov, A.M.	1863	Engineer	L (U)	1880s	Poltava
Tregubov, I.M.	1853	Tolstoyian (R)	L (U)	1869–1928	Poltava
Tregubov, N.M.	1855	Statistician (SR)	L (U)	1878–1921	Poltava
Troitskii, A.I.	1863	Teacher, Sem.	O (P)	1909	Vladimir
Troitskii, S.S.	1881	Teacher, Gym.	L (P)	1898–1910	Kostroma
Tsezarevskii, P.V.	1843	Doctor	A (P)	1906	Voronezh
Tsvetaev, D.V.	1852	Historian	L (U)	1896, 1910	Vladimir
Tsvetaev, I.V.	1847	Professor	L (U)	1911–12	Vladimir
Tsvetkov, A.E.	1847	Doctor	L (U)	1864–1908	Simbirsk
Tsvetkov, I.E.	1845	Art Collector	D, A, L (U)	1866, 1809, 1863–1910	Simbirsk

Name	Born	Profession*	Genre†	Date‡	Birthplace
Tsvetkov, P.E.	1854	Doctor	L (U)	1874–94	Simbirsk
Uspenskii, N.N.	1875	Teacher, Sem.	L (U)	1906–14	Riazan
Uspenskii, N.V.	1837	Writer	A (P)	1889	Tula
Uspenskii, S.N.	1886	Economist	D, L (U)	1897, 1904–13	Riazan
Vasil'ev, A.V.	1851	Writer	L (U)	1890s	Belgorod
Vasnetsov, A.M.	1850	Artist	L (U§), A (P)	1896–1924, 1929	Viatka
Vasnetsov, V.M.	1848	Artist	L (P/U§), D, A-c (U§)	1871–1926, 1909, 1924	Viatka
Veselovskii, N.N.	1901	Clerk	A (U)	1925	Vladimir
Vinogradov, V.K.	1843	Director, Gym.	A (P)	1895	Vladimir
Vishniakov, A.G.	1837	Bureaucrat	L (P)	1863	Vladimir
Vologodskii, P.V.	1863	Lawyer	A (P)	1920	Tobol'sk
Voronskii, A.	1884	Revolutionary (SD)	A (P)	1932	Tambov
Vrutsevich, Mikhail	1845		A (P)	1905	Ukraine
Vvedenskii, A.I.	1844	Lit. Scholar	A (U)	1894	Tver
Vvedenskii, I.I.	1813	Writer	A (P)	1855	Saratov
Zagoskin, M.V.	1830	Writer	F (P)	1876	Irkutsk
Zamiatin, E.I.	1884	Writer (SD)	A (P)	1922–29	Tambov
Zelenin, D.K.	1878	Prof. Ethnography	D, A (U)	1895–1902, 1920–49	Viatka
Zlatovratskii, A.P.		Teacher	L (P)	1857–58	Vladimir
Znamenskii, E.S.	1816	Bureaucrat	L (U)	1830s	Vladimir
Znamenskii, M.S.	1833	Artist	L (U), A (U§)	1848–58, 1864–76, 1880s	Tobol'sk
Zolotarev, A.A.	1879	Writer	L, A-c (U)	1897–1929, 1948	Iaroslavl

* When known, political affiliation: **(R)** = generic Radical (usually Populist); **(SD)** = Marxist; **(L)** = Liberal; **(SR)** = Social Revolutionary; **(M)** = Monarchist.

† A = autobiography; **D** = diary; **L** = Letter; **N** = Suicide note; **C** = Confession to police if autobiographical; **F** = Fictionalized autobiography; **I** = Oral history interview; **O** = Obituary of family member. Sometimes multiple works of the same genre were written by an author. Whether or not the work was published or unpublished is indicated by **P** (published) or **U** (unpublished). An **A** followed by a **c** indicates that the autobiography was commissioned from the author for a collection. Petitions, speeches, and scholarly works by identifiable *popovichi* are not included here as they are not specifically personal texts.

‡ The date a text was written; if that is unknown, a publication date is listed.

§ Written in the pre-revolutionary period and only later published in the Soviet or the post-Soviet period; or if written in the Soviet period, published in the post-Soviet period.

Notes

Abbreviations

Biblioteka VMed A—The fundamental library of the Medical-Military Academy

BV—*Bogoslovskii vestnik*

DCh—*Dushepoleznoe chtenie*

DP RNB—Dom Plekhanova of the Russian National Library, St. Petersburg

GARF—State Archive of the Russian Federation, Moscow

GAVO—State Archive of Vladimir Province, Vladimir

GM—*Golos minuvshogo*

Granat—*Entsiklopedicheskii Slovar' Russkogo biograficheskogo instituta Granat*

IRLI—Institute of Russian Literature (Pushkinskii dom), St. Petersburg

IV—*Istoricheskii vestnik*

IVO [year]—*Izvlecheniia iz vsepoddanneishego otcheta ober-prokurora*

KhCh—*Khristianskoe chtenie*

IVDS—N. Malitskii, *Istoriia Vladimirskoi dukhovnoi seminarii*

MIR—Museum of the History of Religion, St. Petersburg

OR RGB—Russian State Library, Manuscript Division, Moscow

OR RNB—Russian National Library, Manuscript Division, St. Petersburg

PFA RAN—Archive of the Russian Academy of Sciences, St. Petersburg Division

PO—*Pravoslavnoe obozrenie*

PSS—*Polnoe sobranie sochinenii*

RGALI—Russian State Archive of Literature and Art, Moscow

RGIA—Russian State Historical Archive, St. Petersburg

RSP—Rukovodsto dlia sel'skikh pastyrei

RA—Russkii arkhiv

RS—Russkaia starina

SR—Slavic Review

SS—Sobranie sochinenii

Str.—Strannik

VI—Voprosy istorii

VEV—Vladimirskie eparkhial'nye vedomosti

In archival references, I use the following standard Russian abbreviations:

f.—*fond* (collection)

op.—*opis'* (inventory)

d.—*delo* (file)

k.—*karton* (box)

l., ll.—*list, listy* (leaf, leaves)

ob.—*oborot* (backside)

otd.—*otdelenie* (division)

st.—*stol* (department)

ch.—*chast'* (part)

koll.—*Kollektsia* (collection)

Introduction

1. Blagosvetlov, *Vvedenskii*, 6.
2. On the pivotal role of the "new aristocracy" in sixteenth-century England, see Greenfeld, 44–51. On the similar role Jews have played in modern history, see Slezkine, *Jewish*. For a fruitful discussion of the meaning of the ubiquitous term *modernity*, see Cooper, 113–49.
3. On the intelligentsia as a "nascent civil society" see Nahirny. For a discussion of the historiographical usage of the term "intelligentsia" see Leikina-Svirskaia, "Zarubezhnaia."
4. For this definition of the self, see Seigel, 3–44.
5. For a discussion of how reversion to traditional culture can be an act of revolutionary deviance, see Thompson, *Customs*, 9–10. For the phenomenon of "revolution by tradition" within Christianity, see Hill, 3–4, 85–103. Because the clergy was the only estate to share the nobility's widespread access to education, only two intelligentsia cultures developed in nineteenth-century Russia. Although by 1905 a worker intelligentsia had emerged, as well as ethnic intelligentsias representing Russia's national minorities, the late emergence of these new intelligentsias muted their influence on the ethos of the pre-revolutionary intelligentsia.

6. For an informative discussion of "repentant noblemen," see Ovsianiko-Kulikovskii, 8:83–99. On the clergy's independent institutions see Freeze, "Handmaiden." On the nobility as Russia's ruling class see LeDonne.

7. Frank, 156–84. For a similar attack, see Nikolai Berdiaev's 1906 essay (Berdiaev, "Socialism," 107–33). The concept of this shift in the intelligentsia ethos has been widely accepted in the historiography. For an influential analysis of these two juxtaposed intelligentsias, one pre- and one postreform, see Pipes, "Evolution," 47–62. Bazarov's clerical origins (his father was a popovich), which have largely eluded contemporary critics, were immediately recognizable to pre-revolutionary Russian readers. See Belousov, "Vnuk."

8. For a comparable example of a study that looks at the broad range of common assumptions that united German intellectuals who were both pro- and antimodernity, see Ringer.

9. Sarna, 220–24; Eliade, 204–6.

10. Blumenberg, 3–121. On the generalization of religious values during secularization, see Luckmann, 110–13. For contemporary sociological standard use of the term "secularization," see Wallis and Bruce, "Secularization," 8–30.

11. See Kselman; Blackbourn; Harris.

12. For scholars who argue that the modern self is rooted in a secularized form of Christianity, see Abrahms, 12–13, 65–70, 89–91, 217–21; de Certeau, 175–79; Taylor, 41–45.

13. Greenblatt, 7, 9. For religion as a "cultural defense" see Casanova, "Beyond," 25. Whereas Greenblatt defines self-fashioning as the opposite of a clan or caste identity, the use of the term "collective self" by recent anthropologists for the modern era is evidence of a new trend toward describing what could be termed collective self-fashioning, something that this study, in a sense, employs. For the collective self see Herzfeld, 139–70.

14. For a historian who has recently made this assertion, see Slezkine, *Jewish,* 66, 96, 363.

15. For the intelligentsia's self-definition, see Ivanov-Razumnik, 1:1–10.

16. The number of letters sent through the official mail jumped from 5 million in 1825 to 620.5 million in 1896 (this figure includes official correspondence). See Dmitriev, 397, 408, 411. For figures on the numbers of diaries and autobiographies issued in certain publications between 1801 and 1916, see Tartakovskii, 275.

17. Burke, 17–28; Blagosvetlov, "Novye," 89.

18. These non-traditional personal narratives cited in this book are from the institutional archives of the Holy Synod housed in RGIA, the archive of the Imperial police in GARF, and the local church school, seminary, police, and consistory collections in GAVO.

19. See Halbwachs, 48.

20. The approximate percentage of popovichi is based on the number of students studying in clerical schools and the ratio of Vladimir seminarians who left the clerical estate in the nineteenth century. IVO [1852], 62–85; IVO [1882], 78–81 calculations from the records of 7,002 seminarians in Malitskii, *IVDS,* 3:1–336.

21. Resources I used to find published autobiographies included: Zaionchkovskii, *Istoriia,* and *Russkie Pisateli.* On clerical last names, see Boris Uspenskii, 2:164–204. I looked up all common clerical last names in the three-volume *Lichnye.* By using an assortment of biographical guides, such as *Deiateli* and *Spiski,* I compiled a list of popovichi whose papers were potentially preserved in such personal collections. An example of a guide I used to memoirs in an individual archive that lists social origin is Zhitomirskaia. On the relative uniformity of clerical daily life, upbringing, and education in Central Russian provinces, see P.R., "Zametki."

1—The Backdrop

1. Belinskii quoted in Raeff, *Russian,* 256; Pushkin, "Skazka," 497–502; Griboedov, 103–218; Turgenev, 1:420–32; Repin, 74–75; Gippius, "Sumashadshaia."

2. Hertzen, 4–5:79–81; OR RGB, f.322, op.2, d.2, l.18 (V.V. Khizhniakov's undated memoir); Kanatchikov, 3, 5. For depictions by conservative noble memoirists and emigres, see *Rasskazy*, 243; Raeff, "Enticements," 275. For folklore, see *Narodnye*, 2:5.

3. Barnes, 139–58; Zemskaia, "Zametki"; Men'shikov, 112–13; Dal', 2:195–97. The term *bursa* originally referred only to the student dormitory at either level of clerical schools. Alfred Kuhn, vii.

4. Firsov and Kiseleva, 151–52; Meshcherskii; "Vospominaniia Khvoshchinskoi," 166.

5. For the monitoring of clerical behavior by peasant parishioners, see Shevzov, "Popular," 205–7. On the Slavophiles, see Aksakov, 113, 496 (I.S. Aksakov to Aksakovs, 1.7.1844, 2.5.1849); Engelstein, 83, 88–89.

6. For nineteenth-century discourse on the concept of "other," see McGrane. On social estate replicating race in Russia see Kolchin, 8, 170–71, 187. For other examples of historians who use "other" to discuss class, see Chevalier; Eugen Weber, chapter one.

7. Gippius, *Zhivye litsa*, 116–18. For two influential works, see Miliukov, *Religion*; Pipes, *Russia*. For recent recapitulations of this stereotype, see Figes, 67.

8. Bourdieu, 483.

9. Reiser, 150; Markov, no. 3:388; Freeze, *Levites*, 186–204.

10. *Prakticheskoe*, 84–85; Rabinovitch, 182–90; Korelin, 48.

11. Vinogradova, 23; Freeze, *Parish*, 156–59.

12. IVO [1885], 82, 239.

13. G., 73.

14. IVO [1855], 18–19.

15. *Pervaia*, 38–41. In 1880 43.6% of all female teachers in rural schools were popov'ny. "Odnodnevnaia," 194.

16. For an overview of the pastoral care movement see Florovskii, 332–451; Freeze, *Parish*, 192, 389–94. On its origins, see Freeze, "Mission," 115, 128, 135.

17. For clergy teaching in their homes in the prereform period, see GAVO, f.556, op.1, d.2413, ll.28, 63, 281; and d.2138, l.213 (petitions from Vladimir province clergy, 1865–66); and d.1299 (investigation of deacon teaching in 1816). The observation about clergymen teaching in the postreform period is based on the reading of the clerical service records of hundreds of Vladimir province parishes.

18. RGALI, f.904, op.1, d.346, ll.1–163 (Father Emelian's unpublished sermons and *besedy*); GAVO, f.556, op.1, d.1801, l.3, ll.20–22 (reports to Holy Synod from Vladimir province deans, 1856–57). On *besedy*, see Shevzov, "Popular," 144–55.

19. As examples, see GAVO f.556, op.109, d.339, l.3ob, and op.111, d.943, ll.6–8, 99–100, 169, 200–203 (parish service records from deaneries in Vladimir province, 1878, 1885); Berdinskikh, 134–38; David Martin, 279, 282, 288.

20. Pevtsov, 72–75, 148.

21. RGALI, f.904, op.1, d.346, l.117–17ob.

22. For examples of politically radical nineteenth-century clergymen, see *Deiateli*, 2:525, 637, 668, 811, 3:913, 1080, 1183, 1217, 1246, 1373. For political activism among clergymen, see Pisitios, "Dissident"; Pisitios, "Russian."

23. GAVO, f.556, op.1, d.2224, ll.68, 114, 130 (Vladimir province deans' reports, 1863); K.D.; S. Sh., 125, 131. 133, 136; *Obshchii*, 225; Ivan Preobrazhenskii, *Otechestvennaia*, 192, 209, 215–18.

24. *Materialy*, 665–68; Zaburdaev.

25. Calculated from *Materialy*, 154 (V.I. Dobroliubov to N.A. Dobroliubov, 8.9.1854); GAVO, f.551, op.109, d.37, ll.36ob–37 (parish service record for the village of Vashka, Vladimir province, 1850); GAVO, f.556, op.109, d.103, ll.1–2; op.111, d.870, ll.39–40 (parish service records for the city of Pereslavl', 1870, 1876). For secular salaries see Zaionchkovskii, *Pravitel'stvennyi*, 88; RGIA, f.802, op.8, d.175, ll.1–2 (a seminary teacher's petition, 1866). For attempts to regulate the treby system, see Shevzov, "Russian," 83–88.

26. Likhacheva, 356; RGIA, f.797, op.5, d.19196, d.19197, d.19217 (lawsuits by members of sacristans' families who had been misclassified as serfs by landlords, 1835); RGIA, f.802, op.9, r.I, d.3, l.108 (Bishop of Vladimir's report, 1869); P.R., "Zametki," 516; GAVO, f.471, op.1, d.106, ll.22–23, 27, 29 (minutes of Vladimir Church School meeting, 1868).

27. Pevtsov, 156–58; IVO [1857], 17–18.

28. Calculated from GAVO, f.454, op.1, d.554, ll.1–373 (birth certificates of 118 Vladimir seminarians born in 1890s); RGALI, f.1, op.2, d.6, l.3 (N.G. Chernyshevskii's birth certificate).

29. Quoted in Frierson, *Letters*, 47; for example, see GARF, f.102, op.233, d.6, ch.249 (1905 arrest record of N.I. Popov).

30. For the term "proximate other," see Smith, 47.

31. Pushkin, *PSS*, Jubilee edition, 2:482, 11:85, 11:78, 17:65; Antonovich-Mizhueva, 192–94.

32. Katkov, 416–18; Chicherin, 104.

33. Quoted in Panaeva, 176–77. Between 1882 and 1896 16% of individuals who were given hereditary nobility status came from the clergy. Korelin, 28.

34. Kovalevskaia, 58–59; Panaeva, 403.

35. Apollon Grigor'ev, 25–26.

36. A. Miliukov, 204–21.

37. Custine, 3:80.

38. Quoted in Belousov, "Obraz," 57; Kalugin; Ostrovskii, 192–279; Saltykov-Shchedrin, *Gubernskie;* Perov, 7.

39. Fedotov, 27; Polunov; Florovskii, 294–95. On the demeanor of the last two Russian tsars regarding peasant culture, see Wortman, *Scenarios*, 2:177–79, 192, 204–5, 383.

40. *Pis'ma Borodina*, 2:168–70; quoted in Nefedova (Moscow, 1884), i.

41. Zhirkevich, 25.

42. RGALI, f.1248, op.1, d.53, l.2; Glickman, 11–12, 17, 23, 30, 36, 45.

43. Khrenov, 71–87. For other examples, see GAVO, f.704, op.1, d.457, ll.6–9ob (peasant testimonials during a 1905 court case); GAVO, f.410, op.1, d.276, ll.1–10b (Pavel Leont'ev's 1904 obituary of L.A. Leporskii).

44. M.M. Bogoslovskii, 27–28.

45. On this polarized juxtapositioning of the "other," see Slezkine, *Arctic*, 34–35.

46. For the priest's statement, see GAVO, f.556, op.1, d.4355, ll.34–37 (Korshunkov to Bishop of Vladimir, 1903). For the memoirs of seminarians from other social estate groups see GAVO, f.P46, op.1, d.158, l.4 (memoir of S.V. Deltiarev); Aleksandrovskii, 286–92; K.M. Malinin, 10.

47. Korolenko, *Dnevnik*, 2:311. For his fictional portrayals, see his story "Staryi zvonar'."

48. GARF, f.102, op.223, d.1000, ch.10, ll.20ob–21.

49. Manning, 3–57; Vagner, 33; Bogdanovich, 55; quoted in Strakheev, 90.

50. Polovtsov, 2:447.

51. RGIA, f.802, op.16, d.641 (conscription records); GARF, f.102, 1907, op.237, d.62 (1907 arrest record of N.L. Korenko); RGIA, f.796, op.170, otd.6, st.2, d.2578, ll.7–8ob (law regarding popovichi's registration).

52. RGIA, f.1149, op.7, d.3, l.9 (1869 legislation); GARF f.109, op.223, d.34, l.20–20ob (Third Section report, 1869); RGIA, f.797, op.45, otd.1, st.2, d.90, l.1 (1875 ban on Vologda seminarians).

53. Engel'gardt, 3.

54. As examples, see Kokoshkin, 114; Fausek, 79–106; Panteleev.

55. Vengerov, "Blagosvetlov," 3:345–62.

56. As examples, see Naumenko, 30, 36; Figner, "Novorusskii," 12, 14; GAVO, f.410, op.1, d.276, l.1–1ob.

57. As examples, see Alekseenko, 4; Polevoi, "Tri," 137–41; Petrunkevich, 98.

58. Vovelle, 114–25. For insightful challenges to the general use of the two-tiered approach, see Brown; Shevzov, "Letting."

2—Popovichi and Their Fathers Judge Other Social Estates

1. RGALI, f.904, op.1, d.167, ll.8–10, 13, 17.

2. As examples, see Greznov, no. 18:514; Giliarov-Platonov, *Iz*, 1:297; OR RGB, f.356, k.3, d.43, l.20.

3. RGIA, f.802, op.10, d.12, ll.181, 226 (petitions to the Holy Synod, 1902–3); For examples on recognition, see Levkoev, 516; Krasnoperov, *Zapiski*, 74; *Pis'ma Kliucheskogo*, 45 (3.09.1861).

4. RGALI, f.218, op.1, d.55, ll.5, 8, 19ob (undated notes for Zolotarev's manuscript "K istorii Russkogo dukhoventsva"); A.A. Zolotarev, 109–11.

5. Gloriantov, 219–20; *Nasha*, 3–4. For examples of affiliating themselves with these traits, see Vrutsevich, 693–704; GAVO, f.410, op.1, d.121, l.3 (obituary of I.F. Gomerov by A.I. Troitskii, 1909); RGIA, f.802, op.10, d.67, l.19–19ob (draft of memorandum by Ivan Pomialovskii for the ministry of education, 1905). As examples of identifying themselves as "new men," see *Pis'ma Kliucheskogo*, 99 (17.3.1862); Marenin, 1:10–14, 109, 133–43.

6. As examples, see *Pis'ma Kliucheskogo*, 68–69 (27.10.1861); Antonovich and Eliseev, 137; PFA RAN, f.849, op.2, d.1, l.2.

7. Tikhonov, *Dvadtsat'*, 2:98. As examples of their studies, see Golovshchikov; Eliseev; Zelenin, "Seminarskiia slova."

8. For examples of closest friends who were fellow popovichi, see GAVO, f.454, op.1, d.173, l.1983 (birth certificate of G.T. Iakhontov's son, 1864); GAVO, f.40, op.1, d.19177, l.3 (marriage certificate of Ivan Blagonravov, 1896); GARF, f.109, op.1, d.500, l.11 (testimony of I.A. Ametistov, 1870). For other examples of marrying popov'ny, see RGIA, f.802, op.10, d.12, ll.152, 162, 177, 194, 215, 333ob (petitions to Synod, 1902–3).

9. As examples, see Tikhonov, *Dvadtsat'*, 1:30; RGALI, f.602, op.1, d.96, l.1; OR RNB, f.725, op.1, d.3, l.4 (G.K. Solomin's 1938 memoir).

10. As examples, see GAVO, f.454, op.1, d.213, ll.804–5, 822; d.181, ll.901ob–2 (stipends established for Vladimir seminarians, 1884–1885); A.S. Preobrazhenskii, 26–28.

11. Koz'min, 11; reprinted in Samoilov and Vinogradov, 115. Belinskii was actually a clerical grandson, not a popovich. Pavlov's mistake is indicative of his belief that many famous intelligenty were popovichi.

12. RGALI, f.904, op.1, d.16, ll.13ob, 14; GARF, f.102, op.223, d.1000, ch.10, l.19ob (petition by Smolensk seminarians, 1905); DP RNB, f.194, op.1, d.1220, l.3 (Matvei Glubokovskii's 1881 military record); DP RNB, f.1179, op.1, d.1, l.1 (1903 complaint lodged by Professor Aleksandrov); Gloriantov, 219; GARF, f.109, op.1, d.500, l.13ob.

13. *Materialy*, 618–20; RGALI, f.1027, op.1, d.3, ll.34–47ob; Aleksandr Orlov, 110; Dubasov, 190. As examples of returning to the fold, see "Posviashchenie"; "Khronika: Rukopolozhenie."

14. Walker, 336, 339.

15. Bunin, 289. On the redemptive plan in Christian autobiographies, see Henderson, 9. On merchant memoirs, see Kafengauz, 107.

16. Sadov, 2. See also OR RGB, f.250, k.2, d.1, l.1; Rostislavov, *Provincial*, 5.

17. Lepeshinskii, 7.

18. Innokentii, *Bogoslovie*, 3:272–74, 334–35, 338, 408–9, 436; Nikanor, "O khristianskom," 39–40; Khalkolivanov, 148. On the Orthodox definition of salvation, see Petr. On the influence of Pietest texts see Florovskii, 388–90; Nichols, 75–86.

19. Bronzov, *Nravstvennoe*, 107–8; Hedda; in addition to Khalkolivanov, see Soliarskii.

20. For examples of those who did not, see Sergei Zarin, 1:6, 20; "Asketizm." On "worldly asceticism" see Max Weber, *Protestant*, 95–154.

21. Fleri, 29–78; Khalkolivanov, 16.

22. Khalkolivanov, 60, 63; for an example of a saint's life, see *Istoricheskie*, 611; for Christ's biography, see Makarii, *Bogoslovie*, 1:202; Mikhail, 13, 15.

23. "O prazdnosti," 257–58, 263, 265, 290, 295; *Dnevnik sviashchennoslizhitelia*, 1:435.

24. Khalkolivanov, 67, 101, 115, 124, 132, 141.

25. Nikanor, 37–38; Zarnitskii, 502–4; Khalkolivanov, 237.

26. Bazhanov, 85–87; Khalkolivanov, 90, 159–61; Alekseev, 59, 67, 226.

27. Khalkolivanov, 124–25; Pelikan, *Eastern*, 260, and *Medieval*, 25–26; Greenblatt, 2–3.

28. D'iachenko, 325–26. As examples of well-read saints, see *Zhitiia sviatykh na Russkom iazyke*, 11:102; *Istoricheskie*, 570; *Zhitiia sviatykh Rossiiskoi tserkvi*, 9:17–18.

29. Khalkolivanov, 137, 190; Zarnitskii, 452–53; Chel'tsov, 3–5.

30. *Otnoshenie*, 5, 9, 13–17, 20.

31. For one example, see "Schastie," 371.

32. Khalkolivanov, 150, 172, 197, 227–30, 235.

33. D'iachenko, 323; Protopopov, 1692–93; *Otnoshenie*, 20–25.

34. Nikol'skii and Izvol'skii, 20; Khalkolivanov, 135–36, 183, 234, 240; Filaret [Drozdov], 342, 344.

35. I.L., 277–79, 282; Potorzhinskii, 700–702; Khalkolivanov, 207, 226–27, 234–37. On Christ, see Makarii, *Bogoslovie*, 1:203. On the interplay between Russian national identity and Orthodoxy among Late Imperial Russian missionaries, see Geraci.

36. Khalkolivanov, 41, 171, 173, 234; "Razmyslenie," 252–53; Bulgakov, *Obraztsy*, 869.

37. "Zhenskie," 235.

38. Bazhanov, 2:150–51; Khalkolivanov, 237–39, 244; Platon, 2:237, 239.

39. As examples, see OR RGB, f.356, k.3, d.46, l.30; OR RNB, f.725, op.1, d.3, ll.13, 56ob.

40. N.N., 714.

41. *Russkoe*, 419; *Zapiski*, 18.

42. RGALI, f.904, op.1, d.167, l.8; Dobroliubov, "Chto," 314–18; Grekov, 111–12.

43. *Russkoe*, 419; Sergei Solov'ev, 252; Dobroliubov, "Chto," 336–37.

44. For examples of sermons, see Smiriagin, 1392; *Russkoe*, 386. On clerical reforms, see Anatolii, 113.

45. D., 686–87; Dobroliubov, "Zagranichnye preniia," 245; Ponomarev, 496.

46. P.I.T., 34–36; "Posviashchenie," 96; *Zapiski*, 1; Dobroliubov, "Kogda," 96–140; V.A. Dobroliubov, 139; Herzen quoted in Slezkine, *Jewish*, 140.

47. P.I.T., 37, 65; Solov'ev; *Zapiski*, 253.

48. "Sviashchennik," 1365–66. For other examples, see Gusev, 301; Baratynskii, 397.

49. Grekov, 111–12; S.; *Zapiski*, 3–5; M.K. On worker ambivalence, see Steinberg. On merchants emulating noble culture, see Kafengauz, 114, 116; Ruckman, 8.

50. For one example, see Tikhonov, *V otstavke*, 38–39.

51. Malein, 205–11; Aleksandr Orlov, 83. For another example, see Vologodskii, 133–34.

52. Shashkov, no. 30:11; RGALI, f.602, op.1, d.96, l.11–13. For a conservative popovich spurning nobles as friends, see Tikhonov, *Dvadtsat'*, 1:45.

53. N.V. Uspenskii, 12–13; Glickman, 76; Lepeshinskii, 165–67.

54. As examples, see Sychugov, *Zapiski*, 323 (S.I. Sychugov to Tomas, 1.11.1899); OR RNB, f.802, op.1, d.23, l.39ob (S.N. Uspenskii to G.N. Uspenskaia, 1911); RGALI, f.602, op.1, d.96, l.1. On noble ambivalence toward the term, see Kolonitskii, "Intelligentsiia," 184, 194.

55. GAVO, f.704, op.1, d.192, l.97; "Kak dolzhen," 181–82.

56. Karonin, "Obshchestvo."

57. GAVO, f.622, op.2, d.707, ll.1–2 (A.V. Smirnov to A.V. Skalon, 24.4.1882); Mamin-Sibiriak, "Avtobiografiia," 198–99. For enlightened priests in popovichi's fiction see the character of Father Aleksei Mertsalov in Chernyshevskii's novel *What Is to Be Done?* and Karonin's story "Podrezannye kryl'ia." For an example of an intelligent from the nobility defining the intelligentsia as excluding members of the clergy, see Gippius, *Zhivye*, 116.

58. Elpat'evskii, *Vospominaniia,* 29–30, 114; Sergei Solov'ev, 103–8. For examples of "good" noble Slavophiles see Kliuchevskii, "Aksakov," 318; Giliarov-Platonov, "O syd'be."

59. Khalkolivanov, 245–46.

60. Popov, *Pis'ma,* 7, 126–44; Kliuchevskii, "Ob intelligentsii," 299–308. On noble intelligenty's images of the peasantry see Frierson, *Peasant,* 32–54. For examples of popovichi's image of the peasantry, see Dobroliubov, "Cherty," 245, 269; GAVO, f.704, op.1, d.192, l.97. For two examples of the traits clergymen praised peasants for, see Beliaev, 92; Zelenetskii, 1089.

61. Knight; M.R. Popov, 53; Tikhonov, *Dvadtsat',* 1:3; OR RGB, f.23, k.1, d.1, l.2; Bulgakov, *Zametki,* 14–15.

62. OR RGB, f.356, k.3, d.46, l.53ob. For another example, see OR RGB, f.177, d.50.66, l.1. For an example of a noble autobiographer describing the peasantry in ethnographic detail, see Davydov, 2:30–31. On noble intelligenty viewing peasants as an enigma, see Frierson, *Peasant,* 53.

63. Sergei Solov'ev, 274: Tikhonov, *V otstavke,* 41–42; OR RGB, f.356, k.3, d.46, ll.13ob–14.

64. As examples, see Lavrov, 45; "Psalomshchik," 833; RGIA, f.804, op.1, d.11, r.III, l.88ob (response of Vladimir province parish clergy to 1863 questionnaire).

65. *Zapiski,* 32–34, 116, 213.

66. A.M. Vasnetsov, 135; Wachtel, 108–10; Davydov, 1:337, 2:8–9, 13–14. As examples of peasants as their best friends, see Tikhonov, *Dvadtsat',* 1:42; Snezhnevskii, 9; Voronskii, 66.

67. Giliarov-Platonov, *Iz,* 1:151. As examples of good relations with peasants as adults see Malein, 214; DP RNB, f.102, op.1, d.189 (V.I. Brilliantov to A.I. Brilliantov, 1918); RGALI, f.602, op.1, d.96, l.10.

68. RGIA, f.796, op.141, d.367a, l.62ob (minutes of 1860s church school reform committee); S. P—v, 47; Smiriagin, 725. For examples of these complaints about peasants, see RGIA, f.804, op.1, d.14, l.122 and d.18 l.53ob (responses of clergymen in two Vladimir province parishes to 1863 questionnaire); *Zapiski,* 38.

69. As examples, see P.I.T., 35; E.A., 3.

70. Zelenetskii, 1085.

71. A.V., 131–32, 140.

72. Sadov, 3. As examples of watching over peasants, see Kriukovskii, 144(10):63; M. R. Popov, 42, 391–403; Biriukov, 11.

73. GAVO, f.556, op.1, d.2413, ll.37–38, 43.

74. Khalkolivanov, 12, 242; Bazhanov, 2:155; Platon, 2:246. Prior to the midnineteenth century, Church publicists and bishops were generally uncritical of Russia's urban classes. See Freeze, "'Going,'" 217–19.

75. Dobroliubov, "Temnoe," 7–139; Shashkov, no. 30:10–11; *Zapiski,* 4, 12.

76. A.M. Vasnetsov, 127; Shashkov, no.30, 10–11.

77. *IVDS,* 2:169; RGIA, f.802, op.9, d.6, l.5ob–6; Shashkov, no. 30:10–11. For other examples of popovichi, see Tankov, no.25:687; RGALI, f.904, op.1, d.35, l.17 (Ivan Tsvetkov's 1909 memoir). For an example of a clergyman assigning these traits to the two urban estates, see M.V., 92–93.

78. Mikhail, 11–12, 37; Suny, 105–37; Lazurskii, 11.

79. For examples of respectful merchants, see OR RGB, f.250, k.II, d.1, l.79; Milovskii, 203.

80. For examples of fistfights with townsboys, see OR RNB, f.725, op.1, d.3, ll.3–4, 68; Gloriantov, 211; Sychugov, *Zapiski,* 207. For examples of interaction with gymnasium students, see Sadov, 15; Evlogii, 19; Kriukovskii, 144(10):64.

81. As examples, see Gloriantov, 213; Giliarov-Platonov, *Iz,* 1:288; "Obzor," 321.

82. *Entsiklopediia,* 272; GAVO, f.556, op.1, d.4355, l.24. A dean is the highest priestly subrank; he supervises all aspects of clerical life within a group of parishes.

83. Ivanov-Razumnik, 1; Rieber, 402; Manning, 6; Figes and Kolonitskii, 168.
84. See Mosse, 5–6, 8.

3—Prescriptive Norms for the Sacred Estate

1. P.R., "Domashnii," 85–88; Jacobsen, 47–67.
2. Khalkolivanov, 209; Makarii, *Bogoslovie*, 1:203; Wagner, 101–37, 149, 238, 308.
3. Casanova, *Public*, 14–15; Weber, *Sociology*, 162–65.
4. Innokentii, *Pastyrskoe*, 104.
5. Freeze, *Parish*, chapters 5–7.
6. Kirill, 23; *Pamiatnaia*, 22, 25.
7. *Pamiatnaia*, 13, 20–21; "Vazhnost'," 106–11; "Pastyr' tserkvi—obrazets," 315–16.
8. Kirill, 21, 23. On doctors as modern priests, see Perrot, "Family," 123.
9. Iakov, 36, 8, 27, 29–31; Bulgakov, *Nastol'naia*, 2:1010, 1098–99; Kirill, 31, 103; *Pamiatnaia*, 15; "Svet," 281–82; Innokentii, *Bogoslovie*, 1:260.
10. Khalkolivanov, 136.
11. "Domashnaia," 268; Kuliasov, 1–3.
12. "Domashniaia," 270–72; Florovskii, 335–44.
13. P.R. "Vazhnoe," 485, 488; P.R., "Domashnii," 88–90, 93–96; Bogoslovskii, *Vzgliad*, 113. For puritan practices, see Hembrick, 186–93.
14. *Prakticheskoe izlozhenie*, 65; "Vazhnost'," 120; *Pamiatnaia*, 7.
15. Pelikan, *Eastern*, 256; Silber; Popov, *Pis'ma*, 1:98–99; G., 66–67; *Zhizn'*, 4–7, 9, 13; Spasskii, 172–80.
16. P.P., 413; Iakshich, 5, 24.
17. For one example, see A.N., 1–21.
18. *Zhizn'*, 9; Pevnitskii, 68–74.
19. K.D., 25; Broiakovskii, 80; Bulgakov, *Nastol'naia*, 2:1048–49, 1098–99.
20. N.G. Bogoslovskii, 61, 65; "Domashnii," 85–87; *Prakticheskoe*, 131.
21. For example, see "Domashnii," 90–92.
22. Mashkevich, "Prisluga v bytu sel'skogo sviashchennika," 73–79; P.R., "Semeistvo," 554.
23. Iakov, 124.
24. Pevnitskii, 136–38; P.R., "Semeistvo," 555–56.
25. Ponomarev, 492.
26. Runovskii, no. 4:452, no. 5:288–89; Gorskii, 201; Ekzempliarskii, 381.
27. Kheraskov, "Beseda," 539; "Vazhnost'," 109–110.
28. Bronzov, *Nravstvennoe*, 181–84; Stelliatskii, 15; S. P—v, 39.
29. Pevnitskii, "Semeistvo," 550; *Prakticheskoe*, 130; Gromov, 37, 39; "Khronika eparkhial'noi," 612–15.
30. della Cava, 71; Werth, 250; "Prizvanie," 129.
31. Platon, 201–3; O neobkhodimosti, 3–5, 18; Sergii, 4–6, 8.
32. *Svod mnenii eparkhial'nyk*, 14, 29.
33. Anatolii, 115, 118–20, 122, 125; GAVO, f.454, op.3, d.46, l.2; GAVO, f.454, op.1, d.504, ll.1–57; GAVO, f.454, op.3, d.47, ll.1–41. On being a bad influence, see RGIA, f.802, op.10, d.53, ll.79ob–80 (auditor's report on Vladimir Seminary, 1897–1898); RGIA, f.797, op.96, d.162, l.15 (Synodal decree issued in 1901). On protecting seminarians, see RGIA, f.802, op.9, d.66, l.142 (investigation, Ekaterinoslav Seminary, 1886); RGIA, f.797, op.45, 2 st., I otd., d.7, l.3, ll.5ob–6, 8ob (investigation, Arkhangel'sk Seminary, 1875).
34. Khalkolivanov, 210; for an example of puritanical views of children in general, see Kapachinskii, 951: "Domashnee vospitanie detei dukhovnogo," 259.
35. Makarii, *Bogoslovie*, 1:493–95; Gould, 39–52; for an example of the return, see S.S., 83–85.

36. Evsevii, 433–34; Popov, *Obshchenarodnye,* 100; I. E—skii, 149–50.

37. For an example of punishment for children in general see S.S., 142–58. For an example of punishment of clerical children see Polkanov, 132. On clergymen and anger see "Pastyr' Tserkvi v," 519–29. For an example on not spoiling children, see Balakovskii, 339–45. On the "good father" in eighteenth-century Europe see Hunt, 17–52. On Slavophile paternalism see Alexander Martin.

38. Khalkolivanov, 210; for one example, see "O religiozno," 276–77; Tovrov, 17–27; Perrot, "Roles," 205.

39. For one example, see Iakov, 47; Stone, 29–32.

40. "Domashnee vospitanie detei sel'skogo," 108; for example, see *Prakticheskoe,* 130.

41. *Ob"iasnitel'nye,* 11; RGIA, f.802, op.9, r.I, d.3, l.114 (bishop's report for Vladimir Church School, 1869–70); Krasovskii, 347–48.

42. M.E., 169; "O domashnei," 2–3; "Primernoe," 121; Bulgakov, *Nastol'naia,* 2:1048–49; P.R., "Semeistvo," 549.

43. Stites, 11–25; N.G. Bogoslovskii, 52–55; Worobec.

44. Ioann Polisadov, 1:304; S.Sh., 1–3; RGIA, f.804, op.1, d.150. r. I, l.183 (Synodal clerical reform committee, 1870); K.D., 27.

45. For an example of concern, see Troitskii, "K voprosu," 122. For an example of marriage as a matter of the heart, see B., 113–15. For an example of the consequences, see Speranskii, 6–7. On compatability, see *Prakticheskoe,* 83–84. For the Russian nobility's concept of love, see Stites, 11–25. On the early modern Protestant definition of a love marriage, see Stone, 26–28. On the Orthodox clerical definition, see Pevnitskii, 132–33.

46. As examples, see P.R., "Zametki," 519; N.G. Bogoslovskii, 56.

47. Prishvin, 251; RGALI, f.316, op.1, d.169, l.1 (inventory of Father Narkiss's library); Udintsev, 136, 173–74.

48. RGALI, f.316, op.1, d.91, l.8. For example, see the discrepancy between the instructions and contents of Father Sergei Belokurov's 1906 will (OR RGB, f.23, k.1, d.14, ll.11, 39ob–40). As examples of these complaints, see Smiriagin, 1216; RGIA, f.804, op.1, d.14, ll.68, 92ob, 122 (responses of Vladimir province parish clergy to 1863 questionnaire).

49. S.B., 232; Panov, 106.

50. RGALI, f.316, op.1, d.163, ll.1–27, 1–2ob and d.91, ll.13ob–14 (N.M. Mamin to D.N. Mamin, 1870s); MIR, K-I, op.11, no.117, d.I–8, l.423ob (A. Popov to Father Pozdnev, 1902); RGALI, f.904, op.1, d.170, l.11; I.G., 438–39.

51. As examples see *Zapiski,* 158–59, 163, 172–73, 262–63; Smiriagin, 1391; Al'bitskii, 78. For the eighteenth century see Tsapina.

52. RGALI, f.316, op.1, d.163, ll.19ob–20; MIR, f.13, op.1, d.797, l.23 (M.I. Tregubova to I.M. Tregubov, 1870s).

53. Meehan; Rostislavov, *O pravoslavnogo,* 1:552–55.

54. Smiriagin, 724: Chernukha, 209–11; RGALI, f.316, op.1, d.308, ll.1–2 (N.A. Ponomarev's memoir, 1809–11).

55. Beliaev, 391; RGALI, f.316, op.1, d.163, l.27. As examples of childlessness and children's deaths, see Iuzefovich, 399; *Protoierei,* 7.

56. RGALI, f.316, op., d.91, l.5ob; Glebov, 10, 14.

57. RGALI, f.316, op.1, d.91 ll.1–1ob, 3ob–4, 6, 8ob, 16–16ob (N.M. Mamin to D.N. Mamin, 12.06.1874, 8.11.1874, 21.11.1874, 3.01.1875).

58. Mamin-Sibiriak, *SS,* 10: 340 (D.N. Mamin to N.M. Mamin, 8.21.1875).

59. RGALI, f.316, op.1, d.91, ll.5–6, 11 (N.M. Mamin to D.N. Mamin, 21.11.1874, 11.04.1875). For other examples, see RGALI, f.904, op.1, d.168, ll.1–2, 5 (E.P. Tsvetkov to I.E. Tsvetkov, 1866); MIR, f.24, op.1, d.159, l.20ob (I. Subbotin to N.I. Subbotin, 1850s).

60. RGALI, f.316, op.1, d.91, l.7.

61. On biographies and autobiographies as a single genre indicative of the modern self see Burke, 20–24; for some of the tenants of modern self-fashioning, see Seigel, 165–66.

62. As examples see Giliarosvkii, 385; Beliaev, 93, 97; V. G—v, 462–63, 467–68. Not every clergyman's obituary classified under the rubric of one or the other model includes every trait cited. A composite is presented.

63. As examples, see "o. Dmitrii," 390–91; Florinskii, 591; A.M., 522.

64. L—V, 442–49.

65. Filaret [Gumilevskii], 389, 456–57; Makarii, *Istoriia*, 4:247–51; for examples of saints embodying traits associated with the otherworldly type, see *Zhitiia sviatykh Rossiiskoi*, 9:17–18 and 4:2–15; for saints who incorporate characteristics of the proto-intelligent, see *Zhitiia sviatykh Rossiiskoi*, 9:94; and *Zhitiia sviatykh na*, 9:98; Meeks, 13–14.

66. *Startsy*; I.M., no. 7:326, no. 10:494.

67. Zavedeev, 711–13.

68. For a discussion of this dualism in religious genres and old Russian literature, see Likhachev, 90.

69. Khalkolivanov, 50–51; Nikanor, 37; "O krotosti," 348.

4—Clerical Childhood as Heaven on Earth

1. Sychugov, "Nechto," 114; Polisadov, "Ocherki," 199. For examples of clergymen's sons contrasting their childhoods to those of nobles, see V.M. Vasnetsov, 155 (Viktor Vasnetsov to V.V. Stasov, 7.10.1898); "Sviashchennik," 1130. On the politicalization of European childhoods, see Reinhard Kuhn, 67; Maynes, 67–68, 81–83. On the politicalization of Russian childhoods and the components of a noble happy childhood, see Wachtel, 83–130.

2. Gloriantov, 209.

3. Strakhov. On revolution and breaking family ties, see Walzer, 48; Wood, 145–68; Hunt, 17–52, 97; Manning, 42. On stability and the cult of the family, see Stone; Perrot, "Family," 4.

4. Tankov, no. 36:685. For examples of popovichi's genealogies or research on great-grandparents see OR RNB, f.847, op.1, d.740 (Fedor Giliarov's genealogy, 1890s); Chernyshevskii, 1–17; V.M. Vasnetsov, 155 (V.M. Vasnetsov to V.V. Satsov, 7.10.1898). For examples of clergymen's genealogies, see DP RNB, f.253, op.1, d.2, ll.1–12 (sacristan Nikifor Dmitrievskii's genealogy, 1916); Baratynskii, 6:397–98; Florenskii, 270–78.

5. Ellis, 424–26; Gorinov, 35–36.

6. DP RNB, f.194, op. 1, d.1295, l.7 (N.N. Glubokovskii's 1912 obituary of M.N. Glubokovskii); On restorative nostalgia, see Boym, 49–51.

7. Pavlovskii, 155–67, 156; I.M. Krasnoperov, "Moi," 197; OR RGB, f.356, k.3, d.43, l.3. As examples of this charity, see Fedor Polisadov, 567; Tikhonov, *Dvadtsat'*, 1:42–43.

8. RGALI, f.765, op.1, d.188, l.2–2ob (M.S. Znamenskii to A.S. Znamenskaia, 1864); GAVO, f.410, op.1, d.121, l.3 (obituary of I.F. Gomerov by A.I. Troitskii, 1909).

9. A.A. Izmailov, 33.

10. As examples, see Bukh, 43; Aralov, 10; Voroshilov, 93.

11. For a Bolshevik noble's family disdaining material objects, see Krupskaia, 236. For examples of non-radicals bragging about their wealth and lifestyle see Bykov, 30; Tikhonov, "Tikhonov," 37; Roosevelt, 167–73.

12. Bulgakov, *Zametki*, 15. For other examples, see OR RGB, f.356, k.3, d.43, l.3ob; "Pamiati Troitskogo," 13. On the absence of religion in noble memoirs of childhood, see Wachtel, 182. For examples of radical sons of nobles and bureaucrats who claimed their parents were irreligious or agnostic, see Sukhomlin, 324; Hertzen, 1:74–75.

13. As examples, see Glebov, 8; Kniazev, 496; Dobrokhotov, 63.

14. RGALI, f.1248, op.1, d.53, l.2; Sadov, 3–5. On nobles, see Manning, 36; Wachtel, 121–22, 130. On clergy as hired labor, see Polisadov, *Doma*, 3–4; Peshekhonov, "Avtobiografiia," 142–43. On servants see Mamin-Sibiriak, "Iz," 204; OR RGB, f.280, k.1, d.21, ll.1ob–2ob (S.I. Smirnov's 1903 memoir).

15. Voronskii, 14; Vinogradov, 5; Lukanin, 35. For noble autobiographers on nannies, see Wachtel, 105–8.

16. Bulgakov, *Zametki,* 6; OR RNB, f.253, op.1, d.1, l.4 (Dmitrievskii's memoir, 1920s). For examples of singing, see Kriukovskii, 144(10):67; D., 671, 720. For examples on siblings, see Lepeshinskii, 7; RGALI, f.904, op.1, d.17, l.1ob (Tsvetkov's 1866 memoir).

17. Bulgakov, *Zametki,* 15; A.M. Vasnetsov, 125; Evlogii, 15. For examples of discussions and reading, see Mamin-Sibiriak, "Avtobiograficheskaia," 10:195; Lazurskii, 1. For examples of outdoor activities, see OR RGB, f.178, d.7312, l.4ob (Almazov's 1886 memoir); Remorov, 103. On nobles' conception of nature, see Wachtel, 117–25.

18. "Rech', skazannaia," 314; Bulgakov, *Zametki,* 17. On *heimat,* see Applegate, 8, 9, 12–13, 15. On Russian landscapes, see Ely, 198–207. For examples of describing themselves as completely Russian, see Kliuchevskii, "Pamiati," 332; Smiriagin, 1218; V.M. Vasnetsov, 173 (V.M. Vasnetsov to V.L. Kignu, 25 April, 1900).

19. OR RGB, f.177, d.50.66; D.I. Orlov, 29–30; Aleksandr Orlov, 21; Lazurskii, 19–20; Biblioteka VMed A, f.21, op.1, d.133, l.1. For examples of their fathers raising them, see DP RNB, f.102, op.1, d.1, l.1 (A.I. Brilliantov's 1908 memoir); N.N., 713; Dobrokhotov, 63. On nobles, see Wachtel, 96–108, 126–28; Tovrov, 17–27.

20. Voronskii, 15. For examples of Bolsheviks from non-clerical backgrounds who expressed this reverence, see Vinokurov, 78; Krasin, 226; Krestinskii, 232. On French revolutionaries, see Hunt, 28

21. Ostrovitianov, 7; Subbotin, 3.

22. For a discussion of the literary mechanisms of hagiography, see Ziolkowski, 29–30. On how individuality is preserved in typologies, see Lotman, "Decembrist," 72.

23. For his 1897 speech, see Liberovskii, 212.

24. OR RGB, f.356, k.3, d.43, l.20, and d.46, ll.54–56; Elpat'evskii, "Po povodu," 60.

25. OR RGB, f.356, k.3, d.43, ll.5ob, 6ob–7ob, 19, 21–24ob; Elpat'evskii, *O chernosotentsakh.* For examples of other fathers with this type of piety, see Pavlovich, 523–26; Giliarov-Platonov, *Iz,* 1:167. For an example of another father who read only theology, see Potapenko, 67.

26. OR RGB, f.356, k.3, d.43, l.20. For examples of other fathers who were adverse to change, see RGALI, f.904, op.1, d.17, l.8; Dmitrievskii, 779.

27. OR RGB, f.356, k.3, d.43, l.20. For other examples of radical popovichi, see Pribylev, 347–48; 351–52; Gedeonovskii, 58. For examples of noble radicals who did implicate their fathers, see Udilenev, 515; Hertzen, 1:101; Tsvilenev, 515.

28. For examples of fathers who stood out for other reasons, see Subbotin, 3; Sadov, 9. For an example of a repentant nobleman father, see Shebalin, 614–15.

29. Orlovskii, "Sviashchennik," 536–40. Even fathers who lacked any formal education could be described as avid scholars. See Nadezhdin, 50–51.

30. Orlovskii, "Sviashchennik," 535–41. For other examples of fathers who had trouble with their superiors, see Sychugov, *Zapiski,* 28; Tikhonov, *Dvadtsat',* 1:14–15.

31. Zhirkevich, 25.

32. Orlovskii, "Sviashchennik," 538–41; Orlovskii, "Selo," 14. For a similar example, see Barshev, 409.

33. S. P—v, 47; RGIA, f.802, op.9, r.I, d.3, l.108 (bishop's report of Vladimir Church School, 1869–70).

34. Shashkov, no. 28:11–12. For other examples see Krasnoperov, "Moi"; Biriukov, 9. For examples of the absence of corporal punishment, see Pavlovich, 592–93; Tikhomirov, 217; Remorov, 108. For examples of punishment as justified, see Golubinskii, 710–11; Pavel Bobrov, 2; OR RGB, f.178, d.7312, l.8ob. On Kliuchevskii, see Okenfuss.

35. Orlovskii, "Selo," 14; Orlovskii, "Sviashchennik," 535, 538–40. For other examples, see Sychugov, *Zapiski,* 28; D.I. Orlov, 136–37.

36. Orlovskii, "Sviashchennik," 541. For other examples of "proto-intelligent" grandfathers, see Sychugov, "Nechto," 112–13; OR RGB, f.23, op.1, d.1, l.2 (S.A. Be-

lokurov's undated c.v.). For examples of "otherworldly" grandfathers see RGALI, f.904, op.1, d.17, l.8; OR RGB, f.356, k.3, d.43, ll.1–2ob.

37. OR RGB, f.356, k.3, d.43, l.1; Elkhovskii, 130.

38. GAVO, f.556, op.111, d.906, ll.3ob–4 (Vladimir province clerical service records, 1878) and op. 1, d.2413, l.111 (reports from clergymen who taught peasants, 1865–66); Dobrovol'skii, 23. There are examples contrary to the political categorizations of Elpat'evskii and Orlovskii: radicals who portrayed their fathers as proto-intelligent (Sychugov and Shashkov) and conservatives who portrayed their fathers as otherworldly (Tsvetkov and Sadov).

39. Mamin-Sibiriak, "Iz," 203–4; Mosse, 3–39.

40. For examples of popovichi expressing a preference for their grandfathers, see OR RGB, f.356, k.3, d.43, l.2–2ob; Dmitrievskii, 781; Mamin-Sibiriak, "Iz," 229–33.

41. Sychugov, "Nechto ," 110; Evlogii, 9. For an example of being beaten by this mother, see Gloriantov.

42. Greznov, 510–11. For examples of illiterate mothers, see Sadov, 7; RGALI, f.904, op.1, d.17, ll.8–9. For an example of excessively indulgent mothers, see Vinogradov, 4.

43. Dmitrievskii, 781–82; Polisadov, *Doma,* 12; Costlaw, 223–36; Maynes, 78. For the first autobiography, see I.G. Grigor'ev, 12.

44. Bunin, 291. For other examples of happy marriages, see Tankov, no. 25:688; OR RGB, f.178, d.7312, l.2ob.

45. For an example on work, see Mamin-Sibiriak, "Iz," 204. As examples of blind faith, see Sychugov, *Zapiski,* 110; Polisadov, *Doma,* 7; Subbotin, 3.

46. Reinhard Kuhn, 66; Wachtel, 88–92; Pascal, 94.

47. For an early memoir of childhood, see Polisadov's "Mirskaia pomosh'," written when he was twenty-four. On autobiographical novels that are countertypes, see Dobronravov, *Novaia,* 1–2; Blagoveshchenskii, "Na"; Levitov. On the difference between the genres of autobiography and fictional autobiography, see Morson, 47–48.

48. Filonov, *Moe,* 11–17, 20.

49. Filonov, "Iz," 619–23, 655; Filonov, *Kak,* 64.

50. Greenblatt, 255–57; GAVO, Kollektsiia. N 7-k, Strakhagenta 21 uchastka Vlad. Gub, l.3–3ob (N.N. Veselovskii's memoir, 1924) and N 29-k, ll.5–6 (S.N. Kliucharev's memoir, 1924).

51. Elpat'evskii, *Vospominaniia,* 89–90; Rostislavov, *O praovoslavnom,* 2:365.

52. Hoogenboom, 78–93; Slezkine, "Lives," 21.

53. Golubinskii, "Iz," 710; Polisadov, "Mirskaia," 15–24.

54. Barshev, 409–19. For other examples, see Kulzhinskii, 111; M.V. Popov, 50.

55. Dobroliubov, *Sochineniia,* 3:289.

56. Giliarov, 184. On Decembrist childhoods, see Lotman, "Decembrist," 79. As examples of not playing games, see OR RNB, f.253, op.1, d.1, l.15; Vvedenskii's autobiography quoted in Blagosvetlov, *Vvedenskii,* 6; Al'bov, 460–61.

57. Voronskii, 63; Bulgakov, *Zametki,* 20. On playing church, see OR RNB, f.253, op.1, d.1, ll.4–5; "Pamiati Troitskogo" 15; Giliarov, 185.

58. For examples of pious childhoods, see E.A. Preobrazhenskii, 120; Shashkov, no. 30:12; GAVO, Koll. N 7-k, Strakhagenta 21 uchastka Vlad. Gub, l.3. For an example of missing church, see Al'bov, 177. For examples of assisting fathers, see Filonov, "Iz," 622–23; "Pamiati Troitskogo," 14–16; OR RGB, f.356, k.3, d.43, l.24ob. For bishops' disapproval, see RGIA, f.796, op.141, d.367a, ll.61ob–62ob (church school reform committee meeting minutes, 1860–1865). For examples of the ceremony, see Sychugov, "Nechto," 42; Filonov, *Moe,* 9; Rostislavov, *Provincial,* 42.

59. Smidovich, 59: Pretty, 298–99.

60. Zamiatin, 109.

61. Quoted in Bachaldin, *Chto,* 17, 20. For examples of noble preferences see Andreev, 29; Shcheglov, 96; Muizhel, 122. For examples of popovichi's preferences, see Al'bov, 1:460; Voronskii, 31–32; Bogoslavskii, "Chernigovskaia," 96.

62. Ziolkowski, 6–8. As examples, see Giliarov, 178–81; Mamin-Sibiriak, "Avtobiografiia," 198; Giliarov-Platonov, *Iz*, 1:181.

63. OR RGB, f.356, k.3, d.46, l.12; Bachaldin, *Chto*, 7–9; Brooks, 61.

64. OR RNB, f.847, op.1, d.739, l.11; OR RGB, f.356, k.3, d.43, l.7ob; OR RGB, f.280, k.1, d.21 (Smirnov's list for 1895); Mitropol'skii.

65. Bogoslovskii, *Iz*, 11. As examples of childhood veneration, see Kriukovskii, 144(10):61–67; Giliarov-Platonov, *Iz*, 1:181; Shashkov, no. 30:12.

66. Giliarov-Platonov, *Iz*, 1:182; Bachaldin, *Chto*, 19–21.

67. Bachaldin, *Chto*, 18–19; OR RGB, f.356, k.3, d.46, l.11; A.E. Zarin, 216. For examples on Crusoe, see Shashkov, no. 30:12–13; Al'bov, 176–77.

68. Tankov, 649; Polisadov, "Mirskaia," 19–20. On other intelligenty reading saints' lives, see Pretty, 298; Ziolkowski, 18–19, 27.

69. Opul'skii, 21; Toporov, 1:648–50.

70. Opul'skii, 21; Tankov, no. 36:685.

71. *Materialy*, 635; MIR, f.13, op.1, d.797, l.113; GARF, f.1733, op.1, d.2, ll.16–17. On the revolutionary collective as a family, see Clements, 82–83.

5—Martyrdom, Moral Superiority, and a Bursa Education

1. Gloriantov, 210. Epigraph from PFA RAN , f.849, op.2, d.30, l.304–4ob.

2. Pisarev, 50–116.

3. GAVO, f.1294, op.1, d.9, l.23; GAVO, f.622, op.1, d.22, l.18ob; GARF, f.102, op.223, d.1000, ch.10, l.44–44ob; Bachaldin, *Chto*, 19; Gur'ev, 357; Sychugov, "Nechto," 119–20. For a refutation by a popovich who attended the same bursa as Pomialovskii, see *Nasha*, 3–9.

4. A.A. Zolotarev, "Bogastyrskoe soslovie," 108. For an example of love for the bursa, including the church school, see Luppov, 69.

5. *Pis'ma Kliucheskogo*, 73 (27.10.1861); Lepeshinskii, 128.

6. Mamin-Sibiriak, "Iz," 254. As examples of stories of the bursa as their first memories, see Remorov, 108–9; Sorokin, 1; Krasnoperov, "Moi," 178–79.

7. Pribylev, 354–55; RGALI, f.904, op.1, d.16, ll.32ob–33, 39ob, 42, 47. On the percentage of clergymen's sons in secular schools, see Rashin, 72–75.

8. Shadrin quoted in Bachaldin, *Vtoroi*, 24–27; Ostrovitianov, 34–35. On Pomialovskii see Flath, 56–69. For a wealthy popovich who sent his son to the bursa, see DP RNB, f.253, op.1, d.307, l.6 (A.A. Dmitrievskii to V.A. Dmitrievskii, 3.06.1916).

9. Thompson, *Making*; GAVO, f.P46, op.1, d.193, l.1 (A.A. Tikhomirov's memoirs); Sychugov, *Zapiski*, 162–63.

10. As examples of this misconception, see Confino, 134–35; Brower, 74–75; Leikina-Svirskaia, *Intelligentsiia*, 102–3.

11. Preobrazhenskii, "Vnutrennee," 740; Freeze, *Parish*, 384–85.

12. Aleshintsev, 70–73, 128–31, 172, 187–88, 254, 279, 306. On the general curricula in gymnasia and Realschulen, see Sinel, 17, 150, 163.

13. Titlinov, *Dukhovnaia*, 1:200.

14. RGIA, f.796, op.169, d.594, ll.2–5ob (investigation, Vladimir seminary, 1888); Titlinov, *Dukhovnaia*, 1:197–99.

15. RGIA, f.802, op.9, r.I, d.3, ll.423–24ob (Vladimir bishop's report, 1878–79).

16. Shmid, 318–26; RGIA, f.802, op.9, r.I, d.3, ll.310ob, 406, 414ob.

17. Nenarokomov, 36–38; Ganelin, 196; RGIA, f.802, op.8, otd.1, st.1, d.23870, ll.14ob–15 (auditor's report, Tula Seminary, 1860); RGIA, f.802, op.9, r.V, d.6, ll.11ob, 13 and d.12, ll.124–27 (report on Vladimir Seminary, 1887–1888); PFA RAN, f.84, op.1, d.1, ll.8, 32–70, 208ob–9ob (Nikitskii's seminary compositions, 1870s); GAVO, f.454, op.1, d.53, ll.1–198 (Vladimir Seminary library's holdings, 1874–1895).

18. RGIA, f.802, op.9, r.IV, d.3, l.34ob; A. Gusev; Titlinov, *Dukhovnaia*, 2:25–27. For Vladimir Seminary teachers' publications, see *IVDS*, 2:230–94.

19. OR RNB, Q.320, ll.1–2, 4–5, passim; calculated from GAVO, 454, op.1, d.181, ll.815–16 (Murom Church School records, 1868–69); GAVO, f.471, op.1, d.122, ll.5–18 (Vladimir Church School admission records, 1868); RGIA, f.802, op.9, r.V, d.6, l.10; RGIA, f.802, op.9, r.I, d.3, l.50; OR RNB, f.847, op.1, d.739, ll.70–73ob (Giliarov's diary).

20. RGALI, f.904, op.1, d.7, l.1–1ob (Alatyrsk Church School schedule); Kheraskov, "Rech'," 545.

21. *IVDS*, 2:154–55.

22. Musgrave, 257; RGIA, f.802, op.9, r.III, d.3, l.320 and r.III, d.5, ll.173, 292–93ob; "Vozzvanie," 289–94; Evgenii Popov, 84.

23. *Pravila*, 8–10; "Khronika: O," 34–35; *IVDS*, 2:182–83.

24. GAVO, f.454, op.3, d.57, ll.17ob–23 (Vladimir Seminary records, 1915); GAVO, f.479, op.1, d.5, ll.390–94 (Murom Church School records, 1861).

25. GAVO, f.454, op.3, d.47, ll.1–41 and op.1, d.504, ll.1–57 (testimonials of Vladimir seminarians, 1903–1907, 1895–1915). For the traits Lycee students in 1812 were praised and criticized for, see Kelly, 40–41.

26. As examples, see RGIA, f.802, op.9, d.66, l.111 (investigation, Arkhangel'sk Seminary, 1882); RGIA, f.802, op.8, d.24500, l.3 (investigation, Iaroslavl Seminary, 1861); RGIA, f.802, op.16, d.164, l.2 (confidential 1907 Synodal circular); RGIA, f.802, op.9, r.I, d.3, ll.67ob, 230.

27. RGIA, f.796, op.445, d.357, ll.42–44ob (Kherson Church School student's death, 1862); *Sobranie postanovlenii*, 188. For the persistence of flogging, see RGIA, f.802, op.9, d.66, l.22. For postreform punishment, see RGIA, f.802, op.9, r.I, d.3, ll.68–69, 101–101ob, 104ob–5. On punishment in the gymnasium, see GAVO, f.457, op.1, d.115, ll.64–67 (Vladimir gymnasium records, 1888–89); Aleshintsev, 120.

28. RGIA, f.802, op.10, d.67, ll.14–14ob, 19–20.

29. See Elpidifor Barsov, 163.

30. As examples, see OR RGB, f.23, k.1, d.1, ll.2ob–3; OR RNB, f.725, op.1, d.3, l.6; Kriukovskii, 144(10):50. On ear pulling, see GARF, f.102, op.223, d.1000, ch.10, ll.44–44ob, 70–70ob.

31. Gur'ev, 362. For a discussion of the role of public punishment, see Foucault, 63, 67.

32. Filonov, *Moe*, 47.

33. As examples, see Oleinikov, 494; Golubinskii, 10; Vrutsevich, 703.

34. OR RNB, f.725, op.1, d.3, l.6; Baratynskii, 399.

35. Remorov, 116; Ianzhul, 6 (I.E. Tsvetkov to Ivan Iazhul, 1900s). On Christian manliness, see Richards, 32–35.

36. Shchapov, 73; Sychugov, "Nechto," 124; Kazanskii, 18–19; E.M. Ovchinnikov, 137. For examples of the commute and the cold and hunger, see Anastasiev, 334–35; Polisadov, *Doma*, 11.

37. As examples, see DP RNB, f.253, op.1, d.24, l.1; Pomialovsky, 171.

38. As examples, see RGIA, f.802, op.9, d.66, ll.128–30 (investigation, Vladimir Seminary, 1884); RGIA, f.797, op.96, d.195, ll.9–10 (1905 petition of Chernigovsk seminarians).

39. Marenin, 1; M.P. Ovchinnikov, 266–67.

40. OR RGB, f.177, d.20.66, l.2. As examples of gymnasium memoirs, see Filippov, 482; Shatilov, 221–22; Gnedich, 44–74. For examples of the seminary as vastly superior, see A.V. Barsov, 169: Rufimskii, 1134. For examples of their correspondence home, see A.P. Serebrennikov's 1890 letters to his parents (DP RNB, f.692, op.1, d.34) and the Tregubov brothers' letters to their widowed mother (MIR, f.13, op.1, d.797).

41. La Capra, 23.

42. Bogoslovskii, *Iz*, 1.

43. Polisadov, *Doma*, 10.

44. Marenin, 1:78–79. On nobles, see Wortman, *Development*, 209. For examples of abusive landlords, see OR RGB, f.178, d.7312, ll.26–39; N.I. Solov'ev, 378; RGALI, f.904, op.1, d.53, l.2 (I.E. Tsvetkov to Tsvetkovs, 1863).

45. Sadov, 17; RGIA, f.796, op.186, d.173, l.8ob; Mamin-Sibiriak, "Iz," 260; Wachtel, 129–30.

46. Evlogii, 28; Kriukovskii, 146(6):582.

47. GARF, f.102, 1905, op.223, d.1000, ch.10, l.15ob; Barshev, 409.

48. GARF, f.102, 1905, op.223, d.1000, ch.10, l.16ob; Pomialovskii, "Ocherki," 131; Kazanskii, 133; GAVO, f.608, op.1, d.1, l.256ob (E. Znamenskii to Znamenskiis, 1835). For examples of monks as despots, see Krasnoperov, *Zapiski*, 13; Golubinskii, 709; DP RNB, f.102, d.190, l.13 (I.I. Brilliantov to A.I. Brilliantov, 1890s). For praise of a learned monk, see Giliarov-Platonov, *Iz*, 2:341.

49. MIR, f.24, op.1, d.159, l.6, l.1ob (I.I. Subbotin to N.I. Subbotin, 1844). For other examples, see Bronzov, "V dukhovnom," no. 5:721–22; Nardov, 191.

50. Nardov, 188; Gosudarstvennyi arkhiv Tambovskoi oblasti, f.4, op.1, d.6800, l.11ob.

51. Rufimskii, 28; Sychugov, "Nechto," 124.

52. For comparisons, see Titlinov, *Molodezh'*, 11, 126. On uprisings in the prereform period, see Mordovtsev.

53. GAVO, f.457, op.1, d.150, l.38 (Vladimir Gymnasium records, 1893–1896); RGIA, f.797, op.46, otd.1, st.2, d.9, ll.178–79ob (1876 investigation of expelled bursaki); RGIA, f.802, op.9, d.38, ll.85ob–86 (auditor's report, Vladimir clerical schools, 1883–84). A slight majority of the 41 Vladimir seminarians involved in an uprising became clergymen. RGIA, f.802, op.9, d.66, ll.126–36; *IVDS*, 1–336.

54. RGIA, f.802, op.9, d.26, ll.8, 19 and d.42 (investigation, Vladimir Seminary, 1894); RGIA, f.796, op.186, d.336, ll.1–2 (investigation, Tambov Seminary, 1905); RGIA, f.796, op.186, d.340, l.4–4ob (investigation, Vitebsk Seminary).

55. Khitrov, 68. As examples of the "good" teacher, see RGALI, f.234, op.5, d.22, l.1 (Ivanovskii's 1897 memoir); Pavlovskii, 156; Pavlov, 6:441.

56. Dobroliubov, *SS*, 8:440–42; MIR, f.24, op.1, d.163, l.5ob (I.I. Subbotin to N.I. Subbotin, 1844). For examples of clergymen on their favorite teachers, see Oleinikov, 498; Rufimskii, 258.

57. RGIA, f.802, op.9, d.11, l.75ob. As examples of defeated teachers, see Kriukovskii, 146(6):582; M.V. Popov, 44; Polisadov, *Doma,* 16.

58. N.I. Solov'ev, 387. On workers' attitudes toward authority, see Steinberg, 40. For Bolshevik autobiographies, see Bogdanov, 30; Ganetskii, 97–98. For non-Bolsheviks, see Ashenbrenner, 12–13; Bekkarevich, 401–3, 409; Polevoi, "Dva."

59. *IVDS*, 2:167; *Zhurnal*, 28–34; RGIA, f.802, op.10, d.85, l.2ob (Seminary teacher's union, 1905 minutes).

60. RGALI, f.1248, op.1, d.50, ll.3–4. For other examples, see Dubasov, 185; Nadrov, 193.

61. Kazanskii, 110–13, 119–20. For other examples, see Vrutsevich, 695–969; Sychugov, *Zapiski,* 119.

62. Giliarov-Platonov, *Iz*, 2:78. For another example, see Lavrov, 12.

63. As examples, see Pomialovsky, *Sketches,* 195–98; N.I. Solov'ev, 381–88; Izmailov, *V burse*, 67–74.

64. *Pis'ma Kliuchevskogo*, 49 (3.9.1861); Krasnoperov, *Zapiski,* 55; Vinogradov.

65. OR RGB, f.178, d.7312, l.88.

66. As examples, see Malein, 61–64; Sychugov, "Nechto," 121, 123; Golubinskii, 10.

67. Krasnoperov, "Moi;" 187–88.

68. For example, see Kriukovskii, 1911, vol. 146, no. 5:445.

69. As examples, see Gloriantov, 211; Vrutsevich, 697; Gur'ev, 360.

70. Golubinskii, 10–11.

71. For seminarians rioting to protect one of their own, see the Smolensk Seminary rebellion in 1894 (RGIA, f.802, op.9, d.26, ll.2–4ob). On collaborating with gymnasium students, see RGIA, f.797, op.60, otd.I, st. II, d.63, ll.11–14 (1891 internal Synodal memo). For the Union's membership and proclamations, see GARF, f.102, op.223, d.1000, ch.10, ll.8, 14, 18ob, 67. For spurning invitations, see RGIA, f.796, op. 186,

d.173, l.6–6ob (investigation, Ekaterinoslav Seminary, 1905). For their journals, see RGIA, f.797, op.45. otd.I, st.II, d.7, ll.2–2ob, 11ob–12 (Arkhangel'sk Seminary, 1875); GAVO, f.622, op.1, d.22, ll.1–28ob (Vladimir Seminary, 1873).

72. RGIA, f.802, op.16, d.164, l.18; GARF, f.102, op.223, d.1000, ch.10, l.44ob (proclamation of Union of Seminarians, 1905); RGIA, f.802, op.9, d.66, ll.40–41 (confiscated correspondence of Arkhangel'sk seminarian, 1877).

73. GARF, f.102, op.8, d.89, t.2, l.72; GAVO, f.704, op.1, d.576, l.55–55ob.

74. RGALI, f.1248, op.1, d.50, l.5.

75. RGIA, f.802, op.9, d.11, ll.73ob–74.

76. RGIA, f.802, op.9, d.12, l.144; RGIA, f.802, op.9, r.I, d.3, l.70ob–71, 461ob and r.II, d.2, l.39ob (Vladimir bishop's report, 1869–1870, 1878–1879, 1881–1882).

77. Chernavskii, 563–64; Kistiakovskii, 5; OR RNB, Q.320, ll.1, 58.

78. RGIA, f.802, op.9, r.I, d.3, ll.229ob, 231, 459ob–60 and r.III, d.5, ll.290, 307; RGIA, f.802, op.10, d.53, ll.80, 101.

79. Khalkolivanov, 102; GARF, f.102, op.223, d.1000, ch.10, ll.16, 23; RGIA, f.802, op.9, d.66, l.139.

80. "Pamiati Troitskogo," 16–17. For other examples, see Sychugov, "Nechto," 111; PFA RAN, f.849, op.2, d.30, ll.301–3 (Novorusskii's 1892 diary).

81. For examples of popovichi who were not employed in the clerical domain who made such statements, see RGALI, f.904, op.1, d.16, ll.15, 17, 40; RGALI, f.716, op.1, d.125, l.27–27ob (V.M. Vasnetsov to A.M. Vasnetsov, 1900s); RGALI, f.765, op.1, d.188, l.1. (M.S. Znamenskii to A.S. Znamenskaia, 1864).

82. Biriukov, 15; Pomialovskii, *PSS*, 2:275. For examples of radical popovichi reconverting, see MIR, f.13, op.1, d.798, ll.14ob, 24, 27, 80 (N.M. Tregubov to I.M. Tregubov, 1917); DP RNB, f.194, op.1, g.1295, l.2; Bulgakov, *Zametki*, 25–35.

83. D.I. Malinin, 93; Pavlov quoted in Samoilov, 109, and Orbeli, 80. For an example of seminarians' interest in naturalism, see RGIA, f.802, op.9, d.12, ll.130–32 (1888 report on underground library at Vladimir Seminary).

84. GARF, f.102, op.223, d.1000, ch.10, ll.16–18 (petitions from Tula and Vitebsk seminarians); RGIA, f.802, op.9, r.I, d.3, ll.67–67ob, 69–69ob, 460 (Vladimir bishop's report, 1869–1870, 1878–1879); Bogoslavskii, "Chernigovskaia," 96.

85. RGIA, f.802, op.9, d.42, ll.33ob–36, .62ob.

86. GARF, f.102, op.223, d.1000, ch.10, ll.17, 22–22ob, 46, 62ob.

87. Tsezorevskii, no. 7:68; Evlogii, 29. For a sermon delivered at a seminary church that emphasized pastors improving the temporal world, see E.A., 1–6.

88. Billington, 120–34. For religious rites in prison see GARF, f.1733, op.1, d.2, ll.40, 44–45; f.1721, op.1, d.135, l.21 (A.A. Teplov to Teplova, 1907). For Jewish populists converting, see Tan-Bogoraz, 442; Aptekman, 9. For non-popovichi populists, see Morozov, 314–15.

89. N. Smirnov, 137.

90. OR RGB, f.177, d.20.66, l.2. For those who did not condemn the bursa, see Neskovskii, 519; Evlogii, 26. On composition writing, see Shashkov, no. 32:13; OR RGB, f.356, k.3, d.46, l.6–6ob.

91. Pavlov, 6:441. For another example, see Tsezorevskii, no. 2/3:292.

92. A.V. Barsov, 170; Mertsalov, 1–4; "Korrespondentsii," 303. For an example of a non-political seminary kruzhok, see "Pamiati pochivshego," 407. On kruzhki in secular school as exclusively radical, see Morrissey, 25.

93. Blagoveshchenskii, "Biograficheskii," xvi, xxviii, xliii.

6—Holy Exodus

1. *Zapiski sel'skogo*, 1. For this interpretation, see David Martin, 252; Weber, *Peasants*, 352–74; Chartier, 100–101. For Russia specifically, see Leikina-Svirskaia, *Intelligentsiia*, 104; Martynov, 112.

2. Markov, 3:386–411, 592–93, 596, 4:612; *Svod zakonov,* 9:64–67. The last mass draft was in 1853.

3. Calculated from *IVDS,* 3:1–336; RGIA, f.802, op.16, d.159, l.24–24ob (1914 history of seminarians' educational restrictions); *Otchet,* 11; Bulgakova, 24.

4. Rashin, 7

5. *Rukovodstvennye,* 158–59; Shchetinina, "Alfavitnye," 72.

6. Shchetinina, *Universitety,* 200; RGIA, f.802, op.16, d.159, ll.25ob–28; Ivanov, *Studentchestvo,* 68, 69, 72–74.

7. RGIA, f.796, op.141, d.367a, l.23; RGIA, f.797, op.36, d.395, otd.I, st.2, l.99–99ob.

8. RGIA, f.796, op.164, d.909, ll.1–13; for its authorship, see Freeze, *Parish,* 436–37; *Svod mnenii eparkhial'nykh,* 9.

9. "Tekushchaia khronika" (1879), 140–42; Kheraskov, "Pouchenie," 556–58; "Pochemu," 454–55; RGIA, f.802, op.10, d.36, l.1–10b.

10. Kheraskov, "Rech'," 539; *Zapiski sel'skogo,* 24–25, 90. As examples of statistics, see "Raznye," 604–5; "Izvestia," 358–59.

11. *Neobkhodimoe,* 18–19. As examples of these bibliographies and studies, see Golovshchikov; Vladimir Kolosov, 333–462; Pritezhaev.

12. Kheraskov, "Pouchenie," 554–56. For other examples, see Makarii, "Istoriko," 67; *Predsobornoe,* 2:560.

13. N.G. Bogoslovskii, 4.

14. *Materialy* (Bishop Antonii to N.A. Dobroliubov, 12.09.1853), 22–23; Sergii, *Kuda,* 10.

15. As examples, see Troitskii, "Obozrenie," 537; N.A. Kolosov, 1.

16. *Zapiska,* 4–6.

17. RGIA, f.802, op.10, d.12, l.327 (bursa admittance policies, 1902–3); *Praktich-eskoe,* 130.

18. *Byt sviashchennikov,* 16.

19. Khalkolivanov, 151–52.

20. *Zapiski sel'skogo,* 131–32; Tsezorevskii, 4:260. For the service reform of 1869 and subsequent repeals of aspects of it, see Freeze, *Parish,* 315–19, 417–33.

21. Mamin-Sibiriak, "Iz," 204–6. As examples of such petitions, see GAVO, f.454, op.1, d.181, l.272; GAVO, f.454, op.2, d.14, l.46 (Vladimir Seminary, 1868, 1914). As examples of awe, see RGALI, f.34, op.1, d.140, l.1 (Amfiteratrov's 1902 memoir); N.I. Barsov, 174; OR RGB, f.356, k.3, d.43, l.29–29ob. As examples of fathers encouraging sons, see OR RGB, f.250, k.2, d.1, l.17; Lazurskii, 1–2; Greznov, 239–40.

22. RGALI, f.316, op.1, d.91, ll.1–1ob, 6; GAVO, f.622, op.2, d.713, l.21; OR RNB, f.802, op.1, d.76, l.14ob (N.I. Uspenskii to S.N. Uspenskii, 11.11.1907).

23. DP RNB, f.692, op.1, d.52, l.2 (A.P. Serebrennikov's diary).

24. OR RNB, f.725, op.1, d.3, l.89.

25. Chernobrovtsev, 63. Calculated from Chistovich, 1–148. For an example of preference for the theological academy, see Barshev, 411.

26. As examples see Filonov, "Iz," 650; Pavel Bobrov, 1. On priests' sons as more likely to leave, see calculations from Litvinov. Litvinov's records cover the years 1774–1908. Other reasons included higher rates of bursa attrition among sacristans' sons due to financial insolvency and poorer pre-school preparation.

27. GAVO, f.608, op.1, d.1, l.3 (S. Znamenskii to E.S. Znamenskii, 1.08.1835).

28. As examples, see Greznov, 239–40; Pribylev, 346. On altering their plans, see Pokrovskii, 1–2.

29. *Materialy,* 1:6–17 (N.A. Dobroliubov to Dobroliubovs, 6.8.1853, 23.8.1853, 6.9.1853); N.A. Dobroliubov, *SS,* 8:450–53 (diary entry from 15.3.1853). For another example, see Nefedova, xxix (A.I. Levitov to Levitovs, late 1850s).

30. Krasnoperov, *Zapiski,* 108–9, 35–36. For other examples, see Peshekhonov, 144; Aleksandr Orlov, 59.

31. *Zhitiia sviatykh Rossiiskoi,* 8:225; Ziolkowski, 31; Kizenko, 177, 179.

32. Glebov, 3; M. Gn., 361; Dobronravov, "Kto."

33. OR RGB, f.177, d.50.66, l.1; E.A. Preobrazhenskii, 121; Leonid Preobrazhenskii's unpublished memoirs quoted in Gorinov, 32, 35; Ostrovitianov, 171.

34. Shalamov, 76–78.

35. As examples, see Tikhonov, *Dvadtsat',* 1:28–31; Bogoslavskii, "Chernigovskaia," 76–77; Malein, 209. At Vladimir Seminary popovichi held a higher rank at graduation than seminarians who entered the clergy during every period between 1790–1900 except 1841–1850. *IVDS,* 3:1–336. In 1874–1875, nine out of ten of the top students in the two graduating classes of Vladimir Seminary left the clergy. GAVO, f.454, op.1, d.446, ll.99–100.

36. Nefedova, xxxi (A.I. Levitov to M.I. Levitova, late 1850s). On unwillingness to marry, see Giliarov-Platonov, *Iz,* 2:126; OR RNB, f.725, op.1, d.3, l.27; Kazanskii, 108.

37. Tikhonov, *Dvadtsat',* 1:42–43. For other examples, see Vrutsevich, 704; F.L., 2.

38. MIR, f.13, op.1, d.1001, l.10 (I.M. Tregubov to M.I. Tregubova, 1887); d.983, l.2 (I.M. Tregubov to K.P. Pobedonostsev, 6.3.1897). For other examples, see RGIA, f.797, op.96, d.162, l.26 (Smolensk Seminary SD Party to General Tikhomirov, early 1900s); Sychugov, *Zapiski,* 231.

39. Giliarov-Platonov, *Iz,* 2:126–32.

40. GARF, f.102, op.223, d.1000, ch.10, l.62ob; Filonov, "Iz," 650; Kazanskii, 108; Biriukov, 17.

41. Aleksandr Orlov, *Moia zhizn',* 22.

42. Quoted in Zhirkevich, 27. On "good" versus "bad" priests, see Mamin-Sibiriak, "Iz," 254; Ostrovitianov, 20; N.I. Solov'ev, 381–88.

43. RGIA, f.802, op.9, d.66, ll.39–41 (confiscated correspondence of Arkhangel'sk seminarian Shmakov). For other examples, see M.Kh.,1–36; Eliseev, 15–16.

44. Kistiakovskii, 6; I. Dobrogaev quoted in Naumenko, 21; RGALI, f.1027, op.1, d.3, l.36ob.

45. Pavlovskii, 157; RGIA, f.802, op.9, d.11, l.73ob; RGIA, f.802, op.9, r.II, d.2, l.32ob; RGIA, f.802, op.10, d.67, ll.27–51.

46. RGALI, f.904, op.1, d.16, l.15; GARF, f.102, op.223, d.1000, ch.10, l.44–44ob. For examples of specific references to clerical calling, see Bogoslavskii, "Chernigovskaia," 78; Barshev, 411.

47. For this definition of modernity, see Giddens, 5.

48. DP RNB, f.253, op.1, d.307, l.7; Mamin-Sibiriak, *SS,* 10:336–37, 344; Weber, *Protestant,* 80.

49. Manning, 56. On the transfer of service ethic among nobles, see Raeff, *Origins.*

50. Based on calculations of the secular professions of Vladimir seminarians (*IVDS,* 1–36); *Statisticheskiia,* 267, 293–93; Bulgakova, 53; Leikina-Svirskaia, *Intelligentsiia,* 154.

51. Lazurskii, 1; Tikhomirov, 217, 222.

52. Bulgakova, 53; Ivanov, *Vysshaia,* 224; Leikina-Svirskaia, *Intelligentsiia,* 184–85; Pritezhaev, 169.

53. PFA RAN, f.849, op.2, d.1, l.25.

54. Shchetinina, "Alfavitnye," 118; Leikina-Svirskaia, *Intelligentsiia,* 105–6; calculated from Zagoskin, 1:19–219; 2:245–96, 312–48.

55. Calculated from *IVDS,* 3:1–336; Bulgakova, 103; Frieden, 23, 201, 205, 337; calculated from Litvinov.

56. D.I. Orlov, 137; Sychugov, "Nechto," 135. For other examples, see E.M. Ovchinnikov, 143; IRLI AN, f.286, op.1, d.48, l.2 (Aleksandr Smirnov's diary, 1892).

57. Pirumova, 98; MIR, f.13, op.1, d.798, ll.41ob, 44ob (N.M. Tregubov to I.M. Tregubov, 1900s); V.M. Vasnetsov, 147 (V.M. Vasnetsov to V.S. Mamontovaia, 28.12.1897).

58. Pintner, 435; calculated from *IVDS*, 3:1–336; calculated from the records of Shuisk Church School 1818–1886 graduates in Pravdin, 183–273: *K voprosu*, 6.

59. For one example, see Bogoslavskii, 78–79; Shchetinina, "Alfavitnye," 118; *Tomskii*, 148–52; Elpat'evskii, *Vospominaniia*, 33, 38.

60. For examples of depicting the bureaucracy as foreign, see Malein, 5–6; Nadezhdin, 55; Tikhonov, *Dvadtsat'*, 1:18–19. For an example of despising groveling, see Berezskii, 54.

61. F.F. Izmailov, 123. For examples of noting popovichi who were corrupted, see Gloriantov, 216; RGIA, f.804, op.1, d.11, r.III, l.135 (response of Vladimir parish clergy to 1863 questionnaire).

62. *Svod mnenii eparkhial'nykh*, 6, 14, 33; RGALI, f.904, op.1, d.35, ll.21–22. On the numbers of popovichi in commerce, see *Naselenie*, 1:90–118

63. Slezkine, *Jewish*, 50; OR RGB, f.356, k.3, d.46, l.14ob.

64. Weber, *Protestant*, 80, 153–54; Geary, 191–200; Silber, 1, 32, 158–83.

65. OR RGB, f.356, k.3, d.46, l.14ob.

7—The Search for Secular Salvation

1. GAVO, f.704, op.1, d.192, l.97–97ob, and d.292.

2. Quoted in Ginzburg, 40; Vengerov, 6:376.

3. Henderson, 14.

4. Krasnokutskii, 54–79; Paperno, *Chernyshevsky*, 41–42. On French Catholics, see Corbin, "Secret," 498–502, 549–50.

5. For these letters, see Kizenko, 97–150. For an example of a written confession to a clerical relative, see RGALI, f.904, op.1, d.188, l.1 (F.P. Tsvetkov to E.P. Tsvetkov, 28.02.1849).

6. PFA RAN, f.849, op.2, d.2, ll.3, 27.

7. GARF, f.1733, op.1, d.2, ll.40, 44–45.

8. OR RGB, f.280, k.1, d.18, l.2; PFA RAN, f.849 op.2, d.2, ll.8, 12ob, 126; OR RNB, Q.320, ll.22ob–23, .43.

9. OR RGB, f.280, k.1, d.18, ll.2–5; PFA RAN, f.849 op.2, d.2, ll.13ob, 15, 17ob, 18ob, 49–50, 54. For intelligentsia self-loathing, see Paperno, "Diaries," 244.

10. On the genre of religious autobiographies in late Imperial Russia, see Rosen-shield, 317–27.

11. OR RNB, Q.320, l.43; Engelstein, 94; PFA RAN, f.849, op.2, d.2, ll.2, 27, 42ob, 48, 50.

12. Dobroliubov, *Dnevnik*, 104–5; Ginzburg, 60.

13. RGALI, f.904, op.1, d.16, ll.14ob–15; Sychugov, *Zapiski*, 307. Sychugov's auto-biography was written on the basis of his diaries.

14. As examples, see OR RNB, Q.320, ll.1–69; OR RNB, f.608, op.1, d.10, ll.1–13 (Ivan Pomialovskii's diary, n.d.); Paperno, *Chernyshevsky*, 44–48.

15. M. R. Popov, 45; PFA RAN, f.849, op.2, d.2, ll.19ob–20, 26ob, 46, 49; Aleksei Bobrov, 212–13.

16. PFA RAN, f.849, op.2, d.2, ll.54ob, 55, 27.

17. Modestov, 334; Panteleev, 140–41; Bakh, 25. On the general industriousness of worker intelligenty, see Steinberg.

18. Tankov, 797. As examples of this use of temple, see Pavlovskii, 159; Andrievskii, 964.

19. RGALI, f.904, op.1, d.52, l.2ob; RGALI, f.1027, op.1, d.3, l.35ob; RGALI, f.904, op.1, d.35, l.1.

20. Krylov, 108; OR RNB, f. 608, op.1, d.10, ll.1–13. For noble rituals, see Lotman, *Roman*, 35–110.

21. DP RNB, f.253, op.1, d.306, l.15. The word for scholarship, *nauka*, is feminine in the Russian language. As examples of non-popovich radicals, see RGALI, f.1708,

op.1, d.1, l.2 (Karzhanskii's memoir, 1931); Charyshin, 543; Morozov, 307.

22. M.R. Popov, 46. As examples of popovich scientists, see Biblioteka VMed A, f. 21, op.1, d.27 (A.P. Dianin's 1890 statement on the student movement); GAVO, f.410, op.1, d.31, l.3 (K.F. Arkhangel'skii's 1907 obituary).

23. Koialovich, xiv–xv (M.O. Koialovich to Ia.M. Onatsevich, 1856).

24. Tikhonov, *Dvadtsat'*, 1:51; RGIA, f.802, op.9, d.11, l.73.

25. OR RGB, f.280, k.1, d.18, l.4.

26. Teplov, 82.

27. OR RGB, f.157, k.IV, d.7, l.19. For other examples, see RGALI, f.602, op.1, d.96, ll.9–11; GARF, f.1733, op.2, d.2, ll.10, 13. For an example of a non-popovich, see Tan-Bogoraz, 446.

28. Leonov, 491–98; Clements, 32; *Politicheskie*, 64–65, 290, 555, 744–55, 759–76, 768–79.

29. RGALI, f.602, op.1, d.96, l.11; Lazurskii, 13–14. On the hostility of the intelligentsia to political parties, see Haimson, 309–40.

30. GAVO, f.608, op.1, d.1, l.257ob (E. Znamenskii to Znamenskii, 8.9.1836); RGALI, f.904, op.1, d.54, l.16; DP RNB, f.194, op.1, d.1295, l.2. For the populist intelligentsia's use of pravda, see Mikhailovskii, 1:v–vi.

31. MIR, f.13, op.1, d.798, ll.61ob, 67–68ob.

32. E.A. Preobrazhenskii, 126.

33. Tikhonov, *Dvadtsat'*, 1:75, 113, 9.

34. For an example on clothing, see Pavlovskii, 158. For an example on debt, see DP RNB, f.102, op.1, d.190, l.13 (I.I. Brilliantov to A.I. Brilliantov, 1890s). For examples of seeing their financial status as paltry, see Izmailov, "Aleksandr," 35; Biblioteka VMed A, f.21, op.1, d.55, l.35ob (A.P. Dianin to M.A. Rakant, n.d.); Lazurskii, 3.

35. OR RGB, f.356, k.3, d.46, ll.14ob, 20–25ob, 26–28ob, 33ob–34. See also Pribylev, 353; GARF, f.102, op.233, d.XIX 2529, l.24ob (Kostroma seminarians to Georgii Kazanskii, 1906).

36. Hertzen, 1:75; Figner, *Memoirs*, 209, 205; OR RGB, f.356, k.3, d.46, ll.20–21; f.356, k.3, d.45, l.1–2; Vodovozova, 2:,78, 230–31.

37. P.N. Miliukov, "Liubov'"; Malia, 165–66, 173, 176.

38. Corbin, "Intimate," 549, 570; Lystra, 28–55, 257–58.

39. Pomialovskii, *PSS*, 2:276 (N.G. Pomialovskii to Ia.P. Polonskii, 4.11.1862). For the background on his romance, see Glickman, 70; 117.

40. OR RNB, f.847, op.1, d.739, ll.3–4, 7–8ob, 15ob–16, 24, 29ob–30, 33ob, 35.

41. OR RNB, Q.320, l.62. For other examples, see Tikhonov, *V otstavke*, 84–97; OR RGB, f.356, k.3, d.46, l.50–50ob.

42. As examples, see OR RNB, f.725, op.1, d.3, l.106ob; OR RNB, f.847, op.1, d.739, l.13.

43. RGALI, f.904, op.1, d.16, l.29.

44. DP RNB, f.253, op.1, d.306, ll.11, 87 (A.A. Dmitrievskii to A.I. Dmitrievskaia, 1900s), and d.431, ll.l56–57 (A.I. Dmitrievskaia to A.A. Dmitrievskii, 1913).

45. Golubinskii; RGALI, f.1248, op.1, d.50, l.7.

46. Dobroliubov, "Chto," 341–43; Dobroliubov, *SS*, 8:434–39; (1852 diary entries) Aleksandr Orlov, 108–10.

47. Malia, 177; Naiman, 15. For an example on *Kreitserova sonata*, see Semenov, 14, 24–25.

48. Voronskii, 63; Tikhonov, *Dvadtsat'*, 1:99; Rostislavov, *Provincial*, 37.

49. PFA RAN, f.84, op.1, d.1, l.128; GAVO, f. 622, op.1, d.22, ll.15–16.

50. Tsezorevskii, no. 6:284; Semenov, 20.

51. For the virtues associated with both Christian manliness and modern masculinity, see Mosse, 4–5, 8–9, 48, 50, 52.

52. Kropotkin, *Dnevnik*, 89 (28.12.1862). On the crisis of the romantics over love in the 1830s, see Ginzburg, 55–56. On misogyny among worker Bolsheviks, see Pretty,

294–95. On the radical intelligentsia's views of private life before and after 1905, see Naiman, chapter 1; Stites, 17.

53. MIR, f.13, op.1, d.798, ll.6, 10ob–11 (N.M. Tregubov to I.M. Tregubov, 1900s) and d.1000, ll.6–7 (I.M. Tregubov to N.M. Tregubov, 18.6.1914). On Victorian versus modern love, see Kern, 354–55.

54. MIR, f.13, op.1, d.799, ll.30–32, 35 (A.M. Tregubov to I.M. Tregubov, 1880s). For other examples, see Tikhonov, *V otstavke*, 86, 92; Biblioteka VMed A, f.21, op.1, d.48, d.50, d.53, d.55, passim (A.P. Dianin to M.A. Rakant, n.d.).

55. MIR, f.13, op.1, d.799, ll.25, 34–36, 39, 52, 85 (A.M. Tregubov to I.M. Tregubov, 1880s).

56. MIR, f.13, op.1, d.1001, ll.5, 14, 68ob, 85 (I.M. Tregubov to M.I. Tregubova, 1899), and d.975, ll.5, 7, 9 (I.M. Tregubov to E.P. Nakanindze, 1925–1928).

57. Tikhonov, *Dvadtsat'*, 1:82–83; Krylov, 110.

58. MIR, K-I, op.11, no.117, d.1–3, ll.235–38 (Ivan Pozdnev's diary).

59. Tikhonov, *Dvadtsat'*, 1:150–51; Biblioteka VMed A, f.21, op.1, d.79, ll.5, 19–19ob, 21–22, 34ob–35, 56 (E.P. Dianina to A.P. Dianin, 1910).

60. Alexopoloulos, 28–29, 33, 106, 167; PFA RAN, f.1079, op.2, d.30, ll.51–54 (Sergei Malov's wife's memoir, 1950s); Kalashnikova, 9.

61. M.V. Vasnetsov, 90. On the low numbers of clergy leaving Russia, see Andreyev and Savicky, 120. Of the popovichi employed in this study who were alive after 1917, only five appear to have emigrated (a sixth was deported).

62. Chistov, 3. Other examples of popovichi whose careers thrived after the revolution include the geologist P.A. Zemiatchenskii (1856–1942), the ethnographer S.E. Malov (1880–1957), the historian M.N. Kufaev (1888–1945) and the Vladimir province poet D.N. Semenovskii (1894–1960). For other case studies of popovichi's ethos as expressed in their professional lives, see Manchester. The three popovichi examined in the article are Nikolai Dobroliubov, Ivan Tsvetkov, and Aleksandr Smirnov, all of whom died in or before 1918.

63. Firsov and Kiseleva, 29. For a complete bibliography of Zelenin's publications, see "Ukazatel'."

64. PFA RAN, f.849, op.2, d.1, ll.2–3; Ivanova, *Russkaia fol'kloristika*, 140, 142–46, 153, 158–61.

65. Reshetov, "Neizvestnaia stranitsa," 5.

66. Reshetov, "Zelenin," 166. He was held for seven weeks before being vindicated.

67. Ivanova, *Russkaia*, 143, 150; Zelenin quoted in Reshetov, "Zelenin," 9; Ivanova, "Zelenin," 7–8.

68. Gagen-Torn, "Zelenin," 54; Fenomenov, 447; Reshetov, "Zelenin," 162–67; Slezkine, "Ethnography," 476–84.

69. Zelenin, "Narody," 15.

70. Bezhkovich, 367.

71. Reshetov, "Zelenin," 153; A. Zolotorev.

72. Reshetov, "Zelenin," 172; PFA RAN, f.849, op.3, d.486, ll.4, 10, 19, 29, 20, 40ob.

73. Gagen-Torn, "Zelenin," 53, 60–61.

74. Vasina, "Zelenin," 12.

75. Chistov, 4; Tol'stoi, 13, 17, 22, 24–25; Staniukopich and Toren, 158; Raeff, *Abroad*, 15, 198.

76. Vasina, "Zelenin," 14; Vasina and Gagen-Torn, 70; Bezhkovich, 367–68; Chistov, 6.

77. Gagen-Torn, *Memoria*, 53–54; Bezhkovich, 367–68; Vasina, "Uchenyi," 217, 223, 226.

78. Gagen-Torn, "Zelenin," 54; Vasina and Gagen-Torn, 67; Vasina, "Zelenin," 10–20; S.V. Smirnov, 138.

79. As examples, see "Ivan Maiskii"; "Anatolii Miller"; "Fedor Kudriavtsev." Whether these traits are also present in the obituaries of Soviet citizens who were not academics is beyond the scope of this study; if they are, this only strengthens

my point about the continuity of popovichi's ethos and its dissemination to non-popovichi after 1917.

80. As examples, see "Pamiati Porokha"; "Pamiati Lebedeva"; Sobolev.

81. Sakharov, 1:16–17. For family papers, see Vinogradova, 132–42; *Stranitsy,* 755–75; Zemskaia, *Bulgakov.* All include extensive genealogies. For examples of research on popovichi, see Pashkov; Sushko. The word *popovich* is also now used to describe contemporary clergymen's sons. See Dolinin, 203.

82. Kalashnikova, 20.

Conclusion

1. RGALI, f.218, op.1, d.55, l.30; Babkin, 5, 119.

2. See the essays in Hobsbawm and Ranger, eds.

3. Halfin.

4. Hunt, 17–52. Although the French Revolution entailed a terror phase, it palls in comparison with the millions killed as a result of October 1917.

5. On the anti-intelligentsia mood of the common people in 1917, see Figes and Kolonitskii, 177.

6. Berdyaev, 45–53. For examples of recent scholarly works that adhere to Berdiaev's general thesis, see McDaniel; Klinghoffer; Kharkhordin. For a sophisticated and plausible discussion of the conversion of Orthodox belief into radicalism, see Paperno, *Chernyshevsky,* 195–205.

7. Samuel Huntington, among others, has tried to argue the opposite, citing Orthodoxy as a factor in explaining Russia's alleged "deviance" from the "West." See Huntington.

8. On the English Revolution, see Walzer. On the French Revolution, see van Kley. On the American Revolution, see Bonomi. On the enlightenment roots of Stalinism, see Kotkin.

9. Thompson, *Making,* 54.

Works Cited

Archival Sources

Dom Plekhanova of the Russian National Library (DP RNB)
    Fond 102   A.I. Brilliantov's personal papers
    Fond 253   A.A. Dmitrievskii's personal papers
    Fond 692   P.P. Serebrennikov's personal papers
    Fond 1179   A.I. Aleksandrov's personal papers

Institute of Russian Literature (IRLI)
    Fond 286   A.V. Smirnov's personal papers

Library of the Military Medical Academy (Biblioteka VMed A)
    D. XXI   A.P. Dianin's personal papers

Manuscript Division of the Russian National Library (OR RNB)
    Fond 194   N.N. Glubokovskii's personal papers
    Fond 608   I.V. Pomialovskii's personal papers
    Fond 725   G.K. Solomin's autobiography
    Fond 802   S.N. Uspenskii's personal papers
    Fond 847   N.P. Giliarov-Platonov's personal papers
    Q. 320   Petr Smirnov's diary

Manuscript Division of the Russian State Library (OR RGB)
    Fond 23   S.A. Belokurov's personal papers
    Fond 157   S.Ia. Elpat'evskii's article "Mamin-Sibiriak"
    Fond 177   M.Ia. Fenomenov's autobiography
    Fond 178   Almazov's autobiography
    Fond 250   N.P. Rozanov's autobiography
    Fond 280   S.I. Smirnov's personal papers
    Fond 322   V.V. Khizhniakov's personal papers
    Fond 356   S.Ia. Elpat'evskii's autobiography
    Fond 364   M.K. Liubavskii's personal papers
    Fond 520   B.P. Koz'min's papers

Museum of the History of Religion (MIR)
    Fond 13   I.M. Tregubov's personal papers
    Fond 24   N.I. Subbotin's personal papers
    Koll.I, op.11, Bishop Nikola's personal papers
      no.117

Russian State Archive of Literature and Art (RGALI):
 Fond 1 N.G. Chernyshevskii's personal papers
 Fond 34 A.V. Amfiteatrov's personal papers
 Fond 218 A.A. Zolotarev's personal papers
 Fond 234 V.S. Ivanovskii's autobiography
 Fond 316 D.N. Mamin-Sibiriak's personal papers
 Fond 602 K.V. Lavrskii's autobiography
 Fond 716 V.M. Vasnetsov's personal papers
 Fond 765 M.S. Znamenskii's personal papers
 Fond 904 I.E. Tsvetkov's personal papers
 Fond 1027 G.E. Blagosvetlov's personal papers
 Fond 1248 N.E. [Karonin] Petropavloskii's personal papers
 Fond 1708 N.S. Karzhanskii's personal papers

Russian State Historical Archive (RGIA)
 Fond 796 Office of the Holy Synod
 Fond 797 Ministry of Church affairs
 Fond 802 Commission on clerical schools
 Fond 804 Special bureau for the affairs of the Orthodox clergy
 Fond 1149 State council: Legal department

Saint-Petersburg Filial of the Archive of the Russian Academy of Sciences (PFA RAN)
 Fond 84 A.V. Nikitskii's personal papers
 Fond 849 D.K. Zelenin's personal papers
 Fond 1079 S.E. Malov's personal papers

State Archive of the Russian Federation (GARF)
 Fond 102 Department of Police
 Fond 109 Third Section
 Fond 1721 A.A. Teplov's personal papers
 Fond 1733 M.V. Novorusskii's personal papers

State Archive of Vladimir Province (GAVO)
 Fond 14 Office of the Governor of Vladimir
 Fond R-410 L.S. Bogdanov's material collected for a biographical dictionary of Vladimir writers and scholars
 Fond 454 Vladimir Theological Seminary
 Fond 457 Vladimir Male Gymnasium
 Fond 471 Vladimir Church School
 Fond 479 Murom Church School
 Fond 556 Vladimir clerical consistory
 Fond 608 E.S. Znamenskii's personal papers
 Fond 622 A.V. Smirnov's personal papers
 Fond 704 Vladimir province Police Department
 Fond R-1294 Anonymous Vladimir seminarian's diary, 1860s
 Koll., N-29-k People's inquiry office (NSB)

State Archive of Tambov Province
 Fond 4 Office of the governor of Tambov

State Historical Library (GPIB)
 Unpublished volumes 1–25 of Deiatelia revoliustionnogo dvizheniia

Vladimir Party archive
 Fond P-46 Office of "Istpart" for Vladimir province

Published Sources

A.M. "Matvei Semenovich Malinovskii, sviashchennik Kashinskoi Voznesenskoi tserkvi." *Tverskie eparkhial'nye vedomosti* (1903), no. 20:514–27.

A.N. *V zashchitu braka; po povodu "kreitserovoi sonaty" gr. L'va Tolstogo.* St. Petersburg, 1891.

A.V. "Vnutrennee tserkovnoe obozrenie." *Str.,* 1880, no. 9–10:127–40.

Abrahms, M.H. *Natural Supernaturalism: Tradition and Revolution in Romantic Literature.* New York, 1971.

Akinfiev, I.Ia. "Avtobiografiia." In Vengerov, *Kritikobiograficheskii,* vol. 6.

Aksakov, I.S. *Pis'ma k rodnym.* Moscow, 1988.

Al'bitskii, M.S. "Vospominaniia Mikhaila Silycha Al'bitskogo (1814–1890), sviashchennika zhenskogo Feodorovskogo monastyria." In *Stranitsy.*

Al'bov, M.N. "Mikhail Nilovich Al'bov." In Fidler.

Aleksandrovskii, V. "Polveka sredi dukhovenstva." *GM,* 1917, no. 11/12:279–92.

Alekseenko, M.M. "Nekrolog." In *Pamiati Aleksandra Afanas'evicha Potrebni.* Khar'kov, 1892.

Alekseev, Ioann. *Uteshenie v nishchete. Pouchitel'nye slova.* St. Petersburg, 1846.

Aleshintsev, I. *Istoriia gimnazicheskogo obrazovaniia v Rossii (XVIII i XIX vek).* St. Petersburg, 1912.

Alexopoloulos, Golfo. *Stalin's Outcasts: Aliens, Citizens and the Soviet State, 1926–1936.* Ithaca, NY, 2003.

Anastasiev, A.I. "Avtobiografiia." In Vengerov, *Kritikobiograficheskii,* vol. 6.

"Anatolii Filippovich Miller." *VI,* 1973, no. 11:220–21.

Anatolii (Bishop). "Mysli po sluchaiu sovremennyk tolkov o dukhovnykh seminariiakh i dukhovenstve otechestvennoi tserkvi." *Str.,* 1861, no. 12:111–26.

Andreev, L.N., "L.N. Andreev." In Fidler.

Andreyev, Catherine, and Ivan Savicky. *Russia Abroad: Prague and the Russian Diaspora, 1918–1939.* New Haven, CT, 2004.

Andrievskii, M.A. "Autobiograffia." In Vengerov, *Kritikobiograficheskii,* vol. 1.

Antonovich, M.A., and G.Z. Eliseev. *Shestidesiatye gody.* Moscow-Leningrad, 1933.

Antonovich-Mizhueva, M.A. "M.A. Antonovich." In *Izbrannye stat'i,* by M.A. Antonovich. Leningrad, 1938.

Applegate, Celia. *A Nation of Provincials: The German Idea of Heimat.* Berkeley, 1990.

Aptekman, O.V. "Avtobiografiia." *Granat,* vol. 40.

Aralov, S.I. "Avtobiografiia." *Granat,* vol. 41, part 1.

Aries, Philippe, and Georges, Duby (eds.) *From the Fires of Revolution to the Great War,* vol. 4 of *A History of Private Life.* Cambridge, MA, 1990.

Ashenbrenner, M.Iu. "Avtobiografiia." *Granat,* vol. 40.

"Asketizm." *Pravoslavnaia bogoslovskaia entsiklopediia.* 12 vols. St. Petersburg, 1900–1910, 2:54–74.

B. "Trebovaniia otnositel'no braka lits, posviashchaiushchikh sebia na sluzhenie tserkvi." *Tserkovnye vedomosti,* 1888, no. 5:113–15.

Babkin, B.P. *Pavlov: A Biography.* Chicago, 1949; reprint: London, 1951.

Bachaldin, I.S. *Chto chitaiut v dukhovnoi shkole? (Anketa sredi uchashchikhsia).* Vologda, 1912.

———. *Vtoroi tovarishcheskii s"ezd byvshikh vospoitannikov Vologodskoi dukhovnoi seminarii vypuska 1894 goda.* Vologda, 1915.

Bakh, A.N. "Avtobiografiia." *Granat,* vol. 40.

Balakovskii, A. "Prigotovlenie detei dukhoventsva k uchilishchu." *RSP,* 1869, no. 27:334–45

Baratynskii, A.I. "Avtobiografiia." In Vengerov, *Kritikobiograficheskii,* vol. 6.

Barnes, Andrew. "The Social Transformation of the French Parish Clergy, 1500–1800." In *Culture and Identity in Early Modern Europe (1500–1800): Essays in Honor of Natalie Zemon Davis,* edited by Barbara B. Diefendorf and Carla Hesse. Ann Arbor, MI, 1993.

Barshev, Ia.I. "Avtobiografiia." In Vengerov, *Kritikobiograficheskii,* vol. 6.

Barsov, A.V. "Avtobiografiia." *Bibliograficheskii ukazatel' materialov po istorii russkoi shkoly,* 1900, no. 10:169–75.

Barsov, Elpidifor. "Avtobiografiia." In Vengerov, *Kritikobiograficheskii,* vol. 2.

Barsov, N.I. "Avtobiografiia." In Vengerov, *Kritikobiograficheskii,* vol. 2.

Bazhanov, V.B. *Obiazannosti khristianina.* 2 vols. St. Petersburg, 1839.

Bekkarevich, N. "Orenburgskaia gymnaziia starogo vremeni." *RS,* 1903, vol. 116, no. 11:401–17.

Beliaev, Fedor. "Ocherk zhizni protoiereia Mikhaila Gerasimovicha Sokol'skogo." *VEV,* 1891, no. 3:91–98.

Belousov, A.F. "Obraz 'seminarista' v predstavleniiakh i tvorchestve F. M. Dostoevskogo." *Philologia* (1997), 2:56–60.

———. "Vnuk d'iachka." *Philologia* (1994), 1:30–41.

Berdiaev, Nikolai. "Socialism as Religion." In *A Revolution of the Spirit: Crisis of Value in Russia, 1890–1924,* edited by Bernice Glatzer Rosenthal and Martha Bohachevsky-Chomiak. New York, 1990.

Berdinskikh, V.A. "Prikhodskoe dukhovenstvo Rossii i razvitie kraevedeniia v XIX veke." *VI,* 1998, no. 10:134–38.

Berdyaev, Nicholas. *The Origin of Russian Communism,* translated by R. M. French. Ann Arbor, 1960.

Berezskii, P.K. "Avtobiografiia." In *Dvadtsatipiatiletie vrachei byvshikh studentov imp. Mediko-Khirurgicheskoi akademii vypuska 9-go dekabria 1868 g.* St. Petersburg, 1893.

Bezhkovich, A.S. "Dmitrii Konstantinovich Zelenin (1878–1954). Nekrolog." *Izvestiia Vsesoiuznogo geograficheskogo obshchestva,* 1955, vol. 87, no. 4:367–69.

Billington, James. *Mikhailovsky and Russian Populism.* Oxford, 1958.

Biriukov, V.P. *Ural'skaia kopilka.* Sverdlovsk, 1967.

Blackbourn, David. *Marpingen: Apparitions of the Virgin Mary in Bismarckian Germany.* Oxford, 1993.

Blagosvetlov, G.E. *Irinarkh Ivanovich Vvedenskii.* St. Petersburg, 1857.

———."Novye Knigi: 'Iz dal'nikh let vospaminaniia.'" *Delo,* 1879, no. 4: 89–100.

Blagoveshchenskii, N.A. "Biograficheskii ocherk." In N.G. Pomialovskii, *PSS.* 2 vols. Moscow-Leningrad, 1935. vol. 1.

———. "Na pogoste." In *Povesti i razskazi,* by N.A. Blagoveshchenskii. St. Petersburg, 1873.

Blumenberg, Hans. *The Legitimacy of the Modern Age.* Translated by Robert M. Wallace. Cambridge, MA, 1983.

Bobrov, Aleksei. "Iakov Vasil'evich Smirnov, byvshii prepodavate pervo' Moskovskoi Gimnazii (1836–1868 g.) po ego dnevniku." *VEV,* 1880, no. 7:197–215.

Bobrov, Pavel Antonovich. *Iz proshlogo (Pamiatka seminarista, 1835–1852 g.g.).* Saratov, 1913.

Bogdanov, A.A. "Avtobiografiia." *Granat,* vol. 41, part 1.

Bogdanovich, A.V. *Tri poslednikh samoderzhtsa. Dnevnik A.V. Bogdanovich.* Moscow-Leningrad, 1924.

Bogoslavskii, G.K. "Chernigovskaia seminariia 50 let nazad (iz vospominanii byv. seminarista)." *Vera i zhizn',* 1915, no. 5/6:77–98; no. 7:59–79.

Bogoslovskii. *Iz materialov po istorii podpol'noi biblioteki i tainogo kruzhka Vladimirskoi seminarii.* Kostroma, 1921.

Bogoslovskii, M.M. "V.O. Kliuchevskii, kak uchenyi." In *V.O. Kliuchevskii. Kharakteristiki i vospominaniia.* Moscow, 1912.

Bogoslovskii, N.G. *Vzgliad s prakticheskoi storony na zhizn' sviashchennikov. Pis'ma otsa k synu.* St. Petersburg, 1860.

Bonomi, Patricia B. *Under the Cope of Heaven: Religion, Society and Politics in Colonial America.* New York, 1986.

Bourdieu, Pierre. *Distinction: A Social Critique of the Judgment of Taste.* Translated by Richard Nice. Cambridge, MA, 1984.

Boym, Svetlana. *The Future of Nostalgia.* New York, 2001.

Broiakovskii, Serapion. *Sputnik pastyria. Sbornik statei i zametok po voprosam pastyrskogo sluzheniia.* Kiev, 1903.

Bronzov, A.A. *Nravstvennoe bogoslovie v Rossii v techenie XIX-ogo stoletiia.* St. Petersburg, 1901.

———. "V dukhovnom uchilishche." *Str.,* 1908, no. 5:716–27.

Brooks, Jeffrey. *When Russia Learned to Read: Literacy and Popular Literature, 1861–1917.* Princeton, 1985.

Brower, Daniel. *Training the Nihilists.* Ithaca, NY, 1975.

Brown, Peter. *The Cult of the Saints: Its Rise and Function in Latin Christianity.* Chicago, 1981.

Bukh, N.K. "Avtobiografiia." *Granat,* vol. 40.

Bulgakov, S.V. *Nastol'naia kniga dlia sviashchenno-tserkovno sluzhitelia.* 2 vols. Khar'kov, 1913; reprint, Moscow, 1993.

———. (ed.). *Obraztsy sviatootecheskoi i Russkoi propovedi.* Khar'kov, 1887.

Bulgakov, Sergei. *Avtobiograficheskie Zametki.* Paris, 1991.

Bulgakova, L.A. "Intelligentsia v Rossii vo vtoroi chertverti XIX veka: sostav, pravovoe i material'noe polozhenie." Kand diss., Leningrad, 1983.

Bunin, A.A. "Avtobiograficheskie Zapiski." *Voronezhskaia starina,* 1904, no. 4:289–319.

Burke, Peter. "Representations of the Self from Petrarch to Descartes." In *Rewriting the Self: Histories from the Renaissance to the Present,* edited by Roy Porter. London: Routledge, 1997.

Bykov, A.N. "Avtobiografiia." In Maksimov.

Byt sviashchennikov-dedov i ottsov i sviashchennikov-vnukov nashego kraia. Podol'sk, 1897.

Casanova, Jose. "Beyond European and American Exceptionalisms: Toward a Global Perspective." In *Predicting Religion: Christian, Secular and Alternative Futures,* edited by Grace Davie, Paul Heelas, and Linda Woodhead. Burlington, VT, 2003.

———. *Public Religions in the Modern World.* Chicago, 1994.

Chartier, Roger. *The Cultural Origins of the French Revolution,* translated by Lydia G. Cochrane. Durham, NC, 1991.

Charyshin, N.A. "Avtobiografiia." *Granat,* vol. 40.

Chel'tsov, M.P. *Osnovnaia zadacha vysshogo obrazovaniia (Rech' k studentam Instituta grazhdanskikh inzhenerov imperatora Nikolaia 1-go).* St. Petersburg, 1904.

Chernavskii, M.M. "Avtobiografiia." *Granat,* vol. 40.

Chernobrovtsev, I. "Nekrolog. o. Ksenofont Prokhorovich Smirnov." *VEV,* 1905, no. 2:61–65.

Chernukha, V.G. "Memuary stolichnogo chinovnichestva vtoroi poloviny XIX v." In *Vspomogatel'nye istoricheskie distsipliny.* Leningrad, 1983.

Chernyshevskii, N.G. "Avtobiograficheskie otryvki N.G. Chernyshevskogo." In *N.G. Chernyshevskii 1828–1928. Sbornik statei, dokumentov i vospominanii.* Moscow, 1928.

Chevalier, Louis. *Laboring Classes and Dangerous Classes in Paris during the First Half of the Nineteenth Century.* Translated by Frank Jellinek. New York, 1973.

Chicherin, B.N. *Vospominaniia B.N. Chicherina.* Part two of *Russkoe obshchestvo 40–50-kh godov XIX v.,* edited by S.L. Chernova. Moscow, 1991.

Chistov, K.V. "Ot redaktora." *Problemy slavianskoi etnografii (k 100-letiiu so dnia rozhdeniia chlena—korrespondenta AN SSSR D.K. Zelenina).* Leningrad, 1979.

Chistovich, I.A. *Sankt-Peterburgskaia dukhovnaia akademiia, 1858–1888.* St. Petersburg, 1889.

Clements, Barbara Evans. *Bolshevik Women.* Cambridge, UK, 1997.

Confino, Michel. "On Intellectuals and Intellectual Traditions in Eighteenth- and Nine-teenth-Century Russia." *Daedalus,* 101, no. 2 (1972):117–49.

Cooper, Fredrick. *Colonialism in Question: Theory, Knowledge, History.* Berkeley, 2005.

Corbin, Alain. "Intimate Relations." In Aries and Duby.

———. "The Secret of the Individual." In Aries and Duby.

Costlaw, Jane T. "The Pastoral Source: Representations of the Maternal Breast in Nineteenth Century Russia." In *Sexuality and the Body in Russian Culture,* edited by Jane T. Costlaw, Stephanie Sandler, and Judith Vowles. Stanford, 1993.

Custine, Astolphe, Marquis de. *La Russie en 1839.* 8 vols. Brussels, 1843.

D. "Kartiny proshlogo. Iz semeinoi khroniki sviashchennika." *Iaroslavskie eparkhial'nye vedomosti,* 1900, no. 43:685–87.

Dal', V. *Poslovitsy russkogo naroda.* 2 vols. Moscow, 1989.

Davydov, N.V. *Iz proshlogo.* 2 vols. Moscow, 1913–1917.

de Certeau, Michel. *The Writing of History.* Translated by Tom Conley. New York, 1988.

Deiateli revoliutsionnogo dvizheniia v Rossii. Bio-Bibliograficheskii slovar' ot predshestvennikov dekabristov do padeniia tsarizma. Vols. 1–3, 5 in ten parts. Moscow, 1927–1934.

della Cava, Olha Tatiana. "Sermons of Feofan Prokopovich: Themes and Styles." Ph.D. diss., Columbia University, 1972.

D'iachenko, Grigorii. *Dukhovnoe posevy.* 4th ed. Kiev, 1900.

Dmitriev, S.S. "Memuary, dnevniki, Chastnaia perepiska pervoi poloviny XIX v." In *Istochnikovedenie istorii SSSR XIX-nachala XX v.* Moscow, 1970.

Dmitrievskii, A.A. "Pamiati zastatnogo diakona Afansiia Petrovicha Dmitrievskogo i ego suprugi Eleny Fedorovichy." *Astrakhanskie eparkhial'nye vedomosti,* 1913, no. 30:777–86.

Dnevnik sviashchennoslizhitelia. 2 vols. Tula, 1906.

Dobrokhotov, D.N. "Avtobiografiia." In Maksimov.

Dobroliubov, N.A. *SS.* 9 vols. Moscow, 1961–1964.

———. "Cherty dlia kharakteristiki Russkogo prostonarod'ia." *SS,* vol. 6.

———. "Chto takoe oblomovshchina?" *SS,* vol. 4.

———. *Dnevnik,* edited by V. Polianskii. Moscow, 1932.

———. "Dnevnik 1852 goda." *SS,* vol. 8.

———. "Kogda zhe pridet nastoiashchii den?" *SS,* vol. 6.

———. *Sochineniia.* 4 vols. 6th ed. St. Petersburg, 1901.

———. "Temnoe Tsartsvo." *SS,* vol. 5.

———. "Zagranichnye preniia. O polozhenii Russkogo dukhovenstva." *Sochineniia N.A. Dobroliubova.* 5th ed. St. Petersburg, 1896.

Dobroliubov, V.A. *Lozh' gg. Nikolaiia Engel'gardta i Rozanova o N.A. Dobroliubove, N.G. Chernyshevskom i dukhovenstve.* St. Petersburg, 1902.

Dobronravov, I.M. "Kto Prav?" *Zvonar',* 1906, no. 6:35–52.

Dobronravov, L.M. *Novaia bursa.* St. Petersburg, 1913.

Dobrovol'skii, V. "I.I. Orlovskii, ego lichnost' i znachenie v dele izsledovaniia Smolenskogo kraia." Reprinted partially in Zhirkevich.

Dolinin, Aleksandr. "Pamiati A. P. Chudakova." *Novoe literaturnoe obozrenie,* 2005, no. 5:203.

"Domashnaia zaniatiia sviashchennika." *RSP,* 1885, no. 28:265–282.

"Domashnee vospitanie detei sel'skogo dukhoventsva v s——koi gubernii." *RSP,* 1871, no. 3:106–15.

"Domashnii byt prikhodskikh pastyrei." *RSP,* 1869, no. 20:85–103.

Dubasov, I.I. "Iz shkol'nykh vospominanii." In *Ocherki iz istorii Tambovskogo kraia,* by I.I. Dubasov. Moscow, 1884.

E.A. *Zadachi pitomtsev dukhovnoi shkoly.* Kazan', 1902.

Ekzempliarskii, Il'ia. "Russkoe beloe dukhoventsvo, kak soslovie." *RSP,* 1863, no. 28: 381–402.

Eliade, Mircea. *The Sacred and the Profane: The Nature of Religion.* Translated by Willard R. Trask. New York, 1959.

Eliseev, G.Z. *Begstvo seminaristov.* St. Petersburg, 1876.

Elkhovskii, E.A. "Vospominaniia Evgeniia Andreevicha Elkhovskogo (1869–1937), sviashchennika zhenskogo Sviato-Nikol'skogo monastyria." In *Stranitsy.*

Ellis, Harold A. "Genealogy, History, and Aristocratic Reaction in Early Eighteenth-Century France: The Case of Henri de Boulainvilliers." *Journal of Modern History* 58 (June 1986): 414–51.

Elpat'evskii, S.Ia. *O chernosotentsakh.* St. Petersburg, 1906.

———. "Po povodu razgovorov o russkoi intelligentsii." *Russkoe bogastvo,* 1905, no. 3:57–82.

———. *Vospominaniia za 50 let.* Leningrad, 1929.

Ely, Christopher. *This Meager Nature: Landscape and National Identity in Imperial Russia.* Dekalb, IL, 2002.

Engel, Barbara Alpern. "Mothers and Daughters: Family Patterns and the Female Intelligentsia." In *The Family in Imperial Russia,* edited by David L. Ransel. Urbana, IL, 1978.

Engel'gardt, Nikolai. "O. Matvei v russkoi kritike (literaturnaia spravka)." *Novoe vremia,* 16 December 1901, no. 9623:3–4.

Engelstein, Laura. "Orthodox Self-Reflection in a Modernizing Age: The Case of Ivan and Nataliia Kireevskii." In *Autobiographical Practices in Russia,* edited by Jochen Hellbeck and Klaus Heller. Gottingen, 2004.

Entsiklopedicheskii Slovar' Russkogo biograficheskogo instituta Granat. Vols. 40–41. Moscow, 1927.

Entsiklopediia literaturnykh geroev: Russkaia literatura vtoroi poloviny XIX veka. Moscow, 2001.

Evlogii (Metropolitan). *Put' moei zhizni.* Paris, 1937.

Evsevii, [Orlinskii] Archbishop. *O vospitanii detei v dukhe khristianskogo blagochestiia.* 3rd ed. St. Petersburg, 1857.

F.L. *Nashi dukhovnye seminarii v 50-kh g. Vospominaniia.* Pochaev, 1904.

Fausek, V. "Pamiati Vsevoloda Nikailovicha Garshina." In *Pamiati V.M. Garshina.* St. Petersburg, 1889.

"Fedor Aleksandrovich Kudriavtsev." *VI,* 1976, no. 8:220.

Fedotov, G.P. "The Religious Sources of Russian Populism." *Russian Review* 1, no. 2 (April 1942): 27–39.

Fenomenov, M.Ia. "Kniga, kotoraia sozdala ephokhu." *Kraevedenie,* 1927, no. 4: 447–50.

Fidler, F.F. *Pervye literaturnye shagi. Avtobiografii sovremennykh russkikh pisatelei.* Moscow, 1911.

Figes, Orlando. *A People's Tragedy: A History of the Russian Revolution.* London, 1996.

Figes, Orlando, and Boris Kolonitskii. *Interpreting the Russian Revolution: The Language and Symbols of 1917.* New Haven, 1999.

Figner, Vera. *Memoirs of a Revolutionist.* New York, 1968.

———. "Mikhail Vasil'evich Novorusskii." In *Tiuremnye Robinzony,* by M. V. Novorusskii. Moscow-Leningrad, 1926.

Filaret [Drozdov]. *Tvoreniia.* Moscow, 1994.

Filaret [Gumilevskii]. *Istoriia Russkoi tserkvi.* 6th ed. St. Petersburg, 1895.

Filippov, A.A. "Avtobiografiia." *Granat,* vol. 40.

Filonov, A.G. [A. Borisoglebskii]. "Iz zhizni starogo pedagoga." *Gimnaziia,* 1890, no. 8/10:619–55.

———. *Kak ia shel peshkom v Petersburg uchit'sia.* St. Petersburg, 1903.

———. *Moe detstvo.* St. Petersburg, 1864.

Firsov, B.M., and I.G. Kiseleva, eds. *Byt velikorusskikh krest'ian-zemlepashtsev. Opisanie materialov etnograficheskogo biuro kniazia V.N. Tenisheva (po primere Vladimirskoi gubernii).* St. Petersburg, 1993.

Flath, Carol Apollonio. "N.G. Pomialovskii's Seminary Sketches: Context and Genre." Ph.D. diss., University of North Carolina at Chapel Hill, 1987.

Fleri, V.I. *Pravila nravstvennosti.* St. Petersburg, 1847.

Florenskii, Pavel. *Detiiam moim. Vospominaniia proshlykh dnei. Genealogicheskie issledovaniia. Iz solovetskikh pisem. Zaveshchenia.* Moscow, 1992.

Florinskii, N. "Pamiati pochivshogo." *VEV,* 1887, no. 19:591.

Florovskii, Grigorii. *Puti russkogo bogosloviia.* Paris, 1937.

Foucault, Michel. *Discipline and Punish: The Birth of the Prison.* New York, 1977.

Frank, S.L. "Etika nigilizma." In *Vekhi: Sbornik statei o russkoi intelligentsii.* Moscow, 1909. Reprinted in *Vekhi: intelligentsiia v Rossii: sbornik statei 1909–1910.* Moscow, 1991.

Freeze, Gregory L. "'Going to the Intelligentsia': The Church and Its Urban Mission in Post-Reform Russia." In *Between Tsar and People: Educated Society and the Quest for Public Identity in Late Imperial Russia,* edited by Edith W. Clowes, Samuel D. Kassow, and James L. West. Princeton, 1991.

———. "Handmaiden of the State? The Church in Imperial Russia Reconsidered." *Journal of Ecclesiastical History* 36, no. 1 (January 1985): 82–102.

———. *The Parish Clergy in Nineteenth-Century Russia: Crisis, Reform, Counter-Reform.* Princeton, 1983.

———. *The Russian Levites: Parish Clergy in the Eighteenth Century.* Cambridge, MA, 1977.

———. "A Social Mission for Russian Orthodoxy: The Kazan Requiem of 1861 for the Peasants in Bezna." In *Imperial Russia, 1700–1917. State. Society. Opposition. Essays in Honour of Marc Raeff,* edited by Marshall Shatz and Ezra Mendelsohn. Dekalb, IL, 1988.

Frieden, Nancy Mandelker. *Russian Physicians in an Era of Reform and Revolution.* Princeton, 1981.

Frierson, Cathy A. *Peasant Icons: Representations of Rural People in Late 19th Century Russia.* Oxford, 1993.

———, ed. *Aleksandr Nikolaevich Engelgardt's Letters from the Countryside, 1872–1887.* Oxford, 1993.

G. "Tserkovno-obshchestvennye voprosy v nashei zhurnalistike." *PO,* 1876, no. 5: 65–80.

G———v., V. "Protoierei Sergii Sergievich Gromov." *VEV,* 1899, no. 13:462–70.

Gagen-Torn, N.I. "D.K. Zelenin kak pedagog i uchenyi (Leningradskii period)." In *Problemy slavianskoi ethnografii.* Leningrad, 1979.

———. *Memoria.* Moscow, 1994.

Ganelin, Sh.I. *Ocherki po istorii srednei shkoly v Rossii vtoroi polovine XIX veka.* Leningrad-Moscow, 1950.

Ganetskii, Ia.S. "Avtobiografiia." *Granat,* vol. 41, part 1.

Geary, Patrick J. "The Renunciation of Renunciation in Monastic Life." In *Monastic Life in the Christian and Hindu Traditions,* edited by Austin B. Creel and Vasudha Norayanam. Lewiston, NY, 1990.

Gedeonovskii, A.V. "Avtobiografiia." *Granat,* vol. 40.

Geraci, Robert. *Window on the East: National and Imperial Identities in Late Imperial Tsarist Russia.* Ithaca, N.Y., 2001.

Giddens, Anthony. *Modernity and Self-Identity: Self and Society in the Late Modern Age.* Cambridge, UK, 1991.

Giliarosvkii, Ioann. "Nekrolog pamiati pochivshogo sviashchennika sela Voimigi, Suzd. u. o. Flegonta Iv. Giliarovskogo." *VEV,* 1913, no. 18: 385–88.

Giliarov, F.A. "Vospominaniia." *RA,* 1904, no. 1:175–88.

Giliarov-Platonov, N.P. *Iz perezhitogo.* 2 vols. Moscow, 1886.

———. "O syd'be ubezhdenii: po povodu smerti A.S. Khomiakova." In his *Sobornik sochinenii,* 2 vols. Moscow, 1900, vol. 2.

Ginzburg, Lydia. *On Psychological Prose.* Translated and edited by Judson Rosengrant. Princeton, 1991.

Gippius, Zinaida. "Sumashadshaia." *Novyi Put',* 1903, no. 2:71–106.

———. *Zhivye litsa.* Leningrad, 1991.

Glebov, A.A. *Sviashchennik Aleksei Andreevich Glebov (Nekrolog).* Novocherkassk, 1903.

Glickman, Rose. "The Literary *Raznochintsy* in Mid-Nineteenth-Century Russia." Ph.D. diss., University of Chicago, 1967.

Gloriantov, V.I. "Vospominaniia davno proshedshogo vremeni." *RA,* 1906, no. 2: 209–20.

Gnedich, P.P. "Iz proshlogo nashikh gimnazii (zametki klassika semidesiatykh godov." *Russkii Vestnik,* 1890, vol. 207, no. 4:44–74.

Golovshchikov, K.D. *Ocherk zhizni i uchenykh trudov byvshikh pitomtsev Iaroslavskoi dukhovnoi seminarii.* Iaroslavl, 1893.

Golubinskii, E.E. "Iz vospominanii." In *U troitsy v akademii, 1814–1914.* Moscow, 1914.

Gorinov, M.M. "Evgenii Preobrazhenskii: Stanovlenie revoliutsionera." *Otechestvennaia istoriia,* 1999, no. 1:30–47.

Gorskii, A.V. "Po voprosu o nashem dukhovenstve (istoricheskie ocherki)." *Chteniia v obshchestve liubitelei dukhovnogo prosveshcheniia,* 1877, no. 2:196–202.

Gould, Graham. "Childhood in Eastern Patristic Thought: Some Problems of Theology and Theological Anthropology." In *The Church and Childhood,* edited by Diana Wood. Cambridge, MA, 1994.

Greenblatt, Stephen. *Renaissance Self-Fashioning.* Chicago, 1980.

Greenfeld, Liah. *Nationalism: Five Roads to Modernity.* Cambridge, MA, 1992.

Grekov, Fr.G. "Dukhovnoe zvanie v Rossii. Golos sel'skogo sviashchennika." *Dukhovnaia Beseda,* 1859, no. 17:109–30.

Greznov, Evgenii. "Iz shkol'nykh vospominanii byvshego seminarista." *Pribavlenie Vologodskikh eparkhial'nikh vedomostei,* 1901, no. 18:509–16.

Griboedov, A.S. *Gore ot uma* (1823). In *Litso i genii,* by A. S. Griboedov. Moscow, 1997.

Grigor'ev, I.G. "Sovremennye zapiski nadvornogo sovetnika Ivana Grigor'evicha Grigoror'eva, im samim napisannye." In A. Liashchenko, *Zapiski I.G. Grigor'eva.* St. Petersburg, 1899.

Grigor'ev, Apollon. *Vospominaniia.* Leningrad, 1980.

Gromov, P. *Uroki prakticheskogo rukovodstva dlia pastyrei.* Irkutsk, 1873.

Gur'ev, Mikhail. "Vospominaniia o moem uchenii." *RS,* 1909, vol. 139, no. 8:357–71.

Gusev, A. "Polozhenie prepodavatelei dukhovnykh seminarii i uchilishch." *PO,* 1885, no. 11:569–93; no. 12:693–726.

Gusev, N. "Piatidesiatiletnii iubilei." *VEV,* 1898, no. 9:299–302.

Haimson, Leopold. "The Parties and the State: The Evolution of Political Attitudes." In *The Structure of Russian History: Interpretive Essays,* edited by M. Cherniavsky. New York, 1970.

Halbwachs, Maurice. *On Collective Memory.* Translated and edited by Lewis A. Coser. Chicago, 1992.

Halfin, Igal. *Terror in My Soul: Communist Autobiographies on Trial.* Cambridge, MA, 2003.

Harris, Ruth. *Lourdes: Body and Spirit in the Secular Age.* London, 1999.

Hedda, Jennifer Elaine. "Good Shepherds: The St. Petersburg Pastorate and the Emergence of Social Activism in the Russian Orthodox Church, 1855–1917." Ph.D. diss., Harvard University, 1998.

Hembrick, Charles E. *The Practice of Piety: Puritan Devotional Disciplines in Seventeenth-Century New England.* Chapel Hill, NC, 1982.

Henderson, Heather. *The Victorian Self: Autobiography and Biblical Narrative.* Ithaca, NY, 1989.

Hertzen, A.I. *Byloe i Dumy.* 3 vols. Moscow, 1967.

Herzfeld, Michael. "The European Self: Rethinking an Attitude." In *The Idea of Europe: From Antiquity to the European Union,* edited by Anthony Pagden. Cambridge, UK, 2002.

Hill, Michael. *The Religious Order: A Study of Virtuoso Religion and Its Legitimation in the Nineteenth-Century Church of England.* London, 1973.

Hobsbawm, Eric, and Terence Ranger, eds. *The Invention of Tradition.* Cambridge, UK, 1983.

Hoogenboom, Hilde. "Vera Figner and Revolutionary Autobiographies: The Influence of Gender on Genre." In *Women in Russia and Ukraine,* edited by Rosalind Marsh. Cambridge, UK, 1996.

Hunt, Lynn. *The Family Romance of the French Revolution.* Berkeley, CA, 1992.

Huntington, Samuel P. *The Clash of Civilizations: Remaking of World Order.* New York, 1996.

I. E—skii. "Otvet bratu——sel'skomu sviashchenniku na voprosy ego o tom, chemu i kak obuchat' detei do postupleniia ikh v uchilishche." *RSP,* 1864, no. 21:146–57.

I.G. "Iz dnevnika sviashchennika." *RSP,* 1871, no. 49:438–49.

I.L. "Zametki o razvitii u detei liub'vi k otechestvu." *RSP,* 1871, no. 8:274–84.

I.M. "Znachenie khristianskoi very v dele obshchestvennogo blagoustroistva." *VEV,* 1868, no. 7:325–37; no. 10:494–505.

Iakov, Archimandrite. *Pastyr' v otnoshenii k sebe i pastve.* St. Petersburg, 1880.

Iakshich, D. *O nravstvennom dostoinstve devstva i braka po uchenniu pravoslavnoi tserkvi.* St. Petersburg, 1903.

Ianzhul, Ivan. *I.E. Tsvetkov.* St. Petersburg, 1911.

Innokentii, [Pustynskii] Bishop. *Bogoslovie oblichitel'noe.* 4 vols. Kazan', 1859.

———. *Pastyrskoe bogoslovie v Rossii za XIX veke.* St. Petersburg, 1899.

Istoricheskie skazaniia o zhizni sviatykh podvizavshikhsia v Vologodskoi eparkhii. Vologda, 1880.

Iuzefovich, D. "Nekrolog (Diakon Gavriil Maksimovich)." *Poltavskie eparkhial'nye vedomosti,* 1864, no. 36:397–99.

"Ivan Mikhailovich Maiskii." *VI,* 1975, no. 12:212–13.

Ivanov, A.E. *Studentchestvo Rossii kontsa XIX-nachala XX veka.* Moscow, 1999.

———. *Vysshaia shkola Rossii v kontse XIX-nachale XX veka.* Moscow, 1991.

Ivanova, T.G. "D.K. Zelenin i ego nauchnye interesy v 1917–1934 godakh." In *Izbrannye stat'i po dukhovnoi kul'ture, 1917–1934,* by D. K. Zelenin. Moscow, 1999.

———. *Russkaia fol'kloristika nachale XX veka v biograficheskikh ocherkakh.* St. Petersburg, 1993.

Ivanov-Razumnik, Ia.A. "Chto takoe intelligentsiia?" In his *Istoriia russkoi obshchestvennoi mysli,* 2 vols. St. Petersburg, 1908, vol. 1.

Izmailov, A.A. "Aleksandr Alekseevich Izmailov." In Fidler.

———. *V burse.* St. Petersburg, 1903.

Izmailov, F.F. "Iz zapiskok starogo professora seminarii." *PO,* 1870, no. 7:94–124.

"Izvestia i zametki: Seminaristy v Tomskom universitete." *Str.,* 1897, no. 2:358–59.

Izvlecheniia iz otcheta po vedomstru dukhovnykh del pravoslavnogo ispovedeniia. St. Petersberg, 1837–1863.

Izvlecheniia iz vsepoddanneishego otcheta ober-prokurora sr. sinoda po vedomstrvu pravoslavnogo ispovuedeniia. St. Petersberg, 1866–1884.

Jacobsen, Grete. "Nordic Women and the Reformation." In *Women in Reformation and Counter-Reformation Europe,* edited by Sherrin Marshall. Bloomington, Indiana, 1989.

K voprosu ob obezpechenii detei dukhovnogo znaiia, neokonchivshikh kursa I nepoluchivshikh vovse obrazovaniia v nashikh dukhovnykh uchilishchakh. Khar'kov, 1880.

K.D. "Zhena sviashchennika-prikhodskaia matushka." *RSP,* 1875, no. 36:23–27.

Kafengauz, B.B. "Kupecheskie memuary." In *Moskovskii krai v ego proshlom,* edited by S. Bakhrushin. Moscow, 1928.

"Kak dolzhen derzhat' sebia sel'skii pastyr' po otnosheniiu k mestnoi intelligentsii." *RSP,* 1888, no. 23:180–94.

Kalashnikova, R.B. "Iz istorii semei zaonezhskikh sviashchennikov (konets XVIII-pervaia tret' xx v.)." *Knizhskii vestnik,* 2002, no. 7:3–20.

Kalugin, S.F. *Platonik (Stseny iz seminarskoi zhizni).* St. Petersburg, 1863.

Kanatchikov, Semon Ivanovich. *A Radical Worker in Tsarist Russia: The Autobiography of Semon Ivanovich Kanatchikov.* Translated and edited by Reginald E. Zelnik. Stanford, 1986.

Kapachinskii, A. "O religiozno-nravstvennom vospitanii detei." *VEV,* 1865, no. 17:948–57.

Karonin. [N.E. Petroparlovskii] "Podrezannye kryl'ia." *Slovo,* 1880, no. 4–6.

———. "Obshchestvo gramotnosti." Quoted in "Tema intelligentsii v tvorchestve S. Karonina-N.E. Petropavlovskogo" (1887–1892 gg.) by E.F. D'iachenko. In *K voprosam russkoi i natsional'noi filologii.* Stavropol', 1968.

Katkov, Mikhail. "O nashem nigilizme. Po povodu romana Turgeneva." *Russkii Vestnik,* 1862, no. 7:402–26.

Kazanskii, P.S. "Vospominaniia Seminarista." *PO,* 1879, no. 9:100–33.

Kelly, Catriona. *Refining Russia: Advice Literature, Polite Culture, and Gender from Catherine to Yeltsin.* Oxford, 2001.

Kern, Stephen. *The Culture of Love: Victorians to Moderns.* Cambridge, MA, 1992.

Khalkolivanov, Ioann. *Pravoslavnoe nravstvennoe bogoslovie.* Samara, 1872.

Kharkhordin, Oleg. *The Collective and the Individual in Russia: A Study of Practices.* Berkeley, CA, 1999.

Kheraskov, Mikhail. "Beseda s vospitannikami seminarii, pri nachale novogo 1887–88 uchebnogo goda." *VEV,* 1887, no. 18:525–45.

———. "Pouchenie vospitannikam skazannoe rektorom Vladimirskoi Seminarii, protoiereem M.I. Kheraskovym, pred nachalom 1878–1879 uchebnogo goda." *VEV,* 1878, no. 19:548–62.

———. "Rech' vospitannikam skazannaia rektorom Vladimirskoi seminarii, protoiereem M.I. Kherskovym, pred nachalom 1879–1880 uchebnogo goda." *VEV,* 1879, no. 18:536–56.

Khitrov, A. "Tozhe da ne tozhe." *Russkaia shkola,* 1891, no. 7/8:63–75.

Khrenov, Aleksandr. "Vospominaniia o S.S. Troitskom krest'ianina Khrenova." In *Sbornik, posviashchennyi pamiati Sergeia Semenovicha Troitskogo.* Tiflis, 1912.

"Khronika eparkhial'noi zhizni." *Str.,* 1900, no. 8:612–15.

"Khronika: O vospreshchenii ustroistva v dukhovgnoi-uchebnykh zaredoniiakh Kontsertov, spektaklie, chtenii drugikh publichnykh sobranii." *Str.* 1871, no. 7: 34–35.

"Khronika: Rukopolozhenie statskogo sovetnika Feofana Pavlovicha Dragomiretskogo vo sviashchennika." *Str.,* 1876, no. 4:125–33.

Kirill, Archimandrite. *Pastyrskoe bogoslovie.* 2nd ed. St. Petersburg, 1854.

Kistiakovskii, A.F. "Avtobiograficheskii otryvok." In V.P. Naumenko, "Aleksandr Fedorovich Kistiakovskii." *Kievskaia starina,* 1895, vol. 48, no.1: 2–13.

Kizenko, Nadieszda. *A Prodigal Saint: Father John of Kronstadt and the Russian People.* University Park, PA, 2000.

Klinghoffer, Arthur Jay. *Red Apocalypse: The Religious Evolution of Soviet Communism.* Lanham, MD, 1996.

Kliuchevskii, V. O. "I.S. Aksakov." In *Neopublikovannye proizvedeniia.*

———. "Ob intelligentsii." *Neopublikovannye proizvedeniia.* Moscow, 1983.

———. "Pamiati Solov'eva." *Sochineniia v deviati tomakh.* Moscow, 1989. Vol. 7.

Kniazev, N. "Diakon Stefan Kniazev." *Iaroslavskie eparkhial'nye vedomosti,* 1891, no. 31:487–96.

Knight, Nathaniel. "Was the Intelligentsia Part of the Nation? Visions of a Society in Post-Emancipation Russia." *Kritika* 7, no. 4 (Fall 2006):733–58.

Koialovich, M.O. *Istoriia russkogo samosoznaniia.* St. Petersburg, 1893.

Kokoshkin, F. "A.S. Alekseev." *Iuridicheskii Vestnik,* 1916, vol. 14:113–27.

Kolchin, Peter. *Unfree Labor: American Slavery and Russian Serfdom.* Cambridge, MA, 1987.

Kolonitskii, B.I. "Intelligentsiia v kontse XIX-nachale XX veka: Samosoznanie sovremennikov i izsledovatel'skie podkhody." In *Iz istorii russkoi intelligentsii: Sbornik materialov i statei k 100-letii so dnia rozhdeniia V.P. Leikinoi-Svirskoi.* St. Petersburg, 2003.

Kolosov, N.A. "Tipy pravoslavnogo russkogo dukhovenstva v russkoi svetskoi literature 1901–1902 gg." Moscow, 1903.

Kolosov, Vladimir. *Istoriia Tverskoi dukhovnoi seminarii.* Tver, 1889.

Korelin, A.P. *Dvorianstvo v poreformennoi Rossii.* Moscow, 1979.

Korolenko, V.G. *Dnevnik.* 2 vols. Poltava, 1928.

———."Staryi zvonar'." *Volzhkii vestnik,* May 26, 1885.

"Korrespondentsii. Iz Penzy (Seminarskii kruzhok samoobrazovaniia i inspektsiia)." *Krasnyi zvon,* 1909, no. 12:203.

Kotkin, Stephen. *Magnetic Mountain: Stalinism as a Civilization.* Berkeley, CA, 1995.

Kovalevskaia, S.V. *Vospominaniia; Povesti.* Moscow, 1974.

Koz'min, B. "Voskresshii Belinskii, iz neizdannogo literaturnogo naslediia N. A. Dobroliubova." *Literaturnoe nasledstvo* 1951, vol. 57, no. 3:7–24.

Krasin, L.B. "Avtobiografiia." *Granat,* vol. 41, part 1.

Krasnokutskii, V.S. "Dnevniki Gertzena i Russkaia memuarnaia literatura XIX veka." In *A.I. Gertzen khudozhnik i publitsist.* Moscow, 1977.

Krasnoperov, I.M. "Moi detskie gody i shkola." *Vestnik vospitaniia,* 1903, no. 6:174–200.

———. *Zapiski raznochintsa*. Moscow-Leningrad, 1929.

Krasovskii, Petr. "Otvet na stat'iu 'o domashnem obrazovanii detei sviashchennikov'." *RSP,* 1869, no. 33:341–51.

Krestinskii, N.N. "Avtobiografiia." *Granat,* vol. 41, part 1.

Kriukovskii, V.Ia. "Okolo Bursy." *Russkaia Starina,* 1910, vol. 144, no. 10:49–70; 1911, vol. 146, no. 5:437–52, no. 6:579–83.

Kropotkin, Peter. *Dnevnik raznykh let.* Moscow, 1992.

———. *Memoirs of a Revolutionist.* New York, 1988.

Krupskaia, N.K. "Avtobiografiia." *Granat,* vol. 41, part 1.

Krylov, V.P. "Avtobiografiia." In *Dvadtsatipiatiletie vrachei byvshikh studentov imp. Mediko-Khirurgicheskoi akademii vypuska 9-go dekabria 1868 g.* St. Petersburg, 1893.

Kselman, Thomas. *Miracles and Prophecies in Nineteenth-Century France.* New Brunswick, NJ, 1983.

Kuhn, Alfred. "Introduction." In Pomialovsky.

Kuhn, Reinhard. *Corruption in Paradise: The Child in Western Literature.* Hanover, NH, 1982.

Kuliasov, A.K. *Znachenie samoobrazovaniia v zhizni sel'skogo dukhoventsva.* Kazan', 1909.

Kulzhinskii, I.G. "Avtobiografiia." In *Litsei kniazia Bezborodko.* St. Petersburg, 1859.

L———V, "Sviashchennik F. P. Sergievskii (Nekrolog)." *VEV,* 1892, no. 17:442–49.

La Capra, Dominick. *Writing History, Writing Trauma.* Baltimore, 2001.

Lavrov, M.E. *Avtobiografiia sel'skogo sviashchennika M.E. Lavrova.* Vladimir, 1900.

Lazurskii, V.F. *Professor A.F. Lazurskii.* Odessa, 1917.

LeDonne, John. *Ruling Russia: Politics and Administration in the Age of Absolutism, 1762–1796.* Princeton, NJ, 1984.

Leikina-Svirskaia, V.R. "Zarubezhnaia istoriografiia o dorevoliutsionnoi intelligentsii Rossii." *Istoriograficheskii sbornik,* 1978, no. 4:146–65.

———. *Intelligentsiia v Rossii vo vtoroi polovine XIX veka.* Moscow, 1971.

Leonov, M.I. *Partiia Sotsial'stov-revoliutsionerov v 1905–07 gg.* Moscow, 1997.

Lepeshinskii, P.N. *Na povorote.* Moscow, 1955.

Levitov, A.I. "Moia familiia." In his *Sochineniia.* Moscow, 1977.

Levkoev, I.G. "Protodiakon vseia Rossii (semeinoe predanie v razskaze moei pokoinoi matushki)." *IV,* 1912, vol. 128, no. 5: 515–38.

Liberovskii, Dimitrii. "Nachal'nik-otets (Iz lichnykh vospominanii)." *VEV,* 1908, no. 10: 211–13.

Lichnye arkhivnye fondy v gosudarstvennykh khranilishchakh SSSR. Ukazatel'. 3 vols. Moscow, 1962–1963.

Likhachev, D. *Poetika drevnerusskoi literatury.* Moscow, 1979.

Likhacheva, E. *Materialy dlia istorii zhenskogo obrazovaniia.* St. Petersburg, 1883.

Litvinov, V.V. "Pitomtsy Voronezhskoi dukhovnoi seminarii, vyshedshie iz dukhovnogo zvanie." *Voronezhskaia starina,* 1909, no. 9:255–94; no. 12:411–90.

Lotman, Iu.M. *Roman A.S. Pushkina "Evgenii Onegin": Kommentarii.* Leningrad, 1983.

Lotman, Iurii. "The Decembrist in Daily Life (Everyday Behavior as a Historical-Psychological Category)." In *The Semiotics of Russian Cultural History,* edited by Alexander D. Nakhimovsky and Alice Stone Nakhimovsky. Ithaca, 1985.

Löwith, Karl. *Meaning in History.* Chicago, 1949.

Luckmann, Thomas. *Invisible Religion: The Problem of Religion in Modern Society.* New York, 1970.

Lukanin, P.V. "Diadia Mitia." In *D.N. Mamin-Sibiriak v vospominaniiakh sovremennikov.* Sverdlovsk, 1962.

Luppov, P.V. *V dukhovnom uchilishche. Viatskoe Dukhovnoe uchilishche v nachale poslednei chetverti proshlogo stoletiia.* St. Petersburg, 1913.

Lystra, Karen. *Searching the Heart: Women, Men, and Romantic Love in Nineteenth-Century America.* Oxford, 1989.

M.E. "Nechto o religiozno-nravstvennom vliianii na prikhozhan zheny pastyria." *RSP,* 1886, no. 42:169–80.

M.Gn. "O sovremennoi molodezhi i sovremennom vospitanii." *RSP*, 1902, no. 32:353–62.

M.K. "'Obrazovannoe' svetskoe obshchestvo i pravoslavnoe dukhoventsvo." *Str.*, 1909, no. 8:320–31.

M.Kh. *Iz-za seminarskoi skam'i.* 1906.

Makarii, [Miroliubov] Bishop. *Istoriko-statisticheskoe opisanie riazanskoi dukhovnoi seminarii i podvedennoi ei dukhovnykh uchilishch.* Novgorod, 1864.

Makarii, [Bulgakov] Metropolitan. *Istoriia Russkoi tserkvi.* 12 vols. St. Petersburg, 1857–1883; reprint, Moscow, 1996.

——. *Pravoslavno-dogmaticheskoe bogoslovie.* 2 vols. 5th ed. St. Petersburg, 1895.

Maksimov, A.N. (ed.) *Sotrudniki russkikh vesemostei.* Moscow, 1913.

Malein, I.M. *Moi vospominaniia.* Tver', 1910.

Malia, Martin. *Alexander Herzen and the Birth of Russian Socialism.* New York, 1961.

Malinin, D.I. "Iz vospominanii o kruzhke seminaristov." In *Iz partiinogo proshlogo: sbornik vospominaniia o partinoi rabote v Kaluge.* Kaluga, 1921.

Malinin, K.M. *Polveka na postu veterinarnogo vracha.* Moscow, 1961.

Malitskii, N. *Istoriia Vladimirskoi dukhovnoi seminarii.* 3 vols. Moscow, 1900–1902.

Mamin-Sibiriak, D.N. "Avtobiograficheskaia zametka." In his *SS,* vol. 10.

——. "Avtobiografiia." *Voprosy literatury,* 1976, no. 4:198–99.

——. "Iz dalekogo proshlogo." In his *SS,* 10 vols., Moscow, 1958, vol.10.

Manchester, Laurie. "Commonalities of Modern Political Discourse: Three Paths of Activism in Late Imperial Russia's Alternative Intelligentsia." In *Kritika: Explorations in Russian and Eurasian History* 8, no. 4 (Fall 2007):715–48.

Manning, Roberta. *The Crisis of the Old Order in Russia: Gentry and Government.* Princeton, 1982.

Marenin, V.I. *Shkol'nye i semeinye vospominaniia.* 2 vols. St. Petersburg, 1911–1915.

Markov, N. "Deti dukhovenstva: istorickeskii ocherk voprosa ob ikh pravakh." *Strannik,* 1900, no. 3:386–411.

Martin, Alexander M. "The Family Model of Society and Russian National Identity in Sergei N. Glinka's Russian Messenger (1808–1812)." *SR* 57, no. 1 (Spring, 1998):28–48.

Martin, David. *A General Theory of Secularization.* New York, 1978.

Martynov, B.V. "Vospominaniia N.P. Rozanova." In *Mir Istochnikovedeniia: Sbornik v chest' Sigurda Ottovicha Shmidta.* Moscow, 1994.

Mashkevich, Iliia. "Prisluga v bytu sel'skogo sviashchennika." *RSP,* 1887, no. 3:73–79.

Materialy dlia biografii N.A. Dobroliubova sobrannye v 1861–1862 godakh. Moscow, 1890.

Maynes, Mary Jo. *Taking the Hard Road: Life Courses in French and German Workers' Autobiographies in the Era of Industrialization.* Chapel Hill, NC, 1995.

McDaniel, Tim. *The Agony of the Russian Idea.* Princeton, 1996.

McGrane, Bernard. *Beyond Anthropology: Society and the Other.* New York, 1989.

Meehan, Brenda. "From Contemplative Practice to Charitable Activity: Russian Women's Religious Communities and the Development of Charitable Work." In *Lady Bountiful Revisited: Women, Philanthropy, and Power,* edited by Kathleen McCarthy. New Brunswick, NJ, 1990.

Meeks, Wayne A. *The Origins of Christian Morality.* New Haven, 1993.

Men'shikov, A. *Vozzreniia Moskovskogo Mitropolita Filareta po voprosam o tserkovnom zakonodatel'stve.* Kazan', 1894.

Mertsalov, E. *O samovospitanii. (Iz pisem k seminaristu).* Petrozavodsk, 1898.

Meshcherskii, V.P. *Zhenshchiny iz peterburgskogo bolshogo sveta: original'nyi roman.* 3rd ed. St. Petersburg, 1875.

Mikhail. [Semenov] *O schast'e i meshchanstve.* St. Petersburg, 1904.

Mikhailovskii, N.K. *Sochineniia N.K. Mikhailovskogo.* St. Petersburg, 1896.

Miliukov, A. "Bursa v shkole i literature." In *Otgoloski na literaturnye i obshchestvennye iavlenie.* St. Petersburg, 1875.

Miliukov, P.N. "Liubov' u idealistov tridtsatykh godov." In *Iz istorii russkoi intelligentsia: Sbornik statei.* St. Petersburg, 1902.

———. *Religion and the Church.* Translated by Valentine Ughet and Eleanor Davis, vol. 1 of *Outlines of Russian Culture.* Philadelphia, 1942.

Milovskii, N. "Goroda Shui starogo Pokrovskogo sobora protoierei Ioann Alekseevich Subbotin." *VEV,* 1894, no. 9:193–215.

Mitropol'skii, Aleksandr. "*Reestr knig chitannykh mnoiu...*": *krug Chteniia N.A. Dobroliubova 1849–1853 gg. i pervye literaturnye opyty.* Nizhnii Novgorod, 1991.

Modestov, V.I. "Avtobiografiia." In Vengerov, *Kritikobiograficheskii,* vol. 3.

Mordovtsev, D. "Uchastie seminaristov v narodnykh dvizheniiakh proshlogo veka." *Zaria,* 1871, no. 10/11:188–254.

Morozov, N.A. "Avtobiografiia." *Granat,* vol. 40.

Morrissey, Susan K. *Heralds of Revolution: Russian Students and the Mythologies of Radicalism.* Oxford, 1998.

Morson, Gary Saul. *The Boundaries of Genre.* Evanston, IL, 1981.

Mosse, George L. *The Image of Man: The Creation of Modern Masculinity.* New York, 1996.

Muizhel, V.V. "Viktor Vasil'evich Muizhel." In Fidler.

Musgrave, P.W. *From Brown to Bunter: The Life and Death of the School Story.* London, 1985.

N.N. "50-letie sviashchennosluzheniia protoieria o Nikolaia Stepanovicha Rozhnatovskogo." *Pribivaniia k Chernigovskim eparkhial'nym vedomostiam,* 1907, no. 20:704–16

Nadezhdin, N.I. "Avtobiografiia." *Russkii Vestnik,* 1856, no. 2: 49–78.

Nahirny, Vladimir C. *The Russian Intelligentsia: From Torment to Silence.* New Brunswick, NJ, 1983.

Naiman, Eric. *Sex in Public: The Incarnation of Soviet Ideology.* Princeton, 1997.

Nardov, Arkasii. "Vospominaniia o Muromskom dukhovnom uchilishche." *VEV,* 1891, no. 6:183–96.

Narodnye Russkie skazki A.N. Afanas'eva v trekh tomakh. 3 vols. Moscow, 1984–1985.

Naselenie S.-Peterburga po perepisi 10 dekabria 1869. St. Petersburg, 1870.

Nasha svetskaia i dukhovnaia pechat' o dukhoventsve; vospominaniia byvshogo al'ta-solista A. b—a. St. Petersburg, 1884.

Naumenko, V.P. "Aleksandr Fedorovich Kistiakovskii." *Kievskaia starina,* 1895, vol. 48, no. 1:13–43.

Nefedova, D., ed. *Sobranie sochinenii A. I. Levitova.* Moscow, 1884.

Neobkhodimoe ob"iansnenie. Kiev, 1865.

Nenarokomov, I.V. *Otchet o revizii Vladimirskoi Seminarii i tamoshnego dukhovnogo uchilishcha (v 1869 g.).* St. Petersburg, 1869.

Neskovskii, M. "Na rubezhe dvukh epokh. Iz lichnykh vospominanii." *RS,* 1896, no. 3: 511–39.

Nichols, Robert L. "Orthodoxy and Russia's Enlightenment, 1762–1825." In *Russian Orthodoxy under the Old Regime,* edited by Robert L. Nichols and Theofanis George Stavrou. Minneapolis, MN, 1978.

Nikanor, Archbishop. "O khristianskom ideale." *Str.* 1886, no. 1:31–42.

Nikol'skii, N., and M. Izvol'skii, eds. *Sbornik obraztsovykh propovedei, slov i pouchenii.* St. Petersburg, 1896.

"o. Dmitrii Flegontovich Giliarovskii," *VEV,* 1917, no. 49/50: 390–91.

"O domashnei zhizni pastyria Tserkvi." *RSP,* 1891, no. 18: 1–7.

"O tam, chto my dolzhny zhizn' svoiu soobrazovat' s slovom Bozhiem." *Khch* 25 (1827): 342–59.

O neobkhodimosti usileniia tserkovnostii i religioznoi nastroennosti mezhdu vospitannikami dukhovnoi-uchebnykh zavedenii. Khar'kov, 1913.

"O prazdnosti." *KhCh,* 1841, no. 4:255–99.

"O religiozno-nravstvennom vospitanii detei v pervonachal'nom ikh vozraste." *RSP,* 1869, no. 25:269–84.

Ob"iasnitel'nye zapiski k proektu ustava dukhovnykh uchilishch, sostavlennomu komitetom po preobrazovaniiu dukhovno-uchebnykh zavedenii. St. Petersburg, 1867.

Obshchii svod po imperii rezul'tatov, razrabotki dannykh vseobshchei perepisi naseleniia, proizvedennoi 28 ianvaria 1897 goda. St. Petersburg, 1905.

"Obzor zhurnalov." *Strannik,* 1882, no. 6:321–25.

Odnodnevnaia perepis' nachal'nykh shkol Rossiiskoi imperii proizvedennaia 18 ianvaria 1911 16 vols. St. Petersburg, 1916. Vol. 16:16–73.

Okenfuss, Max J. "V.O. Kliuchevskii on Childhood and Education in Early Modern Russia." *History of Education Quarterly* 17, no. 4 (Winter, 1977): 417–47.

Oleinikov, Mitrofan. "Iz vospominanii ob uchilishchnoi zhizni (1859–1865 g.g.)." *Voronezhskaia starina,* 1913, no. 12:492–98.

Opul'skii, Albert. *Zhitiia svytykh v tvorchestve russkikh pisatelei XIX veka.* East Lansing, MI, 1986.

Orbeli, L.A. *Vospominaniia.* Moscow-Leningrad, 1966.

Orlov, Aleksandr. *Moia zhizn' ili ispoved'.* Moscow, 1832.

Orlov, D.I. "Avtobiografiia." In *Ocherk XXV-letnei deiatel'nosti vrachei vypuska 1878 goda imp. Mediko-Khirurgicheskoi akademii,* edited by L. I. Voinov. St. Petersburg, 1903.

Orlov, N.A. "Protoierei Aleksei Vladimirovich Orlov." *VEV,* 1905, no. 23:1–34.

Orlovskii, I.I. "Selo Danilovichi." Partially reprinted in *Smolenskii istoriograf Ivan Ivanovich Orlovskii,* by M.V. Aksenov. Smolensk, 1909.

———. "Sviashchennik Ioann Mikhailovich Orlovskii (Nekrolog)." *Smolenskie eparkhial'nye vedomosti,* 1905, no. 10:533–41.

Ostrovitianov, K.V. *Dumy o proshlom.* Moscow, 1967.

Ostrovskii, A.N. "Bednaia nevesta." (1852) In his *PSS.* Moscow, 1973.

Otchet o glavnom pedagogicheskom institute s 1853 po 1855. St. Petersburg, 1855.

Otnoshenie khristianstva k nauke, gosudarstvu i kul'ture po vzgliadu pravoslavnogo khristianina. Ekaterinoslav, 1898.

Ovchinnikov, E.M. "Avtobiografiia." In *Sbornik biografii vrachei vypuska 1881 goda imp. Mediko-khirurgicheskoi akademii.* St. Petersburg, 1906.

Ovchinnikov, M.P. "Iz moikh narodovol'cheskikh vospominanii." *Sibirskii arkhiv,* 1916, no. 6/8:266–67.

Ovsianiko-Kulikovskii, D.N. *Istoriia russkoi intelligentsii.* In his *Sobranie sochinenii.* St. Petersburg, 1909. Vol. 8.

P.P. "Chto takoe asketizm." *Str.* 1895, no. 11:373–413.

P.R. "Domashnee vospitanie detei dukhovnogo zvaniia." *RSP,* 1861, no. 10:253–67.

———. "Domashnii byt prikhodskikh pastyrei." *RSP,* 1869, no. 20:85–103.

———. "Semeistvo i domochadtsy pastyria." *RSP,* 1869, no. 33:543–68.

———."Vazhnoe znachenie dnevnika dlia prikhodskogo sviashchennika." *RSP,* 1876, no. 16:475–88.

———. "Zametki o byte sel'skogo dukhoventsva v iugo-zapadnom krae Rossii sravnitel'no s bytom ego v vnutrennei Rossii." *RSP,* 1870, no. 15:509–22.

P.I.T. *Istoricheskie vzgliad na uchastie zhenskogo pola v religiozno-nravstvennoi i grazhdanskoi zhizni tserkvi Bozhiei i prilozheniem istorii Iaroslavskogo uchilishcha devits dukhovnogo zvaniia.* Iaroslav, 1871.

"Pamiati Igoria Vasil'evicha Porokha." *Otechestvennaia istoriia,* 2000, no. 2:210–11.

"Pamiati moego dorogogo brata S. S. Troitskogo." In *Sbornik, posviashchennyi pamiati Sergeia Semenovicha Troitskogo.* Tiflis, 1912.

"Pamiati pochivshego o. Mikhaila Il'icha Sokolova." *Arkhangel'skie eparkhial'nye vedomosti,* 1895, no. 16:403–10.

"Pamiati Viacheslava Vladimirovicha Lebedeva." *Otechestvennaia istoriia,* 2003, no. 3:221.

Pamiatnaia knizhka dlia sviashchennika, ili razmyshleniia o sviashchennicheskikh obiazannostiakh. Moscow, 1860.

Panaeva, A.Ia. (Golovacheva). "Vospominaniia. Otryvky." In *N.A. Dobroliubov v vospominaniiakh sovremennikov.* Moscow, 1986.

Panov, Nikolai. "Dnevnik sviashchennika." *DCh,* 1874, no. 5:103–28.

Panteleev, L.F. "Pamiati V. M. Garshina." *Sovremennaia illiustratsiia,* 1913, no. 3 [reprinted in Panteleev, *Vospominaniia,* 645–46].

———. *Vospominaniia.* Moscow, 1958.

Paperno, Irina. *Chernyshevsky and the Age of Realism: A Study in the Semiotics of Behavior.* Stanford, CA, 1988.

———. "Tolstoi's Diaries: The Inaccessible Self." In *Self and Story in Russian History,* edited by Laura Engelstein and Stephanie Sandler. Ithaca, NY, 2000.

Pascal, Roy. *Design and Truth in Autobiography.* Cambridge, MA, 1960.

Pashkov, A.M. "Olenskaia dukhovnaia seminariia i ee vklad v formirovanie intelligentsii Karelii." in *Novoe v izuchenii istorii Karelii.* Petrozavodsk, 1994.

"Pastyr' Tserkvi v srede vrazhduiushchikh chlenov sem'i i obshchestva." *RSP,* 1888, no. 34:519–29.

"Pastyr' tserkvi—obrazets dlia pasomykh." *RSP,* 1874, no. 29:313–20.

Pavlov, Ivan. "Avtobiografiia." *PSS,* 2nd ed. Moscow-Leningrad, 1952.

Pavlovich, M. "Venok na mogilu v boze pochivshego protoiereia Mikhaila Savvicha Pavlovicha (1823–1905)." *Volynskie eparkhial'nye vedomosti,* 1905, no. 16:517–26.

Pavlovskii, A. D. "Avtobiografiia." In *Sbornik biografii vrachei vypuska 1881 goda imp. Mediko-khirurgicheskoi akademii.* St. Petersburg, 1906.

Pelikan, Jaroslav. *The Growth of Medieval Theology (600–1300).* Vol. 3 of *The Christian Tradition.*

———. *The Spirit of Eastern Christendom (600–1700).* Vol. 2 of *The Christian Tradition: A History of the Development of Doctrine.* Chicago, 1971–1989.

Perov, Vasilii. "The First Rank (Sexton's Son Becomes a Collegiate Registrar: Trying on His Uniform), 1861." In *Paintings, Graphics Works,* by Vasily Perov. Leningrad, 1989.

Perrot, Michelle. "The Family Triumphant." In Aries and Duby.

———. "Roles and Characters." In Aries and Duby.

Pervaia vseobshchaia perepis' naseleniia Rossiiskoi imperii. Sbornik svedenii po Rossii. St. Petersburg, 1897.

Peshekhonov, A.V. "Avtobiografiia." In Maksimov.

Petr, Bishop. *Ukazanie puti ko spaseniiu (opyt asketiki).* Sergiev Posad, 1872.

Petrunkevich, Ivan. "Pamiati V.A. Gol'tseva." In *Pamiati Viktora Aleksandrovicha Gol'tseva.* Moscow, 1910.

Pevnitskii, V. "Semeinaia zhizn' sviashchennika." *RSP,* 1885, no. 21:67–76; no. 23:132–40.

Pevtsov, V.G. *Lektsii po tserkovnomu pravu.* St. Petersburg, 1914.

Pintner, Walter M. "The Social Characteristics of the Early Nineteenth-Century Russian Bureaucracy." *SR* 29, no. 3 (Fall 1970): 429–43.

Pipes, Richard. "The Historical Evolution of the Russian Intelligentsia." In *The Russian Intelligentsia,* edited by Richard Pipes. New York, 1970.

———. *Russia under the Old Regime.* London, 1982.

Pirumova, N.M. *Zemskaia intelligentsiia i ee rol' v obshchestvennoi bor'be do nachala XX v.* Moscow, 1986.

Pisarev, D.I. "Pogibshie i pogibaiushchie." *Literaturnaia kritika v trekh tomakh.* Leningrad, 1981.

Pisitios, Argyrios. "Russian Orthodoxy and the Politics of National Identity in Early Twentieth Century." *Balkan Studies* 42, no. 2 (2001):225–43

———. ."The Unknown Dissident: The Prosopography of Clerical Anti-Tsarist Activism in Late Imperial Russia." *Modern Greek Studies Yearbook* 18/19 (2002/2003):63–94.

Pis'ma A.P. Borodina. 4 vols. Moscow-Leningrad, 1927–1950.

Pis'ma V.O. Kliucheskogo k P.P. Gvozdevu. Moscow, 1924.

Platon, [Fiveiskii]. *Napominanie sviashchenniku ob obiazannostiiakh ego pri sovershenii tainstva pokaianiia.* Moscow, 1861.

"Pochemu nasha intelligentsia vrazhdebna po otnosheniiu k dukhoventsvu." *RSP,* 1905, no. 34:451–58.

Pokrovskii, N.V. *Professor Nikolai Vasil'evich Pokrovskii, direktor imp. Arkheologicheskogo instituta. 1874–1909. Kratkii ocherk.* St. Petersburg, 1909.

Polevoi, P. "Tri tipa Russkikh uchenykh (Kunik, Sreznevskii i Grigorovich." *IV,* 1899, vol. 76, no. 4:124–43.

———. "Dva Pedagoga (iz shkol'nykh vospominanii)." *IV,* 1892, vol. 50, no. 12:675–93.

Polisadov, Fedor. "Kovrovskogo uezda, sela Lezhneva Protoierei Lev Ivanovich Polisadov. Biografiia." *VEV,* 1879, no. 19:556–68.

Polisadov, G.A. *Doma i v shkole.* Vladimir, 1915.

———. "Ocherki zhizni i byta sel'skikh sviashchennikov i ikh semeistv v 40-kh i 50-kh godakh nyneshniago stoletiia." *Nizhegorodskie eparkhial'nye vedomosti,* 1892, no. 6:199–215.

———. "Smes'; Mirskaia pomoshch' i sel'skogo sviashchennika." *Str.,* 1860, no. 7:5–31.

Polisadov, Ioann. *Propovedi.* 2 vols. St. Petersburg, 1896.

Politicheskie partii Rossii konets XIX-pervaia tret' XX veka. Entsiklopediia. Moscow, 1996.

Polkanov, Ivan. "Domashnee vospitanie detei dukhoventsva v S——koi eparkhii." *RSP,* 1861, no. 4:131–39.

Polovtsov, A.A. *Dnevnik gosudarstvennogo sekretaria A.A. Polovtsova.* 2 vols. Moscow, 1966.

Polunov, A.Iu. *Pod vlast'iu ober-prokurora: gosudarstvo i tserkov' v epokhu Aleksandra III.* Moscow, 1996.

Pomialovskii, N.G. "Ocherki bursy." In his *SS.* 2 vols. Moscow-Leningrad, 1935.

Pomialovsky, N.G. *Seminary Sketches.* Translated by Alfred R. Kuhn. Ithaca, NY, 1973.

Ponomarev, A. "Zhenshchina v dukhovnoi sem'e: v sviazi s istoriei prikhodskogo dukhovenstva v Rusi." *Str.,* 1895, no. 12:489–97.

Popov, Evgenii. *Obshchenarodnye chteniia po pravoslavno-nravstvenomu bogosloviiu.* St. Petersburg, 1901.

———. *Pis'ma po pravoslavno-pastyrskomu bogosloviiu.* 4 vols. 2nd ed. Perm, 1873.

Popov, M.R. *Zapiski zemlevol'tsa.* Moscow, 1933.

Popov, M.V. "Moia biografiia." In N.N. Glubokovskii, *Sviashchennik M.V. Popov.* Vologda, 1910.

"Posviashchenie v san diakona byvshogo mirovogo sud'i." *Permskie eparkhial'nye vedomosti,* 1895, no. 5:91–103.

Potapenko, I.N. "I.N. Potapenko." In Fidler.

Potorzhinskii, M.A., ed. *Obraztsy Russkoi Tserkovnoi Propovedi XIX veka.* 3rd ed. Kiev, 1912.

Prakticheskoe izlozhenie tserkovno-grazhdanskikh postanovlenii v rukovodstvo sviashchenniku na sluchai sovershenii vazhneishikh treb tserkovnykh. 6th ed. St. Petersburg, 1880.

Pravdin, E.I. *Istoriia Shuiskogo, Vladimirskoi gubernii, dukhovnogo uchilishcha.* Vladimir, 1887.

Pravila dlia zhizni uchenikov Tverskoi Dukhovnoi seminarii. Tver, 1890.

Preobrazhenskii, A.S. *Na pamiat' o tovarishcheskom s"ezde byvshikh vospitannikov Iaroslavskoi dukhovnoi seminarii, vypuska, 1889 god.* St. Petersburg, 1910.

Preobrazhenskii, E.A. "Avtobiografiia." *Granat,* vol. 41, part 2.

Preobrazhenskii, Ivan. *Otechestvennaia tserkov' po statisticheskim dannym s 1840–41 po 1890–91 gg.* 2nd. ed. St. Petersburg, 1901.

———. "Vnutrennee tserkovnoe obozrenie." *Str.,* 1895, no. 11:739–57.

Pretty, Dave. "The Saints of the Revolution: Political Activists in 1890s Ivanovo-Voznesensk and the Path of Most Resistance." *SR* 54, no. 2 (Summer 1995): 276–304.

Pribylev, A.V. "Avtobiografiia." *Granat,* vol. 40.

"Primernoe povedenie sviashchennika v domashnei zhizni." *RSP,* 1872, no. 21:119–27.

Prishvin, M.M. "My s toboi. Po dnevniku 1940." *Druzhba narodov,* 1990, no. 6:236–69.

Pritezhaev, E. "Dukhovnaia shkola i seminaristy v istorii russkoi nauki i obrazovanii." *KhCh,* 1879, no. 2:161–87.

"Prizvanie k sviashchennomu sanu." *KhCh,* 1843, no. 4:125–58.

Protoierei Feodor Aleksandrovich Golubinskii. Moscow, 1855.

Protopopov, D.I. (ed.) *Sbornik obraztsovykh propovedei*. Moscow, 1890.

"Psalomshchik Nikolai Stefanovich Vvedenskii." *VEV*, 1912, no. 40:830–38.

Pushkin, A.S. *PSS*. Jubilee edition. Moscow, 1941.

———. "Skazka o pope i o rabotnike ego Balde (1830)." In his *PSS*. Moscow, 1948, vol. 3.

Rabinovitch, M.G. *Ocherki etnografii russkogo feodal'nogo goroda: grazhdane, ikh obshchestvennyi i domashnii byt*. Moscow, 1978.

Raeff, Marc. "Enticements and Rifts: Georges Florovsky as Russian Intellectual Historian." In *Georges Florovsky: Russian Intellectual, Orthodox Churchman*, edited by Andrew Blane. Crestwood, NY, 1993.

———. "Home, School, and Service in the Life of the Russian Nobleman." In *The Structure of Russian History*, edited by Michael Cherniavsky. New York, 1970.

———. *Origins of the Russian Intelligentsia: The Eighteenth-Century Nobility*. New York, 1966.

———. *Russia Abroad: A Cultural History of the Russian Emigration, 1919–1939*. Oxford, 1990.

———. *Russian Intellectual History: An Anthology*. Atlantic Highland, NJ, 1978.

Rashin, A.G. "Gramotnost' i narodnoe obrazovanie v Rossii v XIX i nachale XIX v." *Istoricheskie zapiski*, 1951, vol. 37:28–80.

Rasskazy babushki. Iz vospominanii piati pokolenii zapisannye i sobrannye ee vnukom D. Blagovo. Leningrad, 1989.

"Razmyslenie: O krotosti i smirenii." *KhCh*, 1832, vol. 48:250–54.

"Raznye izvestiia i zametki: Seminaristy v universitetakh." *Str.*, 1880, no. 12:604–5.

"Rech', skazannaia prepodavatelem seminarii S. F. Arkhangel'skim pri otpevanii V.M. Berezina." *VEV*, 1912, no. 14:314.

Reiser, S.A. "Rodoslovnye razyskaniia (k 150-letiiu so dnia rozhdeniia N.A. Dobroliubova)." *Vspomogatel'nye istoricheskie distsipliny*, 1987, vol. 18..

Remorov, N.I. "Stranichki proshlogo." *Nabliudatel'*, 1900, no. 9:103–24; no. 10:59–72.

Repin, Ilya. "Archdeacon (1877)." Reproduced in *Ilya Repin: Russia's Secret*, by Henk Van Os and Sjeng Scheijen. Groningen, 2001.

Reshetov, A.M. "Neizvestnaia stranitsa iz zhizni D. K. Zelenina." *Etnograficheskoe obozrenie*, 2005, no. 4:130–36.

———. "Dmitrii Konstantinovich Zelenin: Klassik Russkoi etnografii." In *Vydaiushchiesia otechestvennye etnologi i antropologi XX veka*, edited by D.D. Tumarkin. Moscow, 2004.

Richards, Jeffrey. *Happiest Days: The Public School in English Fiction*. Manchester, UK, 1988.

Rieber, Alfred. *Merchants and Entrepreneurs in Imperial Russia*. Chapel Hill, NC, 1982.

Ringer, Fritz. *The Decline of the German Mandarin: The German Academic Community, 1890–1933*. Cambridge, MA, 1969.

Roosevelt, Priscilla. *Life on the Russian Country Estate: A Social and Cultural History*. New Haven, 1995.

Rosenshield, Gary. "The Realization of the Collective Self: The Rebirth of Religious Autobiography in Dostoevskii's Zapiski iz Mertvogo Doma." *Slavic Review* 50, no. 2 (Summer 1991): 317–27.

Rostislavov, D.I. *O pravoslavnom belom i chernom dukhovenstve v Rossii*. 2 vols. Leipzig, 1866.

———. *Provincial Russia in the Age of Enlightenment*, translated by Alexander M. Martin. DeKalb, IL, 2002.

Ruckman, JoAnn. *The Moscow Business Elite: A Social and Cultural Portrait of Two Generations, 1840–1905*. DeKalb, IL, 1984.

Rufimskii, Porfurii. "Iz seminarskikh vospominanii." *Izvestiia po Kazanskoi eparkhii*, 1911, no. 1:25–33.

Rukovodstvennye dlia pravoslavnogo dukhovenstva ukazy, Sviatieishogo Pravitel'stvuiushchogo Sinoda, 1721–1878 g. Moscow, 1879.

Runovskii, N. "Soslovnaia zamknutost' belogo dukhoventsva v Rossii i mery k oslableniiu ee v tsarstvovanie Imperatora Aleksandra II, v sviazi s voprosom o nasledstvennosti dukhovnogo zvaniia." *Str.*, 1897, no. 4:438–55; no. 5:57–68.

Russkie Pisateli: 1800–1917: Biograficheskii slovar'. 4 vols. Moscow, 1989–1999.

Russkoe propovednichestvo; Istoricheskii ego obzor i vzgliad na sovremennoe ego napravlenie. St. Petersburg, 1871.

S. "Novyi tip 'sovremennogo' sviashchennika." *RSP,* 1873, no. 50:479–88.

S.B. "Piatidesiatiletnii iubilei sviashchennika sela Varvarina, Iur'evskogo uezda, o. Dmitriia Andreevicha Orlova." *VEV,* 1909, no. 13/14:231–34.

S.P——v. "Voprosy vospitaniia v srede sel'skogo dukhovenstva." *Zvonar',* 1907, no. 10:39–56.

S.S. *Besedy o vospitanii detei.* Sergiev Posad, 1904.

S.Sh. *Ob uchilishchakh dlia devits dukhovnogo zvaniia.* Moscow, 1866.

Sadov, A.I. "Iz vospominanii o sel'skoi zhizni i shkol'nom byte 60–50 let nazad." *Deistviia Nizhegorodskoi gubernskoi uchenoi arkhivnoi komissii,* 1913, vol. 16, no. 1:1–18.

Sakharov, Andrei. *Vospominaniia v dvukh tomakh.* Moscow, 1996.

Saltykov-Shchedrin, M.E. *Gubernskie Ocherki.* 1856–1857; reprint: Moscow, 1968.

Samoilov, V.O., and Ia.A. Vinogradov. "Ivan Pavlov i Nikolai Bukharin." *Zvezda,* 1989, no. 10:94–110.

Sarna, Jonathan D. *American Judaism: A History.* New Haven, CT, 2004.

"Schastie cheloveka i put' k nemu." *VEV,* 1877, no. 6:311–19.

Seigel, Jerrold. *The Idea of the Self: Thought and Experience in Western Europe since the Seventeenth Century.* Cambridge, UK, 2005.

Semenov, P.V. *Ot Bursy do sniatiia sana.* 2nd ed. Samara, 1913.

Sergii, Archimandrite. *Kuda ia poidu? Rech' K vospitannikam seminarri vypuska 1900 goda.* St. Petersburg, 1900.

Shalamov, V. "Chetvertaia Vologda (Avtobiograficheskaia povest')." In his *Voskreshenie listvennitsy.* Paris, 1985.

Shashkov, S. "Avtobiografiia," *Vostochnoe obozrenie,* 1882, no. 28:11–13; no. 30:10–12; no. 32:11–13.

Shatilov, N. "Iz nedavniago proshlogo." *GM,* 1916, no. 4:205–25.

Shchapov, A.P. "Iz bursatskogo byta." In his *SS.* Irkutsk, 1937.

Shcheglov, I.L. "Ivan L. Shcheglov." In Fidler.

Shchetinina, G.I. "Alfavitnye spiski studentov kak istoricheskii istochnik. Sostav universitetskogo studentchestva v konste XIX-nachale XX veka." *Istoriia SSSR,* 1979, no. 5:110–26.

——. *Universitety v Rossii i ustav 1884 goda.* Moscow, 1976.

Shebalin, M.P. "Avtobiografii." *Granat,* vol. 40.

Shevzov, Vera. "Letting the People into Church: Reflections on Orthodoxy and Community in Late Imperial Russia." In *Orthodox Russia: Belief and Practice under the Tsars,* edited by Valerie A. Kivelson and Robert H. Greene. University Park, PA, 2003.

——. "Popular Orthodoxy in Late Imperial Rural Russia." Ph.D. diss., Yale University, 1994.

——. *Russian Orthodoxy on the Eve of the Revolution.* Oxford, 2004.

Shmid, E. *Istoriia srednikh uchebnykh zavedenii v Rossii,* translated by A. G. Neilisov. St. Petersburg, 1878.

Silber, Ilana Friedrich. *Virtuosity, Charisma and Social Order: A Comparative Sociological Study of Monasticism in Theravada Buddhism and Medieval Catholicism.* Cambridge, UK, 1995.

Sinel, Allen. *The Classroom and the Chancellery: State Educational Reform in Russia under Count Dmitry Tolstoi.* Cambridge, MA, 1972.

Slezkine, Yuri. *Arctic Mirrors.* Ithaca, N.Y., 1994.

——. "The Fall of Soviet Ethnography, 1929–38." *Current Anthropology* 32, no. 4 (Aug.– Oct., 1991): 476–84.

——. *The Jewish Century.* Princeton, 2004.

——. "Lives as Tales." In *The Shadow of Revolution: Life Stories of Russian Women from 1917 to the Second World War,* edited by Shelia Fitzpatrick and Yuri Slezkine. Princeton, 2000..

Smidovich, P.G. "Avtobiografiia." *Granat,* vol. 41, part 2.

Smiriagin, A.P. "Iz pastyrskoi khroniki sel'skogo sviashchennika." *Missionerskoe obozrenie,* 1903, no. 19:1210–18.

Smirnov, N. "Ateizm (Iz perezhitogo)." In *Dukhovnaia shkola. Sbornik.* Moscow, 1906.

Smirnov, S.V. "D.N. Kudriavskii i D.K. Zelenin." *Trudy po russkoi i slavianskoi filologii,* 1968, vol. 12:138–46.

Smith, Jonathan Z. "What a Difference a Difference Makes." In *"To See Ourselves as Others See Us": Christians, Jews and "Others" in Late Antiquity,* edited by Jacob Neusmer and Ernest Frerichs. Chico, CA, 1985.

Snezhnevskii, V.I. "Avtobiografiia." *Deistviia Nizhegorodskogo Gubernskogo uchebnogo arkhivnogo komissia,* 1909, no. 7:9–16.

Sobolev, G.L. "Pamiati Vitaliia Ivanovicha Startseva." *Otechestvennaia istoriia,* 2001, no. 1:220–21.

Sobranie postanovlenii Sviateishego Sinoda 1867–1874 gg. otnositel'no ustroistva dukhovnykh seminarii i uchilishch. St. Petersburg, 1875.

Soliarskii, P.F. *Zapiski po nravstvennomu pravoslavnomu bogosloviiu.* 3 vols. St. Petersburg, 1860–1863.

Solov'ev, N.I. "Kak nas uchili (rasskaz iz dukhovno-seminarskoi zhizni)." *Russkaia starina,* 1899, vol. 100, no. 11: 375–98.

Solov'ev, Sergei. *Izbrannye trudy. Zapiski.* Moscow, 1983.

Sorokin, Gavriil I. *Uchitel' druzhishche.* Kiev, 1902.

Spasskii, A.A. "Iz tekushchei zhurnalistiki: Vopros o monasheshestve." *BV,* 1903, no. 12: 172–80.

Speranskii, S. *Moskovskoe filaretovskoe eparkhial'noe zhenskoe uchilishche, 1832–1882.* Moscow, 1883.

Spiski studentov okonchivshikh polnyi kurs imperatorsskoi moskovskoi dukhovnoi akademii za pervoe stoletie ee sushchestvovaniia (1814–1914). Sergiev Posad, 1914.

Staniukopich, T.V., and T.D. Toren. "Dmitrii Konstantinovich Zelenin." *Sovetskaia etnografiia,* 1954, no. 4:157–59.

Startsy o. Paisii Velichkovskii i o. Makarii Optinskii i ikh literaturno-asketicheskaia deiatel'nost'. Moscow, 1909.

Statitisticheskiia tablitsy Rossiiskoi imperii. No. 2. Nalichnoe naselenie imperii za 1858 god. St. Petersburg, 1863.

Steinberg, Mark. *Moral Communities: The Culture of Class Relations in the Russian Printing Industry, 1867–1907.* Berkeley, CA, 1992.

Stelliatskii, N. *O nachalakh khristiankogo vospitaniia detei v sem'e i v shkole.* Kiev, 1907.

Stites, Richard. *The Women's Liberation Movement in Russia: Feminism, Nihilism, and Bolshevism, 1860–1930.* Princeton, 1990.

Stone, Lawrence. "The Rise of the Nuclear Family in Early Modern England: The Patriarchal Stage." In *The Family in History,* edited by Charles E. Rosenberg. Philadelphia, 1975.

Strakheev, D.I. "Gruppy i portrety." *IV,* January 1907, no. 1:81–94.

Strakhov, Nikolai. "Ottsy i Deti." *Vremiia,* 1862, no. 4:58–64.

Stranitsy istorii Rossii v letopisi odnogo roda (Avtobiograficheskie zapiski chetyrekh pokolenii russkikh sviashchennikov). Moscow, 2004.

Subbotin, N.I. "V sem'e sviashchennika (iz vospominanii detstva)." *Moskovskie vedomosti,* 1899, no. 355:3.

Sukhomlin, Vasilii Ivanovich. "Avtobiografiia." *Granat,* vol. 40.

Suny, Ronald G. "Images of the Armenians in the Russian Empire." In *The Armenian Image in History and Literature,* edited by Richard G. Hovanissian. Malibu, CA, 1981.

Sushko, A.V. "Mentalitet detei dukhovenstva vo vtoroi polovine XIX-nachale XX v." In *Mentalitet rossiianina; istoriia problemy: Materialy semnadtsatoi vseros. zaoch. nauch. konf.* St. Petersburg, 2000.

"Svet i istina." *KhCh*, 1823, 11:270–86.

"Sviashchennik F.N. Sosuntsev. Nekrolog." *Izvestiia po Kazanskoi eparkhii*, 1906, no. 36:1129–36; no. 43:1365–66.

Svod mnenii eparkhial'nykh nachal'stv po voprosu ob otkrytii detiam sviashchhenno— tserkovnosluzhitelei putei dlia obespecheniia svoego sushchestvovaniia na vsekh poprishchakh grazhdanskoi deiatel'nosti. St. Petersburg [186?].

Svod mnenii otnositel'no ustava Dukhovnoi Seminarii, proektirovannogo komitetom 1860–62 godov. St. Petersburg, 1866.

Svod zakonov. St. Petersburg, 1832, vol. 9.

Sychugov, S.I. "Nechto v rode avtobiografii." *GM*, 1916, no. 1:109–36.

———. *Zapiski bursaka.* Moscow, 1933.

Tan-Bogoraz, V.G. "Avtobiografiia." *Granat*, vol. 40.

Tankov, A.A. "Zakonouchitel' Kurskoi muzhskoi gimnazii prot. o. A.A. Tankov (1817–1904)." *Kurskie eparkhial'nye vedomosti*, 1904, no. 36:684–89; 1906, no. 30:791–803.

Tartakovskii, A.G. *Russkaia memuaristika: XVIII-pervoi poloviny XIX v.* Moscow, 1991.

Taylor, Charles. *Sources of the Self: The Making of Modern Identity.* Cambridge, MA, 1989.

"Tekushchaia khronika." *Str.*, 1878, no. 11:241–49.

Teplov, A.L. "Avtobiografiia." *Zemlia rodnaia*, 1959, vol. 22/23:81–82.

Thompson, E.P. *Customs in Common: Studies in Traditional Popular Culture.* New York, 1993.

———. *The Making of the English Working Class.* New York, 1964.

Tikhomirov, D.I. "Avtobiografiia." *Bibliograficheskii ukazatel' materialov po istorii russkoi shkoly*, 1901, no. 11:216–32.

Tikhonov, V.A. *Dvadtsat' piat' let na kazennoi sluzhbe (Vospominaniia otstavnogo china).* 2 vols. St. Petersburg, 1912.

———. *V otstavke (Vospominaniia otstavnogo chinovnika).* St. Petersburg, 1913.

Tikhonov, V.A. "Vladimir Alekseevich Tikhonov." In Fidler.

Titlinov, B.V. *Dukhovnaia shkola v Rossii v XIX stol.* 2 parts. Vil'na, 1909.

———. *Molodezh' i revoliutsiia.* Leningrad, 1925.

Tol'stoi, N.I. "Trudy D.K. Zelenina po dukhovnoi kul'ture." In *Izbrannye trudy. Stat'i po dukkovnoi kul'ture, 1901–1913*, by D.K. Zelenin. Moscow, 1994.

Tomskii universitet. Kratkii istoricheskii ocherk. Tomsk, 1917.

Toporov, V.N. *Sviatost' i sviatye v russkoi dukhovnoi kul'ture.* Moscow, 1995.

Tovrov, Jessica. "Mother-Child Relationships among the Russian Nobility." In *The Family in Imperial Russia*, edited by David L. Ransel. Urbana, IL, 1978.

Troitskii, A. "K voprosu ob uluchsheniiakh v byte dukhoventsva." *PO*, 1862, no. 7:102–29.

———. "Obozrenie sovremennoi literatury po voprosu o dukhovenstve." *PO*, 1860, no. 4:535–59.

Tsapina, Olga A. "Secularization and Opposition in the Time of Catherine the Great." In *Religion and Politics in Enlightenment Europe*, edited by Dale K. Van Kley and James E. Bradley. Notre Dame, IN, 2001.

Tsezorevskii, P.V. "Shestidesiatye gody v dukhovnoi seminarii." *Zvonar'*, 1906, no. 2/3:272–94; no. 6:268–86; 1907, no. 7:48–69.

Tsvilenev, N.F. "Avtobiografiia." *Granat*, vol. 40.

Turgenev, I.S. "*Pop* (1844)." In his *PSS*. Moscow-Leningrad, 1960, vol. 1.

Udilenev, N.F. "Avtobiografiia." *Granat*, vol. 40.

Udintsev, B.D. *D.N. Mamin-Sibiriak: rukopisi i perepiska.* Moscow, 1949.

"Ukazatel' trudov D.K. Zelenina i osnovnoi literatury o nem." In *Problemy slavianskoi ethnografii.* Leningrad, 1979.

Uspenskii, Boris. "Sotsial'naia zhizn' russkikh familii." In his *Izbrannye trudy.* 2 vols. Moscow, 1994.

Uspenskii, N.V. *Iz proshlogo. Vospominaniia.* Moscow, 1889.

Vagner, N.P. "Vospominaniia ob Aleksandre Mikhailoviche Butlerove." In *Aleksandr Mikhailovich Butlerov po materialam sovremennikov.* Moscow, 1978.

van Kley, Dale. *The Religious Origins of the French Revolution: From Calvin to the Civil Con-stitution, 1560–1791*. New Haven, CT, 1996.

Vasina, A.I. "D.K. Zelenin (Kratkii ocherk zhizni i tvorchestva)." In *Opisanie kollektsii rukopisei nauchnogo arkhiva Geograficheskogo obshchestva SSSR*. Leningrad, 1973.

———. "Uchenyi patriot." In *Slovo o zemliakakh: Sbornik*. Izhevsk, 1965.

Vasina, A.I., and N.I. Gagen-Torn. "Dmitrii Konstantinovich Zelenin (K 10-letiiu so dnia smerti)." *Izvestiia Vsesoiuznogo Geograficheskogo obshchestva*, 1966, vol. 98, no. 1:67–70.

Vasnetsov, A.M. "Kak ia sdelalsia khudozhnikom i kak i chto rabotal." In *Apollinarii Vas-netsov. K stoletiiu so dnia rozhdeniia*. Moscow, 1957.

Vasnetsov, M.V. *Russkii khudozhnik Viktor Mikhailovich Vasnetsov*. Prague, 1948.

Vasnetsov, V.M. *Mir khudozhnika: Pis'ma, Dnevniki, vospominaniia, dokumenty, suzhdeniia sovremennikov*. Moscow, 1987.

"Vazhnost' sviashchennogo sana." *KhCh*, 1843, no. 4:106–24.

Vengerov, S.A. "Blagosvetlov, Grigorii Evlampievich." In his *Kritikobiograficheskii*.

———. *Kritikobiograficheskii slovar' russkikh pisatelei uchenykh*. 6 vols. St. Petersburg, 1897–1904.

Vinogradov, V.K. *Avtobiografiia*. Feodosiia, 1895.

Vinogradova, T.P. *Nizhegorodskaia intelligentsiia vokrug N.A. Dobroliubova*. Nizhnii-Nov-gorod, 1992.

Vinokurov, A.N. "Avtobiografiia." *Granat*, vol. 41, part 1.

Vodovozova, E.N. *Na zare zhizni i drugie vospominaniia*. 2 vols. Moscow, 1911.

Vologodskii, P.V. "Iz istorii moei zhizni." *Russkoe obozrenie*, December, 1920, 98–135.

Voronskii, A.V *burse*. Moscow, 1966.

Voroshilov, K.E. "Avtobiografiia." *Granat*, vol. 41, part 1.

"Vospominaniia Eleny Iurevny Khvoshchinskoi (Rozhdennoi Kniazhny Golitsynoi)." *RS*, 1897, no. 4.

Vovelle, Michel. *Ideologies and Mentalities*. Translated by Eamon O'Flaherty. Cambridge, MA, 1990.

"Vozzvanie k pastyriam o luchshem domashnem vospitanii svoikh detei." *RSP*, 1887, no. 9:289–94.

Vrutsevich, Mikhail. "Dukhovnoe uchilishche starykh vremen." *RS*, 1905, no. 121:693–704.

Wachtel, Andrew. *The Battle for Childhood: Creation of a Russian Myth*. Stanford, 1990.

Wagner, William G. *Marriage, Property, and Law in Late Imperial Russia*. Oxford, 1994.

Walker, Barbara. "On Reading Soviet Memoirs: A History of the 'Contemporaries' Genre as an Institution of Russian Intelligentsia Culture from the 1790s to the 1970s." *Russian Review* 59 (July 2000): 327–52.

Wallis, Roy, and Steve Bruce. "Secularization: The Orthodox Model." In *Religion and Modernization: Sociologists and Historians Debate the Secularization Thesis*, edited by Steve Bruce. Oxford, 1992.

Walzer, Michael. *The Revolution of the Saints: A Study in the Origins of Radical Politics*. New York, 1976.

Weber, Eugen. *Peasants into Frenchmen: The Modernization of Rural France, 1870–1914*. Stanford, 1976.

Weber, Max. *The Protestant Ethic and the Spirit of Capitalism*, translated by Talcott Par-sons. New York, 1958.

———. *The Sociology of Religion*. Boston, 1993.

Werth, Paul. "Orthodoxy as Ascription (and Beyond): Religious Identity on the Edges of the Orthodox Community, 1740–1917." In *Orthodox Russia: Belief and Prac-tice under the Tsars*, edited by Valerie A. Kivelson and Robert H. Greene. Univer-sity Park, PA, 2003.

Wood, Gordon S. *The Radicalism of the American Revolution*. New York, 1992.

Worobec, Christine D. *Peasant Russia*. Princeton, 1991.

Wortman, Richard. *The Development of a Russian Legal Consciousness*. Chicago, 1976.

————. *Scenarios of Power: Myth and Ceremony in Russian Monarchy.* 2 vols. Princeton, 2000.

Zaburdaev, N. "Iz semeinoi khroniki Dobroliubovykh." *Volga,* 1977, vol. 12:175–79.

Zagoskin, N.P. *Za sto let. Biograficheskii slovar' professorov i prepodavatelei Imp. Kazanskogo universiteta (1840–1904).* 2 vols. Kazan, 1904.

Zaionchkovskii, P.A. *Istoriia dorevoliutsionnoi Rossii v vospominaniiakh i dnevnikakh.* 13 vols. Moscow, 1976–1989.

————. *Pravitel'stvennyi apparat samoderzhavnoi Rossii v XIX v.* Moscow, 1878.

Zamiatin, Evgenii. "Avtobiografiia." In *Pisateli: Avtobiografii Sovremennikov,* edited by Vl. Lidin. Moscow, 1926.

Zapiska po voprosu ob otkrytii detiam sviashchenno-tserkovnosluzhitelei putei dlia obespecheniia svoego sushchestvovaniia vo vsekh poprishchakh grazhdanskoi deiatel'nosti. St. Petersburg, 1868.

Zapiski sel'skogo sviashchennika. St. Petersburg, 1882.

Zarin, A.E. "Andrei Efimovich Zarin." In Fidler.

Zarin, Sergei. *Asketizm po pravoslavno-khristianskomu ucheniiu.* 2 vols. St. Petersburg, 1907.

Zarnitskii, Ia.I. (ed.) *Sbornik propovednicheskikh obraztsov.* St. Petersburg, 1891.

Zavedeev, Petr. *Lektsii po bogoslovskim naukam (Polnoe rukovodstv o dlia podrotovki k ekzamenu na sviashchennika).* Moscow, 1908.

Zelenetskii, A.A. "Mitropolit Ioannikii i seminaristy-narodniki." *IV,* 1901, vol. 86, no. 10/12:1082–94.

Zelenin, D.K. "Narody krainego severa SSSR posle Velikoi Oktiabr'skoi sotsialiosticheskoi revoliutsii." *Sovetskaia etnografiia: Sbornik statei,* 1938, no. 1:15–52.

————. "Seminarskiia slova v Russkom iazyke." *Russkii filologicheskii vestnik,* 1905, 14:109–19.

Zemskaia, E.A. *Mikhail Bulgakov i ego rodnye: Semeinyi portret.* Moscow, 2004.

————. "Zametki o russkom iazyke, kul'ture i byte rubezha XIX–XX vv. (Po materialam semeinogo arkhiva Bulgakovykh)." In *Oblik slova: Sbornik statei Pamiati Dmitriia Nikolaevicha Shmeleva.* Moscow, 1997.

"Zhenskie tipy dukhovnogo zvaniia v svetskoi literature." *RSP,* 1874, no. 43:234–43.

Zhirkevich, A.V. *Ivan Ivanovich Orlovskii.* Vil'na, 1909.

Zhitiia sviatykh na Russkom iazyke izlozhennye po rukovodstvu Chet'ikh-minei sv. Dmitriia Rostovskogo. 12 vols. Moscow, 1906.

Zhitiia sviatykh Rossiiskoi tserkvi takzhe iverskikh i slavianskikh i mestno chtimykh podvizhnikov blagochestiia. 12 vols. Moscow, 1859.

Zhitomirskaia, S.V. *Vospominaniia i dnevniki XVIII–XX vv. Ukazatel' rukopisei.* Moscow, 1976.

Zhizn' pastyria v mire. St. Petersburg, 1844.

Zhurnaly i protokoly zasedanii vysochaishe uchrezhdennogo predsobornogo prisutsviia. 4 vols. St. Petersburg, 1906–1907.

Zhurnal uchebnogo komiteta pri Sviateishem Sinode s soobrazheniiami po vosprosam, kasaiushchimsia ustroistva vospitatel'noi chasti v dukhovnykh uchilishchakh. St. Petersburg, 1875.

Ziolkowski, Margaret. *Hagiography and Modern Russian Literature.* Princeton, 1988.

Zolotarev, A.A. "Bogatyrskoe soslovie." In "Bogatyrskoe soslovie: A.A. Zolotarev o roli dukhoventsva v istorii Rossii," by V.E. Khalizeva. *Literaturnoe obozrenie,* 1992, no. 2:99–112.

Zolotorev, A. "Retsentsiia." *Istorik Marksist,* 1937, no. 5/6:201–2.

Index

popovichi's representation of parents' marriages, 112; popovichi marrying popov'ny, 40–41; popovichi rejecting, 185–86, 193, 194, 195, 206; popovichi's views on, 168, 181, 197, 198, 199. *See also* Mamin; Tregubov family

Medicine, 57, 71, 74, 169; taught and practiced in bursa, 128, 146; clergy administering, 22, 173; clergy's view of as a profession, 167; popovichi on why chose as a profession, 175, 177; popovichi's contribution to the profession of, 41, 173–74; popovichi doctors, 102, 185. *See also* Elpat'evskii; Krylov; Petersburg Medical Academy; Smirnov family, Aleksandr; Sychugov; Tsezarevskii; Tsvetkov family, Aleksandr

Merchantry, 28, 81, 83, 98, 156, 169; Church publicists' conceptions of, 63–65, 238n.74; attitudes toward of clergymen and popovichi, 64–65, 96

Miliukov, Aleksandr, 27

Missionaries, 77, 128; popovichi as, 151, 160

Modern Self, xii, 8, 79, 118, 202, 214, 216, 217; bursa as one source of for popovichi, 126, 135, 143, 153; defined, 5, 115; and ego-documents of clergy and popovichi, 9–10, 73, 90, 181; how could arise in Russia, 6, 47; how Orthodox theology promoted, 47; popovichi as embodying, 6; popovichi's choices as a sign of, 153, 172. *See also* Intelligentsia; Love

Modernity, 7, 9, 67, 180, 189, 192; binary models and, xii, 8, 214; popovichi shaping in Russia, 4, 216; Orthodox Church's response to, 10, 162, 180

Modernization, 4, 7, 9, 21, 69, 162, 172, 176, 177, 188, 214

Molotov, Viacheslav, 41

Monasticism, 175, 185; bishops, 24; bursa similar to, 126, 131–32; Church publicists' new position on, 73; nuns, 87; parish clergy's animosity toward, 86–88, 167, 177; popovichi compared with, 166, 178; popovichi's condemnation of, 140–41, 144, 150, 151, 169; social background of monks, 24. *See also* Evlogii

Moscow, 28, 54, 108, 174, 176; Archeological Society, 106; Circus, 209, Theological Academy, 27, 137, 181; University, 174, 204

Nadezhdin, Nikolai, 25–26, 35, 226

National identity: books popovichi read as children and, 118–19, 121; Church publicists' concept of patriotism, 49–50; Church publicists on popovichi as exemplifying, 161; contemporary Russian Orthodox Church claiming embodies, 209; defined in late imperial moral theology, 50; as part of "model piety," 97; popovichi as possessing a strong sense of, 119, 174, 175, 191, 211, 212, 213; popovichi on selves as embodying, 43, 54, 100, 102, 110, 211, 212; on peasants as symbolizing, 59; popovichi's use of term homeland, 100, 102. *See also* History, Russian; Popovichi, stereotypes

Nechaev, Sergei, 180

Nekrasov, Nikolai, 30, 56

Nevskii, Aleksandr, 178

"New men" of the 1860s, 3, 30, 40, 95, 183, 192; popovichi viewing selves as prototypes of, 40, 43

Nietzsche, Friedrich, 213

Nikitskii, Aleksandr, 101, 195, 226

Nobility, 17, 18, 43, 57, 71, 136, 156; anti-clericalism of, 5, 14–16; autobiographies of childhood, 94–95, 98–100, 110, 112–13; daily life compared to clergy, 19, 23; Church publicists' attitudes toward, 51–55, 57, 59, 63, 70, 75, 78, 82, 110, 161; clergy's conception of, 51–56, 65, 67, 86, 96, 106, 110, 112, 137; culture as divergent from clerical, 5–6, 44; emulation of popovichi, 28–29, 36; on fathers, 102, 106; generational strife and divide, 9, 11, 95, 166; hostility toward popovichi, 8, 25–28, 33–35; identity of, 26, 185, 211, 212; as parents, 81, 112; popovichi alienated when amongst, 38–39, 55; popovichi on childhoods of, 95, 120; popovichi fashioning selves against, 8, 24, 44, 94, 122, 187, 192, 212, 213; popovichi on as foreign, 3–4, 43, 53–54, 56, 59, 60, 65, 94, 112; popovichi's hatred of, 56, 214–15; popovichi on as indifferent to peasant distress, 175–76, 187; popovichi on intelligenty from, 56–58; popovichi on popovichi who emulate, 116; popovichi resent, 42; popovichi on selves as superior to, 40, 126, 137–38; popovichi on as sinful, 51–53,